I0092031

Learning to Industrialize

This book proposes a new, pragmatic way of approaching economic development which features policy learning based on a comparison of international best policy practices. While the important role of government in promoting private sector development is being recognized, policy discussion often remains general without details as to what exactly to do and how to avoid common pitfalls. This book fills the gap by showing concrete policy contents, procedures, and organizations adopted in high-performing East Asian economies.

Natural resources and foreign aid and investment can take a country to a certain income level, but growth stalls when given advantages are exhausted. Economies will be caught in middle-income traps if growth impetus is not internally generated. Meanwhile, countries that have soared to high income levels introduced mindset, policies, and institutions that encouraged, or even forced, accumulation of human capital – skills, technology, and knowledge. How this can be done systematically is the main topic of policy learning. However, government should not randomly adopt what Singapore or Taiwan did in the past. A continued march to prosperity is possible only when policy makers acquire the capability to formulate policy suitable for local context after studying a number of international experiences.

Developing countries wanting to adopt effective industrial strategies but not knowing where to start will benefit greatly from the ideas and hands-on examples presented by the author. Students of development economics will find a new methodological perspective which can supplement the ongoing industrial policy debate. The book also gives an excellent account of the national pride and pragmatism exhibited by officials in East Asia who produced remarkable economic growth, as well as the serious effort by an African country to emulate this miracle.

Kenichi Ohno is Professor at the National Graduate Institute for Policy Studies, Tokyo. He was born in Kobe, Japan and holds a PhD in Economics from Stanford University, California. He worked at the International Monetary Fund and taught at the University of Tsukuba and Saitama University before assuming his current position.

Routledge-GRIPS Development Forum Studies
Edited by Kenichi Ohno and Izumi Ohno
National Graduate Institute for Policy Studies, Japan

1. **The Rise of Asian Donors**
   Japan's impact on the evolution of emerging donors
   Edited by Jin Sato and Yasutami Shimomura

2. **Learning to Industrialize**
   From given growth to policy-aided value creation
   Kenichi Ohno

Learning to Industrialize

From given growth to policy-aided value creation

Kenichi Ohno

LONDON AND NEW YORK

First published 2013
by Routledge
2 Park Square, Milton Park, Abingdon, Oxon, OX14 4RN

Simultaneously published in the USA and Canada
by Routledge
711 Third Avenue, New York, NY 10017

Routledge is an imprint of the Taylor & Francis Group, an informa business

British Library Cataloguing in Publication Data
A catalogue record for this book is available from the British Library

Library of Congress Cataloging in Publication Data
Ono, Ken'ichi, 1957–
Learning to industrialize : from given growth to policy-aided value creation / by Kenichi Ohno.
p. cm. – (Routledge-GRIPS development forum studies; 2)
Includes bibliographical references and index.
1. Economic development. 2. Industrialization. 3. Industrial policy.
4. Industrialization–East Asia. 5. Industrialization–Developing countries. I. Title.
HD82.O586 2012
338.9–dc23

2012014602

ISBN 13: 978-0-415-59570-4 (hbk)
ISBN 13: 978-0-415-70582-0 (pbk)
ISBN 13: 978-0-203-08553-0 (ebk)

Typeset in Times New Roman
by Graphicraft Limited, Hong Kong

Contents

Figures

Tables

Preface

> Learning without thinking is useless; thinking without learning is insecure.
> (Confucius, 551–479 BC, chapter on politics, *Lun-yu*)

This book proposes a way to learn pragmatic policymaking for developing countries that must cope with the strong pressure of market-orientation and globalization of our time. It points to a realistic method of overcoming a low- or middle-income trap into which many countries seem to have fallen. Such a strategy is not only possible but also already practiced in many parts of the world, especially in East Asia, with different degrees of success. Our main focus is the productive sector of the economy which includes manufacturing, agriculture, services, and logistics, but the general principle advanced here should be applicable to all policy making. This study should be useful for people who are seriously interested in the practice of development policy, such as national leaders, economic ministers, directors and officials of government ministries and agencies, development experts and consultants, policy researchers and students, and even ordinary citizens who are yearning to know what goes wrong with the policies of their motherland and how this can be remedied.

Industrial policy debate is receiving revived attention. The days of minuscule government and unfettered markets are over. It is now widely recognized that free-market crusaders can do much harm to the global economy, and the appropriate involvement of government is essential for sustained growth. Based on this re-emerging view, economists are arguing whether policy should lead or follow markets, whether selective intervention is possible in the twenty-first century, what should be the six steps to compile an industrial strategy, and so on. However, these arguments are a bit too abstract for the practitioners of development policy. I would like to enter the debate from a different angle.

The discussion here is action-oriented rather than theoretical. Many concrete cases and policy measures will be presented, mainly from the current and historical experiences of East Asia, which feature pragmatism, obsession with concrete details, and expectation of graduation from aid. The debate on the proper role of government, for example, cannot be resolved in the theoretical realm alone because theory and practice are intertwined. The answer critically hinges on the policy capability of government and the maturity of the private sector of the country in question. Many industrial strategies have failed not due to the lack of theoretical justification but largely because of crude and inappropriate application. Most promotion measures are globally common but performance differs considerably from one country to another. This book attempts to explain, for instance, why Japan and Taiwan were so successful in absorbing foreign technology and strengthening their small and medium enterprises while most other countries remain ineffective even though their policy menus are similar. Not only that, this book also suggests how policy capability can be built up in pragmatic steps. Early achievers of industrialization did not have to go to school to learn good policies. They struggled through self-study and trial-and-error, and produced spectacular results. But today's latecomer countries may benefit greatly from more explicit and systematic learning. Cataloguing, analyzing, and sharing policy know-how should be one of the central objectives of policy science.

A latecomer country often starts to grow when domestic markets are liberalized and international integration is initiated, but growth stalls when the income level dictated by given advantages—location, natural resources, existing labor, and inflow of foreign funds—is reached. Beyond that point, sustained development to high income will require internal creation of value backed by continuous upgrading of skills, technology, and knowledge. To realize this, government must install policies and institutions that encourage, or even force, human capital accumulation. This is a difficult task that only a handful of countries have accomplished. The enormity of this difficulty is the fundamental reason why income tends to polarize across countries under globalization and also why low- and middle-income traps are so common.

This book emphasizes policy learning. It considers government as a proper (but often still potential) initiator of national transformation in mindset, technology, and industry in a developing country. Weak policy capability does not lead to the conclusion that government should remain inactive but to the counsel on policy learning to overcome this weakness. However, random adoption of policy measures without knowledge of global practice or difference in local contexts is doomed to fail. Policy learning must be based on a systematic collection and comparison of international best policy practices (and even failures), with the objective of enhancing government capability which enables the creation of a policy package most appropriate for the country's unique situation. Three things must be learned: policy content, policy procedure, and policy organization. A more advanced question is what to do with a lazy private sector that fails to respond to good policies introduced by government. These are the issues that will be dealt with in this volume. It may not give definitive answers, but the materials and ideas provided will hopefully be of use to further study.

This book is written in the same spirit as the Growth Report produced by the Commission on Growth and Development in 2008. I totally concur with the statement that there is no single recipe for growth policy and that outsiders can only provide ingredients for a dedicated national team to select and combine to cook a suitable dinner for the country (Commission on Growth and Development, 2008, p. 16). But I go further by comparing alternative methods of industrial policy design and implementation across countries, hinting at how they can be selected and combined, and showing how policy skills can be taught and learned. My perspective is somewhat broader than the Growth Report and includes politics, social mindsets, and administrative hurdles as backgrounds for development policy formulation in each country. Practical cases are drawn mainly from East Asia, which constitutes another special feature of this volume.

The main title of the book, *Learning to Industrialize*, is the same as that of the work by Sanjaya Lall (1987) which surveyed nineteen Indian firms in the cement, steel, textiles, and consultation industries. Lall's main concern was the methods by which individual firms acquired technological capability while policy environment was treated cursorily as external conditions. In my book, government is the learner and I explore the way in which its capability can be strengthened. I hope the reader will find my work complementary to Lall's as it broadens the scope of learning that must be undertaken for economic development.

The book has two parts. The first part contains general discussions in four chapters and the second presents six country studies—five from East Asia and one from Africa—that portray serious governmental effort to establish policies and institutions that accelerate human capital accumulation, each in its own way and with different degrees of success. In-depth case studies are an integral part of policy learning because they can show not just technical aspects of policymaking but, more importantly, the resolve and passion of political leaders and public servants that sustain a nationwide industrialization drive. Development is propelled not by science and technology alone but by the spirit of the people. A vivid and detailed description of how a poor country rose—or is trying to rise—to the status of an industrial economy with advanced technology should move the reader at the heart and enrich him or her in the brain.

Chapter 1 argues that globalization in its natural tendency polarizes income across countries. The crucial factor that divides winners from losers is the amount of skills, technology, and knowledge accumulated in their citizens rather than the initial endowment of natural resources or the amount of foreign funds received. Low or middle income may be attained by economic liberalization or external opening, but a continued march to high income becomes possible only when the country establishes a national mechanism for constant upgrading of human capital.

Chapter 2 shows that many latecomer countries are already willing to learn the nitty-gritty of industrial promotion, but such knowledge is not forthcoming from either academia or international organizations. What they need is a hands-on instruction on how to execute concrete policies rather than a theoretical debate on the justification or desirability of industrial policy. Proactive industrial policy is proposed by which latecomers balance state and market as well as integration commitments and retention of sufficient policy tools. A number of frequently asked questions are reviewed, and commonly encountered issues such as a weak private sector, problems generated by high growth, and politics of development are addressed.

Chapter 3 discusses ingredients of industrial promotion. The concept of policy learning is introduced, policy dialogue with developing countries as practiced by Japan and South Korea is explained, and the meaning of "learning from East Asia" is re-examined. The rest of the chapter is devoted to the exposition of standard policy tools for industrial capability building such as kaizen, shindan, engineering universities and technical colleges, training-industry links, industrial parks, and strategic FDI marketing. More complex policy packages such as small and medium enterprise promotion, integrated export promotion, creation of an entirely new industry, and comprehensive regional development with core infrastructure are also discussed. Some of these policy tools are globally well known but others are special or uniquely developed in East Asia.

Chapter 4 deals with the procedural and organizational aspects of policy-making which are often neglected in existing policy studies. After the critical importance of leadership is stressed, necessary ingredients in policymaking procedure—vision, consensus building, documentation, and stakeholder participation—are explained. Alternative policy organizations are highlighted with concrete international examples, including a technocrat team supporting the top leader, a national council or committee, a super-ministry, a specialized institute as a policymaking hub, and a strong leader without institutionalization. Additionally, standard contents of an industrial policy document are illustrated, and advice on Vietnam's policy procedure and organization is appended as an example.

Chapters 5 to 10 report six different cases of the state's effort to upgrade human capital. The first three cases are reviews of outstanding performance while the remaining three are stories of contemporary struggle.

In Chapter 5, Japan in the second half of the nineteenth century, which internalized Western technology vigorously and effectively, is analyzed from the perspectives of history, politics, and specific policy measures. Chapter 6 narrates Singapore's national productivity movement which started with the top-down initiative but eventually assimilated widely and continues even today. Chapter 7 explains Taiwan's current innovation drive featuring a powerful ministry, technology development projects, research institutes, and science parks. In Chapter 8, Malaysia's intense effort to escape an upper-middle-income trap is described where highly sophisticated policy mechanisms are contrasted with a lackluster response from the private sector. In Chapter 9, Vietnam's awareness of the lack of quality of growth and internal value creation is examined despite its remarkable growth in the last two decades following economic liberalization and global integration. Finally, Chapter

10 documents the policy learning process of Ethiopia, a low-income country with difficult initial conditions, which is backed by an unwavering political resolve and a strong desire to learn from East Asia and not from Washington.

The sample of countries is far from complete, but even this small selection should be enough for the reader to realize the existence of something common among high performers despite enormous diversity of their experiences. The inclusion of Ethiopia, in particular, should prove that the type of policy learning advocated in this book is not a monopoly of East Asia. It is also hoped that their tales will conjure up the same thrill and amazement about policymaking in the reader as they did in myself. The number of countries included also had to be limited by such practical concerns as the acceptable size of the book and my own time constraints. South Korea and Thailand were omitted although interesting information was available on their policy formulation. China and India, the two giants which remain untouched in my study, must be dealt with separately when my research progresses further.

As the reader will surely notice, the people and organizations that supported my policy research over the last two decades are too many to be recognized individually. Instead of listing them one by one, I would like to thank them collectively with the deepest sense of respect and appreciation for their intelligence and dedication to policy making in their respective countries, including those in East Asia and Africa which are not featured in this book. But one person must be specially mentioned. I would like to express my great gratitude to Azko Hayashida, my most productive assistant who supported the policy research during the last ten years. I sincerely hope that her next adventure in life will be as intellectually exciting as the one we shared.

Acknowledgments

The policy research that has produced this book was financially supported, over the years, by Grants-in-Aid for Scientific Research, the 21st Century Centers of Excellence Program, and the Global Centers of Excellence Program of the Japan Society for the Promotion of Science. The Japan International Cooperation Agency provided support as well as partnership to the policy dialogues and surveys in a number of countries conducted by the GRIPS Development Forum and the Vietnam Development Forum. I remain grateful to these programs and organizations.

Kenichi Ohno

Part I

Ideas and methods

1 The developmental trap

1.1 Income polarization

The idea that globalization promotes international income convergence through trade and investment opportunities and technology transfer, and therefore helps latecomer countries in their effort to catch up with early achievers, has long been advanced by a number of officials and scholars. It is also an idea that has been challenged by countless arguments and examples. The controversy over latecomers' advantage under globalization did not originate from the Washington Consensus, a policy proposition championed by the World Bank and the International Monetary Fund, which argued that economic liberalization, privatization, and opening up are good for all countries. Nor was it invented by the scathing critiques of the Washington Consensus by such proponents as Chang (2002), Stiglitz (2002, 2006), Rodrik (2007), and Cimoli et al. (2009a). Conflict of interests over globalization between early achievers and latecomers is an old issue that goes back at least to the nineteenth century.

If left to natural forces, globalization tends to polarize income rather than equalize it. This is a phenomenon that first emerged as a result of the Industrial Revolution in the West. In previous centuries when international trade was long-distance exchange of primary commodities and local specialties with low technology content, free trade did not produce obvious winners and losers. When Europe exported silver in exchange for Chinese silk and spices, trade was a mutually profitable activity between more or less equal partners. However, production of industrial goods by mechanized factories changed the rules of the trading game. Merchandise in large volume, uniform quality, and low cost began to invade the global market in which technology and production scale were decisive factors. Learning, R&D, and patenting in new knowledge became crucial. In the new trading game, where winner-take-all and technology lock-in for late starters are prominent features, early achievers are able to continuously improve technology while latecomers are not even allowed to enter the race. The only way to catch up for latecomers seems to be protection and promotion of domestic industries for a certain period, but imposition of free trade effectively removes this option. The fundamental nature of globalization that enhances the rich-and-poor gap basically remains intact even to this date with a minor modification that knowledge industries and high-value services have been added to manufacturing as leading sectors.

The developing world liberalized its trade regime rapidly and significantly in the 1980s and 1990s under integration, structural adjustment, and systemic transition programs sponsored by the three sister international organizations consisting of the International Monetary Fund, the World Bank, and the World Trade Organization. However, increased openness did not automatically stimulate economic growth in developing countries. An UNCTAD report on least developed countries (LDCs) in 2004 questioned the supposed benefit of trade expansion on economic growth (proxied by per capita private consumption). Among 66 observations on poorest countries in the five-year period of 1990–1995 and/or 1995–2000, exports grew in 51 of them. In 18 of these 51 cases, however, per capita private consumption fell as export expanded (the "immiserizing trade effect"). Only 22 of the 51 cases showed rising per capita private consumption along with export growth, while the export–consumption nexus was ambiguous in 11 of the 51 cases. UNCTAD concludes that "even when the LDCs have increased their overall export growth rate—as many . . . did in the 1990s—better export performance rarely translates into sustained and substantial poverty reduction" (UNCTAD, 2004, p. IV). In a similar vein, after reviewing the "voluminous" literature on the links between trade policy and economic performance, Rodrik finds that "there is no convincing evidence that trade liberalization is predictably associated with subsequent economic growth" (Rodrik, 2007, pp. 215–216).

Back in the mid-nineteenth century when Japan re-opened its ports and began to trade with the West after more than two centuries of feudal rule and severely controlled external trade, Okubo Toshimichi (1830–1878), the first home minister of the reformist Meiji government who initiated an industrial modernization drive, wrote in his policy proposal:

> If we are to turn the tide around and correct the situation [of slow economic progress and trade deficits], we have no choice but to encourage private business and international trade by mobilizing effective policy measures to cultivate fundamental strengths of economic activities and expand commercial profit. If we do not regard this as the duties of the government and leave the matter to people's own devices and simply wait for the results, will the decline ever stop? This is the most pressing of all national issues. Even though such policy may not be endorsed by the orthodox doctrine of political economy, rules must be bent to respond to the urgent needs of our time.
>
> (Okubo, 1876, pp. 79–80)

The orthodox doctrine of political economy to which Okubo referred was the Ricardian theory of comparative advantage with the assumption of given technology in each country. Under this static theory commonly preached by the British delegation to Japan, it could be "proved" that free trade benefited all nations including advanced and backward ones. However, Japanese leaders in the nineteenth century were keenly aware, by instinct and through observing situations in Asian neighbors, of the true nature of free trade imposed on Japan by unequal commercial treaties with the West.[1] They clearly understood the suppressive effects that free trade with advanced countries would have on burgeoning domestic industries, and resulting dominance of the strong nations over the weak—a situation described as *imperialism of free trade* by economic historians.

In 1871, Hirobumi Ito (1841–1909), who later drafted the first Japanese constitution and became Japan's first prime minister, wrote from the United States, where he was staying on an official mission to study American fiscal and monetary systems, that the free trade advocated by Britain was merely an excuse to pursue its own national interest whose adoption would greatly harm an underdeveloped country like Japan. The common practice of *kicking away the ladder* by early industrial achievers to deprive others of the means of climbing after them was eloquently pointed out by the nineteenth-century German economist Friedrich List (1841), and was more recently documented with ample historical evidence by Chang (2002).

Notwithstanding the strong pressure of *imperialism of free trade*, Japan in the late nineteenth century absorbed Western systems and technology well and rapidly developed its industries by employing various policies other than tariff protection. It joined the "Big Five," a group of most advanced nations, by the 1910s and began to attend international conferences that determined the fate of the world. How this feat was achieved will be the main topic of Chapter 5. However, it is important to stress that Japan was a rare exception rather than the rule among latecomers. There was no other non-Western country that caught up with Western industrial powers until the latter half of the twentieth century when Singapore, Hong Kong, Taiwan, and South Korea began to surge. At present, there are a number of "emerging economies," such as China, India and Brazil, that seem to be on a track to catch-up industrialization. Nonetheless, the rest of the developing world has generally and for long remained poor with low industrial capabilities.

Castaldi et al. (2009) summarize global development experience in historical perspective as follows. Since the British Industrial Revolution, there emerged a clear separation of countries between the rich and the poor clubs. Only a small number of countries made up the former while the vast majority belonged to the latter. This was in sharp contrast to the situation in earlier centuries when income levels were more equal at least among Europe, China, and the Arab world. Transition probabilities between the two clubs were not zero but very small, with only a few countries, already mentioned above, rising to join the rich club and even a fewer countries descending from the rich to the poor club. Within subgroups of countries, such as within the already rich OECD members and within the East Asian region, a tendency for collective catching up was observed. But such local convergence was unable to offset the global tendency of income polarization.

In short, most countries remained poor while a small number of rich countries became and remained rich in the last two centuries, with very limited switching of members between the two clubs. The view that globalization promotes international income convergence through new trade and investment opportunities and technology transfer is not only naïve but also rejected by the data. The fact is that an integrated world economy has a natural tendency to polarize income—a tendency which, however, may be resisted and even reversed by well-constructed policies as argued in the chapters to follow.

1.2 Diversity in catching-up ability

East Asia is known as a region that achieved remarkable economic growth *on average*, but not all economies in the region have succeeded in development. The World Bank's *East Asian Miracle* report, which explored the policy secrets of this rapidly growing region, implicitly assumed that all of the ten economies it studied registered impressive growth and deserved admiration (World Bank, 1993). But statistics reveal that this was not the case. Figures 1.1 and 1.2 present real income per head of East Asian economies relative to the United States, the frontrunner country of our time, for the period starting in 1950. Japan began to industrialize very early, in the late nineteenth century, and traveled an entirely different path from the rest of

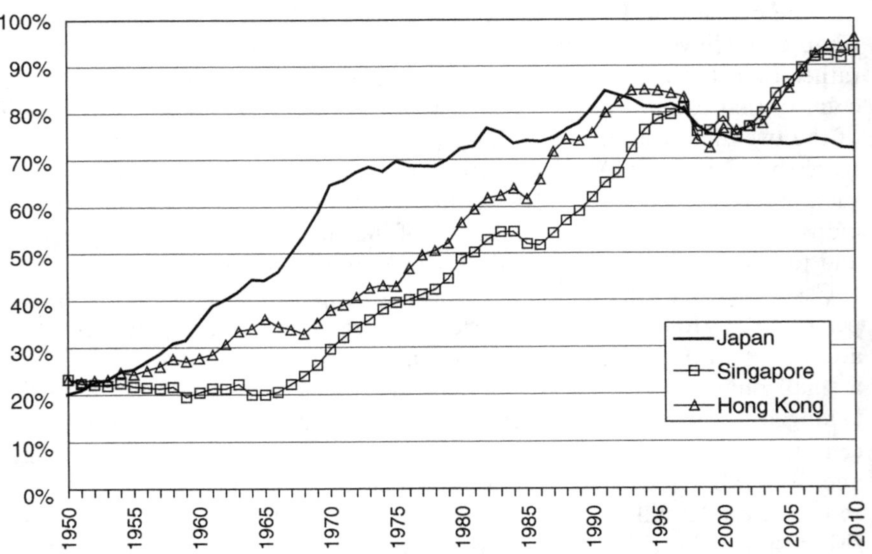

Figure 1.1 Per capita income relative to US: East Asia 1 (measured in the 1990 international Geary-Khamis dollars)

Sources: Angus Maddison (2003) and IMF, World Economic Outlook Database, April 2010 (for updating)

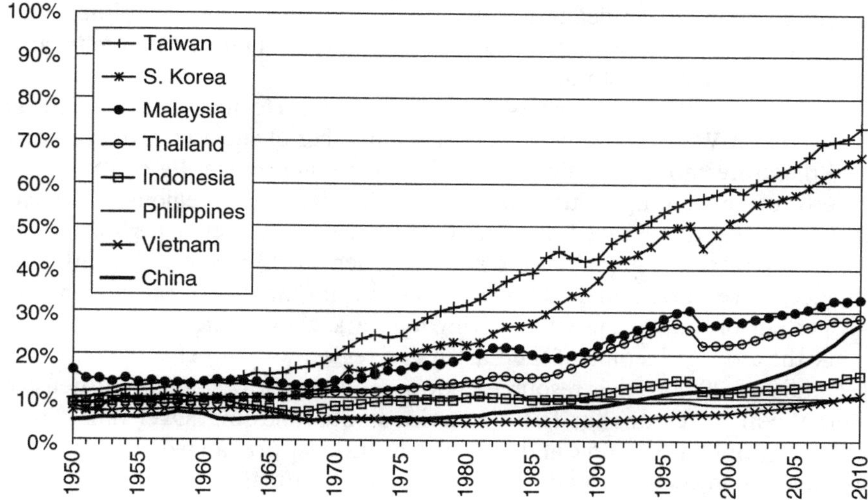

Figure 1.2 Per capita income relative to US: East Asia 2 (measured in the 1990 international Geary-Khamis dollars)

Sources: Angus Maddison (2003), the Central Bank of the Republic of China, and IMF, World Economic Outlook Database, April 2010 (for updating).

East Asia (Ohno, 2006a). Singapore and Hong Kong, two city economies inhabited mainly by ethnic Chinese and currently functioning as information, financial, and transport hubs of the region, rose fast to overtake Japan in recent years. These are the highest income achievers in East Asia.

Other countries in the East Asian region, in Figure 1.2, can be classified into four groups according to their income performance in the post-World War II period. Taiwan and South Korea (the first group) soared rapidly to attain high income and high industrial capability. Malaysia and Thailand (the second group) have risen only to middle income although they started industrialization at about the same time as Taiwan and South Korea, namely in the 1960s. Meanwhile, Indonesia and the Philippines (the third group) have not made any visible long-term catching up relative to the US income. Two transition economies which initially belonged to the third group deserve special mention. China, a socialist giant, took off in the 1980s and made accelerated strides in the 1990s and 2000s. It now belongs to the middle-income group and continues to ascend. Vietnam, another socialist latecomer hampered by prolonged war and economic planning in the past, started to grow fast in the 1990s driven mainly by large inflows of foreign aid and capital.

Figure 1.2 clearly illustrates the fact that different income performance among the first, second, and third groups in East Asia is the result of different speeds of ascent rather than delayed starts. Furthermore, the East Asian region is also a host to several countries, not shown in Figure 1.2, that remain poor and without significant industrial achievement for various political and economic reasons. They are Laos, Cambodia, East Timor, Myanmar, and North Korea (the fourth group).

Yet, despite these disparities in development performance, East Asia is the only non-Western region that has had a number of super growth achievers and therefore shown significant income growth *on average*. By contrast, the records of catching-up industrialization in other developing regions, presented in Figures 1.3 to 1.6, are less remarkable and without stellar performers.

Latin America was part of the relatively rich world in the eighteenth and nineteenth centuries. In 1820, average per capita income of the region was 42 percent of that of the United Kingdom, a leading economy at that time, while the average income of the East Asian region was 34 percent of the UK (Maddison, 2003). Rich resource endowments and low population density were the main reasons for Latin America's initial blessing. Over time, however, as population grew and industrialization effort lagged, the region's average income vis-à-vis advanced economies gradually eroded, and eventually fell to 23 percent of the US income by 2001. The post-World War II period continued to witness the long-term trend of slipping from middle income as shown in Figure 1.3. A large fall of oil-rich Venezuela from high to low income is particularly striking. It may be said that, over the last few centuries, wealth generated from land has been squandered in Latin America without igniting investment in knowledge, skills or technology.

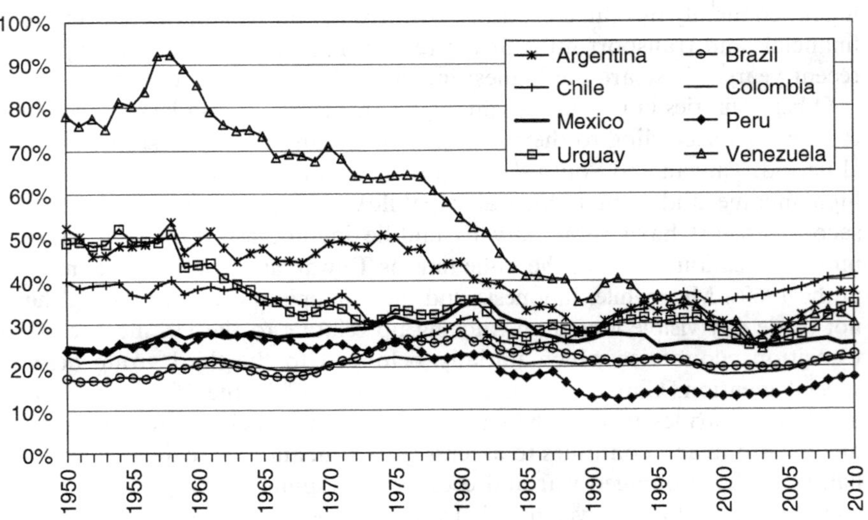

Figure 1.3 Per capita income relative to US: Latin America (measured in the 1990 international Geary-Khamis dollars)

Sources: Angus Maddison (2003) and IMF, World Economic Outlook Database, April 2010 (for updating).

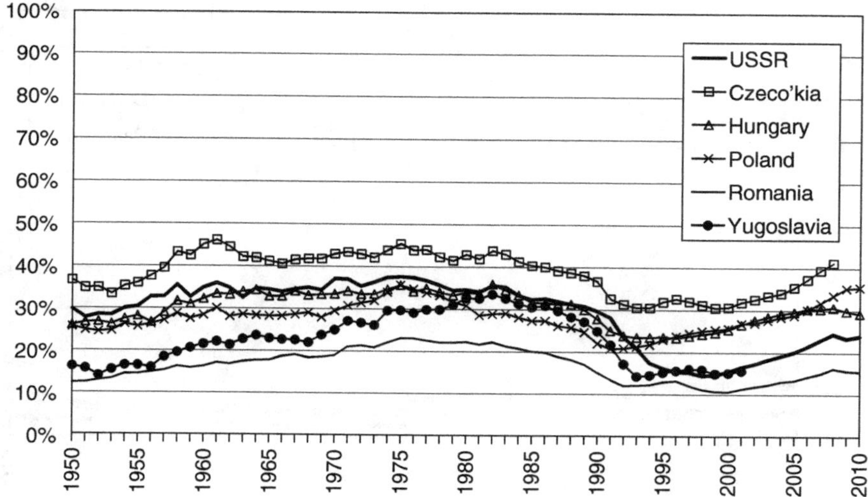

Figure 1.4 Per capita income relative to US: Russia and Eastern Europe (measured in the 1990 international Geary-Khamis dollars)

Sources: Angus Maddison (2003) and IMF, World Economic Outlook Database, April 2010 (for updating).

Notes: Data for Yugoslavia and Czechoslovakia after the break-up are given by aggregating split countries. USSR after the collapse is represented by Russia.

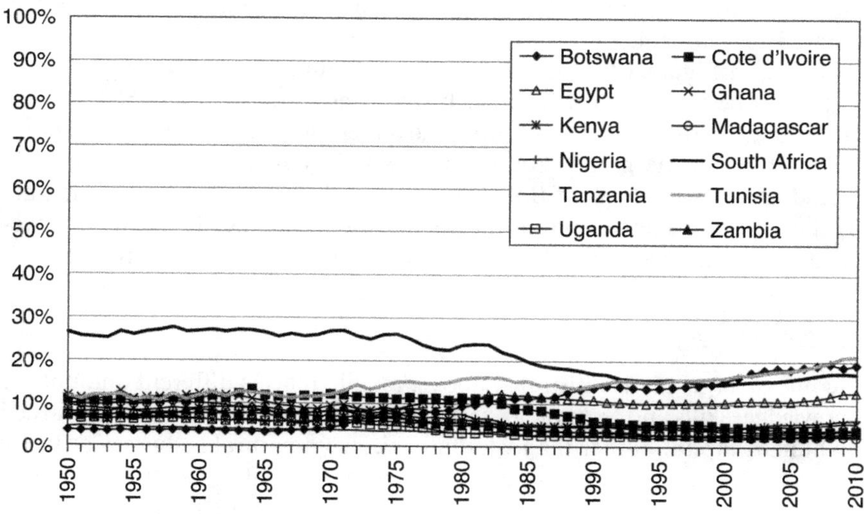

Figure 1.5 Per capita income relative to US: Africa (measured in the 1990 international Geary-Khamis dollars)

Sources: Angus Maddison (2003) and IMF, World Economic Outlook Database, April 2010 (for updating).

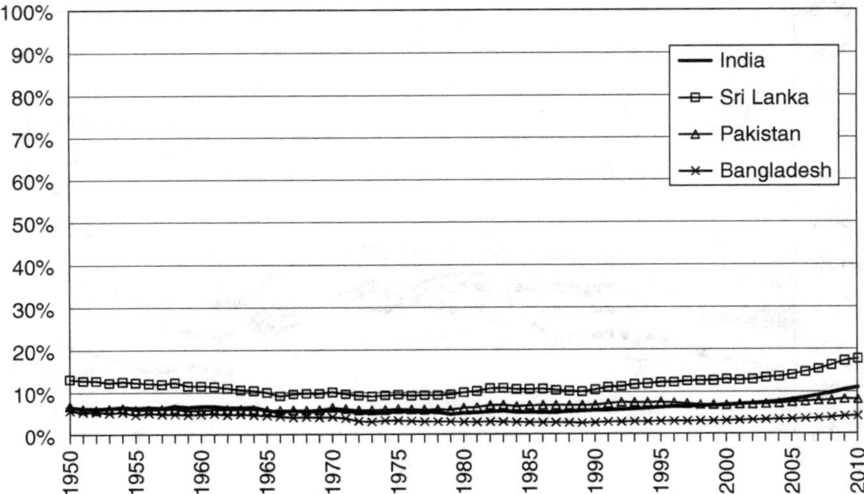

Figure 1.6 Per capita income relative to US: South Asia (measured in the 1990 international Geary-Khamis dollars)

Sources: Angus Maddison (2003) and IMF, World Economic Outlook Database, April 2010 (for updating).

Russia and Eastern Europe are another group of countries that have fluctuated in the middle-income range mostly under the socialist regime. Economic difficulties at the time of the disappearance of the USSR are also clearly visible in Figure 1.4.

Africa, in Figure 1.5, and South Asia, in Figure 1.6, are two regions that appear to be stuck at low income. In both regions, countries are clustered at the bottom of the scale with little movement which gives a highly monotonous tone to the graph. South Africa's mildly high income in the early period and a modest rise of Botswana in recent years are explainable mainly by the export of metals and precious stones. In South Asia, recent improvements in Sri Lanka and India, albeit tiny, deserve to be monitored.

1.3 Knowledge, skills and technology

Income divergence, as illustrated above, mainly reflects different amounts of knowledge, skills and technology accumulated in each country. Income earned by human capital, rather than windfall gain from natural resources or lucky inflows of foreign money, is the key determinant of long-term economic growth. This should be obvious to most readers, but it is still useful to review some statistics, assembled by Castaldi et al. (2009), to re-confirm the obvious. In doing so, two caveats should be noted in advance. For one thing, human capital (or "innovativeness") cannot be directly measured and therefore must be represented by some proxies. For another, causality from human capital to income, or vice versa, cannot be directly proved by correlation. Data may amply illustrate, but cannot rigorously prove, that innovativeness is the mother of high income.

As proxies of innovativeness and technology attainment, Castaldi and others look at the number of US patents granted, labor productivity, firm-level R&D, number of researchers, expenditure on IT, diffusion of ICT, and concentration of R&D activities by foreign affiliates. These data are selectively presented in Table 1.1. The authors observe that "irrespectively of the chosen proxy, the picture which emerges is one with innovation highly concentrated in a small group of countries" (p. 40). Just as the club of rich countries has been exclusive, the club of innovating countries has also been small with restricted entry and a slow pace of change in relative ranking in the last two centuries. Again, Japan in the early twentieth century and South Korea and Taiwan in the late twentieth century are mentioned as the only new major entrants to the innovation club. Since income and innovativeness are closely related, overlapping membership in the two clubs is not at all surprising.

One of the proxies highlighted by Castaldi and others is the number of US patents granted to non-US countries since 1883. The authors admit that this is a narrow definition of human capital. Upgrading of knowledge, skills, and technology can occur not only through inventive discovery and patenting but also through emulation, reverse engineering, adoption of capital-embodied innovation, learning by doing, incremental productivity enhancement at factories, organizational innovation, and so on. Nevertheless, a significant link exists between invention and gross domestic product (GDP) per capita which is reasonably robust over different historical periods. The link is particularly strong between 1913 and 1970 as well as in the 1980s and 2000s. Correlation between the *growth* of US patents per capita and the *growth* of GDP per capita among 14 OECD countries was 0.05 and statistically insignificant in 1890–1913 but became large and statistically significant at 5 percent level in later periods: 0.67 in 1913–1929, 0.58 in 1929–1950, and 0.71 in 1950–1970. Then it evaporated in the turbulent oil-shock years of 1970–1977 to 0.16 with no statistical significance. A more recent and larger dataset containing 21 OECD countries basically paints the same picture with the following correlation coefficients between the growth of US patents per capita and the growth of GDP per capita: 0.18 (insignificant) in 1970–1977, 0.82 in 1977–1984, 0.89 in 1984–1991, 0.30 (statistically insignificant) in 1991–1998, and 0.64 in 1998–2006.

If the *level* of US patents per capita and the *level* of GDP per capita are used instead of growth rates, correlation between them is consistently positive (ranging from 0.50 to 0.88) and significant at 5 percent level throughout 1929–2006 but not in the early years of 1890 or 1913. Similarly, correlation between the level of R&D per capita and the level of GDP per capita is always positive (ranging from 0.49 to 0.79) during 1963–2006 (no data are reported before 1963). These mutually supportive results confirm the existence of a strong link between innovation and R&D on the one hand

Table 1.1 Selected indicators of innovativeness

	US patents granted (% of non-US recipients)				Labor productivity relative to US			Mean years of schooling		Number of researchers (per 1000 labor force)	IT expenditure as % of GDP	Internet users (per 100)
	1883	*1929*	*1973*	*2007*	*1913*	*1973*	*2007*	*1970*	*2000*	*2003*	*2006*	*2004*
OECD												
Australia	1.11	1.96	0.89	1.63	106.4	71.7	77.3	10.2	10.9			65.3
Austria	2.62	2.47	1.05	0.59	56.4	61.4	77.1	7.4	8.4		2.8	47.5
Belgium	1.59	1.30	1.25	0.67	71.9	75.5	86.9	8.8	9.3		2.8	40.2
Canada	19.94	10.25	5.95	4.27	86.9	85.8	77.2	9.1	11.6			62.3
Denmark	0.56	0.71	0.68	0.50	68.6	66.5	75.0	8.8	9.7		3.2	50.4
France	14.22	9.76	9.47	4.03	56.0	76.4	86.0	5.7	7.9	7.1	3.1	39.3
Germany	18.67	32.36	24.68	11.64	58.7	72.2	66.8		10.2	6.8	2.9	42.7
Italy	0.24	1.19	3.35	1.67	40.6	69.5	72.7	5.5	7.2	3.0	1.7	46.8
Japan	0.16	1.40	21.82	42.90	20.9	56.9	71.1	7.5	9.5	10.1	3.4	62.2
Netherlands	0.24	1.57	3.03	1.61	80.4	82.4	72.6	7.8	9.4		3.3	61.6
Norway	0.32	0.71	0.37	0.32	46.7	63.9	83.3	7.2	11.9		2.4	39.0
Sweden	0.95	3.19	3.37	1.36	50.2	68.2	76.9	8.0	11.4	10.6	3.8	75.5
Switzerland	1.75	4.46	5.86	1.33	65.0	82.4	65.2	8.5	10.5			
UK	34.55	22.23	12.61	4.23	84.8	65.6	78.5	7.7	9.4		3.5	47.0
US	–	–	–	–	100.0	100.0	100.0	9.5	12.0	9.1	3.3	63.0
NICs												
Israel			0.37	1.42		61.2	65.7	8.1	9.6			21.8
Singapore			0.03	0.51		39.5	74.2	5.1	7.1	9.3		57.9
Taiwan			0.00	7.88		28.7	71.6			6.7		
South Korea			0.02	8.10		21.3	61.7	4.9	10.8	6.6		65.7
Hong Kong			0.07	0.43		43.3	94.7	6.3	9.4			50.3
India			0.09	0.70		6.1	18.9					3.2
China			0.04	0.99		4.8	10.9			1.1		7.2
Latin America												
Argentina			0.12	0.05		52.9	40.7	6.2	8.8	1.8		16.1
Brazil			0.08	0.12		27.9	19.4	3.3	4.9	0.9		12.0
Mexico			0.19	0.07		45.9	30.7	3.7	7.2	1.9		13.4
Venezuela			0.03	0.02		92.4	46.4	3.2	6.6	0.5		8.4

Source: compiled from Tables 3.1, 3.3, 3.8, 3.9, 3.10, and 3.11 in Castaldi et al. (2009).
Note: Data for NICs and Latin America in the 2007 labor productivity column are actually 2006 data.

and income per head on the other at least for OECD countries (Castaldi et al., 2009, pp. 45–47).

Individual countries that deserve special mention in Table 1.1 include Japan which sharply increased its share of US patents granted from 1929 onward, and Taiwan and South Korea which did the same from 1973 onward. Labor productivity relative to the US reveals similar trends with Japan rising greatly from 1913 and East Asian tigers following suit in more recent decades. It is also notable that the four Latin American countries fell significantly in relative labor productivity in recent decades. Thus the stories about innovativeness of nations are basically the same as the stories of relative income catch-up illustrated in Figures 1.1 to 1.6 above. The same countries are repeatedly mentioned as outstanding achievers in both human capital and income per head because the two are inseparable.

These historical results lead to the conclusion that knowledge, skills, and technology do not flow naturally from high-level to low-level countries even in a world with low barriers to trade, investment, capital mobility, labor migration, and information in printed and electronic media. Globalization does not automatically support convergence in the quality or quantity of human capital across countries but rather tends to widen and solidify the gap between innovative countries and others.

Knowledge relevant to human capital accumulation cannot be bought off-the-shelf because improvement requires internalization of foreign knowledge by local residents. A toolkit for efficient factory management or a textbook on strategic marketing have little impact unless it is effectively put to use in the local context. This in turn calls for a complex socio-economic process involving a merger of two systems—a foreign system introduced from outside and an existing local system—which are often initially incompatible (Ohno, 2000). Friction, hostility, and rejection which arise in a forced systemic merger must be managed properly by modifying both systems for a better fit without diluting the desired benefits of the imported system. Maegawa (1994, 2000), an economic anthropologist who studies the meeting of "civilization" (dominant technology and systems) and a "culture" (local society), calls this process *translative adaptation*.

> [M]any nations and societies have adopted Western institutions and objects from without in order to survive (or by their own choice). However, it is important to recognize that they did not accept Western inventions in their original forms. Any item in one culture will change its meaning when transplanted to another culture, as seen widely in ethnography around the world. Not only cosmology, religious doctrine, rituals, but also the family system, the institution of exchange, and even socio-economic organizations like the firm exhibit the property of adapting to external institutions and principles with the existing cultural system maintaining its form of structure. The essence of what has been called "modernization" is the adaptive acceptance of Western civilization under the persistent form

> of the existing culture. That is, actors in the existing system have adapted to the new system by reinterpreting each element of Western culture (i.e., "civilization") in their own value structure, modifying yet maintaining the existing institutions. I shall call this "translative adaptation."
>
> (Maegawa, 1994, English translation pp. 174–175)

Translative adaptation does not naturally arise from the market mechanism. To succeed, the process must be managed with careful deliberation and trial-and-error. Mindsets and institutions that facilitate a smooth systemic merger must be designed and installed. The principal coordinator of this change should be the central government of the latecomer country in question. Individuals and private firms who produce and invest are the key actors of economic development, but they themselves cannot stand outside the arena to plan, implement, monitor, or adjust the process of systemic merger. To establish a national innovation mechanism, the government must acquire sufficient expertise to guide and assist the private sector. Only when this public–private cooperation reaches a certain critical point, private-sector capabilities begin to accumulate in a significant way. The difficulty of this policy learning is the fundamental cause of the exclusive membership of the innovative country club as well as the rich country club.

It must be added that innovation most pertinent to latecomer countries at low and lower middle-income levels is the creation of something new *in the home country* and not the creation of something entirely new in the world. Acquiring and assimilating knowledge, skills, and technology that are already widely known and practiced in advanced economies is extremely important and forms the core of learning that latecomer countries must do. This should be achieved by importing, digesting and transforming existing bodies of industrial knowledge through translative adaptation. It is emulation, not innovation in the narrow sense, that is required of latecomer countries in the process of industrial catching up. Similar caveats apply to the pursuit of ICT, high-tech, software, bio-tech, nano-tech, new materials, solar technology, and other fancy terms that are thrown randomly into the plan documents of many developing countries. In order to achieve early industrialization, countries should mainly focus on improving discipline and reducing wastes in factories (kaizen), better marketing, strategic business planning, building enterprise networks, and other ordinary and non-proprietary knowledge to raise productivity and competitiveness (Chapter 3) instead of trying to become a leader in frontline technology. Innovation in the narrow sense will become increasingly important for upper-middle and high-income countries but emulation should be the key strategy for other countries.

Emulation is somewhat similar to, though much broader than, what Rodrik calls *self-discovery*.

> Diversification of the productive structure requires "discovery" of an economy's cost structure—that is, discovery of which new activities can

> be produced at low enough cost to be profitable. Entrepreneurs must experiment with new product lines. They must tinker with technologies from established producers abroad and adapt them to local conditions. This is the process that Ricardo Hausmann and I called "self-discovery."
>
> (Rodrik, 2007, pp. 104–105)

However, emulation is not confined to the introduction of a new product at lower cost for diversifying the product mix. As Schumpeter (1934) eloquently analyzed, it can occur through new products, new production method, new markets, new input procurement, and new industrial organization. Emulation can work miracles when properly applied to the improvement of a factory-floor organization or the creation of linkage between farmers and the food processing industry, for example.

On the other hand, Krugman (1994)'s contention that Asian miracle is a myth because its growth has depended heavily on *perspiration* (accumulation of factors of production such as labor and capital) rather than *inspiration* (growth in total factor productivity) seems to be off the mark. Catch-up industrialization of latecomer countries, especially in its early stages, is always driven more by accumulation of human and non-human capital—education and investment—than productivity growth as measured by TFP. That is the right way to start development, and the fact that so many East Asian countries could do this while most other developing countries cannot is a wonder worth genuine praise and serious investigation.

1.4 The curse of natural resources and foreign money

It may seem that having a large amount of natural resources is an advantage for industrialization because the nation can earn foreign exchange for industrial investment. But history shows that this is not the case. Correlation between natural resource abundance and economic stagnation is a well-documented fact in development economics. All of the top income achievers in East Asia—Singapore, Hong Kong, Japan, Taiwan, and South Korea—are people-rich and resource-poor. On the other hand, it is rare to see countries endowed with large deposits of energy, minerals, and other natural resources relative to population size—Argentina, Mexico, Venezuela, Bolivia, Zambia, Angola, and the Gulf states, for example—to experience a sustained march in national income or boast globally competitive manufacturing industries. True, there are exceptions such as Botswana which manages its diamond wealth reasonably well and Malaysia which has a large FDI-based electronics industry *despite* natural resource abundance (but see Chapter 8 for Malaysia's malaise). Nevertheless, data confirm that countries with few natural resources on average perform better than resource-rich countries. After controlling for past growth trends and geographic factors, Sachs and Warner (2001) conclude from their regression analysis that linkage between natural resource abundance and lackluster growth is robust.

We must, however, beware of the winners' bias. Countries that have succeeded in industrialization look resource-poor *ex post facto* even if they started with the same degree of natural resource dependence as others. For example, Japan in the mid-nineteenth century was an exporter of raw silk and dried tea leaves, and Taiwan before it established Hsinchu Science Park in 1980 was a major producer of rice, sugar, and bananas. These economies look less dependent on natural resources today because their industries grew much faster than agriculture or mining. However, this bias can be avoided if we compare natural resource dependence of each country at some past point with its subsequent growth performance.

Figure 1.7 plots natural resource endowment in 1970, measured by exports of fuels, ores, and minerals in percent of GDP, against average per capita real growth in the subsequent three decades for all countries for which data are available in the World Bank database (81 countries including both developed and developing). The majority of countries are resource-poor and clustered on the left-side of the diagram. They exhibit a wide range of growth performance from negative to very high. From this diagram, we cannot detect any positive association between resource abundance and high growth. In fact, extremely resource-rich countries, on the right-side of the diagram, have been condemned to low or even negative long-term growth. The same results were obtained from a similar diagram of Sachs and Warner (2001) which compared resource endowment in 1970 and average per capita real growth in the subsequent 19 years.

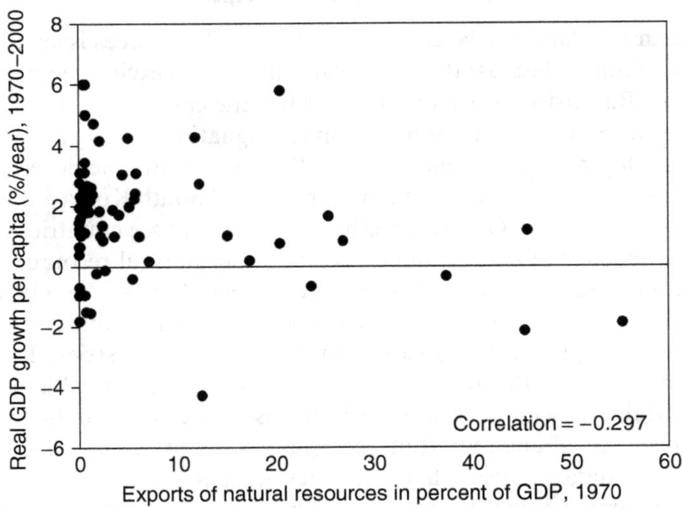

Figure 1.7 Growth and natural resource endowment

Source: Author's calculation using data from World Bank, *World Development Indicators & Global Development Finance*, April 2010.

Reasons for the curse of natural resources are many. Some point to laziness and complacency associated with unearned wealth whilst others emphasize corruption and political capture spawned by the availability of large rents. In the 1970s, unfavorable terms of trade for resource exporters were frequently cited as the cause of their impoverishment, based on the argument that the prices of primary commodities tended to decline relative to the prices of industrial goods in the long run.

However, the most convincing explanation of the curse, at least economically, is that a rise in the natural resource sector crowds out the manufacturing sector. Large export earnings from natural resources inject additional purchasing power into the national economy which pushes up the prices of non-traded goods and non-traded factors of production such as services, wages, land rents, and industrial service costs. Meanwhile, the prices of manufactured goods, which are traded internationally and cannot deviate from global norms, remain the same. As a result, the manufacturing sector loses international competitiveness due to high input costs relative to output prices. Moreover, the domestic factors of production, such as managers, engineers, workers, and capital (if capital mobility is less than perfect), are competed away to the expanding resource sector. Faced with a reduced supply and higher costs of domestic inputs, the manufacturing sector shrinks as natural resource export rises. Industrialization is inhibited.

The loss of industrial competitiveness can occur whether the exchange rate is fixed or floating. If it is fixed, rising domestic demand gradually exerts inflationary pressure on the non-tradable sector while the prices of manufactured goods are anchored globally. The Netherlands discovered off-shore natural gas in the 1960s when major currencies were fixed under the Bretton Woods currency system. As natural gas was extracted, domestic income and spending expanded, investment was redirected toward the natural gas sector, and Dutch wages and prices began to rise. Over time, Dutch industrial products became too costly to compete, and the manufacturing sector shrunk. This phenomenon, in which the Netherlands acquired natural gas but lost manufacturing, was called the "Dutch Disease."

Under a floating exchange-rate regime, the negative impact of resource export may come more quickly and dramatically because of the amplification effect of market expectations. Soon after the major currencies started to float in the mid-1970s, the UK discovered and exploited the North Sea oil fields. Since the oil price was on a rising trend at the time, people expected the UK to earn a large amount of foreign exchange in the future. But even before these earnings were realized, currency speculation pushed up the British pound suddenly and sharply. The resulting loss of price competitiveness severely damaged the British manufacturing sector. From the mid-1970s to the early 1980s, the share of North Sea oil and gas in British GDP rose from 0 to 5 percent while the share of manufacturing in British GDP fell from about 30 percent to 24 percent. In a world with floating currencies and free capital mobility, natural resource abundance not only damages the manufacturing sector but also magnifies macroeconomic instability.

Economic performance of a country that relies heavily on resource exports is strongly influenced by the gyration of commodity prices. According to Hirano (2009), correlation between oil-rich Nigeria's nominal GDP and the price of crude oil, both expressed in US dollars, from 1970 to 2007 was as high as 0.942. Among countries whose nominal GDP shows similarly high correlation with the oil price are Trinidad and Tobago (0.947), Saudi Arabia (0.925), Kuwait (0.914), and Russia (0.891). Figure 1.8 visually presents per capita nominal GDP and the price movement of main export commodity of Zambia (copper), Côte d'Ivoire (cocoa), Venezuela (oil), and Uganda (coffee). The high correlation between the two variables is truly remarkable.

The correlation between the aggregate GDP of Sub-Saharan Africa and oil price is also as high as 0.902. The gross regional product of Sub-Saharan Africa, which continued to stagnate around US$300 to 350 billion during 1990–2002, suddenly began to soar in 2003 to reach nearly US$900 billion by 2007. Much of this "growth" was explainable by the oil price that jumped 2.8 times between 2002 and 2007 and inflation of other extractive commodities. While income per head of many African countries made great advances in official statistics at that time, living conditions of subsistence farmers on the continent were little affected. Growth driven by global commodity markets is fragile and unsustainable. Hirano concludes that

> in its post-independence history, Africa's economic growth was realized only when the prices of oil or metals increased. Economic growth of Sub-Saharan Africa in the 2000s was also brought about by a surge in the prices of mineral resources including oil . . . which leads to a suspicion that this growth will come to an end when resource prices stop rising.
>
> (Hirano, 2009, p. 209)

If a large injection of purchasing power into the national economy causes de-industrialization and macroeconomic instability, similar problems can occur not only with natural resources but also with other large receipts such as foreign direct investment (FDI), financial investment in bonds and stocks, property investments, big infrastructure projects, and development and military aid. Problems may be generated even by workers' remittances, illegal money from drugs and other crimes, and the money that foreigners in aid business and military operation spend for consumption, housing, transport and personal security in the country if they are a sufficiently large relative to GDP.

As capital accounts were liberalized in many developing countries in the 1990s, generalized Dutch Diseases caused by excessive inflows of foreign funds of one kind or another and their subsequent withdrawal became frequent and globally more synchronous. Inflows such as investment in bonds, stocks, and property projects are particularly volatile and subject to the whims of market psychology. Countries that receive large foreign funds relative to GDP experience temporary growth acceleration accompanied by the symptoms of overheating—i.e., consumption boom, construction boom, land speculation,

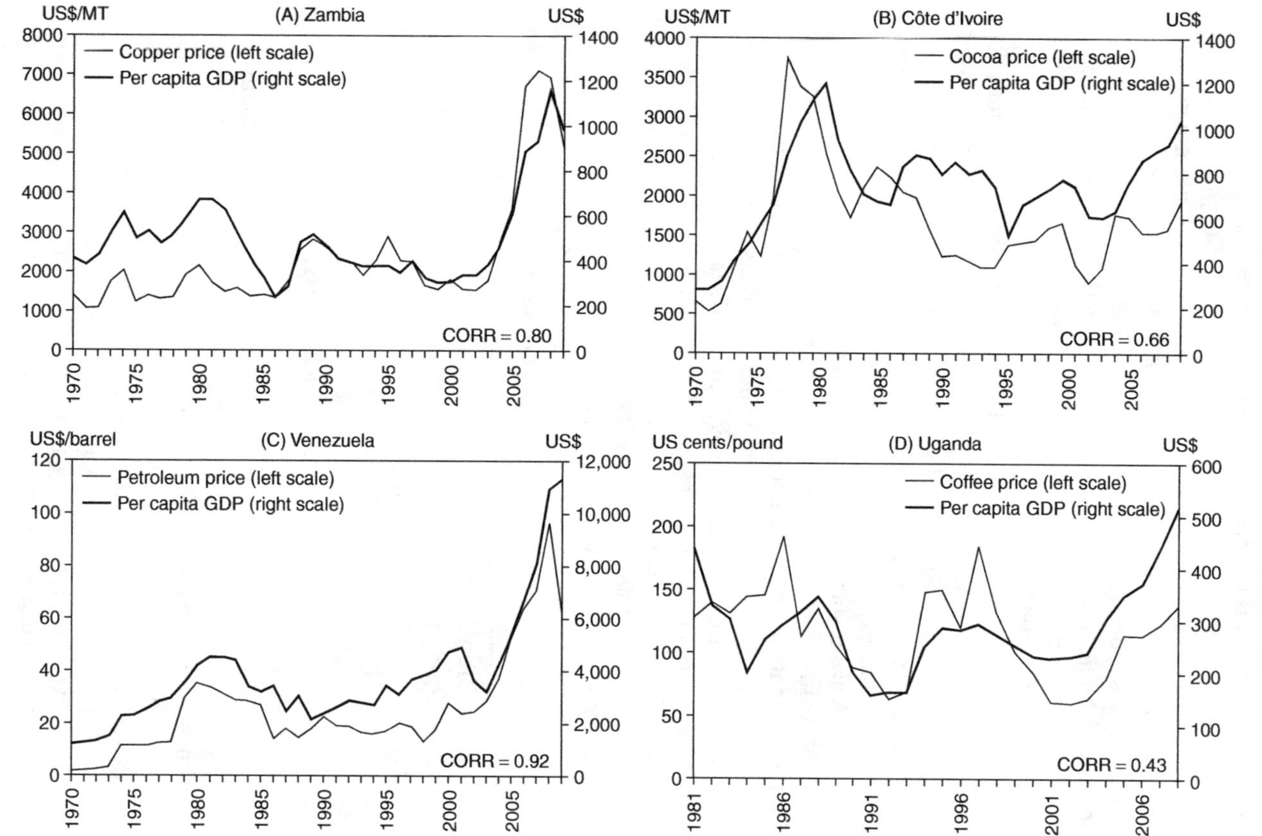

Figure 1.8 Per capita income and commodity price: (A) Zambia, (B) Côte d'Ivoire, (C) Venezuela, (D) Uganda

Source: International Monetary Fund, *International Financial Statistics*, August 2010.

stock-market bubbles, inflation, current-account deficits, *rising* international reserves, and a loss of international competitiveness. This mix is troublesome enough, but the real risk is the possibility of post-bubble crisis if this situation proceeds too far. A severe reversal may occur as commodity prices fall, asset markets collapse, investors leave the country, the currency plummets, and bad debt mounts. The Asian financial crisis of 1997–1998 was a severe regional crisis caused by a sudden and massive withdrawal of short-term commercial bank loans which had a strong regional contagion effect. Ephemeral foreign money also played havoc with Mexico (1994), Russia (1998), Brazil (1998–1999), Turkey (2000–2001), and Argentina (2001–2002).

More recently, around 2007, much of the world experienced economically good times. Even Sub-Saharan Africa, which had stagnated for long, enjoyed a collective growth spurt. The main driver of this boom was global financial glut, and commodity inflation ignited by it, which stimulated the economies of the countries that exported energy, minerals, and primary commodities such as Russia, Kazakhstan, Mongolia, UK, Nigeria, Zambia, South Africa, Botswana, Mauritania, and Angola. Swollen resource money flowed into global financial centers which transformed it into other forms of purchasing power and spread the boom globally. The financial markets of the UK, US, and UAE, which received this resource money, expanded vigorously. Meanwhile, China and Vietnam, on the receiving end, faced inflows of foreign funds in various forms such as robust export earnings, workers' remittances, big public and private projects, and portfolio investment. This global financial and commodity bubble came to an end by the Lehman Shock originating in the United States in 2008 and further deflated by the European crisis in 2011–2012.

With all these facts and possibilities in front of us, it is hard to avoid the conclusion that natural resources and foreign money are hazardous to one's economic health. Growth spurts driven by a discovery of new energy or mineral resources, large foreign investment in construction or telecom, massive aid programs for a fragile state, or a jump in the price of the commodity a country exports, are not only temporary but also divert the attention of policymakers and private investors to activities that are not desirable or sustainable. Natural resources and foreign money may make you rich, at least for a while, but they do not make you innovative or hardworking.

This is not to argue that receiving a large amount of foreign exchange is always and everywhere a bad thing. But it will easily turn to a negative factor in development unless proper policy mechanisms are in place to avoid the known pitfalls. Additional policy issues for resource-rich countries and large receivers of foreign money include: (i) diversification of export base, (ii) a stabilization fund to smooth the fluctuation of commodity revenue, (iii) fiscal, monetary, and exchange-rate management to cope with severe balance-of-payments shocks, (iv) channeling windfall gains to productive investment in line with a consistent long-term development strategy, and (v) when feasible, processing of natural resources instead of exporting them in raw form. If these extra issues are well handled, abundant natural resources and attraction of foreign money may even become a positive factor for the development of latecomer countries. However, this is hardly a universal proposition as success requires high additional policy capability. Availability of unearned resources is neither a sufficient nor necessary condition for economic development driven by knowledge, skills, and technology.

1.5 Overcoming middle income (and other) traps

A developmental trap is a situation where a country is stuck at an income level dictated by given resources and initial advantages and cannot rise beyond that level. The level of income where the trap may occur depends on the size of a country's windfall gain. If unearned income is small relative to population, the country will be caught in a poverty trap. If the country enjoys abundant natural resources or foreign money relative to population, income per head will be high without expending any development effort. If the country has moderate resources and advantages, it will most likely be caught in a middle-income trap.

Determinants of the level of a developmental trap include natural conditions such as soil, climate, topography, water supply, coastal access, forest and marine resources, extractive energy and minerals, and frequency of natural disasters. Potential income is also influenced by external political and economic factors such as inflows of foreign investment and aid, global and regional trade regimes, colonial legacies, geopolitical positions, and regional conflicts and crises. These are more or less given conditions beyond the power of domestic citizens or the government and define the starting point of development for each country. Some countries are naturally rich while others face poverty and hunger. Lucky people may conjure up envy but not necessarily respect or admiration. But even high-income countries endowed with large unearned advantages must face the challenge of using them to build an internal value-creating mechanism as advantages do not usually last eternally.

Growth that depends on unearned advantages will sooner or later come to an end. As the government stops suppressing the economy and liberalizes it, the country automatically rises to the level corresponding to its given factors. But this can hardly be called successful development. Development, in the true sense, must come from the upgrading of human capital. A continued march to high income is possible only when people improve capabilities and work hard to overcome existing constraints and create new value. A country may rise to a certain income level with little effort but will eventually get stuck in that income category—or even gradually slips from that category—unless it builds a national mindset and institutions that encourage constant improvement of its human capital. To establish these, policy must lead the way because the other two determinants of income performance—given advantages and private sector dynamism—cannot be the initiating force.

Geological, geographical, or geopolitical advantages are unevenly distributed across countries in our unfair world. This is a fact that cannot be altered and therefore must be accepted by policymakers. Private-sector dynamism also differs from one country or one ethnic group to another. This includes inherent vitality of private agents in commerce and industry as well as effectiveness with which they respond to policies. This point may be hard to take for those who believe that all humans are created equal in their ability to seize economic opportunities and that all farmers and merchants are the same in their response to economic incentives. A Western economist who visited East Asia for the first time for a conference strongly protested against the statement made there that Korean workers were superior to Thai workers in their productivity and discipline on the factory floor even under the same management—a fact too obvious for veteran executives of any multi-national corporations operating in East Asia. Whether politically correct or not, it is an undeniable fact that people are different in their ability to create commercial networks or manufacture industrial goods just as they are differently competent in football matches or musical composition. Chinese merchants are all over the world taking risks and opening new frontiers even without the aid of their government, but ethnic Malays lack vigor and ingenuity in business dealings even at home—this is the controversial argument made by Mahathir bin Mohamad before he became the prime minister of Malaysia (Mahathir, 1970). The issue of cultural differences will be discussed more fully in Chapter 2.

Although the level of private-sector dynamism is given at any moment in any country, it is not immutable. Just as with athletic or musical ability, talent and effort both matter. Over time, lazy people can be made more hard-working and industrious people even more so. It is well to recall that a Japanese government labor survey conducted more than a century ago found Japanese workers only half as productive as American workers with such lamentable characteristics as low saving, lack of work discipline, dearth of skill, and frequent job hopping (Ministry of Agriculture and Commerce, 1903).

Policy capability is also unevenly distributed across countries. Governments in fragile states are often too occupied with maintaining power and social order to be able to seriously discuss long-term economic strategies, let alone execute them. On the other hand, there are some countries whose leaders seem to have the knack for managing development politics and economics and making progress through decisive action and pragmatic trial-and-error. To be successful, such leaders must be supported by elite technocrats who concretize and implement their visions (Chapter 4). East Asia has abounded in such developmental leaders and technocrats, and other regions also have seen them occasionally. But the capacity of most countries falls in between; they are capable enough to draft five-year plans and industrial master plans but without sufficient expertise to effectively fine-tune and implement them.

Although economic development must fundamentally be driven by private producers and investors, just letting markets loose in a country that lacks human capital and is struggling with globalization pressure may not see a spontaneous rise of private dynamism with innovativeness and international competitiveness. In such a case, the first impetus for growth must come from the government which stirs up a sleepy and undeveloped private sector into investment, risk-taking, and learning. In theory, non-government actors such as business associations, chambers of commerce and industry, and individual business leaders could also become catalysts for industrial development. In late-nineteenth-century Japan, these private actors did play key roles in industrialization in close cooperation with government policies. However, in today's remaining latecomer countries such private initiatives may not automatically arise or make strong impact on national development. Asking a lethargic private sector to discipline itself does not seem a valid answer.

Policy capability can be strengthened if there is a strong political will and a systematic cataloguing and learning of relevant facts and policy measures. This book argues that such policy learning is possible, and illustrates how it can be done—by comparing historical and contemporary best practices and extracting common patterns from them, then building capability to create from these best practices a policy package most stable for each country. Well-instructed policy learning should be the entry point for overcoming a middle-income trap or any other developmental trap that may occur, rather than an ideological debate over the relative size of market failure versus government failure. Through such policy learning, a nationwide mechanism should be established to encourage constant human capital accumulation. This will be the main topic of Chapters 2 to 4. Subsequent Chapters 5 to 10 will give concrete and remarkable examples in this effort.

1.6 Summary

Globalization has a natural tendency to polarize income among countries. It helps rich countries to solidify their lead and maximize the benefit of their industrial strength through free but lopsided trade and investment. Meanwhile, knowledge does not flow freely from high-level to low-level countries, and latecomers are not given a chance or sufficient time to catch up in skills and technology. It is foolish to deny the polarizing tendency of globalization in our age. But it is also not advisable to attack globalization as the principal enemy of development.

The proposition advanced in this book is as follows. Countries that earn a high income are those that have succeeded in installing a national mechanism that encourages constant upgrading of human capital. While production, investment, and trade should in principle be carried out by the private sector, private agents in latecomer countries cannot build such a system without the leadership and guidance of the government. Thus, the role of policy in assisting private dynamism becomes crucial. Since most governments in latecomer countries do not initially have knowledge or capability to do this, policy must be learned systematically from concrete international experiences with appropriate selectivity and adjustment for each country and sector. This is a two-step approach to national capacity building; improve the government's capability to guide the private sector first, then improve the capability of private agents.

Even in our world of the early twenty-first century where globalization has greatly deepened in comparison with the recent past, policy measures that can resist or even reverse the tendency of income polarization are available. They mainly focus on developing industrial human resources in a way that does not violate any international rules or regional agreements. Such policy measures, which I shall collectively call *proactive industrial policy* in the following chapters, are different from past industrial policies including infant industry promotion which featured import protection and export subsides. Proactive industrial policy is already practiced widely in East Asia and elsewhere and producing results. This should be learned and implemented by countries in all developing regions.

The development model that deserves serious attention and research is not growth based on natural resource abundance or geopolitical advantage but an internal mechanism that continuously generates new sources of growth within a country. While natural resources may be depleted or become obsolete over time, human capital never wears out by use. In fact, the more intensively it is used, the greater capability it will acquire. The construction of a national mindset and institutions that strengthen human capital is the most important task of the government in a developing country. It should also be the main objective of international development cooperation.

2 Industrial policy in the age of globalization

Any policy, be it industrial or otherwise, must be crafted and executed in the context of a particular age, society, and international relations. The world of the early twenty-first century in which we live is different from past ones. In order to achieve industrialization, some policies frequently employed in the nineteenth century or even a few decades ago are no longer permitted or effective today. Conversely, public intervention that was unknown previously may have to be invented and fortified to take advantage of new situations. Industrial policy formulation consistent with the needs and constraints of a particular place and time must start with the understanding of the shifting political, social, and global environment in which such policy must operate.

2.1 Eager to learn

When I attended an international conference in a low-income African country, an economic advisor to the prime minister of that country, whom I happened to meet in a lunch buffet queue, said to me: "We need action-oriented policy advice, not purely academic research. Do you have any concrete studies from East Asia that are useful for us?" This country already had an industrial development strategy for several years, and partially implemented it through self-study, dispatch of young researchers to South Korea, and donor support. The country has embraced benchmarking and business process re-engineering as key productivity tools, and drafted a few sectoral industrial master plans with technical assistance from foreign experts. Following the Korean model, a monthly export steering committee presided over by the prime minister was set up to monitor progress and solve problems. But industrial performance, while visible in a few small sub-sectors, was not satisfactory to its leaders.

On another occasion I was in a conference co-hosted by the World Bank and the government of an industrializing country in East Asia with the attendance of the prime minister. The topic was how this country should revise its growth model to generate internal value and secure a strategic position in the regional production network. Renowned economists from

Washington, DC explained the general features of a middle-income trap with ample data and proposed a six-step approach to prevent it. Reaction from the policymakers and economists of this country was not very enthusiastic. They felt that the presentations by the prominent guests were too general and the proposed steps were too crude and mechanical. The country had already attained the lower-middle-income status and the government had begun to study the future risk of growth slowdown. The country was desperately looking for concrete industrial measures for the next ten years to avoid this fate. At this late stage in policy formulation a general illustration of what middle-income traps were was no longer very informative.

Nowadays developing countries seriously considering or actively implementing industrial policies are many. Not only the two countries mentioned above but also a large number of countries and regional organizations in Asia, Africa, Latin America, and elsewhere have already graduated from an ideological debate over state versus market and are struggling to draft and execute policies to level up industrial capabilities and strengthen targeted sectors. Industrial master plans and numerical targets have multiplied on paper. However, the quality of industrial policy is often low and effective implementation remains elusive.

In East Asia where industrial policy has long been accepted and practiced, the question is not whether industrial policy is valid but how to continuously improve its design and implementation in order to cope with new global trends and compete effectively with China, India, and other rival economies. More surprising is the fact that industrial policy is no longer taboo even in other developing regions which experienced a forced introduction of economic liberalization, privatization, and international integration in previous decades. In Africa, Botswana, Egypt, Ethiopia, Namibia, Rwanda, Tanzania, Tunisia, and Zambia are some of the countries that are keenly interested in learning and adopting industrial policy. In Latin America, Brazil has led the industrial policy drive while other countries, such as El Salvador, are showing willingness to follow. Global re-focusing on industrial policy and issues is evident.

The situation is similar with regional development organizations. The African Union proclaims that "No country or region in the world has achieved prosperity and a decent socio-industrial life for its citizens without the development of a robust industrial sector" (African Union, 2008, p. 1). Its Strategy for the Implementation of the Plan of Action for the Accelerated Industrial Development of Africa (AIDA) contains seven program clusters, 16 programs, and 49 projects to bolster industry in the member countries (African Union, 2007). This strategy is comprehensive and covers seven areas including policy and institutional frameworks, productivity and trade, infrastructure and energy, technical skills, innovation and R&D, financing, and environment. This policy menu, at least on paper, overlaps significantly with what East Asian governments do (Chapter 3). The general policy direction is already agreed. The challenge, of course, is how to carry out these ambitious programs and projects effectively and who will finance them. The question of what role a regional organization such as the African Union should play when most industrial policies are conducted at the national level also remains.

We can safely declare that the days of ideological debate over the two naïve extremes—free markets versus state-led growth—which marked much of the 1980s and 1990s are over. While emotional rejection of the term "industrial policy" still remains in some parts of the world,[1] the global development community seems to have regained balance. A new consensus has emerged that the government in a latecomer country has an important role to play in supporting private-sector-led development and that the quality of public policy matters greatly. Acceptance of the market principle and globalization should go hand-in-hand with the capacity building of policy-makers who must handle these trends and retain sufficient policy tools for latecomer industrialization. The World Bank seems to be split between entrenched neoclassical believers who loathe the very idea of industrial policy and those who embrace it under certain conditions. A continued debate with the remaining soldiers of the Washington Consensus may be academically interesting but it is no longer indispensable for taking the next pragmatic step forward in global development strategy.

The argument for industrial policy cannot be settled through theoretical debate alone as its validity depends critically on the accumulation of successes on the ground. Theory must be supported by practice, and practice must inform theory. The two are interrelated and inseparable. The fact is that many developing countries have already accepted the idea of industrial policy and are eager to learn its practical essentials. For such "converts," what is needed is not a theoretical justification for government intervention, which most of us already know (externalities, coordination failures, information failures, and other various market failures), but concrete and systematic instructions as to how policy should be constructed and executed and how common pitfalls could be avoided. This must be done with a deep understanding of local circumstances to prevent imposition of one-size-fits-all solutions. Unfortunately, development economics does not teach such operational details. There is a serious discrepancy between policy recommendations provided by development economists, which are often too naïve, general, and mechanical, and what policymakers of latecomer countries really need in terms of intellectual input.

In the past, countries that have succeeded in industrial catch-up did so through self-study, improvisation, and trial-and-error. With no systematic instruction from outside, only those countries that happened to possess the right policy mindset and a dynamic private sector could launch themselves onto a path to high income. The fact that only a small number of countries achieved this feat proves the inherent difficulty of this self-improvement approach. By now, all latecomer countries that had these propitious properties—the United States, France, Germany, Japan, Singapore, Hong Kong, Taiwan, South Korea, and the like—have already moved up to join the rich club. Meanwhile, countries that are still "developing" today lacked necessary properties at the starting point. Their catching-up is doubly difficult because globalization has deepened significantly today and because their domestic capabilities in the private and public sectors fall short of those of the countries that have already graduated from the poor club.

Collecting micro-level data and running regressions, development economics may be able to prove the importance of, say, educational achievements of company owners or technical training of workers for economic growth. But this "discovery" is hardly enough to guide policymakers who need to calibrate teaching curriculums, design incentives for parents, students, and teachers, and establish links between training institutions and hiring firms. Developing countries eager to introduce effective industrial policy usually face ad hoc and fragmented advice from experts and academics. Nowadays the number of economists who support industrial policy is increasing, but few teach pragmatic details on how key policy components should be designed and implemented and in what sequencing. But this is precisely where a developing country stumbles. What is missing is systemic learning on industrial policy formulation backed by international experiences and at the same time tailored to each country's policy capability and socio-economic situation. Early industrializers did not have to go to school, but today's latecomers may benefit greatly from such formal instructions.

When an industrial master plan is drafted for, say, the agro-processing or garment industry, formulation of its contents and structure are often left to a small group of people who happened to be assigned to the task, which may be officials of the ministry in charge, local academics or foreign consultants (there is a large supply of domestic researchers and foreign-consultant companies in this particular branch of the aid industry). Oftentimes the government of a developing country is not actively involved in setting visions, roadmaps or action plans but only makes cosmetic comments on the policy draft prepared by a few. In this process, expertise in policy design and implementation is not internalized and public–private partnership is not activated. Such superficial and passive policymaking cannot ensure implementability. It must be replaced by an approach based on strong country ownership, systematic research, and active stakeholder participation.

Moreover, political leaders and policymakers sometimes jump at policy advice which happens to be presented to them without serious consideration of compatibility with the domestic and external conditions of the country or a review of alternative possibilities in solving a particular problem. Partial knowledge of what Japan or South Korea did in the past, be it postal saving, export drive or heavy industrialization by huge conglomerates, is insufficient as an intellectual input to policy formulation. A more comprehensive study of various international best practices is needed because all countries are different and one country's success at a certain point in time cannot be directly copied and pasted to another context.

Such casual attempts at industrial policy, which seem to be proliferating in recent years, often fail not because fundamental direction is wrong but because details—policy content, procedures, and organizations—are not set up properly. Without swimming lessons or a piano tutor, it may be difficult for a child to acquire sufficient skills to become a good swimmer or a professional musician. But this fact should not lead us to the conclusion that the child has no talent in these subjects. In the initial stage, well-structured lessons by an experienced instructor are useful until the child masters basics and reaches an intermediate level, at which it can begin to establish its own style.

Additionally, it should be recognized that mimicking the stylized facts of already highly industrialized countries does not lead to the optimal development path for latecomer countries. Studying how Mozart composed piano concertos does not help ordinary people to improve their musical skills very much. For the uninitiated, what early comers did spontaneously and what was obvious to them need to be learned more explicitly and systematically.

2.2 Changing the world or living in it

There are basically two approaches to an evil world. The one is fighting for correction and the other is discovering a way to live in it. According to many authors, globalization erects barriers to catch-up industrialization by latecomers and tends to perpetuate income polarization between the rich and poor countries (Chapter 1). Should all developing countries of the world unite for justice and equal treatment, or should they resign and despair? My suggestion for the twenty-first century latecomer countries is to adopt a two-part strategy: collectively fight for a fundamental change in global development architecture but simultaneously adopt policy measures for industrialization that do not violate existing international rules (this includes taking full advantages of loopholes and waivers in the World Trade Organization (WTO), regional integration, and bilateral agreements). Changing the world usually takes time. Meanwhile, there are many policy options that latecomers can learn and adopt individually and immediately.

In his book *Kicking Away the Ladder* (Chang, 2002), Ha-Joon Chang cites a large number of historical cases to prove, quite convincingly, that the policies and institutions currently recommended to developing countries—deregulation, privatization, transparent and efficient bureaucracy, protection of private property rights, and the like—were actually not adopted by the developed countries when they themselves were developing. In the past, early comers actively availed themselves of the so-called *infant industry promotion policy* featuring temporary tariff protection which was supplemented by other public interventions such as export subsidies, tariff rebates, conferring of monopoly rights, cartel arrangements, directed credits, investment planning, manpower planning, and R&D supports. According to Chang, current prohibition of (some of) these measures, and the call for small government and full acceptance of market forces in an early stage of development, effectively removes the means by which latecomers climb up the ladder of industrialization. He wants a radical change in the International Monetary Fund (IMF) and

World Bank loan conditionalities to recognize that "many of the policies that are considered 'bad' are in fact not so, and that there can be no 'best practice' policy to which everyone should adhere." He also demands the re-writing of the WTO and other trade rules "in such a way that a more active use of infant industry promotion tools (e.g., tariffs and subsidies) is allowed" (Chang, 2002, p. 141).

Dani Rodrik agrees with Chang, saying that "countries dismantle trade restrictions as they get richer . . . today's rich countries, with few exceptions, embarked on modern economic growth behind protective barriers, but now have low trade barriers" (Rodrik, 2007, p. 217). He criticizes the WTO as well as avid integration crusaders for confounding the means (trade liberalization) with the goal (development). He contrasts Vietnam, which grew rapidly under restrictive trade in the 1990s, with Haiti, whose economy stagnated after undertaking comprehensive trade liberalization in 1994–95. With a proper choice of time period for each country, similar contrasting examples can be presented between China, India, South Korea, Malaysia, etc., which recorded high growth under gradualism of one sort or another, and Kyrgyzstan, Mongolia, El Salvador, Bolivia, etc., which suffered from lackluster growth under free trade. Rodrik says that "the benefits of trade openness are now greatly oversold. Deep trade liberalization cannot be relied on to deliver high rates of economic growth and therefore does not deserve the high priority it typically receives in the development strategies pushed by leading multinational organizations." He concludes that the world should move away from viewing free trade as an end itself, and allow for diversity in institutions and standards that support development of each country (Rodrik, 2007, pp. 225–228). But, according to him, this privilege should be available to "democratic" countries only.

Similarly, Cimoli et al. (2009c) find faults with the current WTO regime and the TRIPS agreement that benefit a subset of industrial interests in the developed world at the cost of latecomer countries and global consumers. They also criticize bilateral trade agreements, especially ones concluded with the United States, as a device to fill remaining loopholes and exceptions in the WTO and TRIPS rules that give welcoming breathing space for developing countries. The authors propose a reform of global economic governance consisting of: (i) greater provision of "managed trade" not for protecting vested interests of first-world lame ducks but for nurturing infants in the developing world; (ii) removal of anti-developmental bias of agricultural trade policies in developing countries; (iii) a reduced use of intellectual property rights protection; and (iv) a new global labor standards concerning child labor, work conditions, the right to unionize, and environmental respect.

The general direction in which these authors want to go is clear. I also happily endorse global effort to regain more policy space for latecomer countries. Without negating the value of collective bargaining for global justice, however, this book emphasizes another area of action available to latecomer countries. That is the introduction of a large number of policy measures which are permitted under the current global rules of trade and investment but remain largely unexploited due to the lack of knowledge and experience. For developing countries with a strong will to learn, there are many policy measures that can be implemented selectively and quickly without waiting for the success of a collective action on global development architecture. Many East Asian governments already practice them with good results, and governments in other developing regions should also study and introduce them.

2.3 Re-visiting industrial policy debates

In attending policy dialogues and conferences featuring industrial policy all over the world, one cannot but notice that the same questions are raised all the time. Four of such frequently-asked questions, which are interrelated, are listed below together with rejoinders from the East Asian perspective.

FAQ1: *Are past experiences of East Asian countries really useful for us? Is it not better to create our own policy package than copying the policies of other countries?*

The cliché has it that each country is different and times have also changed. To my knowledge, there is no government that does not declare that "our country is unique" and policies of other countries cannot therefore be copied directly. We also hear that infant industry promotion (temporary tariff protection of domestic industries while they grow) widely practiced by early industrializing countries is no longer available to developing countries under the globalization pressure of the twenty-first century.

As a general description of the contemporary world, I have no disagreement with any of these statements. No reasonable person would advise that what South Korea did in the 1960s be repeated in Tanzania today. Our age is unlike the past, and Tanzania is not South Korea. However, there is a risk in stressing this obvious fact because insistence on the uniqueness of each country may become an excuse to turn a blind eye to the rich policy experiences of other latecomer countries without which good policy is difficult to construct. The very purpose of an in-depth study of international experiences is to craft a realistic and workable industrial policy package appropriate for the country in question from a broad and practical menu. A policy document drafted without such a study is likely to be crude, unimplementable, and ineffective.

International experiences from other countries and different times are useful building blocks for industrial policy for two reasons. First, the general contents of good policy are not radically different from one case to another. For example, the key ingredients of successful industrial estates, small and medium enterprises (SME) consultation systems, or science and engineering universities, are basically the same across time and countries although modifications must be made in details and at the margin to reflect the reality of the host country. Second, a comparative analysis of international experiences will illuminate factors that contribute to successful policymaking as well as warn policymakers of pitfalls and mistakes that must be avoided. Concrete experiences of other countries in any policy area should thus be regarded as raw materials which policymakers can select, modify, combine, or improve to create their own policy package.

FAQ2: *Is industrial policy possible at all in our age of globalization? Can governments do anything when cross-border private flows of goods, services, and capital are so huge?*

People who are not trained to face the world with its perpetual diversity and conflicts tend to jump from one extreme to the other without staying in the middle. The general director of a previously state-owned steel company in an emerging economy with previously socialist tradition stated, with a sigh of grief, that all polices were now futile because global market forces determined everything and the government nothing. In his opinion, policy was impotent in dealing with foreign dumping, bottlenecks in port capacity, or mutual destruction of steel mills through over-investment and price wars. His pessimism cannot be justified because the end of planning is not the same thing as the beginning of unrestrained markets. While the state should get out of production and investment in the steel sector, it has an important role to play in market management—for example, in projecting demand, setting quality, safety, and environmental standards, encouraging skill formation and technology transfer, and avoidance of excess entry, over-investment, and illegal sales.

The world today is certainly more integrated than the world of the 1950s or 1960s, but to argue that industrial policy is no longer possible is a gross overstatement. On the contrary, "more interdependent economies are likely to require *more* and *more sophisticated* measures of policy intervention by the weaker economies" (Cimoli et al., 2009c, p. 542) if they are to catch up in income and technological capabilities. Raising tariffs, subsidizing exports, imposing local content requirements, and free copying of foreign technology are no longer permitted officially, so policy space did shrink in comparison with yesteryear. But the rest of industrial policy remains intact. Global and regional integration does not penalize or prohibit a vast majority of policy tools related to, for example, visions and roadmaps, education and training, enterprise consultation, logistics and transportation, power supply and energy efficiency, banking and securities markets, product standards and tests, industrial cluster formation, business associations, and numerous others (Chapter 3).

As proposed earlier, twenty-first century latecomers should adopt the two-part strategy in which they collectively lobby international organizations for the expansion of policy space and at the same time individually implement policy measures consistent with the current global rules. As a matter of fact, none of the policy measures proposed and explained in this book violates any of the global, regional, or bilateral economic rules in principle—that is to say, unless they are imposed in such a distorted way that intentionally discriminates against foreign firms or otherwise damages foreign interests. To put it differently, what developing countries should aim at is infant industry promotion without violating any of the international rules of the early twenty-first century.

FAQ3: *Shouldn't industrial promotion be general rather than sector-specific? Governments should not pick winners because they cannot distinguish infants from zombies and because policies are easily captured by interest groups.*

Anne Krueger, the former World Bank chief economist and champion of trade liberalization, once remarked that official promotion of a specific industrial sector, be it garment, automotive, or electronics, would most likely fail due to *policy mistake* and *political capture*, which are two perennial problems associated with state intervention. In her own words:

> The problem with the [infant industry] argument, as a basis for policy, is that it fails to provide any guidance as to how to distinguish between an infant that will grow up and a would-be producer seeking protection because it is privately profitable . . . The infant industry argument also is an excellent example of a theory that is nonoperational because criteria for bureaucrats to identify cases have not been put forward.
>
> (Krueger, 1997, p. 12)

> No matter how careful economists are, special interests always will seize their research results in supporting their own objectives. And, no matter how sophisticated and careful research findings are, there always will be politicians formulating, and non-economists administering, policies.
>
> (Ibid., p. 19)

Today, neoclassical ideology no longer holds sway and few would support Krueger's extreme pessimism over the capacity and intention of the government. Furthermore, as mentioned above, industrial promotion in our age is—and should be—conducted with an array of WTO-consistent policy instruments rather than high tariffs and non-tariff barriers. Even so, the risks highlighted by Krueger are real and should not be dismissed lightly. Where I differ from Krueger is policy conclusion. The fact that bureaucrats may not know the selection criteria and policy may be hijacked by rent seekers should not lead us to abandon sector-specific industrial support. Policy capability is not given but can be improved over time. With proper instruction, governments can learn to avoid these obvious risks of selective industrial policy. East Asia abounds in such "wise" governments, but their policy capabilities were acquired through learning and not by inheritance.

The risks associated with selective industrial policies are real when the government's policy capability is low. When officials do not understand what private firms want or where the industry is headed, they invariably impose policies in a top-down manner which are detested or rejected by investors. However, this problem melts away as policy learning advances. If effective channels of public–private partnership are established, government and private firms come to trust each other and can constantly share information on global and domestic situations as well as strengths and weaknesses of local industries. The ministry of industry comes to know the business strategy of each company and even conflict of interest among them. Meanwhile, government–business relationship is kept at arm's length by proper institutional mechanisms. As government and private firms jointly draft sectoral master plans, public will and private intention are no longer separable. Policymakers can sometimes propose visions and strategies which overcome shortsightedness or coordinate different interests that prevail among producers. Such intervention is readily accepted and even highly welcomed by the private sector. In political science, such strong, well-informed, and interest-neutral government is said to possess *embedded autonomy* (Evans, 1995). That this is not a scientific fiction but normal practice in a number of countries is demonstrated by studying the policymaking processes of Singapore, South Korea, and Malaysia (Chapters 6–8), among others.

Official guidance is not necessarily at odds with private-sector development. In fact, they complement each other in advanced policy formulation. Dispute over "picking winners" becomes irrelevant for proud, impartial, and competent policymakers striving to become one with the private sector for national development. If the business community still rejects official policy, that simply means that government has not perfected its policymaking skill.

At the practical level, industrial policy instruments overlap greatly with instruments to promote the policy purposes supported by all donors and researchers—such as private sector development (PSD), technical and vocational education and training (TVET), human resource development (HRD), investment climate improvement, capacity development, marketing, integration into global value chains, and building industrial clusters (see Chapter 3 for concrete industrial policy instruments). This means that many industrial policy measures are already accepted and practiced under different labels, and the gap between government-led industrialization and private sector-led growth is more apparent than real. All are talking about the same policies.

Moreover, the line between general and selective promotion becomes fuzzy in actual implementation. Thailand focuses on skill formation in the automotive sector as a result of private-sector demand backed by a long history of development of this sector in the country. The Singaporean government assisted Binh Duong Province of Vietnam to train electronics workers because the training center was adjacent to an industrial estate hosting a large number of foreign electronics manufacturers. Should these actions be condemned as sectorally biased, and should Thailand and Vietnam conduct training in all sectors, not just automotive or electronics? Hardly. Under resource constraints that developing countries inevitably face, prioritization and targeting are common practice recommended by all development partners.

FAQ4: *Should industrial policy in developing countries conform to comparative advantage or defy it?*

This question, closely related to the previous one, was debated between Justin Lin and Ha-Joon Chang, two leading development economists from Asia (Lin and Chang, 2009). Both agree that technology upgrading and structural change are key to the catching-up of latecomer countries. They also recognize the important role of government as a facilitator of private investment because hands-off policies are not likely to attain this goal. The concept of "comparative advantage" in this debate must be interpreted as a dynamic one in which new industries and products are expected to emerge in a way consistent with the historical path and existing factor endowments of the country in question, not a static one in which technology and endowments of each country are given.

The two differ in the type of industries that should be supported by the government. Lin asserts that policy support—removal of market failures and provision of basic growth functions such as education and training, infrastructure, and incentives for pioneer firms—should be given to "encourage the emergence of firms, industries, and sectors that, once launched, will make effective use of the country's *current* comparative advantage" (p. 486, italics in original) based on existing skills, technology, capital stock, natural resources, and so on. By contrast, Chang contends that industrial capabilities are acquired through concrete production processes unique to each industry which can be started without past heritage. According to him, confining the policy scope to extrapolation of past trends is too narrow and cannot accelerate technological upgrading or structural transformation. In order to catch up in income and technology, a latecomer country must create new comparative advantages, not just follow obvious ones. In this way, Lin cautions against careless choice of industries while Chang stresses creativity and risk-taking in policymaking.

Although the two positions seem far apart, actual differences may not be so large and the debate may be more rhetorical than substantial. In reality, except for white-elephant projects that "deviate too much from one's comparative advantages" (p. 491), it is difficult to tell whether an industry is conforming to a country's (dynamic) comparative advantage or defying it. This is particularly true with manufacturing industries which rely heavily on management, skills, technology, large-scale investment, finance, and other non-natural factors. In fact, looking at the same global firms such as South Korea's Pohang Steel and Finland's Nokia, Lin assures that their emergence is a natural evolution from existing capabilities in each country while Chang sees a clear break from past trends (pp. 493–494 and pp. 497–498).

Future industrializing possibilities of a developing country are broad. For example, Vietnam has attained initial agglomeration in food processing, garment, footwear, electronics, and motorcycles. For this country, possible next steps include upgrading and branding of coffee and shrimp exports, a fashion-apparel industry with new Asian design, production of consumer electronics or eco-car components, a regional center for high-quality die and mold, and many others. All require a big jump in management and technology from their existing industrial base. *Ex ante*, none of them seems impossible if concentrated policy effort and private-sector effort are combined for a number of years. But all may not be pursued simultaneously due to limited resources and policy capability. It is not meaningful to ask which one of these possibilities conforms to Vietnam's dynamic comparative advantage and which one does not. The important question is whether policymakers can summon sufficient will, knowledge and resources to change any of these possibilities into reality.

Even in industries for which natural conditions dominate, such as Chilean salmon or Brazilian Cerrado agriculture, official support is instrumental (Chapter 3). Spectacular success in each case was achieved only after technology, training, marketing, and production scale necessary for commercialization were introduced by the hands of government, development partners, and private enterprises. Although Chile had labor and natural conditions suitable for salmon farming, this potential remained unexploited and no salmon was raised until the semi-official Chile Foundation and Japanese private and public cooperation and investment provided missing ingredients. "The miraculous development [of the Chilean salmon industry] was not realized through autonomous private investment alone" (Hosono, 2010, p. 154). Similarly, vast tropical savanna in central Brazil remained barren until the Brazilian government and the Cerrado Institute, also backed by Japanese technical and financial assistance, turned this land into a new bread basket of the world.

In sum, industrial potentials of any country, which are many, can become reality only when they are accompanied by proper policy actions to eliminate technical, financial, or institutional bottlenecks. Whether or not the targeted industry is in conformity with dynamic comparative advantage is a theoretical question that has little policy relevance to a country that has already made up a short list of candidate sectors through careful study and private-sector consultation. Political will and vision, appropriate policy procedure and organization, and prioritization and sequencing under resource constraints are what are required for turning potentials into reality. It would even be better to avoid the term "comparative advantage" entirely in industrial policy debate as it only adds to confusion and solves no substantive problems.[2]

2.4 Proactive industrial policy

Catch-up industrialization requires a solid combination of *private dynamism* and *good policy*. For any country, the amount of private dynamism is more or less given at any moment (the problem of a lethargic private sector is discussed in the following section) but policy can be improved more quickly if a government guided by a visionary and well-informed leader and staffed by reasonably competent officials is in place. Required industrial actions are more aggressive than past policy recommendations of the IMF and the World Bank featuring deregulation, privatization, integration, good governance, and good business environment. More aggressive actions are both necessary and possible even in the twenty-first century when globalization has deepened and WTO rules and proliferation of regional and bilateral trade arrangements have narrowed the policy space of latecomer countries.

I propose to use the term *proactive industrial policy* to denote a collection of such policy actions. Proactive industrial policy is different from any of the past development strategies including socialist planning, state-led heavy industrialization, market-friendly selective intervention, or big-bang liberalization under minimalist government. It is also different from infant industry promotion practiced by virtually all industrializing countries in the past centuries or even FDI-led industrialization of Southeast Asian countries such as Malaysia and Thailand in the 1980s and 1990s. In the last two strategies, tariff barriers and investment restrictions were lifted gradually as domestic industrial capabilities were built up. But today's developing countries are asked to do away with them from the beginning.

Proactive industrial policy must continuously balance state and market and reconcile globalization pressure with the need to retain sufficient policy tools. It obliges government to learn policy in order to help and prod the private sector to upgrade technology and management. It calls for establishment of close and productive relationship between government and businesses. More precisely, proactive industry policy must satisfy all of the seven conditions below:

(i) *Market-driven development under globalization*—production, investment, and trade must be carried out primarily by the private sector under an open competitive environment generated by the market mechanism and the globalization process. Privatization, WTO rules, and regional integration are to be embraced. State-owned production is not adopted except in cases where no private agents have yet emerged to take over the state's role and only temporarily.

(ii) *A strong state*—the state assumes a strong and active role in guiding and supporting development despite the fact that all productive activities are in principle to be conducted by the private sector. The state will mobilize necessary policies to reward value creation and innovation, punish unproductive rent seeking and corruption, and lead the private sector toward a consistent national vision. A great economic transformation must be orchestrated by the state because market participants cannot design or initiate such a transformation.

(iii) *Retaining sufficient policy instruments for latecomer industrialization*—although globalization is willingly accepted, this does not mean that all industrial policy instruments must be given up and replaced by market forces. This simply means that the policy toolbox for the twenty-first century is different from those of Japan, South Korea, or Singapore in the past. It also implies that enlargement of the market sphere must be in proper steps to ensure the availability of necessary policy capability and instruments, and that international pressure to open up must be consistent in scope and speed with the development strategy of the latecomer country.

(iv) *Dynamic capacity development*—improving policy capability and private dynamism, both of which are often weak in early stages of development, must be the central focus. Policy must set concrete goals and aim at enhancing potential strengths of the country rather than improving governance or capacity in general without specific goals. The policy scope and measures should be gradually expanded in accordance with the enhancement of policy capability and private dynamism (Ohno and Ohno, 2012). The country must eventually graduate from aid.

(v) *Internalizing knowledge, skills, and technology*—the principal method of attaining industrialization must be internalization of knowledge, skills, and technology embodied in the human capital of citizens. This must be by far the most important objective of industrial policy. Resource extraction, FDI, official development assistance (ODA), big projects, and geographic advantages are also important, but they must be given secondary positions in support of human capital development (Chapter 1).

(vi) *Effective public–private partnership (PPP)*—when a strong state guides the private sector, there is a risk of market distortion and suppressed entrepreneurship which leads to economic stagnation. To avoid this risk, effective cooperation between government and businesses *in substance* based on mutual trust and close engagement must be built. Holding symposiums and receiving comments on policy drafts are not enough. Through effective contacts, state policy and private intention merge and strategies initiated by the state should be willingly supported and implemented by the private sector.

(vii) *Sharing deep knowledge of the industry*—to avoid policy mistakes and political capture, government must accumulate sufficient knowledge of the industries in which it intends to intervene. Leaders and policy practitioners of the government must go extra miles to acquire latest practical knowledge and desires of the business community to make intelligent and well-informed decisions. Knowledge can initially be outsourced from consultants, academicians, or foreign experts, but unless it is digested by policymakers themselves the quality of industrial policy cannot improve.

These conditions are consistent with and overlap largely with the current global development thinking which replaced the Washington Consensus in recent years. For example, the Growth Report by the Commission on Growth and Development (2008, pp. 2–7) states that sustained economic growth must be supported by: (i) country-specific and dynamically evolving strategies; (ii) an increasingly capable, credible and committed government staffed with sufficiently competent public servants; (iii) setting priorities for effective implementation under resource constraints; (iv) market-based resource allocation; (v) full exploitation of the world economy in knowledge and trade opportunity; and (vi) inclusiveness and coping with inequality, among other things. Proactive industrial policy can be regarded as a pragmatic attempt to operationalize these widely agreed principles in the area of industrialization. It studies concrete policy ingredients and suggests a way to select and combine them in order to create an industrial policy package most suitable for the country in question.

Proactive industry policy is far more complex than simply unleashing market forces or planning everything by the state machinery. It aims to strike a delicate and ever-changing balance between state guidance and market orientation, between globalization commitments and policy capability, and between strong state leadership and the need to listen to private voices. Some may consider this to be contradictory, but one needs complex policy formulation to deal with complex reality. Furthermore, proactive industrial policy is not a theoretical imagination. East Asia abounds in various cases of proactive industrial policy—in Singapore, Taiwan, South Korea, Malaysia, and Thailand as well as in the long-established industrial support menu of Japanese ODA (selective and concrete components of proactive industrial policy are explained in Chapter 3). It should also be emphasized again that none of the measures proposed by proactive industry policy violates WTO rules or regional or bilateral integration commitments.

Proactive industrial policy requires simultaneous learning by the government and the private sector. The logic of such double learning is as follows. In countries caught in a developmental trap, technology will not be upgraded and industrial structure will not be transformed by spontaneous activities of free markets alone. The government must assist as a guide and facilitator. However, both the government and the private sector are underdeveloped in such countries. Under these circumstances, the chicken-and-egg problem must be solved by the initiative of the government. Political leaders and policy practitioners must first learn how to conduct industrial policy effectively in order to better lead and serve the private sector. This is a two-step approach in which capacity building of the private sector is the end and capacity building of the government is the means. This general formula should be applicable to any latecomer country whether it is Singapore, Kazakhstan, or Zambia.

Proactive industrial policy must be based on the strong policy ownership of the national government, which is often missing in countries heavily dependent on natural resources, FDI, or foreign aid. Every donor, whether bilateral or multilateral, stresses the importance of education and training,

SME promotion, agriculture and rural development, and so on, but no policy capability is acquired unless these universal measures are envisioned, designed, and executed at the hands of a developing country and properly integrated into the national development strategy. Passive acceptance of foreign aid and investment does not lead to the breakthrough of a developmental trap. For any developing country, installation of proactive industrial policy itself should be the first step toward building strong policy ownership.

Proactive industrial policy is dynamic for it does not allow a country to stand still. Policy measures it recommends are comprehensive (Chapter 3) and policy procedure and organization it requires is complex (Chapter 4). A latecomer country with primitive policy capability should start with a few basics instead of trying to master all items at once. As policy learning progresses, policy scope and instruments should be expanded accordingly as Ethiopia is trying to do (Chapter 10). In building skills and technology, low-income countries should mainly focus on emulation of existing general knowledge—including such management and factory operation techniques as 5S, kaizen, logistics, strategic marketing, etc.—rather than competing directly in frontline technology. Innovation, in its narrow sense of bringing something entirely new to the world, will become a core issue as income rises to an upper-middle level and beyond. A country may even graduate from proactive industrial policy as high income is attained and the private sector matures. Then strong state guidance is no longer needed. Taiwan and South Korea have already gone through such a process.

2.5 Coping with a weak private sector

The prime minister of a Sub-Saharan African country posed a question to a policy delegation from Japan: "I have studied East Asian policies and implemented some of them. Our industrial policy has improved in the last several years, rewarding value creation and penalizing rent seeking. Why do my people continue to pour money into property speculation and not manufacturing? Why do they not build more factories?" He wanted to know how East Asian governments turned shortsighted private agents into long-term producers and investors with technological learning.

Difference in national character is a sensitive matter that should be treated carefully. According to the hypothesis of homo economics, all humans behave rationally regardless of race or nationality. Some assume that all farmers and workers respond equally to economic incentives. This leads to the conviction that any failure of development relative to initial conditions should be blamed on the government and its policies, not people. While this view may be politically correct, it is not borne out by facts.[3] In reality, all nations are not equal in the vitality and nimbleness with which they pursue economic goals. Some people are good at playing football and others excel in philosophy. It is also not surprising to see some people better at producing cars and consumer electronics than others. We must start with the premise that different people are good at different things. Without reference to differences in private-sector capability, it is difficult to fully explain why some countries attain high income quickly while others are stuck at a certain income level.

Malaysia has come a long way in improving economic administration and delivering good policies to their citizens (Chapter 8). In many aspects, including morale, professionalism, reform mindset, academic achievements, and presentation skills, Malaysian officials are superior to their Japanese counterparts. Despite this, Malaysia has reached only (upper) middle income after half a century of industrializing effort unlike South Korea and Taiwan which are already in the rich country club. This is not because of a late start but because of slow ascent (Chapter 1). Malaysia's industrial output and export continue to rely heavily on Japanese, Korean, and Western brands and multinational companies mainly because Malay businesses lack dynamism. At the risk of oversimplification, it may be said that Malaysia has been a country of high-quality policy combined with a weak private sector.

In his controversial 1970 book *The Malay Dilemma*, Mahathir bin Mohamad, who later became prime minister in 1981–2003, argued that the value system of the indigenous Malays—fatalism, respect for formality and ritual, and abhorrence of hedonism—formed through history and engraved in genes put them in a disadvantageous position vis-à-vis commercially more active Chinese residents, so much so that they feel dispossessed in their own land.

> The people who left the shores of China to seek their fortune abroad were hardened and resourceful . . . The Malays whose own hereditary and environmental influence had been so debilitating, could do nothing but retreat before the onslaught of the Chinese immigrants. Whatever the Malays could do, the Chinese could do better and more cheaply. Before long the industrious and determined immigrants had displaced the Malays in petty trading and all branches of skilled work. Calling on their previous experience with officialdom in their own homeland, the Chinese immigrants were soon establishing the type of relationship between officials and traders which existed in China.
>
> (Mahathir, 1970, pp. 24–25)

Mahathir's proposal was that policy preferences should be given to the Malays to effectively compete with the Chinese immigrants because legal equality alone was not sufficient to reverse the situation.

In fact, following the 1969 racial riot, Malaysia introduced ethnicity-based affirmative action in favor of *Bumiputra* (indigenous Malays) against other ethnic groups, especially the urban rich Chinese. The New Economic Policy of 1970 imposed comprehensive rules in allocating public positions, business ownership and management, workforce, and other privileges to Bumiputra. When Mahathir became the prime minister in 1981, he introduced a series of industrial drives. The *Look East* policy (learning from Japan and South Korea), heavy industrialization, and a large inflow of manufacturing FDI turned Malaysia into a major electronics exporter by the early 1990s. All this happened under the Bumiputra policy still in place (ethnic privileges were moderated, but only slightly, in 1986).

Measures favoring ethnic Malays may have maintained social harmony but they did not send Malay firms out invading the global market. Proton, Malaysia's heavily supported national car company established in 1983, did produce popular vehicles for the protected domestic market, but it did not become competitive enough for export. Malaysia continues to receive foreign technical assistance to level up its local component industries. The contrast with South Korea's Hyundai is striking. The South Korean car company also received strong policy support and foreign technical assistance initially, but it was soon able to send Japanese engineers home. In 1975, Hyundai Pony, the first South Korean-developed car, was produced. In 1986, Hyundai entered the US market with Excel and set the record of selling the largest number of cars (126,000) in the first year of business in the US. South Koreans are now one of the few independent automobile producers in the world and the most formidable rival for Japanese auto makers. Mahathir's lament on the lackluster performance of Malay businesses after receiving generous support for over three decades is understandable (Mahathir, 2001).

Only countries that can combine proactive industrial policy with private dynamism can soar quickly and break the middle-income trap. Japan, South Korea, and Singapore were such cases. Meanwhile, there are active people without support from home governments who often go abroad to conduct dynamic businesses. Traditionally, Chinese and Indians were such people. Although their governments have replaced planning with liberalization in recent decades, they have a long way to go before their policies can be called proactive. What about a country whose people are not as dynamic or innovative as these Asians? Good policy helps, but it may not be able to cover fully for the lack of energy in its citizens.

National characters formed through history are slow to change, but they are not immutable. The only thing that can be said generally is that both genes and effort matter, a maxim that is equally applicable to art, sports, or manufacturing. More than a century ago, an official survey of factory workers in Japan found that Japanese workers were lazy, unskillful, and unspecialized with a low propensity to save and high inclination to job hopping (Ministry of Agriculture and Commerce, 1903). Their labor productivity was only half that of American workers. To accumulate skills and retain workers, Japanese large manufacturing firms began to introduce internal incentive and promotion mechanisms in the 1910s. Transformation of footloose workers into loyal employees was further carried out by government orders during the war years (1937–45). After World War II, the Japanese had turned into hard workers with a high saving propensity and a lifetime dedication to their companies.

More recently, Singapore succeeded in inculcating the spirit of productivity into its residents (Chapter 6). From the beginning, productivity was high on the agenda of the Singaporean government. The Productivity Unit was created in 1964, which was upgraded to the National Productivity Center in 1967 and to the National Productivity Board in 1972. In 1979, Prime Minister Lee Kuan Yew remarked that "Workers here are not as proud of or as skilled in their jobs compared to the Japanese or the Germans." In 1981, the Productivity Movement was launched and multitudes of programs were introduced until even taxi drivers talked about productivity. The slogan "Together We Work Better" and the mascot character of Teamy Bees were adopted, November was designated as the Productivity Month, and the prime minister delivered his productivity speech for seven consecutive years. Model companies were scaled up, firm consultancy schemes were established and training of workforce was provided. Japan assisted this effort with its first large-scale cooperation in productivity enhancement from 1983 to 1990. Strong political will and policy persistence transformed Singapore into a very competitive nation with high productivity. By the early 1990s, Singapore began to teach productivity skills to developing countries in East Asia, Africa, and Eastern Europe.

If stalled industrialization is due to the weakness of private-sector response, policy must go much deeper than just providing infrastructure or unleashing the power of markets. The country must engage in a national campaign to transform people's value, mindset, and aspiration as Japan and Singapore did with their workers (see Chapter 3 for more discussion). What is required is a spiritual revolution in a country where relaxed attitude toward production and services rules. There is no need to succumb to economic determinism, but resolve and patience are required to alter national characters.

2.6 Coping with high growth

Proactive industrial policy that cultivates internal sources of value and growth is only one component of a broader policy system essential for sustainable growth. The other two components are coping with growth-generated problems and enhancing macroeconomic management under integration. These policies, though as important as proactive industrial policy, lie beyond the scope of this book. However, a passing remark on growth-generated problems may be made.

In East Asia, the dominant view is that growth policy and the policy to cope with growth-generated problems are in principle separable. The latter includes measures to manage income and wealth gaps, internal migration, urban and traffic planning, environment, cultural shifts, and corruption. While both are necessary, growth acceleration and solving growth-spawned problems can—and should—be designed and administered separately. While environmental and other social checks must be in place for every industrial project, justification of industrial projects must be based on industrial objectives. In the West, on the other hand, the currently popular view is that these two goals must be integrated so that all growth strategies must be inclusive, and gender and environmental concern must be embedded in every industrial policy. According to this view, equality and grassroot participation are indispensable ingredients of industrial policy formulation instead of waiting for the fruits of industrialization to bring these desirable changes in the future.

In East Asia, there are two groups of high-growth economies. The first group includes Japan (in the 1960s and 1970s), South Korea, and Taiwan. In these countries, income and wealth gaps narrowed as the economy grew rapidly, making every farmer and worker happy and look to the bright future because their real income, although still low, continued to rise every year. Japan had business cycles and land bubbles, but income convergence continued despite these macroeconomic instabilities. During South Korea's high growth, the ratio of per capita incomes between the richest urban area and the poorest province remained virtually unchanged at 2.0 from 1971 to 1981 and subsequently declined to 1.75 by 1991 (Chapter 3). Farmers were not left behind in South Korea's economic miracle. In Taiwan, strong performance of SMEs created the social condition in which everyone could rise together and share the fruits of growth.

The second group of countries includes China, Thailand, and the Philippines. These countries also grew relatively fast, and sometimes very fast, but their income remains polarized across regions, occupations, and individuals. High-growth benefits a small segment of population while the majority of farmers and workers feel left behind and frustrated. As long as average growth is high, dissatisfaction may not surface immediately. But if polarization continues for a long time, there is a risk of social schism and explosion. Yasusuke Murakami, a Japanese political economist, once wrote that industrialization policy would surely fail if the deprivation of people left behind and their emotional discontent were not properly dealt with

> if urban [migrant] workers feel aggrieved that the emotional strain of their detachment from home is not adequately rewarded by being able to take part in the fruits of industrialization, tension will develop into social discontent . . . Similarly, in rural areas, if villagers think that industrialization only brings poverty and devastated landscapes, support for industrialization will be lost and protest is likely to erupt. Enraged people will become more receptive to calls for social reform through violent means . . . If such disturbances gather momentum and develop into a powerful political force, the road to industrialization will be effectively closed.
>
> (Murakami, 1994, ch.6, English translation p. 194)

Therefore, growth policy and social policy must be promoted in tandem although they do not have to be an integrated policy package designed by a "democratic" government. Murakami suggests that this perhaps explains why communist guerrillas attracted a certain amount of popular support in the Philippines and Latin America. In his view, the February 26 Incident of 1936, a failed coup attempt in pre-World War II Japan, to replace a "corrupt" government that benefited only fat capitalists with a military rule for the sake of poor farmers and workers, was also incited by military officers from farming villages who were upset by the deteriorating rural life. More recently, popular outrage and the toppling of a few entrenched dictators in Middle East in 2011 also arose from similar causes.

2.7 The making of a developmental state

For a poor developing country, progress toward high income must begin with a transformation of politics because developmental failures occur not only from mistaken policies but also, more fundamentally, from political shortcomings such as the lack of political will, national unity, and effective leaders and coalitions that can promote growth. A predatory, neo-patrimonial state which regards a nation's resources as private wealth to be distributed among rulers and their friends must be replaced by a developmental state that encourages value creation and suppresses unproductive rent seeking. Political transition is not easy because the old regime has taken deep root through institutional complementarity (mutual dependence of institutions in which removal of only one institution hardly changes the system), strategic complementarity (strong incentive for individuals to adhere to existing rules and play the existing game), and path dependency (difficulty of deviating from the system which was chosen and subsequently solidified). It is the government that must initiate systemic national transformation because free markets alone are unable to overcome formidable structural inertia.[4]

To succeed, the state must be not only developmental but also action-oriented, being able to mobilize resources to targeted sectors decisively and respond quickly to changing circumstances. In the early stages of development, human and financial resources are limited. They must be mobilized effectively to a small number of key projects and programs for visible results instead of spreading over too many goals. Moreover, a late starter country must guard itself from fragile social and ethnic balance and external shocks arising from globalization. When these shocks occur, remedial action must be taken quickly and flexibly in order for the government, and the country, to survive.

Development is not just an economic process but a highly political one (Leftwich, 2000, 2009). It succeeds only when both aspects are fully integrated in complex interaction. Here, the politics of development refers to *what can be done* under the political landscape and constraints as well as the administrative capacity of the country, whereas the economics of development refers to *what should be done* in terms of policy content to move the economy forward given its initial conditions. Simply put, the former is about the feasibility of development policy and the latter is about its desirability. Not all feasible policies are desirable and not all desirable policies are feasible.

To be relevant and realistic, a policymaker at any level or in any organization must rack his or her brains for a narrow and delicate path that satisfy both feasibility and desirability.

The development strategy for any nation must include not only technicalities of policy measures (Chapter 3) and policymaking procedure and organization (Chapter 4) but also the way non-economic factors such as passion, nationalism, and the sense of pride and humiliation are strategically mobilized under strong leadership to form a driving force of catch-up industrialization. Because all countries are different, no one-size-fits-all solution can apply. Since the first best solution from the viewpoint of economics is often impossible from the viewpoint of politics, compromise must be made and a detour may have to be taken. Policymaking is a complex game, and any plan that looks only at one aspect is certain to fail. While this general point may seem obvious, it must be stressed because the lack of awareness of this obvious fact constitutes a major cause of failure in development policy advice.

Some foreign advisors seem to believe that their job is to find an economically sound solution while implementation is the problem of the host government. The fact is that most policymakers already know the pressing economic problems of their countries and even their solutions. Re-discovery by foreign experts may accentuate their importance but gives little clue as to how these solutions should be initiated and carried out. If policy advice is meant to be practical rather than academic, counsel not based on (implicit) feasibility analysis can hardly be useful regardless of whether proposed actions are a few or many, or whether they are globally common or tailor-made to a particular country. From this perspective, the shortcomings of the IMF's macroeconomic conditionalities and the World Bank's good governance crusade, in which each country is rated by six growth-friendly criteria, are clear enough and need no further elaboration. By now, few economists defend an international organization that imposes a long list of globally common policies on countries struggling with macroeconomic crisis or popular discontent. By the same token, growth diagnostics advanced by a few Harvard economists (Hausmann et al., 2005, 2006) with a mechanical procedure to discover a small number of most binding economic constraints, can also be faulted for the lack of consideration of political feasibility.

Rodrik (2006, 2007) asserts that policies and institutions for igniting and sustaining economic growth should be diverse across countries but democracy as a political institution must be embraced universally by all countries regardless of income or development stage. In his words, "I do not subscribe to the idea that you need to delay democratization just so that you can actually have growth or that you can have democracy only when you can afford it" (Rodrik, 2006). However, it is difficult to justify such a dichotomy between economics and politics. Markets and democracy are similar in the sense that they need enabling mindsets, rules and institutions to take root and grow. These enabling elements must be created consciously and cumulatively in the social context of each country and cannot be imposed suddenly from outside.

Historical experiences of successful latecomers, whether Germany and Japan in the late nineteenth century or East Asian tigers in the post-World War II era, indicate that economic growth based on technology and finance is "easer" to realize than political and social reforms which must be supported by changes in values, attitudes, and social structure at a deeper level (Tominaga, 1990). Invariably, industrialization in these countries was initiated under "outdated" political and social systems.

In her study of South Korean democratization, N.T.T. Huyen (2004: 74) defines the *developmental threshold for democracy* as "a point in the development process when conditions are right for democracy to be installed and sustained." This also implies that democracy introduced before this point would be superficial. According to Huyen, economic growth accompanied by urbanization, industrialization and modernization generates a new *political culture* and a new *social structure*. The former means emergence in people's minds of a desire for political participation and acceptance of equality, moderation, and compromise in political processes in place of terror and violence. The latter refers to the rise of social strata such as urban workers, students, and professionals who support democratization and the shrinkage of classes such as military, capitalists, and landlords who favor the old regime. These changes in popular attitude and population structure increases pressure for political reform until the government succumbs and begins to introduce democracy. Watanabe (1995) calls this a "successful dissolution" of the authoritarian regime as a result of economic development. In South Korea, this happened in 1987 when Chun Doo Hwan, the last military dictator, accepted a presidential election to take place for choosing his successor. By that time South Korea's real income had risen from US$1,105 in 1960 to US$5,670 (measured in the 1990 international Geary-Khamis dollars). Transition to democracy was impossible in 1960 when 80 percent of South Koreans were poor farmers, but became possible and even imperative by 1987 when the urban middle class and workers in support of democratization formed over 90 percent of the population.

Besides South Korea, a number of East Asian countries—Taiwan, Singapore, Malaysia, Thailand, Indonesia, China, and so on—adopted authoritarian developmentalism of various sorts as a temporary regime for accelerating development in the second half of the twentieth century. A charismatic leader rose to assume power, sometimes legally but often by force, to establish a new regime with the purpose of achieving rapid economic growth to maintain national unity and defend the nation from external threat. Such a leader himself became the most powerful driving force of development (it was always *he*, not *she*, who ruled this way in East Asia). He was backed by: (i) a competent technocrat team to faithfully concretize his vision; (ii) national ideology that glorified material advancement; (iii) unwavering belief in upgrading technology and industrial competitiveness; and (iv) political legitimacy and popular

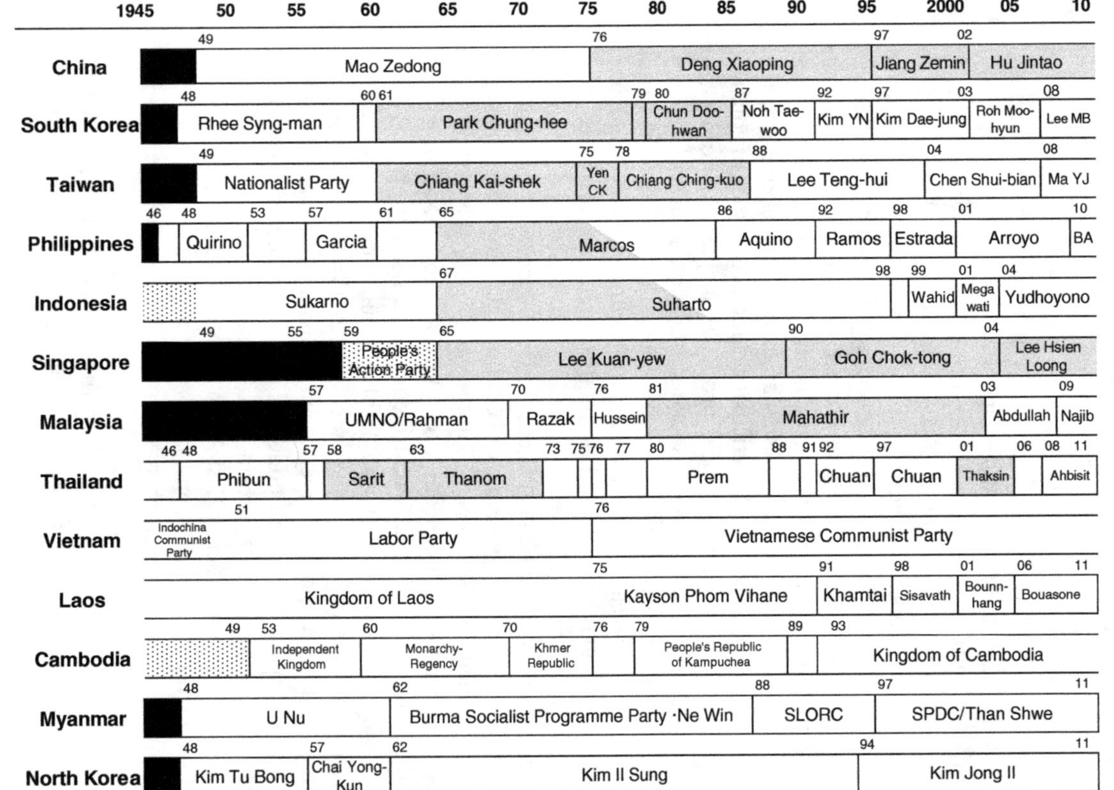

Figure 2.1 Authoritarian developmentalism in East Asia

Source: Information in Suehiro (2000), p.115 was revised, updated, and expanded by the author.

Note: The grey area shows authoritarian developmental leaders and the dark area indicates pre-independence periods. For China, the most influential leader among those holding highest positions is indicated.

support based on industrial results rather than democratic procedure (Watanabe 1995; Ohno 2008a; Banno and Ohno 2010). Military-like discipline imposed from above largely wiped out corruption, nepotism, and incompetence of the previous regime. However, growth performance differed significantly among countries adopting authoritarian developmentalism. As income rose, some have graduated from this regime and democratized. Others still maintain the regime.

The strategy of generating growth first and letting the fruits of growth bring democracy later is often defended, and even recommended, in East Asia as the most realistic sequencing of latecomer development—in sharp contrast to the democracy first principle frequently insisted by the West. However, authoritarianism is no longer permitted in our age. In the early twenty-first century, all countries regardless of income are obliged to embrace some sort of democracy—which usually means multi-party elections and minimum guarantee of human rights and freedom—as the prerequisite to join the global community and receive favorable trade treatment, investment and aid.

In fact, the majority of developing countries have already introduced democracy in form, if not in spirit and substance. Figure 2.2 shows the

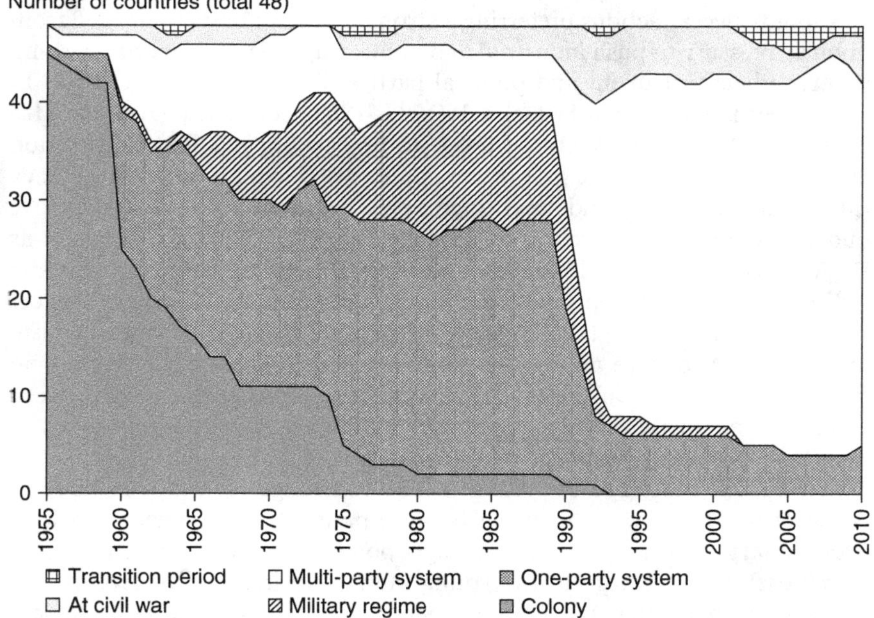

Figure 2.2 Political regimes in Africa

Sources: Created by the author using the following materials: Miyamoto and Matsuda (1997); Ndulu et al. (2008); CIA, *World Fact Book* (various issues); and Japanese Ministry of Finance, *Basic Data of Countries* (various issues).

evolution of political regimes on the African continent from the colonial years to present. Military regimes and one-party rule proliferated in the Cold War era when siding with one ideological camp or another was the name of the game. Developing countries could receive military and economic aid and other strategic benefits from the chosen patron without any conditionalities imposed on domestic political reform. However, the collapse of the USSR in 2001 completely changed the nature of global development politics. Convergence to "international best practices" (Western-style market and democracy) became compulsory. As a result, developing countries in Africa and elsewhere adopted multi-party democracy in droves. This may be regarded as a great achievement from the viewpoint of human rights and political modernization. However, viewed from other angles, all is not well. There are at least three issues to be considered here.

First, democracy which values procedure and participation tends to slow down policymaking and restrain government's hands. Whatever the inherent merits of democracy may be, which are many, speed and agility are not among them. Consensus building takes time, and compromise and unpredictability are inevitable under a democratic rule. This must be weighed against the need for a poor developing country to mobilize limited resources effectively and respond to shocks quickly.

The problem is hardly new. The government of Meiji Japan (1868–1912) was split between factions preferring a strong executive branch shielded from popular pressure to push industrial and military agenda and factions wishing to strengthen parliament and political parties (Banno and Ohno, 2010). In 1882, German Emperor Wilhelm I (1797–1888) counseled Hirobumi Ito (1841–1909), who was visiting Europe to prepare Japan's first constitution and who later became the first prime minister of Japan, to adopt autocracy rather than democracy and never to give parliament the authority to approve budgets. German legal scholars hired by the Meiji government, such as Rudolf von Gneist (1816–1895) and Karl Friedrich Hermann Roesler (1832–1894), were of the same opinion. British sociologist Herbert Spencer (1820–1903) also advised the Japanese delegation for conservative gradualism and against "too large an installment of freedom." These counsels may no longer be acceptable in the twenty-first century, but the dilemma between promoting democracy at high speed and retaining sufficient room for policy maneuver for the government is still with us.

Second, the substance of politics is slow to change even though its form is renewed. This is not surprising because political development is a long evolutionary process realized thorough policy effort and transformation of mindset and structure of the voting public. In many cases, leaders and bureaucrats managing the new democracy are the same folks as before and popular sentiments toward politics also have changed little. The global stampede toward democracy in the early 1990s was externally driven. It was a strategic response by developing country governments to the shifting global rules and constraints for the purpose of continuing to secure political and economic assistance. While a change in form of politics may become a good first step toward a change in substance, we should not expect an instant improvement.

In many developing countries, politics continues to be characterized by radicalism and instability even if democracy is formally in place. Based on extensive qualitative research, Paul Collier reports that democracy has not yet produced accountable and legitimate governments and has rather increased political violence in many developing countries, especially in the societies of the "Bottom Billion" (Collier, 2009). This is because governing rules are yet to be institutionalized and authority has not been firmly established and accepted in such societies. In countries where there is no consensus on how democratic principles should be applied in reality, the incumbent government can exercise much discretion in managing human rights, budgetary allocation, and relationship with parliament. Equally, opposition groups can challenge any action by the government. Under such circumstances, even election becomes a political game of confrontation rather than a device to legitimize the government through popular opinion.

Third, democracy has no automatic tendency to enhance the capability of government to promote development. In this sense, democracy and development are separable. Policy capability for economic development must be strengthened additionally and separately—hence the importance of conscious policy learning. The previous choice between a good dictator who accelerated development and a bad one who did not has been replaced by the problem of how to inspire a slow and mediocre government into developmental action. Latecomer countries must now solve the same fundamental problems in economic development—leadership, elite coalitions, alliance with the private sector, skills and technology, finance, infrastructure, integration, social protection, and the like—under new rules and constraints. Can a democratic state be developmental at the same time? Can it be decisive, quick, and flexible in policymaking? We do not have the final answer.

Both democracy and development are worthy goals, and one should not be sacrificed for the sake of the other. However, interaction between the two is a complex, and sometimes conflicting, process. Promoting one goal may accelerate or deter the other, depending on the country's social fabric and stage of development. External environment also matters, and democratic developmentalism of our time is no more independent from the prevailing world system than authoritarian developmentalism of the 1970s. The only thing we can say with confidence is that an installation of either Western-style democracy or traditional dictatorship, detached from each country's social and historical context, will not work. Harder thinking is required for a complex problem such as this. A continuous balancing act based on realism and relativism, rather than sticking to an extreme position with ideological conviction, should lead to the discovery of a reasonable path.

3 Ingredients of proactive industrialization

When asked about the most severe constraint of growth, the most popular answer from both government officials and business people in developing countries is the lack of finance. In reality, however, what is seriously lacking in those countries is often not financial means but the knowledge and mechanism for mobilizing available human and non-human resources toward productive purposes. Dropping money onto governments or enterprises that have no such knowledge or mechanism is not likely to improve the situation. The fact is that investors and donors will surely know when a country improves its capability to absorb skills and technology and will happily finance investment or learning in such a country.

As stressed in previous chapters, the key to sustained development toward high income is upgrading a nation's ability to build and use its knowledge, skills, and technology. For this, two kinds of learning are required. First, the government must learn how to provide policies and institutions that encourage and support private dynamism. Second, the private sector, assisted by policy, must learn to vigorously acquire knowledge, skills, and technology. Policy learning by the government and acquisition of productive capabilities by the private sector must go in tandem to produce visible results. Market forces alone are not sufficient for igniting industrialization in latecomer countries of the twenty-first century because the private sector, without any guidance or training, is generally too weak to satisfy demanding market needs or compete with global giants. The creation of a wise government is undoubtedly a difficult task, but without it there is little hope of catching up. While early industrial achievers such as Japan, Singapore, and Korea improvised through self-effort and trial-and-error, today's latecomers may need more systematic learning to improve policy capability than their predecessors.

This and the next chapter will explore the making of a developmental state from the perspective of policy methodology.[1] For any country, there are countless studies and reports recommending various policy actions needed to accelerate growth. But a "do" list—whether short or long—will not help very much unless the government knows how to design and implement proposed policies in concrete and realistic steps. In development policy research, what is lacking is not advice on what to do, but advice on *how* it should be done. In this chapter, the way to improve policy content is explored. In the following chapter, policy procedure and organization that can generate appropriate policy content are examined. The arguments and cases in these chapters do not come from academic theories but from a comparison of different best policy practices in East Asia and other regions, some of which are documented in later chapters. In this sense, they are all proven methods which are implementable under certain conditions. To facilitate the learning of policymakers in developing countries, these valuable but scattered experiences should be gathered, compared, and presented systematically.

3.1 Policy learning

Learning from East Asia should not mean copying policies adopted in some East Asian country at some point in time—be it Meiji Japan's engineering education, South Korea's integrated export promotion, or Taiwan's science parks—to another country without considering the latter's local context. The same can be said about learning from the West or any other advanced region or country. Random copying rarely works because the situation each country faces is different.

Studying East Asia or the West should not lead to a flat rejection of foreign models as irrelevant because "our country is unique" (I have never been to a developing country where this statement is not heard) or a blind acceptance of what international organizations or foreign economists advise without pondering local consequences. Both attitudes shut out the country from the possibility of policy improvement. What is critically needed for latecomer countries is systematic and pragmatic learning of alternative international best practices for the purpose of enhancing the capacity to create their own policy packages.

At the general level, the policy menu for sustained industrial development is not very different from one country to another. Presuming reasonable political and macroeconomic stability, the importance of education and training, acquisition of technology, supporting small and medium enterprises, agricultural and rural development, quality and safety standards, and construction of infrastructure such as power and transportation can hardly be disputed. Institutional supports for these policy objectives, such as administrative capacity, legal framework, and fiscal and monetary systems, must also be in place. For countries rich in natural resources, proper management of export revenues for productive investment and smoothing price and demand shocks should be added to the list. In fast industrializing countries, growth-generated problems such as inequality, internal migration, urbanization, congestion, and environmental damage must also be dealt with. The industrial policy menu of any developing country should not deviate greatly from the above although weights attached to individual items may differ. This is so even in the twenty-first century when globalization and market orientation have penetrated virtually every country. Although some measures such as import protection and export subsidies are no longer permitted under the WTO regime, the validity of all other measures—discussed below—remains intact.

Furthermore, as far as industrial policy menus are concerned, Africa and East Asia are not far apart. The seven program clusters, 16 programs, and 49 projects envisaged by the African Union to advance industrialization in its member countries (African Union, 2007), mentioned in Chapter 2, coincide largely with policies pursued by the high-performing East Asian economies although they may be called somewhat differently. The fact that policies in Africa remain mostly on paper while similar policies are actually implemented and producing results in many East Asian countries cannot be attributed to the difference in the policy menu. The success and failure of industrialization depends not so much on the different choice of policies but mainly on how well a country carries out common developmental tasks on the ground.

While the industrial policy menu itself is universal, local context matters greatly in deciding the details of how these common issues are tackled. Policy actions must be differentiated in design and implementation to reflect the social, economic, and historical background of each country. Consider promotion of small and medium enterprises (SMEs) as an example. Japan has since 1948 combined technical, managerial, and financial support under the leadership of the SME Agency, with about 20,000 state-certified SME consultants (*shindanshi*) offering advice to SMEs all over the country and connecting them to policy support and commercial bank loans. In South Korea, financial and non-financial SME supports are integrated in one policy agency (Small and Medium Business Administration) and one implementing organization (Small and Medium Business Corporation) but they work only with manufacturing SMEs as non-manufacturing SMEs are assisted by another mechanism. In Malaysia, the National SME Development Council chaired by the prime minister sets policies, the Ministry of International Trade and Industry is the lead ministry, and SME Corporation Malaysia offers one-stop service to a wide range of measures provided by 15 ministries and 60 government agencies. Malaysia promotes manufacturing and non-manufacturing SMEs alike under the same mechanism.

Such diversity in policy configuration comes partly from historical evolution and partly from different purposes and capacities of individual countries. Some variations enhance policy effectiveness but others are limitations that must be overcome. For a latecomer country preparing to install an SME policy mechanism from scratch, the scope, speed, sequencing and content of the mechanism must be chosen carefully to match the capability of the government and the requirements of the domestic business community. Haphazard adoption of the Japanese, Korean, Malaysian, or any other model without examining local context will surely lead to non-implementation or less-than-expected results. Systematic preparation is required to reduce this risk.

Latecomer countries should learn four things which are essential for sustained development: *leadership*, *national mindset*, *policy content*, and *policy procedure and organization.* Among these, leadership is by far the most important but the hardest to learn. A shift in national mindset is needed in countries where the private sector, when left alone, is not greatly interested in long-term investment in knowledge, skills, and technology. Both leadership and national mindset touch on politics and social ethos which, though not immutable, are not readily amenable to quick social engineering. By contrast, policy content and policy procedure and organization are technical in nature and easier to learn with good instruction and guidance.

The best way to learn these lessons is through a comparison of international best practices. Concrete cases from different countries should be catalogued and analyzed not for adopting them hastily or rejecting them as irrelevant but for the purpose of acquiring internal capability to create a policy package suitable for the home country using foreign experiences as references or building blocks. Foreign models must be selected, modified, combined, or improved before they are applied to any country. International comparison will not only provide a large number of raw materials for review but also give a good perspective to identify common success factors and pitfalls, ways to adjust basic models to local situations, and how to simplify advanced institutions. Such pragmatic instruction on industrial policymaking is currently not available. This book can offer some hints only. It would be nice if such a program, which would require enormous time, resources, and networking, were to be constructed by an international organization through mobilizing current and retired national leaders and policymakers with first-hand experiences.

Besides comparison of international best practices, policy learning requires a few other conditions for effectiveness. First, it must be backed by strong policy ownership. It is policymakers of the developing country, not foreign consultants or international organizations, who must set priorities, decide policy content, create necessary institutions, and be directly responsible for implementing and monitoring projects. The proper role of foreigners is to support a national development strategy from the sideline. In turn, the challenge for a developing country is to prepare a development strategy worthy of such support—which may require initial tutoring as discussed below. Strong policy ownership in turn must be driven by a desire for national pride and global recognition as well as a sense of humiliation over the current inability to compete effectively. Such national aspiration must be given concrete direction and form by a capable national leader. Industrialization should not merely be a technical strategy proposed by government officials but an obsession that engulfs all entrepreneurs, engineers, and workers. Industrialization in many of the East Asian economies was indeed propelled by a collective zeal for assent.

Second, policy must be learned through concrete industrial projects rather than generally and aimlessly. Policy learning is a process that must coincide with the industrialization process itself, not a precondition for industrial take-off. Many of the high-performing East Asian economies enhanced policy capability through hands-on struggles to attain specific targets rather than for raising their ranking in investment climate contests or fulfilling externally imposed conditionalities or governance criteria. Training was conducted, institutions were created, funds were raised, and officials and advisors were mobilized to execute particular projects stipulated in five-year plans, sectoral master plans, or a blueprint for regional development. This pragmatic approach has several advantages including concentration of limited human and financial resources on truly needed areas, clear criteria by which to assess performance, flexible reshuffling of resources and organizations in response to initial results and changing circumstances, and the sense of pride and achievement that emerges as concrete projects are accomplished one by one.

In 1997, the World Bank in its *World Development Report* proposed a strategy which may be dubbed as *policy-capability matching* (World Bank, 1997). It argued that countries with advanced institutions might try "difficult" policies such as selective intervention but those without them should first build general institutional capabilities in (i) effective rules and restraints, (ii) greater competitive pressure, and (iii) increased citizen voice and partnership. Countries in elementary stages should content themselves with easy policies ("fundamentals") and leave difficult ones for later when their institutions are upgraded.[2] This advice, which may look similar to the counsel given in the preceding paragraph, is based on the belief that institutions and capabilities can be built up independently from (or before deciding) the particular development path that the country chooses to tread. However, such unfocused effort may be too difficult to rally politically and too broad in the light of limited funds and administrative capacity. The same problem is encountered in the World Bank's more recent approaches in Good Governance and Ease of Doing Business where Western yardsticks are applied to assess each country's position vis-à-vis global averages, year by year, without reference to specific growth strategy adopted by that country. My advice to low-income countries is not to worry too much about your annual ranking.

Third, policy scope and instruments must be expanded as learning progresses. As with any learning, the novice must start with basics and climb up the ladders steadily. Jumping lessons, which is what some countries try to do upon hearing East Asian miracle stories, is hardly advisable. Take export promotion, for example. Korea's integrated export drive in the 1960s and 1970s employed a large number of policy actions in marketing, technology imports, export credit system, export association, export insurance, etc. Institutional support was provided through master plans, trade-promotion agencies, monthly export steering committee chaired by the president, a special fund for export-promotion activities, the Export Information Center, and the Export Idea Bank (Lim, 2011; also see below). An average latecomer country, for which quick installation of all these measures and institutions is impossible, must start with a simpler mechanism such as export incentives and international technical assistance targeted to a few selected sectors (see the Ethiopian case in Chapter 10). Although such measures unaccompanied by other policy components are not very effective, it is a good place to start. By knowing the complexity of working with local producers and foreign customers, the country can take a small but meaningful step forward in business support.

In this regard, policy dialogue with experienced officials and industrial experts from advanced countries may prove useful for countries just starting to learn industrialization—and this is our fourth point. International assistance in policymaking is being offered via various channels including lectures and seminars, expert dispatches, training at home and abroad, and tours and visits. These can provide ample ideas and cases on different policies, but industrialization also requires ability to integrate individual policy components into a coherent whole which fits the reality of the country in question. This undertaking is highly complex and difficult to learn through standardized manuals or technical assistance with narrowly prescribed terms of reference. For countries wondering where to start, a private tutor who understands the strengths and weaknesses of the pupil, gives clues on what to look for, takes any questions, and guides the beginner toward an initial learning path, will be a great help. Policy dialogue between a developing country and an advanced one, held regularly over a few to several years with an open and evolving agenda, can fill that role. For any art, sport, or science, a student must learn basic techniques from an instructor until he or she is proficient and confident enough to break new grounds and establish his or her own style. Random struggle without assimilating established wisdom is unlikely to produce results. It is the same with the art of making industrial policies.

Japan has conducted policy dialogue with many developing countries in various modalities with respect to purpose, scale, participants, duration, and frequency (Table 3.1). It usually starts with a national leader of a developing country requesting Japan to discuss development strategy generally and/or teach and transfer the secrets of East Asian development. South Korea offers the Knowledge Sharing Program to developing countries on a similar request-base where bilateral policy consultation (joint research, study tours, and seminars) and development of policy modules (information kits on particular policy measures) are the two main pillars (Table 3.2).[3] Although South Korea's policy teaching is more recent, it aims at more standardized, institutionalized, and publicized knowledge transfer than Japanese one which conducts policy dialogue on a more case-by-case basis. Other Asian countries, such as Singapore and China, also provide bilateral coaching on industrialization, but their programs are more issue- or country-specific (assistance in raising productivity, narrating lessons from Chinese industrialization, etc.) and less interactive and responsive to the particular needs of a learner country. Besides this, intellectual cooperation from one developing country to another ("South–South cooperation"), such as Malaysia helping Zambia and Vietnam assisting Mozambique, is now popular though it rarely deals with the issue of overall policymaking as Japanese and Korean programs do.

Policy dialogue is also conducted by Western donors and international organizations but topics tend to be less industrial and more towards

Table 3.1 Japan: policy dialogue with developing countries (selected list)

Country	*Period*	*Head/key players*	*Purpose and content*
Argentina	1985–1987 1994–1996 (follow-up)	Saburo Okita (former foreign minister)	Comperehesive study on agriculture and livestock farming, industry, transport and export promotion
Thailand	1999	Shiro Mizutani (former MITI official)	Study on the master plan for SME promotion policy
Vietnam	1995–2001	Shigeru Ishikawa (professor)	Large-scale joint study on macroeconomy, industry, agriculture, enterprise reform, crisis management, etc.
Vietnam	2003–current	Japanese embassy, JICA, JETRO, JBIC	Bilateral joint initiative to improve business environment and strengthen competitiveness through two-year monitoring cycle of action plans
Indonesia	2000	Shujiro Urata (professor)	Policy recommendation for SME promotion
Indonesia	2002–2004	Takashi Shiraishi and Shinji Asanuma (professors)	Policy support for macroeconomic management, financial sector reform, SME promotion, private investment promotion, democratization, decentralization and human resource development
Laos	2000–2005	Yonosuke Hara (professor)	Study on macroeconomy, finance, state enterprise, FDI and poverty reduction, etc.
Myanmar	1999–2002	Konosuke Odaka (professor)	Study on agriculture, rural development, industry, trade, finance, ITC, etc.
Mongolia	1998–2001	Hiroshi Ueno and Hideo Hashimoto (World Bank economists and professors)	Study on the support for economic transition and development
Ethiopia	2009–	GRIPS Development Forum and JICA	Kaizen, basic metals and engineering, productivity movement, policy procedure and organization, export promotion, technology transfer, etc.

Source: author's research.

Abbreviations: MITI (Ministry of International Trade and Industry), SME (small and medium enterprises), JICA (Japan International Cooperation Agency), JETRO (Japan External Trade Organization), JBIC (Japan Bank for International Cooperation), GRIPS (National Graduate Institute for Policy Studies).

Note: This table lists policy dialogues that are large-scale or worthy of special attention. Besides these, Japan offers policy advice through dispatching advisors to heads of state or ministers, expert dispatches, drafting reports on development strategy, training courses and site visits, conferences and seminars, etc. in various scale and duration.

Table 3.2 Korea: Knowledge Sharing Program (summary)

Establishment	*2004*
Responsible bodies	The Ministry of Strategy and Finance is the responsible ministry while the Korea Development Institute and the Korea EximBank, and subsidiary organizations under them, implement the program (however, see also the note below).
Objective	The overarching goal of this technical assistance is to enhance national development capacities and institutional restructuring efforts of development partner countries by sharing Korea's development experiences.
Consultation areas	Economic development strategy, industrialization and export promotion, knowledge-based economy, economic crisis management, and human resources development.
Project cycle and modality	The project cycle consists of (1) demand identification, (2) policy research, (3) policy consultation, and (4) monitoring and evaluation. There are usually two reporting workshops (interim and final) supplemented by policy practitioners workshop, senior policy dialogues, and dissemination seminar. Officials of developing countries are also invited to visit Korea. The standard cycle is one year with possible extension with follow-up consultation projects.
Output	A policy recommendation paper which contains consultation findings.
Partner countries in 2011	Vietnam, Cambodia, Indonesia, Uzbekistan, Mongolia, Peru, Ghana, Dominican Republic, Laos, Kazakhstan, Brazil, Gabong, South Africa, Myanmar, Bolivia, Sri Lanka, Ecuador, Ethiopia, Honduras, Equatorial Guinea, Tanzania, Panama, Philippines, United Arab Emirates, and Saudi Arabia (25 countries). Until 2010, the Knowledge Sharing Program was involved in research and consultations with approximately 20 countries.

Source: extracted by the author from the official website (www.ksp.go.kr).

Note: Information in this table relates to the Knowledge Sharing Program conducted by the Ministry of Strategy and Finance. There are also similar programs implemented by the Ministry of Foreign Affairs and Trade with the Korea International Cooperation Agency as an implementing agency, which are not called the Knowledge Sharing Program. For the latter programs systematic information or an organized website is not available.

macroeconomic, legal, social, or governance aspects. When industrial subjects are discussed, they are usually cross-sectoral issues such as ICT, globalization, environmental protection, labor rights, and enterprise reform rather than sector-specific targeting or planning. Policy dialogue with Japan or South Korea is unique in the sense that it aims directly at strengthening the state's role and capacity in industrialization rather than reducing the scope of sectoral intervention by government.

Some economists continue to come up with ready-made answers for industrialization such as "benchmark the industries of a country that is twice as rich as yours" or "take the following six steps to overcome a middle income trap." I am afraid that this is a new type of "one-size-fits-all" advice that needs to be avoided. Industrial policymaking is such a complex and country-specific process that no prescribed formula applies and micromanaging it from the center (say, Washington) is hardly helpful. Economic theories and historical cases should be treated as raw materials for each developing country to choose from and combine. We must recall that East Asian high performers industrialized in many different ways. Straitjacket instruction should be replaced by an interactive method which allows teacher and student to understand each other and jointly work toward agreed goals through improvisation and adaptation. The process of interactive learning is more important than the policy conclusion which is temporary and has to be revised and updated anyway. Policy dialogue, set up properly, will do the work while the rigid policy matrix or flowchart offered to every developing country will not.

To conclude this section, several "don'ts" are listed. A development strategy not backed by strong will and clear vision of a national leader will be ineffective. Policies drafted within a narrow circle of government officials, without deep involvement of other stakeholders, will not be implemented. Haphazard adoption of foreign models without examining local context will do more harm than good. Outsourcing of entire policymaking to outside consultants or academics, with policymakers only making comments and revisions, will not enhance policy capability. Bottom-up collection of targets drafted by different ministries will end up in unconnected chapters and too many priorities. Unfortunately, these are frequently observed mistakes in policy formulation of developing countries. Refraining from these practices should be the first step toward industrial policy learning.

3.2 Learning from East Asia

Although model countries for policy learning can in principle be from any region, East Asia presents itself as a particularly interesting case to study for the following reasons.

First, it is natural for latecomer countries to want to learn from successful cases than from failed ones. While East Asia's growth performance and development strategies are fairly diverse across countries (Chapter 1), it is the only developing region that has collectively and significantly caught up with the West with a number of stellar performers such as Japan, Singapore, Taiwan, and Korea—and giant China is also rising rapidly.

Second, most East Asian economies have adopted a developmental approach that emphasizes the essential role of government in industrialization, a pragmatic and evolving view of state guidance and intervention in the private sector, and the vision of market and democracy embedded in the culture and history of each society. For an average developing country immersed in the Western doses of developmental advice featuring liberalization, privatization, integration, good governance, and democracy, learning from East Asia can lead to the expansion of policy space in the double sense of bringing in a new perspective and enlarging the sphere of public policy. Since Western advice cannot be said to have produced great results in Africa and other remaining developing regions, to put it mildly, this should be a highly welcome move so long as the governments of latecomer countries know how to combine the two approaches in an effective and complementary manner.

Third, the guiding principles of East Asia's development cooperation are likely to be more conducive to the industrialization of latecomers than the approach derived from the historic experience of the West. While the World Bank's development strategy has shifted drastically from big-push industrialization to basic human needs, macroeconomic balance and structural adjustment, liberalization and integration, poverty reduction, institution-building and governance, and renewed interest in infrastructure and growth, Japan's aid strategy has been stubbornly constant ever since its ODA program began in 1954. As the first non-Western country to catch up with the West and provide a large amount of ODA, Japan strongly believes that aid must support, rather than discourage, the "self-help" of developing countries to foster industries, raise income, and eventually graduate from aid. A large bulk of Japanese ODA has been—and continues to be—poured into building infrastructure and upgrading human capital. It features hands-on pragmatism and patience for achieving prescribed targets, profound interest in individual sectors and concrete projects at *gemba* (a place where real action takes place such as factories and crop fields), and joint work with local officials and entrepreneurs for knowledge transfer through "on-the-job" training. Japan's aid principles are largely shared by emerging East Asian donors such as Singapore, Korea, China, Malaysia, and Thailand. In East Asia, economic aid is a means by which old teachers help new students to produce excellence even at the risk of creating formidable rivals. This dynamic view of mutual ascent through cooperation and competition is fundamentally different from the religion-backed concept of humanitarian aid where a rich man's obligation is sharing his fortune with the hungry and poor at the risk of creating aid dependency.

However, there is one aspect of East Asia which is difficult to apply directly to other developing regions: intra-regional economic dynamism. East Asian growth was attained through the very existence of the region as an arena for interaction and training among its members. Linked by trade and investment and supported by aid, international division of labor with clear order and structure has emerged. Industries are passed from the first-tier countries to the next and down the line. Since this industrial passing occurs mainly through FDI, countries wishing to strengthen their positions court FDI vigorously. The term *flying geese* referred to these systematic supply-side developments. Japan was the first bird to transfer its production capacity widely in the region, followed by the Asian Tigers (Singapore, Hong Kong, Taiwan, and South Korea), China, and a few other countries such as

Malaysia and Thailand. For latecomers in East Asia, industrialization is tantamount to jumping into this regional production network and becoming one crucial link in it. Each country is under competitive pressure from the countries moving above as well as behind it, forcing it to continuously climb the technological ladders. No other developing region has created such a dynamic interdependence as East Asia, and lead birds that can activate industrialization in neighboring countries are difficult to find elsewhere. For this reason, imitating the flying geese pattern should not be the primary objective in transferring East Asian experience to Africa or any other developing region.

Instead, Japan and East Asia's emerging donors can provide industrial policy support to Africa and other developing regions via the following entry points (GRIPS Development Forum, 2008a). First, for countries with sufficiently strong policy ownership and a reasonable industrialization strategy, policy instruments commonly used in East Asia, as explained below, can be mobilized. In this regard, there should be no distinction between East Asian and other latecomer countries. Second, for countries unsure about where to start or wishing to learn East Asian methods systematically, policy dialogue as discussed in the previous section can be initiated. Third, comprehensive regional development can be engineered around core infrastructure such as transport and power projects and through close cooperation among central and local governments and developing partners (section 3.5.4). Finally, assistance can be provided to supply missing components required by proposed large-scale foreign manufacturing projects, whether it is training, connectivity, administrative reform, or quality standards and testing centers. In fact, these entry points are not new or fundamentally different from the ways in which East Asian countries assist each other.

3.3 Standard policy measures

As stressed earlier, the policy menu for industrialization does not differ greatly across time and place as far as broad categories are concerned. For example, SME promotion, technical and vocational education and training, and technology transfer can hardly be omitted from the industrial strategy of any country. The purpose of this short section is to list up a number of standard measures. The list is meant to be introductory and evolving rather than final or complete. Nevertheless, such tabulation may prove useful for latecomer countries that hope to get a glimpse of available measures before selecting the ones they want to work on initially, just as a diner may want to consult the entire menu before placing an order. This should help them make an informed choice more quickly than when they do it randomly. Terminologies we use here are those frequently used in East Asia. However, these measures are hardly monopoly of East Asian countries as measures with similar functions, sometimes with different names, exist in virtually every developing region.

Table 3.3 shows an inventory of measures that enhance industrial human resource and enterprise capability, an objective that should be at the core of a nation's industrialization strategy. In addition, there are also other important industrial measures concerning infrastructure, logistics and distribution, social and environmental issues, and regional development which are not included in this table. None of the measures shown here violates WTO rules or any other international or regional obligations of FTAs and EPAs *in principle*—that is to say, unless they are deliberately and artificially misused for cross-border discrimination. What WTO prohibits are trade and investment measures that discriminate against imports or foreign firms to the advantage of domestic producers. If these measures are employed normally and applied to all firms including domestic and foreign ones, they should be fully consistent with globalization rules of the twenty-first century.

Table 3.3 Standard policy menu for industrial capability enhancement

Objective	*Policy measure*
(1) Legal and policy framework	Provision of necessary laws and regulations Designation or creation of lead ministry/agency for priority policy Inter-ministerial coordination mechanism Effective public-private partnership (PPP) Policy structure consisting of vision, roadmap and action plan Monitoring and evaluation mechanism National standards for quality, safety, skills, environment, etc. Framework for technology transfer and intellectual property rights Industrial statistics and database Strategic mobilization of international cooperation
(2) Industrial human resource (education and training)	Technology and engineering universities and institutes Polytechnics and industrial colleges Technical support in specialized skills for engineers Technical and vocational training for new and/or current workers Subsidies and incentives for worker training Skill certification, competition, and awards
(3) Enterprise capability (management and technology)	Introduction of kaizen or productivity tools (5S, QC circles, elimination of muri and muda, suggestion box, just-in-time system, etc.) Benchmarking, business process re-engineering, and other management tools Management or technical advisory service (by visiting consultants, short-term) Enterprise diagnostic and advisory system (institutionalized shindan or technical extension services) Short-term courses and tours for enterpreneurs and managers Quality standards and certification, testing services and centers Awards and recognition for business excellence, productivity, competitiveness Subsidies & incentives for upgrading management, technology, marketing, ICT . . .

Table 3.3 (cont'd)

Objective	*Policy measure*
(4) Finance	Development financial institutions Subsidized commercial bank loans for targeted firms (two-step loans) Special loans and grants for priority products and activities Credit guarantee system Equipment leasing Enterprise credit information system Linking loans with enterprise diagnostic and advisory system (see (3) above)
(5) FDI attraction	Clear announcement of preferred investors, sectors, regions, etc. Effective investor information package and website Investment promotion seminars, missions and offices abroad Provision of high-quality infrastructure services (power, transport, land, water, waste water and solid waste treatment, etc) One-stop investor support service (both before and after investment) Development and management of industrial estates including EPZs, SEZs and special zones for priority sectors, high-tech firms, etc. Rental factories for local and/or foreign SMEs Support for labor recruitment, matching, housing, commuting, healthcare, etc. Negotiation and provision of special incentives for attracting targeted anchor firms
(6) Marketing and business linkage	Support for domestic and export market development Trade fairs and reverse trade fairs Enterprise database (SMEs, supporting industries, sectoral) Incentives and subsidies for FDI-local firm linkage and technology transfer Official promotion/intermediation of subcontracting Establishment and strengthening of industry/business associations and local firm networks
(7) Innovation	Business start-up support Support for R&D, branding, patenting Business incubation centers Venture capital market Innovation clusters among industry, research institutes and government Incentives/subsidies for designated activities and products

Source: Author's ongoing research.

Note: These are a subset of industrial support measures aimed at enhancing human and enterprise capabilities. Measures concerning infrastructure, logistics and distribution, social and environmental issues, and regional development are not included.

To successfully implement any one of the measures in Table 3.3 would be a big challenge for a latecomer country. It requires solid preparation in policy design and organization and well-monitored implementation as well as mobilization of sufficient human and financial resources. Each measure would warrant a full book detailing technical and procedural issues, supporting institutions and common pitfalls distilled from a number of international best practices and failures. Just as all dishes on the menu cannot be consumed at once, a latecomer should be realistic and wise in its learning sequence. It should start with a small number of measures that are relatively easy to adopt and at the same time relatively important for the country. Exercising selectivity is an important component of policy learning.

Measures for stimulating innovation, at the bottom of Table 3.3, are particularly important for countries that have reached upper middle to high income. As argued in Chapters 1 and 2, however, innovation in the narrow sense of bringing something entirely new to the world may be too difficult for latecomers at low or lower middle income and therefore should not be the top priority at those levels of income. Innovation in this sense is a higher objective that will become vital only after a latecomer has mastered all "basics" and strengthened its general policy capability and private-sector dynamism.

In the next section, several policy measures will be discussed more concretely to illustrate how East Asian countries typically conduct industrial policy. The later Chapters 5–10 will give a fuller country-by-country account of how industrial policy is carried out in the social and historical context of each country.

3.4 Industrial policy measures: selective discussion

Six measures discussed below are among the most popular policy instruments for enhancing industrial capability in East Asia. Some may be unheard of in other regions, others are vaguely known in their names but not in detailed contents, and still others are globally recognized tools which may have certain East Asian twist. Explanation of these measures in this section is hardly sufficient for serious policy learning. It is only meant to be a preview for those with little exposure to policy formulation in East Asia so they may be able to sense differences between the Eastern way and the orthodox policy package prescribed by Western donors and international organizations. Fuller studies of individual measures are being prepared at the GRIPS Development Forum and the Vietnam Development Forum.[4]

3.4.1 Kaizen (quality and productivity improvement at factories)

Kaizen is a Japanese word for improvement. In Japanese management, kaizen means continuous and participatory improvement in quality and productivity involving the entire company from top management to middle managers and production-line workers. It aims at establishing an endogenous and permanent process of eliminating *muda* (unnecessary action, time, processes, etc.) and maximizing the use of existing human and nonhuman resources inside the company. It contrasts sharply with methods that stress one-time drastic improvement initiated by top management and hired consultants which may require high consultation fees and additional capital investment (GRIPS Development Forum, 2009).

The origin of Japan's kaizen movement was the statistical quality control method imported from the United States in the post-World War II period. The management theories and lectures of Professors W.E. Deming and J.M. Juran were particularly important. Japan quickly assimilated and modified this technique into its own management practice which became uniquely Japanese and began to produce results which even surpassed performance of American manufacturers. Compared with the original US model, the adapted method emphasized process orientation, worker participation, and hands-on pragmatism. This method, which came to be known as kaizen, spread rapidly among Japanese companies, large and small, to form a core of Japanese *monozukuri* (making things) spirit. The key to success was the dynamic response of Japanese companies to the imported method which led to spontaneous internalized learning and adaptation from the outset. This private-sector-led effort was assisted by three non-profit organizations (NPOs)—the Union of Japan Scientists and Engineers, the Japan Productivity Center, and the Japan Management Association—which sponsored lectures, discussions, foreign tours, productivity and quality awards, and other supporting mechanisms (Kikuchi, 2011).

Subsequently, kaizen spread overseas as Japanese manufacturing firms expanded their production bases to the rest of the world. By now, kaizen assistance is one of the standard tools of Japanese industrial support in developing countries. Japanese assistance in kaizen, which is often called quality and/or productivity projects, is conducted through both private and public channels. Many Japanese companies teach their overseas factories and local component suppliers through classroom and on-site training, dispatch of Japanese technicians, training at the mother factory in Japan, and organizing skills competition for local engineers and workers. There are also fee-based instructions provided by private consulting firms such as the Kaizen Institute. Kaizen is also promoted widely by official organizations such as the Japan International Cooperation Agency (Table 3.4), the Japan Overseas Development Corporation, the Association for Overseas Technical Scholarship, and the Asian Productivity Organization in addition to the three NPOs mentioned above. While kaizen activities are most popular in Southeast Asia where Japanese manufacturing firms have strong presence, it is also taught and practiced in other regions including South Asia, Latin America, and Eastern Europe. A number of Sub-Saharan African countries such as Burkina Faso, Ethiopia, Ghana, Kenya, Tanzania, and Zambia are also interested in kaizen as a method that complements Western management techniques.

Table 3.4 JICA's cooperation for systematic introduction of kaizen

	Country	*Start*	*End*	*Counterpart organization*	*Estab.*	*Project type*
1	Singapore	1983	1990	National Productivity Board	1972	Developmental
2	Philippines	1991	1994	Productivity Development Center, Development Academy of the Philippines	1967	Developmental
3	Thailand	1994	2001	Thailand Productivity Institute	1962	Transition
4	Hungary	1995	1999	Hungarian Productivity Centre	1994	Start-up
5	Brazil	1995	2000	Brazilian Institute of Quality and Productivity in Parana	1995	Start-up
6	Costa Rica	2001	2006	Technical Instructor and Personnel Training Center for Industrial Development for Central America	1992	Developmental
7	Tunisia	2006	2008	National Quality Programme Unit	2005	Start-up
8	Paraguay	2007	Ongoing	Paraguayan Quality and Productivity Center	2005	Start-up
9	Egypt	2007	Ongoing	Productivity and Quality Improvement Center	2006	Start-up
10	Argentina	2009	Ongoing	National Institute of Industrial Technology	1957	Developmental
11	Ethiopia	2009	Ongoing	Ethiopian Kaizen Institute (upgraded from Kaizen Unit in 2011)	2011	Start-up & developmental

Source: Ueda (2009) with updates and editing by author.

Note: This table lists projects, conducted by the Japan International Cooperation Agency (JICA), which are exclusively focused on introducing kaizen and strengthening its executing agency. These projects are often called "productivity development" or "quality and productivity" projects. JICA also provides a large number of kaizen supports as part of other projects or for improving targeted companies and organizations without institutionalizing kaizen. Ueda (2009) classifies comprehensive kaizen projects into start-up, developmental and transition stages. The developmental stage aims to enhance government capability to carry out kaizen while the transition stage devolves the function to non-state organizations.

According to Masaaki Imai, chairman of the Kaizen Institute who introduced the idea to the international audience with his books (Imai, 1986, 1997), kaizen is an umbrella concept that encompasses a large number of Japanese business practices. It is not just a technique but a philosophy toward life and work. It instructs how management and workers can jointly change their mindset to improve productivity. There are many overlapping tools that belong to the kaizen toolkit such as 5S, suggestion system, quality control circles (QCC), total quality control (TQC), total quality management (TQM), Toyota Production System (TPS), Just-in-Time (JIT) system, kanban system, lean production, and so on. Among these, 5S ("five S"—*Seiri*, *Seiton*, *Seiso*, *Seiketsu*, and *Shitsuke*, which can be translated as *Sort*, *Straighten*, *Shine*, *Systematize*, and *Standardize*, though other English renditions also exist) is considered to be the very basic that must be embraced by all companies as the first step toward improvement. It is a concise checklist and reminder for order, efficiency, and discipline in the workplace rather than a sophisticated method requiring high-level education or statistical knowledge to understand. It starts with such instructions as "Keep the factory floor clean and free of rubbish," "Remove all unnecessary tools and materials," "Place remaining things in marked positions for easy pickup," "Draw lines on the floor to distinguish work area and transport area," and other seemingly mundane suggestions which can nevertheless work wonders in quality and productivity at any average factory without spending a penny on new investment.

Kaizen is usually taught by an industrial expert with extensive experience who makes weekly visits to the factory in a cycle of three to six months. Classroom instructions may be organized initially to give basic information and select candidate companies. For screening, the general director of the company is interviewed for his or her business vision and willingness to learn.[5] Then a team is formed inside an eligible company to implement kaizen in a chosen production process which will be expanded to the entire company in steps. The team is asked to identify problems and suggest solutions with assistance from the kaizen expert. Weekly homework is often given for this purpose. Kaizen is considered successful if the company internalizes the process and can sustain kaizen activities permanently after the expert leaves.

Two common questions raised about kaizen in developing countries are transferability across cultures and complementarity with Western methods. Some question the validity of kaizen in countries where low literacy, short-terminism, lack of upward mobility, and inattention to details prevail. In societies where hierarchical structure is deeply rooted, it may not be easy to induce workers to contribute ideas to their supervisors. While these arguments are theoretically plausible, experience of numerous kaizen experts, including Mr. Imai, shows that there is no country where kaizen fails to improve quality and productivity. Improvements are immediate and clearly visible in profits or cost saving even though the number of highest performers may vary across cultures. As to the compatibility between kaizen and other methods such as benchmarking and business process re-engineering, the two should in principle be complementary because the former internalizes gradual improvement within a company while the latter aims at a jump in performance. However, it is not clear whether bottom-up processes required by the former can co-exist with top-down decision making assumed in the latter. Another practical concern is over-burdening of management and workers when two different methods are introduced simultaneously in a company.

3.4.2 Shindan (enterprise management consultant system)

Shindan (literally, diagnosis in Japanese) is a state-authorized and supported system of enterprise diagnostics and advisory services targeted mainly at SMEs in both manufacturing and services. Unlike business advice provided by MBA holders and management consultancy companies on a profit basis, shindan pursues the public purpose of strengthening a large number of SMEs to form a solid foundation of a country's industrialization. For this reason government initiative is justified in creating and maintaining the system even though most shindan services are offered commercially and subsidies are a relatively minor part of state intervention. It can be regarded as management support for SMEs in a highly institutionalized form (Do and Pham, 2010; Ohno, 2010).

Japan's shindan system has a long history dating back to the early postwar years. Since the establishment of the Small and Medium Enterprise Agency in 1948, shindan (enterprise diagnostics and advice) and shindanshi (enterprise consultants) have been promoted by legislation, official assistance, and enhancement of supporting organizations. In 1952, the Minister of International Trade and Industry began to certify outstanding consultants and actively mobilize them in SME promotion policies. In 1954, the Japan Small and Medium Enterprise Management Consultants Association (J-SMECA) was founded as a nationwide professional association of shindanshi which was headquartered in Tokyo with a branch in every prefecture of the country.

As the system proved highly successful, it attracted growing interests and higher expectations. The scope of shindan activities was expanded from public to private domain. The mission of the system gradually shifted to private-sector-led development and utilization of management consultants. To implement this policy shift, the Small and Medium-sized Enterprise Basic Act was amended in 1999 and an additional law, the Small and Medium-sized Enterprise Support Act, was enacted in 2000. In 2004, state support organizations were merged into the Organization for Small and Medium Enterprises and Regional Innovation, Japan (SMRJ). In 2006, the system was revised for further institutional improvements such as giving a more flexible time frame for taking exams and renewing registration and placing more emphasis on the actual practice of shindan as a condition for renewal. As of 2008 Japan had about 19,000 registered shindanshi and the number is increasing every year. Many of the Japanese experts that teach kaizen in developing countries are registered shindanshi.

SME Universities under SMRJ are the most important organizations for shindanshi training. Tokyo SME University, its flagship campus, was founded in 1962 and eight additional campuses were established in various regions in the 1980s and 1990s. They provide practical know-how in business operations as well as courses for updating knowledge, methods, and related laws for registered shindanshi. Under the current system, all applicants seeking certification as shindanshi must pass the primary exam, then choose to either

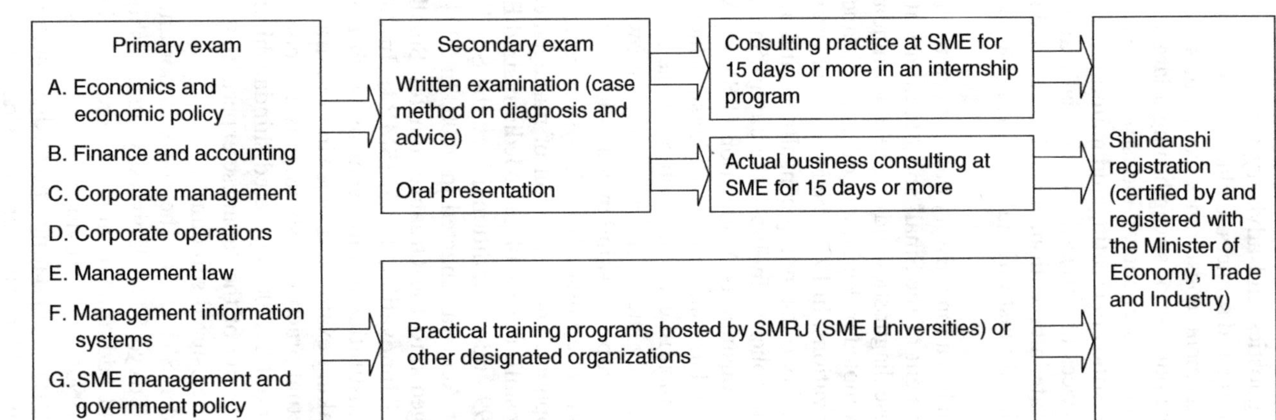

Figure 3.1 Japan: Shindanshi exam and registration scheme

Source: Japan Small and Medium Enterprise Management Consultants Association.

take the secondary exam or study at an SME university. The six-month training program at an SME university is divided into two parts: Business Consulting I and II. In Business Consulting I, students study specific management aspects and acquire related diagnostic and advisory skills. In Business Consulting II, practical diagnostic and advisory skills covering companywide management issues are obtained. To receive a certificate of completion, students must attend over 90 percent of the courses with proper attitude and satisfy minimum standards set by the university. The certificate of completion at an SME university automatically entitles the holder to a shindanshi certificate and a registration number issued by the Minister of Economy, Trade and Industry.

A shindanshi certificate is valid for five years. In order to renew it, a registered shindanshi must complete two requirements within the five-year period of registration: taking at least five courses organized by J-SMECA and engaging at least 30 days in consultancy business.

J-SMECA currently boasts more than 9,000 shindanshi members. Business Clinic, a human resource information program on its web (www.j-smeca.jp), provides matching service between shindanshi and SMEs free of charge. However, consulting fees arising from the contract must separately be decided by the two parties.

When shindan advice is combined with loan application, the triple-win situation is created among SMEs, shindanshi, and financial institutions, making diagnosis and advice offered by shindanshi truly effective. The fact that a firm is receiving or has received analysis, assessment, or advice from shindanshi is important information that positively affects the financial institution's decision to grant a loan. The Japan Finance Corporation (JFC), a government-owned institution created in 2008 by merging four state financial organizations, plays a vital role in extending financial support to SMEs. Reports submitted by shindanshi are an important consideration for JFC in evaluating projects and offering loans. These reports also function as a credit guarantee for loans provided by JFC or other financial institutions. Access to commercial bank loans is also greatly facilitated by receiving shindanshi's advice.

Japan's shindan system is effective thanks to over 60 years of institutional evolution, consistent state backing, a wide array of supporting institutions, and a large number of active shindanshi engaged in domestic and international shindan works. Shindan in its fully developed form is a sophisticated system requiring long experience and high policy capability to run. Nevertheless, support for SMEs is a common agenda for all countries. Some Asian countries try to replicate the Japanese system in a simplified and modified form to fit their socio-economic situations.

In 1999, in the aftermath of the Asian financial crisis, the Japanese government implemented a five-year program to introduce a shindan system in Thailand and produced about 450 Thai shindanshi. Since then, the Thai private sector has taken over to continue to provide various training programs for shindanshi. In Indonesia, the industrial support program of the Japanese government was initiated in 2003. Consultants were trained and a study was conducted in preparation for institutionalizing a training program and a state certification scheme, and responsible offices at local levels were also founded. The Indonesian shindan system was officially inaugurated in 2006 and about 300 shindanshi have been certified. In Malaysia, as part of technical cooperation following the Japan–Malaysia Economic Partnership Agreement signed in 2005, Japanese experts conducted a series of training courses for government officials for two and a half years from 2006 and produced 68 "SME counselors." Meanwhile, when the Japan–Philippines Economic Partnership Agreement was signed in 2006, Japan promised to help the Philippines develop a shindan system and pilot projects were launched in five of the country's provinces. Vietnam, a latecomer in comparison with the above-mentioned countries, has also been working with Japan for developing its supporting industries (parts and component suppliers) since 2008. As part of this effort, Japan's shindan system and similar systems adopted in neighboring countries have been reviewed to assess the feasibility of transplanting the system to Vietnam. In all cases, Japan directly assisted the training of shindanshi or introduction of the shindan system.

3.4.3 Engineering universities and technical colleges

The establishment of leading universities and colleges in science and technology which can teach both theory and practice is absolutely necessary to replace foreign experts and engineers by domestic nationals, create more internal value, and gain technological ownership. The making of such institutions is a long-term endeavor over many decades which usually requires state support and international cooperation. However, private effort can also play an important role as we see in the case of Thailand below.

After feudal Japan was opened up to the Western world in the middle of the nineteenth century, the Meiji government (1868–1912) at first hired foreign managers, engineers and workers in turn-key contracts, management contracts, and technical advice for industrial and infrastructure projects. However, this proved very costly and severely strained the state coffer. To import-substitute foreign experts, the best students were nominated by the government to go abroad to study latest technology at first-rate universities in Europe and America on (relatively meager) official scholarship. To produce competent engineers on a large scale at home, the Ministry of Industry established Kobu Daigakko (Institute of Technology) in central Tokyo in 1871 to function as the nation's top academy for absorbing Western technology. Henry Dyer, a British engineer, was appointed as its first principal, and classes were conducted mainly in English. Courses in civil engineering, mechanical engineering, shipbuilding, telecom, chemistry, architecture, metallurgy, and mining were offered. The six-year program comprised two years each of preparatory study, specialized study, and internship. Many of its first graduates were hired by the government to design and implement industrial policies. The Institute is now part of the Faculty of Engineering of the University of Tokyo. In addition, technical high schools were created all over the country to produce a cadre of mid-level engineers, greatly contributing to the technical absorptive and modifying capacity of the nation (Ohno, 2006a; also see Chapter 5).

Much later in Thailand, the King Mongkut's Institute of Technology Ladkrabang (KMITL), established in 1961 as a small telecom training center with 23 students, has developed into a leading engineering research and education university with special strength in information and comunications technology (ICT). Comprehensive Japanese cooperation, both public and private, in four phases over 40 years was critical to its creation and growth. Japanese cooperation included technical cooperation agreements (1978, 1987, 1992, and 1997), academic exchange agreements (1977, 1992, and 1997), scholarship system (1971), practical factory-based training (1977), and construction scholarship system (1989), as well as campus expansion, human resource development, research promotion, and bilateral research and education via satellite. By 2010 KMITL had seven faculties in engineering and a graduate school with a total of about 22,000 students and 1,000 instructors. KMITL actively accepts students from neighboring countries including Cambodia, Laos, Myanmar, and Vietnam (VDF and Goodwill Consultant, 2011).

In Thailand, technical training is also provided by non-state initiative. The Technology Promotion Association (TPA) is a local NPO established in Bangkok in 1973 by Thai returnees who studied science and technology in Japan. It has long offered management and technical education and training, language courses, and published textbooks. After 34 years of preparation and saving, TPA realized its original plan of establishing the Thai–Nichi Institute of Technology (TNI), a private university to teach Japanese-style manufacturing in both theory and practice with a strong emphasis on the latter, in 2007. TNI was financed by TPA's accumulated profits and bank loans. TNI has three departments in Engineering, IT, and Business Administration as well as MBA courses in Industrial Management and Executive Enterprise Management. In 2011 it reached the full student capacity of 4,000 and produced its first graduates.[6] TNI emphasizes the spirit of *monozukuri* (making things), enterprise internship, Japanese language and culture, and cooperation with Japanese and local companies. Japan has assisted TPA and TNI from the sideline via non-financial channels such as dispatching experts, linking them with Japanese businesses, and providing equipment in kind. Management and financial resources of TPA and TNI remain local with strong Thai ownership (Mori, 2010).

In Singapore, Nanyang Polytechnic (NYP), established in 1992 by merging various institutes created by German, French, and Japanese cooperation in the 1970s and 1980s, has grown into a leading polytechnic in the country with about 78,000 current students. It provides both Pre-Employment Training (PET, for students) and Continuing Education and Training (CET, for workers). Regarding PET, seven schools of NYP run 47 full-time courses for three-year diploma in engineering, IT, business management, interactive and digital media, design, chemical and life sciences, and health sciences. CET at NYP offers formal diploma courses, customized courses, and degree programs with overseas universities. The government provides full funding for administration and operations of NYP (except for the small part covered by tuition fees). Meanwhile, NYP is free to use its revenue from services provided to industry for any activities or investments. Collaboration between industry and NYP is solid and extensive. NYP carries out many industrial projects on a commercial basis in R&D, product design and development, and innovative solutions for industry, as well as teaming up with the government to support start-up technopreneurs. Such collaboration is "win–win" for both industry and NYP because the former can benefit from reduced cost and risk for R&D and start-up investment and because the latter can have ample opportunities for staff capability development and student training in frontline technology in addition to earning money. NYP also offers various kinds of training for management staff and specialists of TVET institutions around the world including China.

3.4.4 TVET–industry linkage

The quality of technical and vocational education and training (TVET) is gauged not by advanced teaching materials and methods but by the degree of matching between the training program and labor demand by targeted industries. Since skill requirements for industrial labor change over time and vary by sector and even from one enterprise to another within a sector, labor matching requires constant and customized consultation and adjustments between industry and TVET institutions. Mere installation of an imported TVET framework will not suffice because strong private initiative and effective public support with attention to details are crucial. Only those countries that can establish a national mechanism to achieve continuous labor matching will succeed in producing relevant workforce for industrialization.

In Singapore, the National Manpower Council (NMC) chaired by the Minister of Manpower identifies the country's human resource needs in the medium to long run and maps out strategies to meet these needs. Numerical targets are set for specific skills and the number and type of students to be graduated from universities and polytechnics over the next four to five years. State funding to educational institutions and industry worker training is closely linked to this manpower planning. However, Singapore is a well-managed city state with a population of five million. It may be difficult to replicate such a sophisticated human-resource strategy in developing countries with an average policy capability.

One of Singapore's international cooperation projects is the Vietnam–Singapore Industrial Park (VSIP) in Binh Duong Province in Southern Vietnam. With efficient management and marketing expected of Singaporean assistance, Phase I of this bilateral national project, started in 1996 with 500 hectares of land in the suburbs of Hochiminh City, has become one of the most successful industrial estates in Vietnam attracting 242 companies with strong representation of electronics and precision machinery sectors. VSIP continues to expand to other locations in Vietnam in three more phases. To supply workers to VSIP Phase I, the Vietnam–Singapore Technical Training Center was built near the industrial park to provide training required by tenant companies in the industrial estate. Students who completed the 12th grade receive five-month training before being placed in factories. The center also offers three-year training for 9th graders. The curriculum, originally based on the Singaporean model, is revised every year by the curriculum committee consisting of tenant companies. For recruitment, a list of graduating students is circulated among companies in the industrial estate which will organize interviews with desired candidates. All students, except those who wish to leave the area, can find jobs in VSIP Phase I. In 2006, the center was merged with the provincial technical school and its ownership and management were transferred from Singapore to the provincial government of Binh Duong. As of March 2007 the merged center had 1,500 full-time students.[7]

The State of Penang, a small island in Malaysia, has a large agglomeration of multi-national semi-conductor firms such as Advanced Micro Devices, Intel, Motorola, Fairchild Semiconductor, and Seagate. This industrial cluster was created by the state government's strategic FDI marketing in the late 1980s (Chapter 8). In order to cope with the shortage of skilled labor, wage pressure, and job hopping arising from increased labor demand, the Penang Skills Development Centre (PSDC) was established in 1989 in unique joint effort among industry, government, and academia. While it is a non-profit organization reporting to the state government, private initiative has been the main driving force in its creation and operation. The management and administration of the PSDC are entirely in the hands of its corporate members while the federal and state government fund and support it without intervention. Key members of the PSDC's management council are CEOs of multinational corporations (MNCs) who contribute their time and knowledge to the improvement of curriculums and fostering of local supplier networks. Strong trust and cooperative spirit that exist between industry and the Malaysian government are the main reason for the enormous success of the PSDC (Mori, 2005; Ohno, 2006b). However, when the PSDC model was scaled up to the federal level it met with less success due to the lack of strong private initiative in other locations in Malaysia.[8]

3.4.5 Industrial estates

Development of industrial clusters, where producers locate and interact in geographical proximity, is a popular measure among policymakers around the world but it has many different interpretations and approaches. Industrial clusters can mean trade villages where a large number of micro and small businesses produce the same product; a region of a country where relatively large firms of the same sector (say, garment or electronics) gather to share works, information, labor, materials, or markets; a vertically integrated production hub with many component suppliers surrounding a large assembler firm; or a city that promotes innovation through policy-guided cooperation among local government, businesses, and universities.

In East Asia, establishment of industrial estates that can attract a large number of foreign manufacturers has been a common practice. While a country should ideally be able to offer attractive investment climate everywhere, this is practically impossible in latecomer countries where physical and institutional impediments to businesses abound. Industrial estates are the means to provide exceptionally good business conditions in confined areas to attract foreign investors in the early years of industrialization. Kaohsiung Export Processing Zone in Taiwan, established in 1966, was the first such successful industrial estate in the world (Chapter 7). Subsequently, all high-performing economies in East Asia used industrial estates of various kinds as one of the key tools for industrialization. Later, as industrialization deepens and the aim of industrial policy shifts from quantitative expansion to qualitative improvement, high-tech industrial clusters that can produce leading-edge products become increasingly important.

One of the largest industrial parks in Southeast Asia is AMATA Nakorn Industrial Park, a Thai-owned private industrial estate in Chonburi Province in the southeast suburbs of Bangkok, Thailand. It constitutes a part of Eastern Seaboard Development, a gigantic national industrial development plan carried out mainly in the 1980s, with easy access via expressway to Laem Chabang Deep Seaport and Suvarnabhumi International Airport. Built in 1989, the industrial park has been operated and expanded by AMATA Corporation.[9] It has grown in nine phases into a complete city equipped with full infrastructure services such as condominiums, commercial areas, logistic support, banking, schools and kindergartens, a medical center, and a golf course. Major customers of AMATA Nakorn are manufacturing firms from Japan (60 percent), Thailand (17 percent), and Europe (7 percent) by nationality, and automotive (33 percent), steel, metal, and plastic (26 percent), and electronics (14 percent) by sector. It is the largest agglomeration of supporting industries (parts and component suppliers) and a critical production hub of the Thai automotive and electronics industries, together with final assembler firms scattered around Bangkok and Eastern Seaboard areas.

Akifumi Kuchiki summarizes the standard procedure for creating successful industrial estates in a sequential list of actions and players (Kuchiki, 2005; Kuchiki, 2007; Kuchiki and Tsuji, 2008). In his flowchart approach (Figure 3.2), the first step is *agglomeration*, in which an industrial zone with essential services and support is established to invite an anchor firm, while the second step is *innovation*, in which tripartite cooperation among industry, government, and universities and research institutions generates high value. Relevant players in these steps are local and central governments, NPOs, semi-government organizations, and private enterprises.

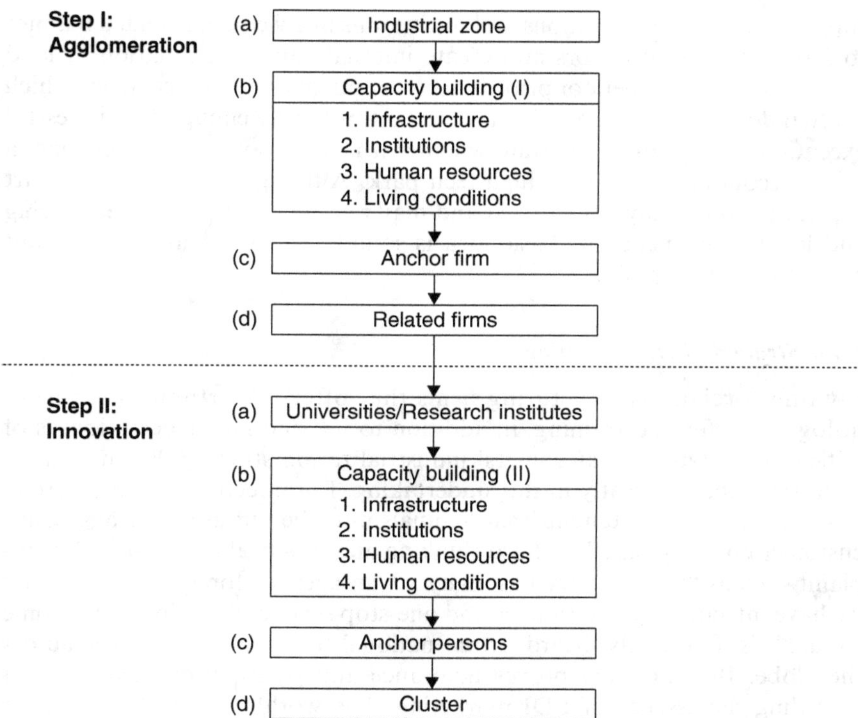

Figure 3.2 Kuchiki's flowchart approach to industrial clusters

Source: Kuchiki (2007).

The first step proceeds as follows. First, an industrial zone must be created, if it does not already exist, and a responsible agency is assigned. Second, essential conditions for smooth production must be provided by appointed players, a process which Kuchiki calls "capacity building." This includes physical factors such as power, water, telecom, and transportation as well as institutional factors such as taxes and incentives, one-stop investor service, and good living conditions. Third, an anchor firm (a large foreign manufacturer with extensive upstream linkage) must be invited which will automatically bring a large number of related firms. When these tasks are completed, sufficient production concentration and linkage will be established in and around the industrial estate and policymakers can proceed to the second stage.

Kuchiki (2007) uses his flowchart to analyze several industrial clusters in Asia including the printer cluster in Northern Vietnam, the automotive clusters in Tianjin and Guangzhou, China, the science and technology cluster in Zhongguancun, Beijing, and the (not so successful) automotive cluster in Malaysia. Kuchiki's formula clearly points to the vital importance of supplying necessary conditions and institutions in a well-coordinated manner to attract foreign investors and create internal value. Designation of land plots and announcement of priority sectors and investment incentives, which is often done in the name of FDI attraction, is hardly enough for successful execution of an industrial estate whether it is an export processing zone, a special economic zone, or a high-tech park. Although Kuchiki's flowchart is perhaps too rigidly constructed and may require more flexible sequencing and local adjustments, its basic idea is sound and can form an important part of industrial policy.

3.4.6 Strategic FDI marketing

Inviting foreign manufacturing firms that offer opportunities for technology transfer and training, in addition to job and income creation, is of critical importance to latecomers' industrialization strategy. But not many countries succeed greatly in this undertaking. For effective FDI marketing, abstract theory and standardized manuals must be put aside for aggressive customer courting based on hard thinking and practical experience. A complaint such as "Our country has many advantages for foreign investors and we have introduced all incentives and one-stop service. Why don't they come to us?" is frequently heard from national investment agencies across the globe. But this only proves ignorance and passivity of such agencies regarding the essence of FDI marketing. The world is a battleground for two-hundred-plus countries competing to attract best foreign manufacturers. Provision of fast procedures and financial incentives, or opening a nice website, is hardly enough to put the country on the radar screen of sharp-eyed foreign investors.

It must be cautioned that absorbing FDI does not automatically promote industrial capability. First, it is manufacturing FDI—not mining companies, real-estate developers, or big infrastructure projects—that can contribute significantly to the upgrading of a nation's industrial capability. Gigantic investments in power and telecom sectors or extractive concessions, whether public or private, can bring hard infrastructure or foreign currency to the country, but little can be expected in the accumulation of knowledge, skills, and technology in the population at large. Second, even with manufacturing FDI, technology transfer is far from spontaneous. In low-income countries, foreign manufacturers are often attracted by cheap labor, tax and import duty incentives, and various locational advantages, not necessarily by the prospect of teaching local managers and workers for productivity. While developing countries often covet "high technology," proprietary knowledge is a corporate secret guarded by intellectual property rights and will not be transferred to developing country partners freely. What can be learned effectively from FDI manufacturers are work ethics, factory operation and maintenance, marketing, kaizen, and other non-proprietary knowledge that can greatly improve performance. However, even this learning will not happen automatically; it requires a combination of proactive policies and serious efforts by local managers and workers for a number of years.

To integrate manufacturing FDI into the national development strategy, there must be a coherent industrial strategy with clear vision and concrete action plans of which FDI policy is a part. FDI marketing must be aggressive and target specific sectors and products, countries, or cities within countries, or even individual companies. Countries with low policy capability can improve business conditions generally and create a level playing field. Countries with higher capability will offer flexible and customer-oriented services that attract and support individual investors. Countries with the most advanced capability will not even publish their incentive policies; they approach foreign companies they want to court directly and negotiate special incentives individually in exchange for investments that support their national objectives.

The Malaysian Investment Development Authority (MIDA) is a highly efficient one-stop central service agency that issues investment licenses and provides investment incentives (Chapter 8). The main incentive schemes in Malaysia are "pioneer status" (corporate income tax exemption), investment tax allowance, and reinvestment allowances. Import duty and sales tax exemptions are also available for imported raw materials, components, and equipment for manufacturing firms only. The list of eligible products and activities, which are quite diverse and detailed, and approval procedure are constantly updated and electronically accessible in English, Japanese, Chinese, Arabic, and Malay. To receive any incentive, activities or products must not only be on the list but also individually screened by MIDA's sectoral departments and approved by its weekly committee.[10]

In Thailand, the Board of Investment (BOI) offers similar centralized investor-friendly services and aligns FDI policy to the nation's development strategy. For over a half century, FDI laws and policies have been revised every five years to meet new demands and challenges. Like Malaysia, investment incentives is differentiated geographically where projects in rural areas are given more privileges than those in suburban or urban areas. Also like MIDA, policies, incentives, application materials, economic and cost data, and so on are conveniently presented in the brochure, website, and slides in six languages which are updated frequently. BOI believes that its welcoming attitude is the greatest asset that attracts foreign investors. It thinks that measures to require technology transfer to foreign corporations are "tricky" since overregulation irritates investors and causes them to leave the country.[11]

In Singapore, the Ministry of Trade and Industry (policymaker) and the Economic Development Board (one-stop agency for FDI marketing and industrial development) work together to attract FDI, foster "industry verticals" (suppliers of intermediate inputs), and enhance business environment. Singapore ranks very high in the ease of doing business. It has the top position in the World Bank's Doing Business Report ranking consecutively from 2007 to 2012. In attracting FDI, Singapore uses both broad-based and targeted approaches. Besides improving business environment generally, it offers targeted, company-specific support and incentives through individual negotiations. This is called the "queen bee" approach where inviting the queen bee automatically brings a large number of other bees into the country (equivalent to the "anchor firm" in Kuchiki's flowchart approach). A good example in this regard is the attraction of world-class aerospace firms such as Rolls-Royce, Pratt & Whitney, and ST Aerospace to Seletar Aerospace Park with an area of over 300 ha, which prompted the arrival of related maintenance and repair services.

3.5 Comprehensive approaches

The cases explained above are individual policy measures. Industrialization also requires policy packages that encompass a large number of policy measures that complement each other, which are obviously more difficult to plan and implement. Due to the multiplicity of tasks, a well-structured policy procedure and organization is essential for interaction among different components (Chapter 4). For this reason, the pursuit of complex policy packages is a good entry point for advanced policy learning. Four examples are briefly discussed below.

3.5.1 SME promotion

The development of SMEs is a very popular policy goal around the world but its content and performance differ greatly across countries. Required policies are comprehensive and largely overlap with the standard policy menu for enhancing industrial capability shown in Table 3.3 above. Many governments produce little result because they lack capability to conduct a large number of policy components simultaneously and interactively.

SME promotion has two distinct and separable purposes. One is the generation of income and job opportunities for the general population (poverty reduction) and the other is selective creation of excellent SMEs to become the drivers of internal value and innovation (competitiveness). Both objectives are important and may be pursued in parallel, but the goals, strategies, and instruments they require are significantly different. For poverty reduction, SMEs in all size and sectors should be supported with simple procedure and with no conditionalities attached. For competitiveness, selection criteria, screening, and monitoring are essential and only those enterprises that demonstrate upward mobility should be promoted. As a country moves from low income to middle and high income, policy focus usually shifts from poverty reduction to competitiveness. In high-performing economies in East Asia, creation of competitiveness is the primary purpose of SME promotion. Each country should clearly define its own objective for SME promotion and design policy instruments and mechanisms accordingly.

In Japan where both large enterprises and SMEs are well developed, the purpose of SME policy in the post-World War II period shifted gradually from the protection of SMEs against exploitation by large parent firms to the encouragement of innovation by SMEs as a source of global competitiveness. Japanese policy instruments and mechanisms for SME promotion are highly complex, combining public–private partnership, participatory policymaking through "deliberation councils," technical assistance, financial support, repeated consultation, and so on. Probably this model is too difficult for most developing countries to adopt initially.

In Malaysia and Thailand, where the economy is highly industrialized but still dominated by foreign MNCs in electronics, automobile, and other machinery industries, the main policy goal is to increase internal value and replace foreigners with local managers, engineers, and designers. SME promotion is at the core of this strategy together with R&D, education and training, technology transfer, national branding, etc. In particular, Malaysia elevates SME policy as one of the key instruments of the New Economic Model for overcoming the middle-income trap (Chapter 8). Its formulation and execution are directed by the National SME Development Council chaired by the prime minister and coordinated by SME Corporation Malaysia, a one-stop service agency under the Ministry of International Trade and Industry which harmonizes SME-related activities of 15 ministries and 60 government agencies.

In a poor country where local industries remain primitive and absorption of manufacturing FDI is minuscule, SME promotion covers virtually the entire policy space for industrialization because almost all domestic producers are micro or small. The term SME promotion may be too broad and ambiguous for such a country. Goals, targeted firms, and policy instruments must be realistic and selective in light of limited policy capability and financial resources, and relevant to the local situation. Its SME policy package must be simpler than and quite different from those in more advanced countries.

3.5.2 Integrated export promotion

The minister of trade and industry of an African country asked a visiting Japanese policy dialogue team of which I was a member how East Asian high-performing economies coped with the situation where export incentives were given to individual firms but they did not fulfill their export targets. Our answer was that such a situation never arose in East Asia because export incentives were not provided in advance or unconditionally and because export targets were set for products or markets but not for individual exporting firms. No firm was penalized for not achieving its target or allowed to grab the subsidy and run. This exchange shows that some latecomer countries do not fully understand the essence of export promotion policy.

South Korea is a country that succeeded brilliantly in its export drive in the 1960s and 1970s. In an article that portrays the Korean success as joint discovery and upgrading of comparative advantages, Wonhyuk Lim (2011) stresses that export promotion must be an integrated national strategy encompassing a large number of measures and not just incentives and subsidies. Incentives and subsidies were only a small part of South Korea's export policy and their effects were largely offset by currency overvaluation. Studying these measures in isolation does not give a full picture or lead to appropriate policy learning.

In South Korea, export promotion policies included marketing, technology imports, export credit system, export association, and export insurance. Moreover, institutional support were provided through visions, strategies, and action plans; trade-facilitating agencies such as the Korea Trade Promotion Corporation and the Small Business Corporation; export promotion meetings chaired by the president; the Export Promotion Special Account Fund which generated financial means for export promotion activities, the Export Information Center, and the Export Idea Bank. Together with incentives and subsidies, these instruments collectively enhanced the effectiveness of the entire policy and institution package. Export incentives took the form of readily scalable rewards based on performance in a competitive setting rather than rewards contingent on the accomplishment of pre-announced targets (Lim, 2011).

Among the Korean measures mentioned above, the monthly export promotion meeting is particularly interesting as a tool for imparting activism and improving coordination among ministries and between government and the private sector. At the request of the minister of commerce and industry, President Park Chung Hee agreed to chair this meeting on a trial basis in 1965 which was institutionalized in the following year. This meeting, attended by high-ranking officials and business leaders, provided a forum to monitor progress and solve problems as they arose under the president's strong leadership.

> At each monthly meeting, the minister of commerce and industry gave a progress report on export performance by region and product relative to the targets set out in the annual comprehensive plan for export promotion. The minister of foreign affairs gave a briefing on overseas market conditions. Government officials and business representatives then tried to identify emerging bottlenecks and constraints that impeded export performance and devise solutions to these problems. Subsequent meetings monitored progress. Export insurance was one of many institutional innovations that were introduced as a result of recommendations from monthly export promotion meetings.
>
> (Lim, 2011, p. 195)

At present, Ethiopia replicates this high-level monthly meeting for export promotion as a result of policy learning from Korea (Chapter 10). Prime Minister Meles presides over this and several other monthly meetings where progress is monitored and problems are solved. Each ministry in Ethiopia is required to meet internally twice monthly, once to prepare reports to the high-level export meeting and another time to "de-brief" the results and take action within the ministry.

3.5.3 Strategic policy intervention to create a new industry

As argued in Chapter 2, debate over whether the state should be a creator or follower of a nation's comparative advantages carries little practical relevance as far as manufacturing is concerned. This is because modern industries depend less on climate or geography and more on the combination of proactive policy and private dynamism to realize a country's potential. Future manufacturing possibilities are wide and overlapping across many developing countries. It is difficult to assign product A to one country and product B to another whether we are talking about assembly of new electronic gadgets, electric car components, brand-name food products, or fashion garment. Even for products that depend heavily on natural conditions, realization of their potential again depends on the effectiveness of public–private partnership without which no industry is created. In either case, what is important is strategic policy intervention for supplying basic growth functions (infrastructure, human capital, supporting institutions, etc.) and avoiding market failures rather than discovery of a country's exclusive comparative advantage based on its history and natural conditions.

Chile has a long and complex coastal line, a large supply of labor, and a fishmeal industry, which put the country in a potentially suitable position for salmon farming. However, no salmon was raised or exported before the 1970s. To create a Chilean salmon industry from scratch, transfer of technology in fish raising and processing with local adjustments, training of fishery engineers and managers, and a sufficient market size for economies of scale and cost reduction were necessary. The involved cost, risk, and gestation period were so great that no private firm could undertake the enterprise. The Chile Foundation, a semi-official body that acted as an incubator of new enterprises through technological and financial support, played a critical role in overcoming these hurdles. Technical support was also provided by Japanese ODA (through the Chile Foundation) and private fishery firms from Japan and Norway. Capabilities had to be built and technologies had to be transferred for 20 long years before private firms finally began to invest in salmon farming in large scale. By now Chile has become a large exporter of salmon competing with Norway for the top position (Hosono, 2010).

Cerrado agriculture in Brazil is another case in point. Vast tropical savanna with an area of 2 million km^2 was so unproductive that it was said that as much as four hectares of land was needed to fill the stomach of one cow. Turning this barren land into one of the largest granaries of the world was impossible by market forces alone. The Brazilian government's strategic intervention through the Cerrado Institute, supported by Japanese cooperation for over 20 years, was instrumental in achieving this. As Brazil emerged as one of the largest exporters of cereals thanks to the success of Cerrado agriculture, overtaking the United States, the structure of the global grain market was changed fundamentally. In addition to grain, diversification into vegetables and fruits is also underway. The case of Cerrado agriculture demonstrates that even a negative factor can be turned into a great advantage by persistent policy intervention. At present, Brazil and Japan are cooperating to replicate this miracle in the northern and least developed provinces in Mozambique.

3.5.4 Comprehensive regional development with core infrastructure

Large-scale infrastructure projects such as transport corridors, deep seaports, or large power supply can be the core for comprehensive regional development provided that they are effectively combined with necessary complements such as education and training, agricultural and rural development, industrial estates, logistic efficiency, environmental technology, and planning capability of central and local governments. Large infrastructure should always be built for this purpose and not as a stand-alone project or for serving one large industrial customer.

Examples of comprehensive regional development with core infrastructure which were supported by Japanese ODA include Eastern Seaboard Development in Thailand mentioned above, the Brantas River Basin Development Project in Indonesia, and the expansion of La Union Port in El Salvador.

Among these, the last case offers an interesting contrast between the Japanese approach and the approach of a group of Harvard economists. In one of the earliest exercises in growth diagnostics, Hausmann and Rodrik (2005) concluded that El Salvador's lackluster growth, despite its bold social and economic reforms, was caused by "inadequate private returns to self-discovery by both local and foreign investors" (i.e., insufficient private incentives to explore and start new businesses). As to hard infrastructure, it was not judged as a bottleneck because the country already had fairly good air, sea, and land links by Central American standards. However, the Salvadorian Foundation for Social and Economic Development (FUSADES), a local think tank, countered that the source of national competitiveness should be created by improving the already good infrastructure to serve as a logistic hub of the region. At the core of this plan was upgrading of La Union Port in the country's eastern region to offer modern container, bulk cargo, and passenger facilities with a capacity large enough to handle Post-Panamex vessels (ships that can carry 4,800 20-foot containers or more). In the first decade of this century, the Japanese government supported this idea by a comprehensive cooperation package whose central pillar was construction of new La Union Port. In addition, an old bridge at the Honduras border was rebuilt for better connectivity, and digital map technology, urban planning for La Union City, and a master plan for eastern region development were offered. This was further complemented by social and human-resource development projects such as a training center, primary and math education, clean water, rural electrification and solid waste control; and support for productive sectors such as SME promotion, aquaculture, small-scale agriculture and livestock production, and reservoirs and irrigation.[12]

Comprehensive regional development planning may cross national borders. The Greater Mekong Subregion Development is an international project strongly supported by Japan and the Asian Development Bank which centers on construction of international roads and river water management in Southern China, Thailand, Vietnam, Cambodia, Laos, and Myanmar. Another example is the initiative of "industrial corridors" launched recently by the Japanese Ministry of Economy, Trade, and Industry which features public–private partnership in building infrastructure, logistic efficiency, and the creation of new industrial regions. Northern Vietnam, Southern India, and the Bangkok-Hochiminh City corridor are some of the regions targeted for this initiative.

3.6 National movement for mindset change

Finally, let us consider policy in a different dimension, one that addresses an intricate problem of less-than-expected response of the private sector to policies introduced by the government. This is an issue which is in principle separable from enhancing policy capability of the government and can become a serious obstacle to industrialization—as seen in Malaysia's limited success with Bumiputra policy discussed in Chapter 2 and further explained in Chapter 8.

Some policy areas require a fundamental change in popular mindset before results are obtained. Good policy alone may not induce dynamic growth if the private sector is generally content with passivity, short-terminism, and foreign-product worship. An unfettered market may favor real-estate speculation and job hopping instead of long-term investment in technology and skills. If mindset change is not forthcoming spontaneously from the private sector, the state may have to force it from the top until it becomes part of national culture. While permanent state guidance detached from market force or popular sentiment is inconsistent with the development of a market economy, temporary use of such an approach is not only permissible but may even be highly effective in the early stage of economic take-off. Such top-down persuasion has produced significant lasting performance in some countries as well as failure in others—as seen in socialist production drive with collective farms and state-owned factories. National movement is a double-edged sword. If it is to be adopted, systematic policy learning is essential to avoid mistakes.

National movement usually aims at elevation of productivity and competitiveness by instilling the spirit of activism and cooperation into the public.

Examples include Japan's Rural Life Improvement Movement (1948–) and factory kaizen (quality and productivity) movement (1950s–), Singapore's Productivity Movement (1960s–), Korea's Saemaul (new village) Movement (1970s–), Malaysia's Look East Policy (learning from Japan and Korea, 1980s–), Botswana's Productivity Movement (1990s–), and Rwanda's ICT drive (2000s–). These movements usually evolve from pilot projects to full-scale mobilization, institutionalization, broadening and shifting of scope, and sharing lessons with other countries. Some movements initiated decades ago are still practiced and disseminated in advanced forms. For this reason, the end point of a successful national movement is more difficult to identify than the starting point.

Mindset change requires a national movement and not just collection of individual projects. Policy will bear no fruit if its spirit and goals are shared only within a narrow circle of political leaders, government officials, and experts and academics. To be successful, a comprehensive and self-sustaining system of principles, implementing mechanisms, and necessary resources backed by the state's will and popular passion are required. In Singapore's productivity movement, which will be examined in Chapter 6, even taxi drivers were made fully aware of importance of improving productivity—and that is really the way it should be.

As an example, I take up South Korea's Saemaul Movement launched in 1970 as a response to an emerging gap between rapid urban industrialization and persistent rural poverty and backwardness. It was driven by President Park Chung-hee's strong personal interest in rural development through mass campaigns. Its objectives included not just improvement of rural life and income but, more fundamentally, achievement of these through a value shift of farmers from passivity to activism. In September 1971, President Park defined the movement as "a fundamental concept of national development, one in which economic development and spiritual enlightenment go together hand-in-hand" (Park 1979, pp. 83–84). The three slogans of *diligence*, *self-help*, and *cooperation* were hammered into all rural residents.

The Saemaul Movement, as a goal-oriented top-down rural development program, started with an experimental free distribution of 335 bags (13.4 tons) of cement to every village of the country from October 1970 to June 1971 with the condition that they should be used only for communal projects. President Park ordered that government funds be directed toward those who demonstrated the right spirit. By 1973, all villages were classified into three categories: 18,415 basic villages, 13,943 self-helping villages, and 2,307 self-sufficient villages in ascending order of achievement. Assistance was continued to be given mainly to the last two categories while "lazy" villages and villagers were repudiated or removed from further assistance (Kim, 2004, pp. 134–35).

The Saemaul Movement was most vigorously pursued in the 1970s in stages. After experimentation with free cement distribution in 1970–71, the years 1972–73 were spent on institutionalization and full-scale implementation supported by a hierarchical administration, guidelines which formalized procedure for project selection and evaluation, and training programs. The period from 1974 focused on self-development, enrichment, and broadening of the movement which included the introduction of Urban Saemaul Movement.

The Saemaul Movement was guided by the Central Consultative Council chaired by the Minister of Home Affairs. Under the Council, there were five administrative layers consisting of central government, provinces, counties, townships, and villages. Through this vertical mechanism the central government provided in-kind and financial aid as well as technical advice on management, farming technology, and project preparation and execution to worthy villages. At the bottom the Village Development Committee in each village, chaired by a Saemaul leader and with 15 elected villagers as members, proposed communal projects which were to be approved by the general assembly of the village as well as at the township level.

For education and training, the Saemaul Leaders Training Institute was opened in 1972 providing one- to two-week intensive courses to village leaders. Eventually 85 such institutes were established across the country with the Institute in Suwon assuming the model role. In 1974 the scope of trainee was expanded to include those in managerial positions in all sectors such as cabinet ministers, religious leaders, university presidents, and media executives. Its standardized curriculum covered Saemaul philosophy, national security and economy, project planning, case studies, field tours, and group discussion. All trainees, which numbered 822,900 in the first ten years of 1972–1981, stayed on the premise and slept in the dormitory during the course. In addition, short-term training without lodging was offered extensively.

Some criticize the Saemaul Movement as President Park's political device to fortify his dictatorial rule under the so-called Yushin Reform and inculcate the entire population in support of it. Others argue that the movement benefited wealthy farmers more than poor ones (Han 1987, p. 48). There was protestation against homogeneous Saemaul leader training which emphasized military-like discipline and morning jogging over specialized knowledge (Kim, 2004, p. 136). These are probably all valid criticisms, but the Saemaul Movement should also be judged by the enormous progress that South Korean villages made in income and living standards, along with urban residents, in sharp contrast to the dismal state of North Korea which also adopted similar top-down popular movements under Kim Il-sung. As average income per capita grew 1.7 times from 1971 to 1981 in South Korea, the ratio of per capita income between the richest urban area and the poorest province remained almost unchanged at 2.01–2.05 and subsequently declined to 1.75 by 1991.[13] Farmers were not left behind in South Korea's economic miracle. Spectacular economic performance may not completely justify forced national movement, but to a large degree it does.

From South Korea's Saemaul Movement and experiences for productivity improvement in other countries, the following factors can be distilled for successful execution of a national movement for mindset change.

First, the movement must be launched and sustained by strong personal interest and commitment of the top leader. Second, the movement must start with top-down instruction for grassroots participation. This may sound contradictory, but contradiction will later evaporate if the movement "catches" and begins to attract genuine interest of private participants because they see benefits of the movement instead of their reluctant obedience. While elements of coercion cannot be eliminated entirely in national movement, it should be regarded as success if intended economic performance is attained even with a certain amount of compulsion. Third, performance-based rewards should be given to villages, firms, or workers that produce good results according to transparent criteria. Highly visible incentive and recognition mechanisms should also be installed at the national and local levels. Fourth, supporting institutions must be created. This includes establishment of a national council or committee presided by the top leader; a central ministry or agency as the lead organization and the secretariat to the national council or committee; regional-, district-, and community-level offices; and staffing and budgetary arrangements. Fifth, authorized and well-designed training programs must be created to educate government officials in charge as well as private leaders and participants of the movement in the frontline of implementation. Sixth, the movement must continue for a sufficiently long time, typically over a decade or more, with evolving emphasis. A project lasting for only a few years will not be enough.

4 Policy procedure and organization

Success in industrial policy formulation depends not only on the proper choice of policy measures as discussed in the previous chapter but also, more fundamentally, on policy procedure and organization from which good policies are produced and executed. This chapter looks at institutional aspects of policymaking which are an important object as well as an essential background for policy learning. The purpose of studying various international best practices in policy procedure and organization is basically the same as studying alternative policy measures in the previous chapter. Rich foreign examples are to be regarded as building blocks from which procedural and organizational arrangements most suitable for the country in question should be created under the principles of selectivity, modification, combination, and improvement. As always, haphazard adoption of foreign models without a systematic survey of local contexts should be avoided.

4.1 Leadership

Our discussion starts with national leaders. High-quality leadership is the most vital ingredient of national development, a fact that can hardly be overemphasized. However, another sad fact is that great developmental leaders are few and far between and most countries at most times must manage development under mediocre (or worse) leaders. A good leader is crucial because he or she is the primary driving force of national development that can create all other conditions of industrialization if they are initially missing. Major reforms are not possible by bottom-up processes alone unless the top leader takes up the main responsibility. This principle applies generally to all organizations including a nation, local governments, ministries and agencies, political parties, firms, universities, research institutions, and civil society organizations.

There are two aspects of national leadership worthy of attention. The first is the quality of the leader or the leading group, and the second is the dynamics of coalition formation among contesting leaders and leading groups.

A national leader must be equipped with a strong will and passion as well as a genuine belief in productivity and excellence for the whole country instead of being interested in personal influence or wealth accumulation. He or she must have sufficient political savvy and networks, personal integrity and discipline, intellectual ability, and pragmatism. A top leader must be personally committed to a nation's priority policies and use his or her full power and authority to push them to completion. In short, a national leader must be developmental, not predatory. I expect that the reader will find this obvious but convincing.

National leadership comes in different forms including personal leadership of a charismatic figure, organizational leadership among multiple ministries and agencies, and inherited leadership by the only or dominant political party with changing heads. Government structure may be centralized and suppressive or "democratic" and pluralistic. Despite these differences in governing style, common success factors for great developmental leadership include (i) projection of clear visions backed by strong personal beliefs; (ii) creation and effective use of administrative machinery such as committees, councils, and task forces that pursue visions with strong mandate and responsibility; (iii) a mechanism by which a top leader hears, directs, and coordinates problems worked and reported by ministries and agencies in charge; (iv) insulation of this mechanism from political pressure and vested interests; and (v) capacity to communicate national visions to the general public and rally popular support toward them. If these conditions are satisfied, alternative policy organizations discussed in the rest of this chapter will function equally well despite apparently diverse structures and divisions of labor.

An effective developmental leader must be able to mobilize various state and non-state developmental actors—elite technocrats and officials, experts and academia, business executives and associations, NPOs and civil society, etc.—by giving them proper space and sufficient authority as well as pride and satisfaction to serve the nation. A great leader has ample ability to provide frameworks, incentives, and recognition that force every actor to do its part and move collectively toward a common developmental goal. To put it differently, prime ministers and presidents who stay aloof of key developmental issues, make sporadic top-down decisions without deep thinking or consultation, or micromanage everything without trusting their ministers and advisors, are unlikely to go down in history as great leaders.

One evident problem with installing a good national leader is that no one can consistently select such a leader in the complex political process of any country whether it is democracy or otherwise. Who will be the next prime minister or president and how powerful or effective that person will be is highly uncertain even among candidates, let alone for individual citizens, officials, or business persons. Yet there are indirect ways to influence the quality of national leaders in the long run. These include leadership and elite education, comparative studies in development politics, systematic analysis of technical aspects of effective policymaking (to which I hope this book contributes), well-calculated cooperation and pressure from foreign governments and aid agencies, regional contagion of good leadership through imitation and competition, and publishing biographies of admirable national leaders of the world. Humans are driven by both reason and emotion. While social sciences should do much to reveal the anatomy of wise and effective leadership, intimate knowledge of works and words of excellent leaders in different countries and periods, presented vividly and concretely, is certain to raise consciousness of what is wanted among voters and political candidates.

The second issue that should be examined is coalition forming among leaders and leading groups, both formal or informal, which is a crucial political process that drives development in any political regimes. Coalitions here are not confined to the alliance of political parties to form a government but covers broader cooperation among individuals or organizations such as bureaucrats, businesses, labor unions, military, regional and ethnic groups, academics, professionals, residents, civil society organizations, and so on. In most cases—this includes even dictatorship and one-party dominance—a single person or political entity is unable to pursue its aim unless it forms a coalition with other groups or organizations through negotiation, compromise, and sharing of benefits (for the case of late-nineteenth-century Japan, see Chapter 5). The importance of politics in development has been recognized in general but the systematic analysis of how this "black box" works and how its operational implications can be used in policy formulation remain rudimentary.

One of such attempts is the Developmental Leadership Program (DLP) organized by Adrian Leftwich (York University) and Chris Wheeler (AusAID) and supported by a number of donors and NPOs (Leftwich, 2009). DLP aims to collect and analyze concrete cases of developmental coalition dynamics from all over the world to extract policy implications and concrete operational guidelines for development partners and civil society organizations. Its research stands on the premise that the good governance drive by the World Bank has failed to produce any significant result and a different approach to developing country politics is required. For bilateral and multilateral aid organizations, "working politically" in developing countries should not mean conspiring a regime change or imposing a Western model in total disregard of local context. Since any aid action will influence power relation and coalition formation among political, official, and civil society organizations in the host country, aid providers must fully understand their influence and work consciously but subtly and quietly to become enabling agents for desired change based on deep local knowledge and a judicious choice of entry points and counterparts. In the first phase of the DLP, the importance of context specificity, brokering and convening functions of donors, and the role of secondary and tertiary education, among others, were highlighted from the case studies of Botswana, China, Egypt, India, Indonesia, Jordan, Mauritius, South Africa, Uganda, Yemen, Zimbabwe, and others.[1]

Additionally, a balance between agential and structural factors, or relative weight between producing high-quality leaders and institutionalization of good policies, must be borne in mind. An outstanding leader may rise to propel the nation toward development for a while but he or she will not stay forever. If progress depends solely on personal leadership, the whole thing may collapse when a next leader of average quality or less arrives. In the worst case, the next head of state may revoke whatever the previous one did just for political revenge or self-expression. In order to reduce this risk, good policies started by an excellent leader must be institutionalized. That is to say, staffing, budgeting, policy procedures, and policy organizations must be cemented as much as possible by laws, regulations, and agreed practices among multiple stakeholders. On the part of an incumbent national leader, it is necessary to delegate sufficient authority to various people and organizations and prepare early on the succession problem. Oftentimes, an "excellent" leader finds it difficult to do so because his or her self-confidence and desire for continued power monopoly outweigh the need for institutionalization of good policy practices.

4.2 Policy procedure

In policy formulation, procedure by which policy is made is often more important than the final document which is drafted and approved. While all policy documents must be revised and updated as time passes, the process that governs the drafting and revision can remain and continue to be fortified as experiences accumulate. This process should not be improvised for each occasion or left to a small group of drafters which happen to be assigned to the task. The process must be owned and institutionalized by policymakers even though background studies and drafting can be outsourced as long as basic goals and directions are laid out clearly. While concrete procedure varies significantly from one country to another, as we will see below, the basic ingredients of successful policymaking are surprisingly common and include a leader's vision, strong participation of state and non-state stakeholders, an effective consensus building mechanism, and designation of a focal organization with clear mandate to coordinate interests and produce policy.

Policy formulation must begin with the vision produced by the top leader. This vision, which must come from the deep personal conviction of the top leader, needs to be communicated to the people and eventually win their approval through election or other political means. It is also the vision by which his or her government is judged. The existence of a seriously committed policy vision is the prerequisite for making any high-priority strategy without which policy tends to be *ad hoc*, reactive, and scattered.

After the leader's vision is provided, the vision must be given more concrete forms in terms of goals, time frame, major directions, and key issues to be overcome by the discussion and agreement among all stakeholders, both government and non-government. When this consensus is formed, drafting work follows. In these processes the two crucial procedural requirements are *inter-ministerial coordination* and *stakeholder involvement*. Figure 4.1 illustrates

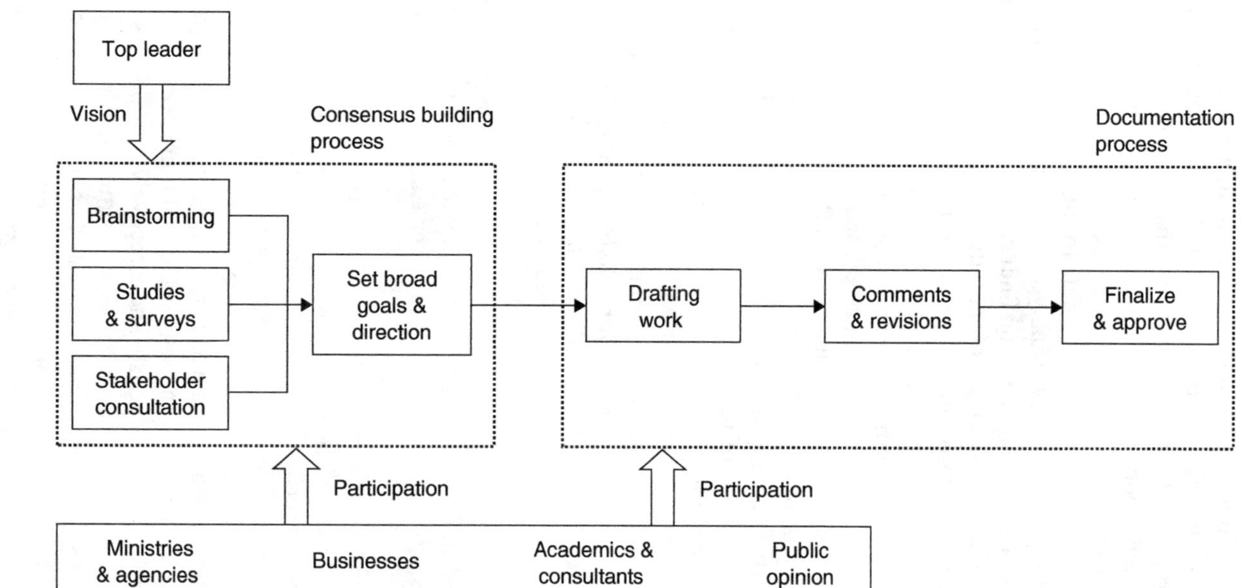

Figure 4.1 Standard policymaking procedure

Note: The entire process is coordinated by a lead ministry or agency.

the standard policymaking procedure recommended generally for any country at any level of development, including those engaged in policy learning.

Any key industrial policy in developing countries—whether it is small and medium enterprise promotion, building industrial human resource, quality and productivity movement, or creation of industrial clusters—normally covers multi-sectoral issues managed by more than one ministry or agency. Thus intra-government coordination becomes imperative if the policy is to be effectively designed, budgeted, and implemented. A lead ministry or agency must be designated and given a clear mandate to formulate the policy. While the ministry in charge of industry usually takes main responsibility, other ministries in charge of national planning, finance, ODA and FDI, education and training, science and technology, transportation, infrastructure, agriculture, urban development, and so on must also be on board. Since one ministry or agency is unable to direct or overrule other ministries and agencies horizontally, there should be a higher mechanism that supervises the whole process, gives full authority to the lead ministry or agency, and provides a forum in which multi-sectoral issues are deliberated and solved. Alternative organizational arrangements that ensure this will be the topic of the next section.

Besides cooperation among ministries and agencies, policymaking must receive active participation of non-government players. For the purpose of industrial policy formulation, by far the most important players are domestic and foreign firms that carry out investment and production as well as their business associations. Without their willing participation, any industrial policy is doomed to fail. Since not all firms share the same business interests or sectoral goals, a mechanism must also be in place to coordinate various voices among them. In addition, domestic and foreign academics, consultants, and industrial experts should be mobilized for conducting surveys, analysis, and international comparison, as well as drafting and commenting on policy documents as needed. Depending on the issue at hand, local residents, downstream user firms, consumers, NPOs, and other stakeholders may also be involved.

It should be stressed that mobilization of non-government stakeholders must be substantial with sufficient time and opportunities provided for contact and input. Nominal participation, such as hearings in which official views are unilaterally communicated or a large-scale symposium where little time is allocated for interaction with the floor, does not contribute much to the betterment of policy formulation. Public–private dialogue will become an important policy mechanism only when it goes beyond setting a formal framework and begins to incorporate private opinions seriously and effectively into policies.

Many governments in East Asia succeeded in institutionalizing government–business interactions for information sharing and policy coordination (Weiss and Hobson, 1995; Weiss, 1998; Kondo, 2005). Large flows of high-quality information between the public and private sector contributed greatly to building mutual confidence, credible commitments, and predictability. In each country, the nature and intensity of government–business coordination have evolved over time as the private sector has improved its capability and graduated from direct public intervention.

Through strong inter-ministerial coordination and stakeholder involvement, all major parties inside and outside the government must participate in policy formulation leading to a growing sense of shared ownership and responsibility as well as willingness to cooperate in implementation. This fact is far more important than producing documents which may be comprehensive and theoretically advanced but are not supported by concerned organizations. In the early stage of policy learning, agreed policy may be relatively simple with only a small number of specified actions (see the Ethiopian case in Chapter 10). Even in that case, if the drafting process matches with existing policy capability and local context, the resulting policy can be unique, ambitious, and at the same time feasible for the country in question. Indeed, this is the very process in which policymaking is learned. If the process is outsourced in its entirety to a group of domestic or foreign consultants, little learning will take place within the government.

This also has an implication for appropriate speed with which policy should be drafted. Some governments set unreasonably short deadlines for policy documents. This compels the ministry in charge to either rush to produce the document internally without regards to quality or contract out the drafting work to outside experts and consultants, which militates against policy learning described above. While the situation varies across countries, if proper internal and external consultation is conducted, a realistic amount of time needed to revise an existing policy is about one year, and for creating a new policy it may take two to three years. This includes lost time due to administrative delays and political cycles which are inevitable aspects of policy formulation. Quality, not speed, should be the main objective of policymaking. Quality here means that, based on sufficient information and analysis, all key aspects of the policy have been agreed among major stakeholders through persuasion and compromise so that the policy, once adopted, will be strongly supported and willingly implemented.

An example is given from Thailand. The Thai automotive industry boasts the largest production volume in Southeast Asia (1.65 million vehicles in 2010) and has expanded strongly despite frequent national, regional, and global economic crises in 1997–98, 2008–09, and 2011. Its policymaking is competently coordinated by the Thailand Automotive Institute (TAI), one of the ten sector-specific non-profit organizations established by the Thai government which are required to be financially autonomous from the government budget (see section 4.3.4). The main content of the Thai automotive policy was given succinctly in the Executive Summary of the Automotive Master Plan 2007–2011 which emanates from Vision 2011[2] and branches out to four objectives, five strategies, and 12 action plans. The most important part of the Master Plan is the exposition of the 12 action plans.

The drafting of the Thai automotive master plan takes about a year, which is genuinely a joint process between private firms and the Ministry of

Industry. Close-knit networking among all stakeholders is ensured by TAI. The drafting process begins with the "CEO Forum," an informal discussion forum among foreign and domestic firms, government officials, and academics that agrees on basic directions and identifies key areas to be worked on (in the 2007–2011 automotive policy, the five key areas were human resources, productivity, marketing, engineering, and investment and linkage). Production and export targets are proposed by the industry, not the government. After a broad consensus is formed, the Automotive Master Plan Steering Committee will commission studies on the above key areas to "focus groups." Finally, the master plan is drafted by TAI staff after all major aspects of policy revisions have been agreed among stakeholders and detailed studies have been submitted. TAI serves as a secretariat throughout the entire process and provides administrative and logistic support. Mr. Vallop Tiasiri, President of TAI, meets foreign and local producers at least twice a month formally and meets them more often informally.

From the perspective of effective policymaking, common mistakes include: (i) the lack of a clear vision from the leader; (ii) drafting by a few designated officials without building consensus or facilitating interaction among all stakeholders; (iii) outsourcing of the entire policy drafting to outsiders with the role of policymakers limited to making comments and revisions; (iv) bottom-up collection of subdocuments drafted by various ministries which ends up in unconnected chapters with too many priorities for implementation. These negative practices must be consciously avoided as a first step toward policy learning.

4.3 Policy organization

What organizational arrangements are necessary to realize inter-ministerial coordination and stakeholder involvement discussed above? An international comparison of policymaking points to different policy organizations that can equally attain good policy procedure. The choice should fundamentally depend on the unique characteristics and existing policy capability of the country in question. Below, five alternative policy organizations for conducting high-priority development policies are explained with concrete examples. Again, the intention here is to provide raw materials from which policy organization for each country can be constructed under the principles of selectivity, modification, combination, and improvement.

It should be noted that organizational arrangements are not mutually exclusive. There are countries that adopt more than one arrangement to execute different national strategies. It is also important to recognize that high-performing economies in East Asia did not possess strong institutional bases at the beginning of their rapid growth. Policy procedure and organization were strengthened during, and not before, their high-growth periods. State-building is a dynamic process in which the government has to accumulate industrial policy capability through concrete hands-on efforts and trial-and-error in the actual process of industrialization.

4.3.1 A technocrat team supporting the top leader

One of the key ingredients of the "East Asian Miracle" was the strong alliance between the top leader and the technocrat team (Campos and Root, 1996; Ohno and Shimamura, 2007). Many countries in East Asia established a semi-permanent technocrat group that directly supported the prime minister or president in executing his top national programs. Examples include Korea's Economic Planning Board (EPB), Malaysia's Economic Planning Unit (EPU), Taiwan's Kuomintang elites, Indonesia's Berkeley Mafia, and Thailand's National Economic and Social Development Board (NESDB).[3] Among these, Malaysia's EPU and Thailand's NESDB still exist while others have been disbanded as income and private-sector dynamism rose and new policy organization replaced the old.

These technocrat groups were created by convening well-educated and highly experienced officials, scholars, and business leaders as the policymaking brain of the country. Many of them had high degrees from foreign countries or had been summoned from prominent positions in foreign countries. These elites had full trust of the top leader while ministries were placed under them as implementing agencies. Their authority and directives became a central coordination mechanism for formulating, implementing, and monitoring development policies (Kondo, 2005).

This policy organization model works best under a strong and wise leader who exercises power for a relatively long time. Korea's EPB and Malaysia's EPU were the supporting arms of their charismatic leaders, namely, President Park Chung-hee (in power 1961–79) and Prime Minister Mahathir bin Mohamad (in power 1981–2003). The policy structure of Korea in the 1960s and 1970s is illustrated in Figure 4.3.

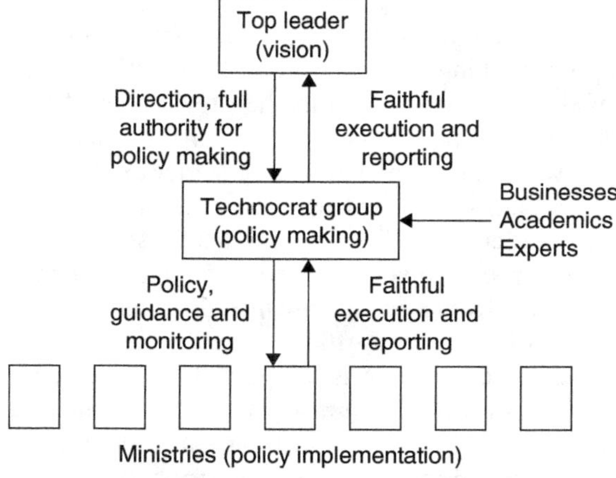

Figure 4.2 Technocrat team supporting top leader

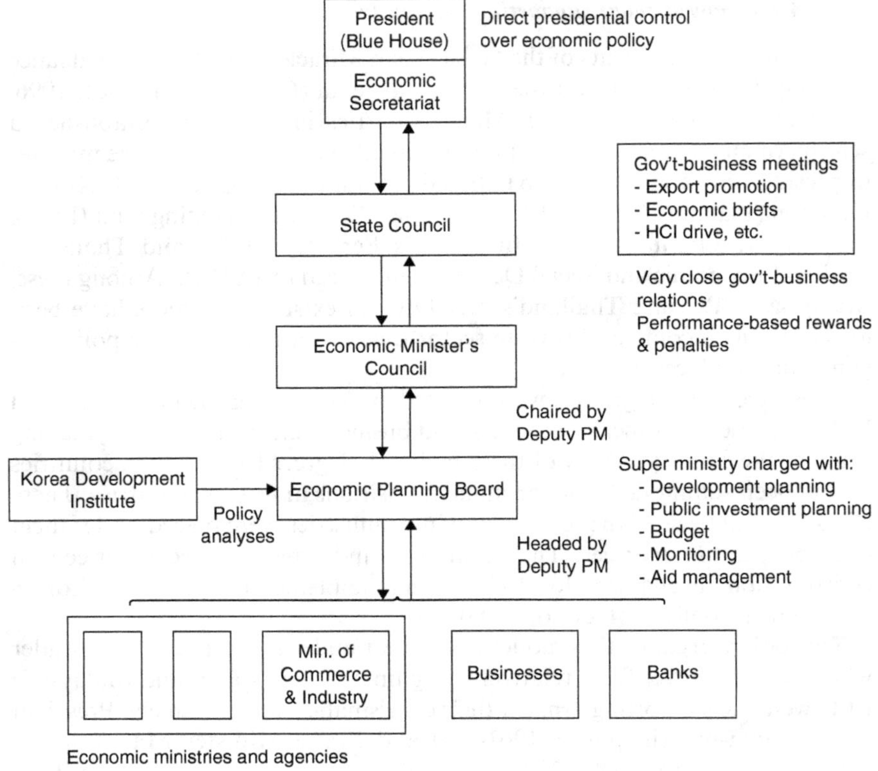

Figure 4.3 South Korea 1960s–1970s: Economic Planning Board

4.3.2 A national council or committee

A national council of committee—the precise name does not matter—is a less permanent policymaking arrangement that can replicate strong coordinating functions of the technocrat team in the previous model. This approach may be adopted by a strong, long-serving leader but it can also work effectively in a country where no such charismatic leader exists. In this model, the task of policy formulation is taken up by a national council or committee headed by the top leader himself, a near-top leader such as vice president or deputy prime minister, or someone trusted and appointed by the top leader. Its members are selected from a broad base including ministers or vice ministers, business people, scholars, retired officials, civil society leaders, media, and so on. The council or committee is supported by a secretariat staffed by seconded officials from various ministries which conducts administrative and logistic works. Working groups (or task forces) prepare studies, reports, and draft chapters in designated topics. Unlike a technocrat team discussed above, these councils or committees are normally organized around a specific mission and are terminated when the policy objective is achieved or there is

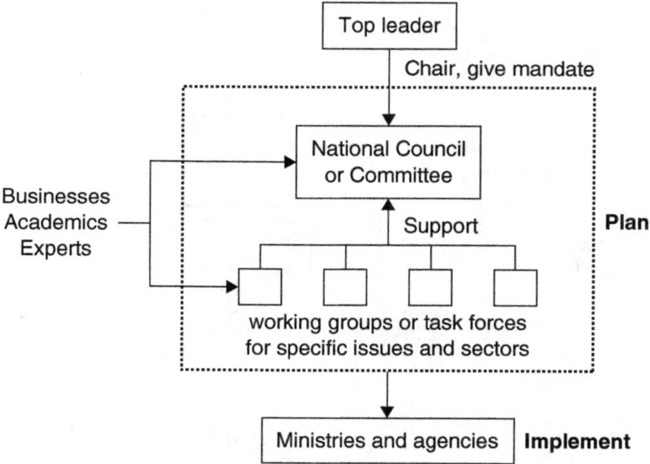

Figure 4.4 National council or committee

a change of government. Councils and committees can be more than one, each working on an assigned issue.

In this model, concerned ministries and agencies can participate in the policy process in three ways: (i) through the minister's membership in the national council or committee; (ii) as official experts in working groups or task forces; and (iii) as implementing bodies. Compared with the technocrat model, this configuration may be more acceptable for ministries and agencies wanting to participate in policy formulation extensively rather than receiving top-down instructions from the elite group and being confined to policy implementation.

The national council or committee approach is used widely with flexible adjustments and variations. Three examples are given below from Singapore, Malaysia, and South Korea. This approach is adopted to carry out a small number—usually up to several—of top-priority programs in each country.[4]

In Singapore, productivity has long been a top national agenda (Chapter 6). In recent years productivity began to receive renewed attention in the context of lagging productivity of aged or foreign migrant workers, the recent rise of China and India, and the aftermath of global economic crisis. To propose basic policy directions, the Economic Strategies Committee (ESC) chaired by the finance minister issued a report in January 2010. It recommended a drastic shift from factor-driven to productivity-driven growth and set an annual productivity growth target of 2–3 percent and an average GDP growth target of 3–5 percent in the next ten years. The main thrust of the ESC Report was endorsed by the prime minister and reflected in annual budgets.

One of the key recommendations of the ESC Report was establishment of the National Productivity and Continuing Education Council (NPCEC). The NPCEC was formed in April 2010 as a policymaking body for creating a productivity-led economy (Figure 4.5). It is chaired by the deputy prime

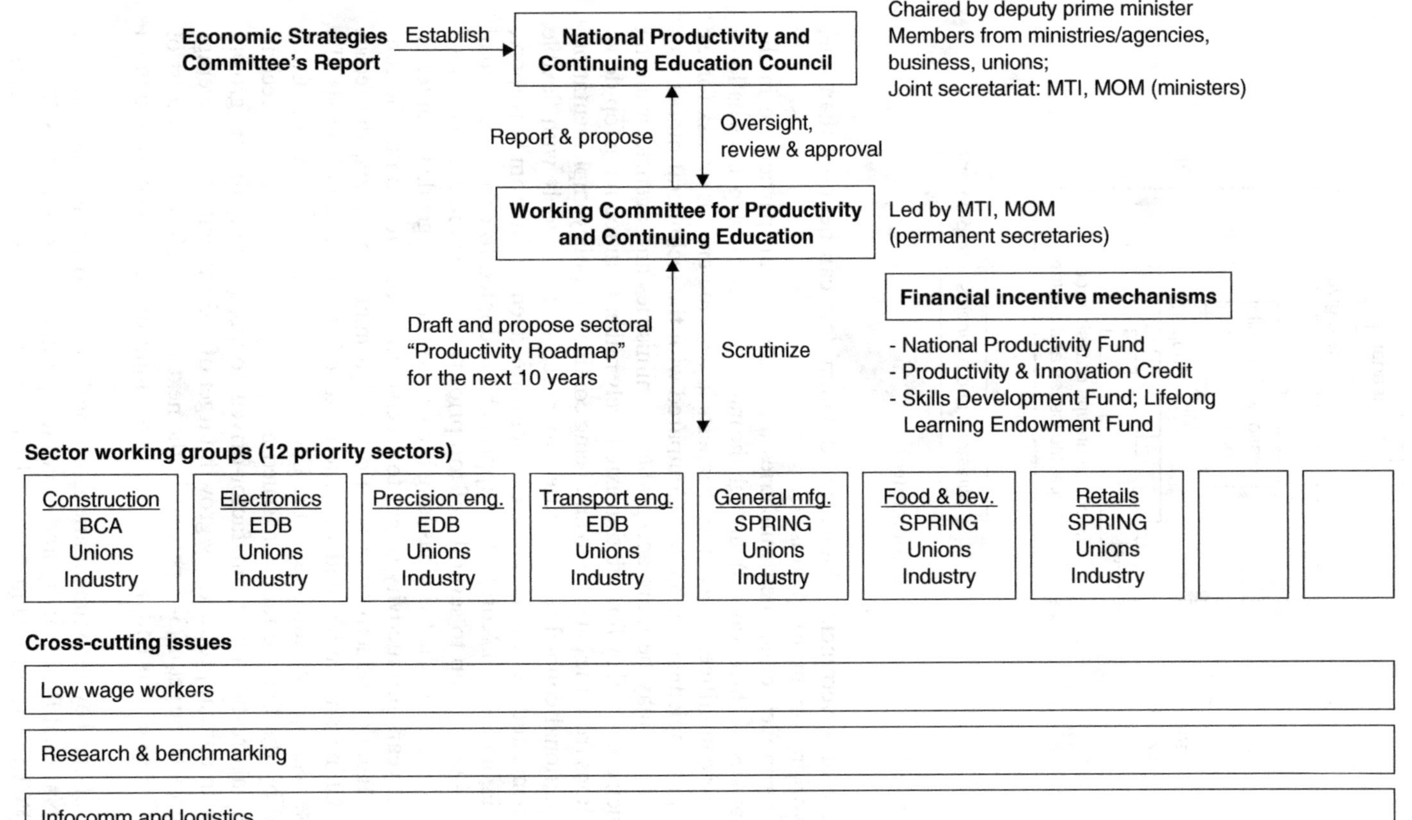

Figure 4.5 Singapore: National Productivity and Continuing Education Council

minister with its members coming from government, business community, and labor unions. The Ministry of Trade and Industry (MTI) and the Ministry of Manpower (MOM) act jointly as the secretariat. Under NPCEC, two layers of organizations are created: (i) the Working Committee for Productivity and Continuing Education (WCPCE) led by the permanent secretaries of MTI and MOM; and (ii) sectoral working groups and horizontal thematic working groups. Three financial mechanisms fund incentives and subsidies for firms and individuals that implement productivity-enhancing actions and training based on their performance.

NPCEC has selected 12 priority sectors that have large contribution to employment and GDP and high potential for productivity gain. Each sector group is required to draw up a productivity roadmap for the next ten years. They are reviewed by the WCPCE and submitted to the NCPEC for approval. A ministry or an agency is assigned to oversee each priority sector. In addition, horizontal working groups work on cross-cutting issues such as low-wage workers, research and benchmarking, and infocomm (ICT) and logistics. In all of these working groups, tripartite representation of government, businesses, and labor unions is ensured.

In Malaysia, the government puts high priority on SME development as an instrument to shift the growth engine from large MNCs to autonomous and innovative indigenous firms (National SME Development Council of Malaysia, 2008, preface). SMEs are to play key roles in job and income creation as well as moving the country out of the middle-income trap and into high income. The National SME Development Council was established in 2004 as a leading body that sets the policy direction for cohesive SME development. It is chaired by the prime minister and brings together 15 ministries and 60 government agencies to work together toward this goal. Initially, Bank Negara Malaysia (central bank) served as the secretariat of the Council; set three policy pillars (enabling infrastructure, capacity building, and financial access), five-year targets, and common SME definition; and published the Annual SME Integrated Plan of Action and the SME Annual Report. The Council also improved National SME Database and SME training and marketing and introduced new financial products for SMEs (Chapter 8).

In 2009 the SME Corporation Malaysia (SME Corp.) was created as a central coordinating agency at the operational level by upgrading the previous functions of the Small and Medium Industries Development Corporation (SMIDEC) which belonged to the Ministry of International Trade and Industry (MITI), a lead ministry for SME development (Figure 4.6). As the new secretariat to the Council, SME Corp. serves as a central reference point for all SME matters and undertakes impact studies on SME policies and programs across all economic sectors. Malaysia has a large number of SME-related ministries, agencies, and private-sector partners whose activities are now brought under the vertical policy organization consisting of the Council, MITI, and SME Corp.

In present South Korea, presidential committees serve as a key instrument for economic policymaking. Upon assuming power, every president establishes a small number of presidential committees as a vehicle to concretize, implement,

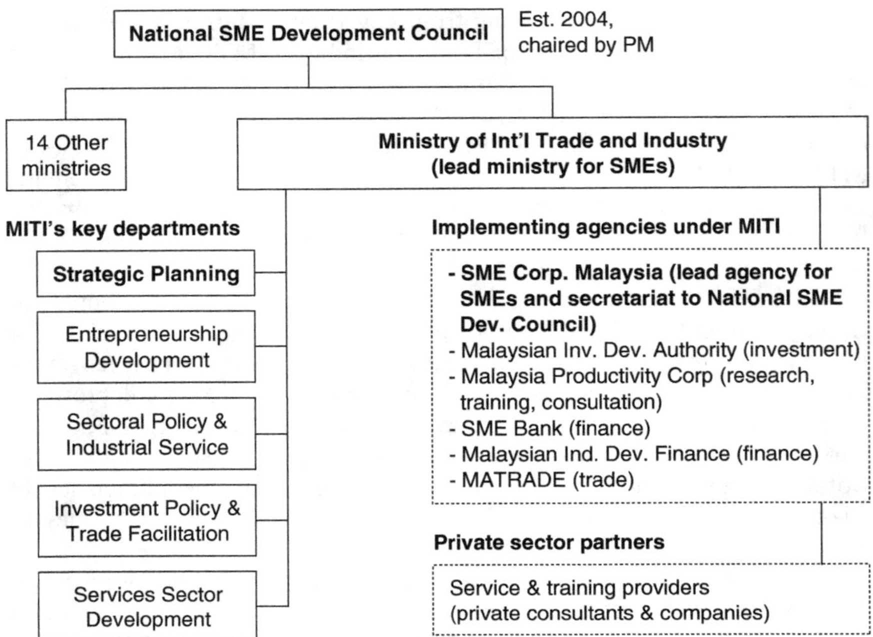

Figure 4.6 Malaysia: National SME Development Council

Note: Bank Negara Malaysia (central bank) served as a secretariat to the National SME Dev. Council until the establishment of SME Corp. Malaysia in 2009.

and monitor the priority agenda during his five-year term. Each presidential committee is headed by a person who has expertise in the chosen subject and enjoys the strong confidence of the president as well as secretarial support by staff seconded from various ministries.

President Lee Myung-bak, who assumed office in February 2008, established four presidential committees for Future and Vision, Green Growth, National Competitiveness, and Nation Branding (Figure 4.7). The most important among them was the Presidential Council for Future and Vision (PCFV), established in May 2008, which advised the president on designing overall national strategies and setting policy priorities. It was chaired by Professor Seung Jun-kwak of Korea University, and had 26 members drawn from vice ministers, academia, NGOs, legal experts, and business leaders. The Council met on a need basis without any fixed schedule. PCFV was supported by the Executive Office of the Council, a secretariat of about 30 staff comprising seconded officials from various government ministries and agencies. The secretariat is charged with drafting of policy documents, inter-ministerial co-ordination, and related administrative works. In addition to four presidential committees mentioned above, a temporary (one-year) presidential committee was created to host the G-20 Summit which took place in Seoul in November 2010.

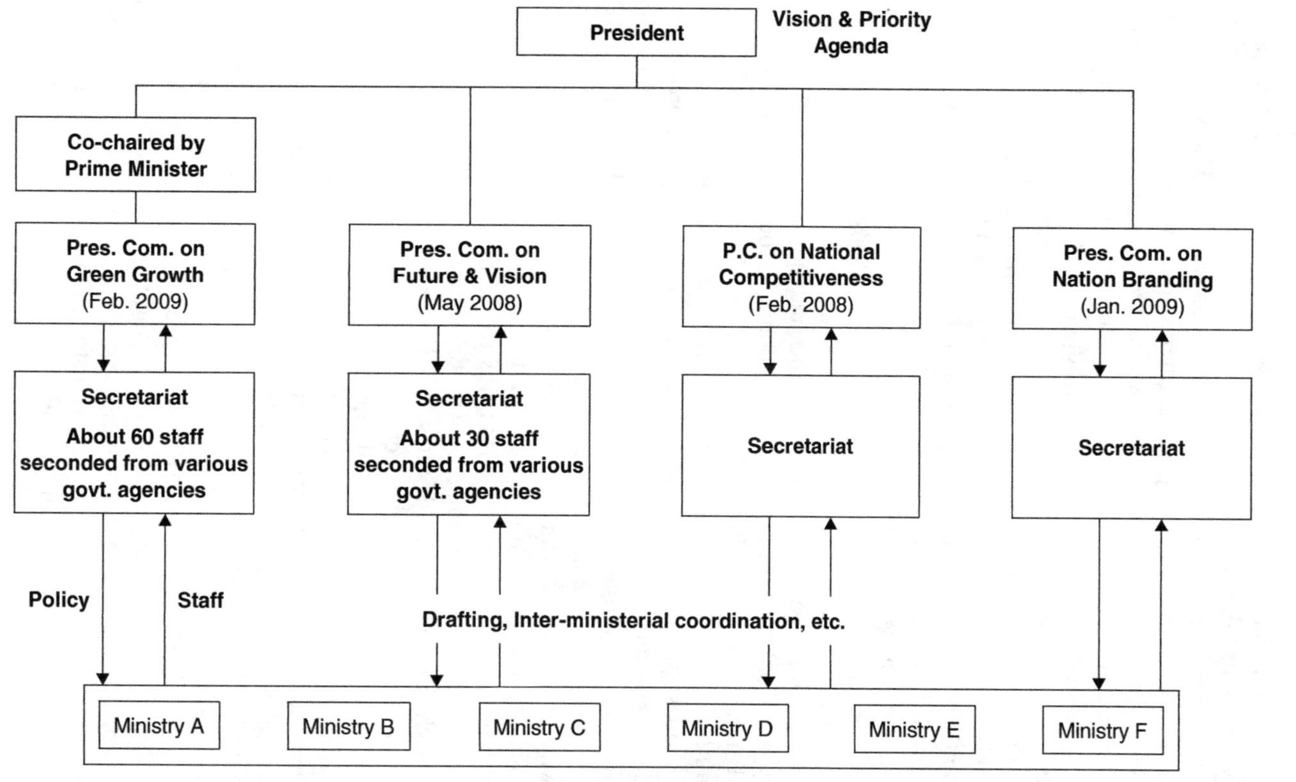

Figure 4.7 Korea: presidential committees

4.3.3 A super-ministry

Another way to secure dynamism and consistency in industrial policy is to give broad responsibility to one ministry and let this ministry do the designing and implementation of industrial strategies as well as additional works such as interface with political parties, interaction with non-government stakeholders, preparation of necessary laws and regulations, impact studies, and dissemination of policy objectives and outcome. While this ministry is just one among many ministries in legal standing, it has sufficient authorities and policy tools to become a one-stop house for initiating and carrying out industrial strategies. As long as the general direction of industrialization is agreed, this approach may not even require a strong and wise national leader to constantly supervise the process since the ministry can internally and autonomously produce coherent visions and strategies with its highly motivated officials and extensive information network.

Japanese industrial policymaking from the late 1950s to the early 1970s was the prime example of this model. The Ministry of International Trade and Industry (MITI) was created in 1949 by merging the Ministry of Trade and Industry, the Coal Agency, and the International Trade Agency to become the lead ministry for post-World War II industrial catch-up.[5] MITI had broad authority over creation of visions and strategies; individual sectors such as textiles, steel, machinery, and electronics; technology and productivity; trade promotion and negotiation; product, quality, and safety standards; intellectual property rights; competition and anti-monopoly policy; SME development; policy finance; restructuring of sunset industries; and energy and environment. Legal frameworks and policy tools needed to promote these policy areas were created during the 1950s.

According to Okimoto (1989), MITI was the *de facto* super-ministry for Japanese industrial policy. Compared with the fragmented industrial policymaking mechanism in the United States, MITI was distinctive in having broad jurisdiction over many industrial sectors and functional issues as described above, as well as having both vertical (industry-based) and horizontal (cross-sectoral) bureaus in its organizational structure (Figure 4.8).

As the lead ministry for industrialization, MITI worked closely with the Economic Planning Agency (EPA) under the Prime Minister's Office and the Ministry of Finance (MOF). The former was in charge of national economic planning and assessment and the latter was responsible for budgeting and financial issues. MITI, EPA, and MOF collectively assumed the primary role in formulating and executing medium- and long-term national visions and economic plans. In addition, EPA and, subsequently, the Land Agency (established in 1974), under the Prime Minister's Office, formulated spatial plans that included corridors, industrial zones, and land use and regional development plans.

In Japan, deliberation councils functioned as a key instrument for vision making, policy consultation and coordination, and information sharing within and outside government. Deliberation councils were also extensively used

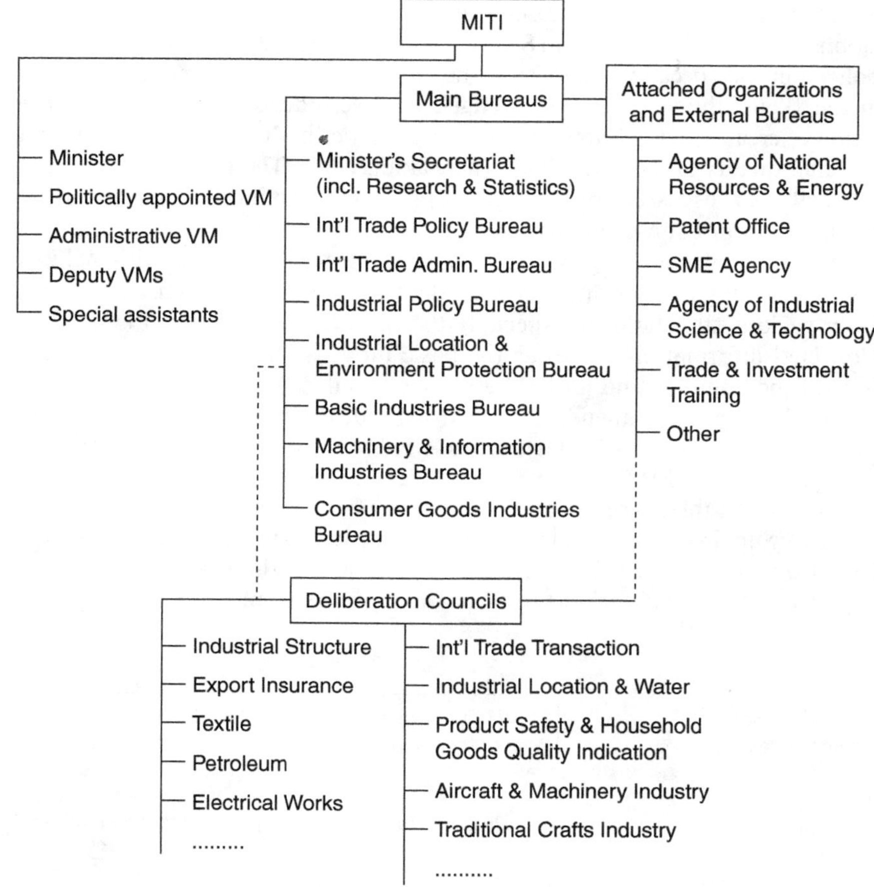

Figure 4.8 Japan: organizational structure of MITI

Source: Adapted from Okimoto (1989), p. 117, Figure 3.2.

within MITI. They provided a forum in which government and businesses met and discussed policy issues and business trends, and built consensus (World Bank, 1993). They were similar to national councils and committees discussed above but they were organized and managed by a super-ministry rather than the top leader, with MITI itself serving as the secretariat. Members of any deliberation council included representatives from related ministries, business leaders, experts, and academicians. Additionally, the structure of deliberation councils reflected both vertical and horizontal bureaus within MITI. This contributed to enhancing MITI's capacity to aggregate diverse interests (Okimoto, 1989).

Among deliberation councils, the Industrial Structure Council, established in 1964, was most influential as it oversaw industrial policy in its entirety with the participation of representatives from the public and private sectors (Johnson, 1982). The Industrial Structure Council drafted a vision for industrial policies in each decade. It published the vision of heavy and chemical industry in the 1960s, the vision of knowledge-intensive industries in the 1970s, the vision of creativity and knowledge-based industries in the 1980s, and the vision of better quality of life in the 1990s (Kawakita, 1991). The Industrial Structure Council also discussed measures to support pioneer industries and ensure the transition of sunset industries.

Japanese policymaking process was bottom-up. It started with MITI's junior officials gathering and analyzing data and conducting intensive hearings from various stakeholders, especially the business community (Figure 4.9). Collected information served as the basic input for subsequent discussions in the subcommittee and the deliberation council, each of which drafted and finalized policy recommendations. Throughout the process, deputy division directors (officials in their mid-thirties) were at the center of communication flows both inside MITI and between MITI and the private sector and thus had a considerable voice in determining the policy direction (Okimoto, 1989).

Akira Suehiro, a leading expert on East Asian development, stresses the Fiscal Investment Loan Program (FILP) and a close link between technical support and financial support to SMEs as Japan's two most successful policy

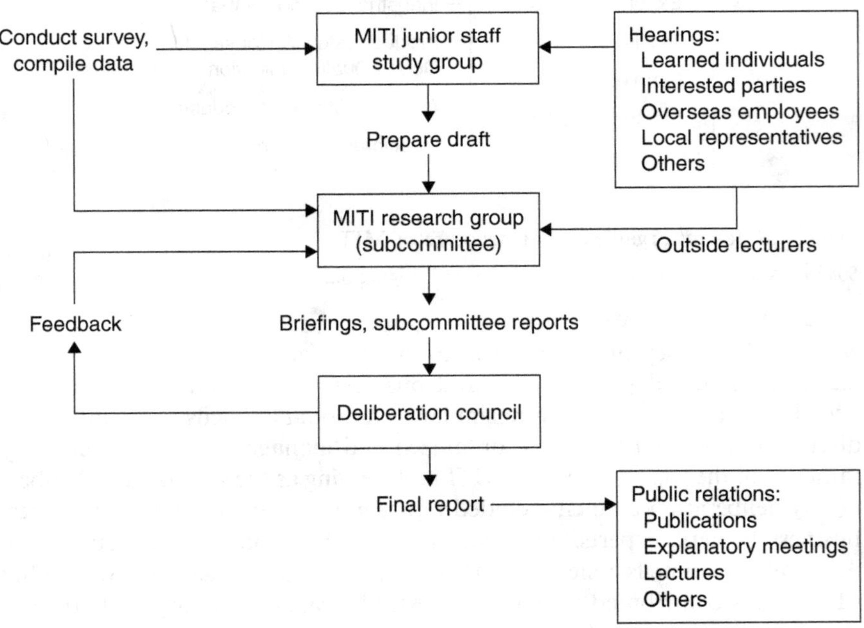

Figure 4.9 Japan: MITI's policy formulation (late 1950s–early 1970s)

Source: Ono (1992).

instruments for high growth in the post-World War II period. FILP was a mechanism in which funds from postal savings and pension contributions from the private sector were mobilized to conduct investment and loans having public nature (typically infrastructure construction and business support) through state institutions and credit mechanisms. Its financial resource was at times as large as half of the central government's general budget. Part of FILP was combined with MITI's industrial policy, where policy formulation and technical support to SMEs were provided by MITI and financial support for SMEs was provided by the Japan Development Bank under MOF using FILP funds. *Shindanshi* (state-certified SME management consultants—see Chapter 3) played a key role in linking management and technical support to SMEs with loans by the Japan Development Bank and commercial banks (Do and Pham, 2010; Ohno, 2010).

During Japan's high-growth period from the late 1950s to the early 1970s, there was no charismatic leader who ruled for a long time. Under the leadership of MITI, key economic ministries and agencies worked in collaboration and maintained close contact with political leaders to formulate visions and concretize them into various plans and policy measures.

A policy organization similar to Japan's MITI in the 1960s and 1970s is replicated in Taiwan where the powerful Ministry of Economic Affairs dominates the making and execution of industrial policy. The functions and organization of Taiwan's innovation drive is fully explained in Chapter 7.

4.3.4 A specialized institute as a policymaking hub

While industrial visions and broad direction should be set by the government, detailed plans, master-plan drafting, and daily contact and consensus building among stakeholders for any particular sector or issue can be delegated to a specialized, neutral, and non-profit organization. Thailand adopts such an approach, together with other approaches, for industrial policy formulation.

The Asian financial crisis of 1997–1998 prompted the Thai government to conduct a comprehensive industry review. The Industrial Restructuring Plan (IRP) was quickly formulated for enhancing industrial competitiveness with due attention to social conditions (this was conducted by the national council approach discussed above). The IRP consisted of the Master Plan, the Strategic Plan, and the Action Plan for industrial restructuring, and included as its objectives upgrading labor skills in target industries, supporting SMEs, relocating high pollution industries, and promoting clean technology. The Ministry of Industry (MOI) was the lead ministry which facilitated involvement of various stakeholders such as the public sector, businesses, and academicians. Although the IRP was formulated and implemented within the framework of structural adjustment loans of the World Bank and the Asian Development Bank, the Thai government took full initiative in developing its content.

Table 4.1 Thailand: specialized institutes

Name	*Start-up date*	*Organizations*
Thailand Productivity Institute	Jun. 1995	Originated from MOI industry promotion dept. 20 Board members, 161 staff.
Thai–German Institute	Nov. 1995	Financial cooperation from KfW, GDC. Technical training (CNC, CAM/CAD, etc.), 12 Board members, 79 staff, 5 German experts.
Thailand Textile Institute	Jun. 1997	Based on MOI industry promotion dept. and industry association. 20 Board members, 27 staff.
National Food Institute (NFI)	Oct. 1996	Based on MOI industry promotion dept. and industry association. 20 Board members, 27 staff.
Management Systems Certification Institute (MSCI)	Mar. 1999	Originated from Thai Industrial Standard Institute (TISI). 14 Board members, 55 staff.
Thailand Automotive Institute (TAI)	Apr. 1999	Supporting industry development. 20 Board members, 28 staff.
Electrical & Electronics Institute (EEI)	Feb. 1999	Supporting industry development. 29 Board members, 28 staff.
Foundation for Cane & Sugar Research Institute	Apr. 1999	Originated from Cane & Sugar Research Institute. 13 Board members.
Institute for SME Development	Jun. 1999	Modeled on Japan's SME Univ. Operated by Thammasat Univ. in cooperation with 8 local universities. 21 Board members.
The Iron & Steel Institute of Thailand	Dec. 1998 (cabinet approval)	Aimed at joint marketing promotion of four steel companies (oversupply).

Source: Higashi (2000).

To implement proposed plans, ten specialized institutes were established or re-created to design concrete measures for targeted industries and issues and to cope with problems arising in the implementation process. They were initially operated jointly by the public and private sectors, each with its own staff and board. They acted as a hub of information sharing and consultation between government and businesses and in some cases formulated industry-specific master plans. Some institutes were created by the Industry Promotion Department of MOI while others were transformed from existing agencies or established with donor assistance. As shown in Table 4.1, they included six industry-specific institutes (textile, food, automobiles, electrical and electronics, cane and sugar research, and iron and steel) and four thematic institutes (productivity, technical training, management and certification, and SME development). After five years of establishment, these institutes were required to become financially independent from the government budget.

Performance varied across these institutes. Among them, the previously mentioned Thailand Automotive Institute (TAI) has been highly successful as a policymaking and implementation hub connecting the Thai tripartite of government, businesses, and experts. TAI conducts policy study and advice, supports clustering of auto parts makers, and promotes export. It provides training for factory engineers and workers, runs an automotive testing laboratory, and serves as the secretariat for consensus building and drafting policy documents. TAI cooperates with MOI, MOF, the Ministry of Commerce, and the Ministry of Science and Technology as well as researchers from ten universities in Thailand. It provides research and information services and manages a website for automotive part makers supported by Asia-Pacific Economic Cooperation (APEC), a regional cooperation forum. At the beginning it was financed jointly by the government and the private sector. By now it has become a self-financing organization. As of November 2009, about half of its 91 staff were at the testing laboratory and the remaining half were in policy research and training.

As the secretariat of master plan drafting, TAI supplies not only administrative support but, more fundamentally, initial ideas for policy direction and coordination of different interests between government and businesses as well as among businesses. The idea of subsidizing Eco-Car production was one of such ideas emanating from TAI and accepted by government and industry in the 2007–2011 automotive master plan. The process by which TAI drafts the master plan has already been explained in section 4.2.

Figure 4.10 depicts Thai policymaking for specific policy areas adopted under Prime Minister Thaksin Shinawatra, a strong leader who ruled the country from 2001 to 2006. The prime minister produced highly vague visions, such as becoming the "Detroit of Asia" or the "Hub of Tropical Fashion," for relevant ministries to concretize and implement. A specialized institute functioned as a policy hub among the tripartite at the operational level while an industry-specific committee approved and adjusted policies at a higher level. The private sector could influence policy through these institutes and committees, and it also had direct access to the prime minister. Even after the strong leader was removed in 2006, the Thai policy system continues to function basically in the same way as before because these specialized institutes are already institutionalized. Its operation does not hinge critically on the existence of a strong leader.

The institutional hub approach works well in the case of the Thai automotive sector because there is deep trust among all stakeholders, because TAI has build solid relations with them, and because Thai policymaking is pragmatic and flexible without too many bureaucratic requirements. According to Thai MOI officials, the Thai automotive sector is already sufficiently developed and the role of government has shifted from direct support to the industry

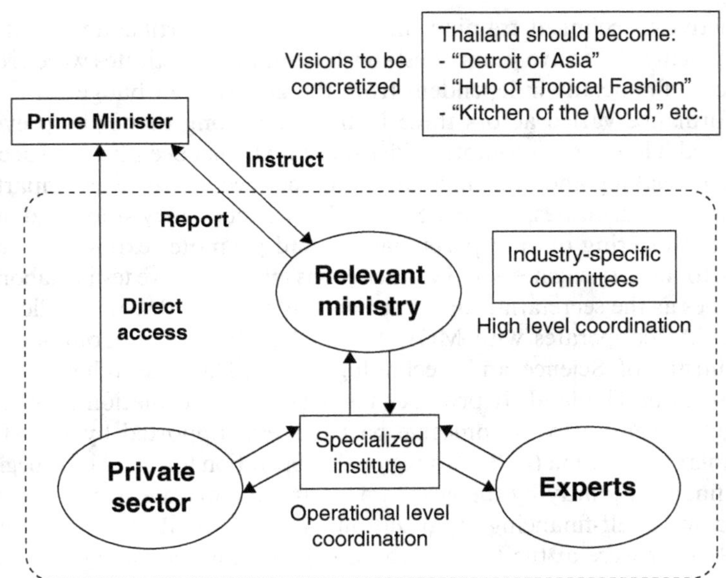

Figure 4.10 Thailand: specialized institute approach (under Thaksin Government 2001–2006)

to general policymaking. At present and in the future, managerial, technical, and financial support for managers, engineers, and workers is to be conducted by private service providers and private financial institutions. However, in a country where the private sector is weak, where mutual trust between government and businesses does not exist, or where policymaking is highly rigid and hierarchical, assignment of policymaking authority to a neutral non-profit organization may not work as effectively as in Thailand.

4.3.5 A strong leader as policy driver without institutionalization

A very different type of policymaking is possible with the existence of a strong and economically enlightened leader without institutionalization. In this case, the head of the state (or a similarly high-level actor) plays an instrumental role in all policymaking functions. This includes vision and strategy making, coordination among ministries and agencies, implementation and monitoring, solving problems and coping with shocks, mobilizing the private sector, and dealing with foreign investors and development partners. Policies become action-oriented and coherent if the leader's mind is lucid and dynamic. Actions of different ministries become mutually consistent even though ministers do not talk to each other. The private sector and foreign investors will know where the country is headed and international cooperation will be made to align with the national development plan. All this is possible because the top leader personally directs every player in the game.

This type of policymaking depends heavily on the personal capacity of one particular individual and, for that reason, can be quickly realized if such a leader assumes power. In the early stage of economic take-off, a leader who sets everything right is highly welcome since the nation has no time or resource to build strong enough systems for sustainable growth. But the risks of this approach are also clear. Without institutionalization, the exit of a capable leader will stagnate and even reverse economic gain and no learning by policymakers will take place. To avoid this fate, the capable leader must work even harder not only to conduct good policies but also to create new laws, systems, and organizations that cement the way of policymaking which he or she has started. This is indeed an enormous demand even on the wise leader. An example of such policymaking is provided in the Ethiopian policy formulation discussed in Chapter 10.

4.4 Policy structure[6]

While policy documents such as industrial master plans and strategies do not have one "correct" format applicable to all countries, structural variation must come from conscious choice based on local context and policy purpose at hand rather than by chance. If a policy document is produced without serious consideration of overall design, it may end up reflecting the whims of particular drafters—ministerial officials, academics, or foreign consultants—that happened to be assigned to the task. As argued in section 4.2 above, basic visions and policy direction must be established through a consensus-building process involving major stakeholders before the drafting of a policy document is commissioned. Drafting itself is a relatively easy task that can be delegated to anyone as long as key contents have been agreed among all.

The standard components of an industrial master plan are illustrated in Figure 4.11 and discussed individually below. Each of these components may occupy either one chapter or a number of chapters. Selection and order of these components are somewhat flexible. For example, targets may be inserted after situation analysis and policy issues. However, the vision should most properly be stated at the outset and the action plan matrix should come at the end (unless specified in another document or mechanism). Terminology is also flexible and substitutable by other phrases of similar connotations. Besides these basic components, there may be additional materials such as preface, table of contents, lists of tables and figures, executive summary, introduction, drafting procedure and organization, appendices, and so on.

4.4.1 Vision

A master plan must clarify the purpose of industrial promotion. This includes why this particular industry is important in national development, what role it should play in stimulating other sectors, what positioning it should take in the global, regional, and national economies, and so on. If these purposes

Vision	Importance, role, orientation, and positioning of industry in national development
Targets	Long- and medium-term numerical and/or qualitative targets
Situation analysis	Current status, potentials and obstacles of the domestic industry in the national, regional and global context; tables and graphics for data, surveys, international comparisons, etc.
Policy issues	A small number of selected issues should be identified, prioritized, and analyzed in preparation for designing policy action
Action plan or action mechanism	A large matrix that pre-specifies actions, sub-actions, expected output, success criteria, deadlines, and responsible organizations; procedure for monitoring and reporting should also be specified. Alternatively, a monthly high-level committee chaired by top leader, or a well-focused and well-coordinated budgeting and project approval process may substitute the action plan matrix.

Figure 4.11 Standard ingredients of an industrial master plan

are already presented in other documents and widely shared among stakeholders, they can be mentioned briefly without spilling much ink. On the other hand, if these are not yet sufficiently expressed, the master plan should clearly and concisely state the importance of the sector in question. This section should be no more than a few pages. One way to state the vision is to present it as part of the introductory chapter. Vision is sometimes stated in a layered structure consisting of vision, missions, and objectives. This is acceptable but not obligatory. It should also be noted that national policy vision is different in nature from vision, missions, and objectives adopted routinely by public or private organizations.

4.4.2 Targets

Long- and medium-term targets, quantitative or qualitative, should be presented with a clear time frame, which should normally extend over a few to several years.[7] These targets should be ambitious but realistic. Numerical targets should be higher than simple extrapolation of the present course but also reachable with serious exertion of government and business effort and cooperation. The appropriate number and levels of these targets, including how many numerical targets should be set with how much detail, depend critically on the characteristics of the sector in question as well as the capability of government and the private sector of that country. For this reason, there is no fixed template applicable to all master plans for all countries. Generally speaking, there should be fewer (numerical) targets if the industry is not capital-intensive, markets and prices are unpredictable, the industry produces final consumer goods, the domestic private sector is mature, policy capability is weak, or the private sector does not trust the government. Targets are useful if the opposite is true. Before setting any targets, policymakers should have a thorough discussion with all stakeholders, including businesses and experts, and conduct necessary studies for the proper configuration of such targets.

4.4.3 Situation analysis

The master plan must analyze the current status, potentials, and obstacles of the domestic industry in question. Data should be presented in tables and graphics, and the results of surveys and benchmarking should be reported if relevant. Information should not be thrown in randomly but must be inserted with a clear purpose of making certain points. Routinely reviewed issues include the past performance of output, capacity, demand, export and import, and localization of inputs; product mixes and producer profiles; regional distribution of production; productivity and competitiveness; demand forecasts; and global, regional, or domestic market trends that may impinge on the development of the industry. The appropriate selection of these analyses depends on the degree of understanding and consensus among stakeholders. If businesses, policymakers, and experts generally agree on the current position of the domestic industry, situation analysis can be brief or even skipped. If, on the other hand, policy formulation is in an early stage and stakeholders do not yet share basic information, situation analysis becomes an integral part of the master plan. I do not particularly recommend SWOT analysis which tabulates strengths, weaknesses, opportunities, and threats. Filling obligatory cells mechanically does not produce any new information. What is important here is provision of basic materials for extracting a few key issues (next subsection).

4.4.4 Policy issues

After the industry situation is reviewed comprehensively, specific aspects that need to be fortified by policy action to realize vision (i) and targets (ii) above must be identified and analyzed. These issues may call for removal of negatives or strengthening of positives. Obviously, which issues need to be included cannot be prejudged because this is highly contingent on the circumstances of the sector or the country. Here, some of the common focal issues are listed by way of examples: skills and technology, cost reduction, quality improvement, product design and development, input procurement (localization and supplier policy), upstream investment, marketing, export promotion, infrastructure, financing, labor supply and quality, and so on. The most relevant topics for the industry should be identified and agreed among stakeholders, and studies should be conducted for each of them (as in the Thai automotive industry discussed in sections 4.2 and 4.3.4 above). It is important to work on prioritized issues only rather than cover all issues broadly and superficially. Issues raised here should be given concrete solutions in the following action-plan section.

4.4.5 Action plan or action mechanism

An action-plan matrix or an action mechanism is essential for ensuring implementation. An action-plan matrix is a large table that translates analyses and proposals conducted in previous chapters into concrete actions. It may be included in the master-plan text or prepared in a separate document. Either way, it is crucial that its progress is monitored and reported to the government at regular intervals and any problems are attended to as they arise. The action-plan matrix typically contains the following cells: actions, sub-actions, deadlines, expected output, performance criteria (success indicators), main responsible organizations, and other cooperative organizations. An extracted sample format from Zambia is given in Table 4.2. The implementation procedure, such as who will report what to whom by when, must also be specified along with the action plan matrix.

Alternatively, an action mechanism, such as a high-level monthly committee chaired by a top leader or minister, or a well-focused budgeting and project approval process coordinated by an effective hub organization, can be adopted. Compared with the action-plan matrix approach which stipulates all actions in advance, these process-oriented approaches are more flexible in coping with shifting circumstances. However, their success requires strong and effective guidance by the leader or the designated hub organization. In cases where political support and administrative capability for policy execution are weak, the action-plan matrix approach may be preferable.

4.4.6 General remarks

An industrial master plan must be implemented and supported by all stakeholders. A policy document, however professionally written, is just paper if it is not implementable. To close this section, general features that must be satisfied throughout a policy document can be reiterated. These can be attained more easily if proper policy procedure and organization discussed in the previous sections are already in place.

First, relevance and conciseness should be the criteria for including any information in policy documents. All text and data should support the main arguments and proposals of the master plan. Statistics that have little informational value, abstract words with no concrete target or mechanism such as "improve," "strengthen," and "level up," and general statements applicable to any industry in any country should be removed as much as possible. If all chapters are logically connected, it is possible to summarize relations among key targets, strategies, and actions in one diagram or table—as done in

Table 4.2 Zambia: action plan matrix format for the Triangle of Hope project

Recommendation (action)	*Activities (subaction)*	*Status*	*Expected output*	*Status*	*Activity period*	*Responsibility*	*Monitoring indicator*
Promote investment in cotton production by allocating land to appropriate producers	1. Identify land to be held in trust	Little progress	Land for cotton production identified and secured	Not yet started	Jun. 2007	MACO (main), MoL (sub)	Monthly report
	2. Write to MOL for title deed	Not yet started					
	3. Develop adm mechanism for farm blocks	Done					

Note: Extracted and edited by the author. The entire action plan matrix occupies 41 pages. The Triangle of Hope Project aims at improving investment climate and establishment of an industrial zone.

Thailand's supporting industry master plan in 1995 and automotive industry master plan 2007–2011. Generally speaking, a compact document of less than 100 pages is more effective in communicating policy to stakeholders than a thick volume that no one reads. The above-mentioned Thai supporting industry master plan, which is old but still used as a reference material for policy action, is only 37 pages long including appendixes.

Second, flexibility and adaptability must be ensured across countries, sectors, and time. Since all industries are different and countries face different challenges, cookie-cutter molds cannot be applied to the making of industrial strategies and master plans. Even for the same industry in the same country, shifting circumstances will call for policy revisions over time. In particular, the relative scope of government intervention must be set properly. The optimal borderline between state and market must continue to be re-drawn for each industrial master plan. Industry's characteristics such as capital intensity, gestation period, product type, and market volatility should influence the appropriate weight of state intervention. In addition, the maturity and dynamism of the private sector and government's policy capability should also be taken into account. Creativity is needed to fit policy documents to the changing reality of the industry in question.

Third, proper balance between fulfilling committed actions and flexibility in implementation must be pursued. In general, the higher is policy capability, the more flexibility should be given to policymakers. In the early stages of policy learning, it is a good idea to regularly and strictly monitor the progress of each pre-agreed action. This will increase the percentage of actions implemented, but at the cost of less agility as situations change and enormous energy and time that must be spent on the production and execution of policy documents. As implementation is assured and policy response to shocks is learned, rigid policy matrices should give way to the improvise-as-you-go approach. For this reason, low-income countries usually spell out proposed actions in large tables while advanced countries prefer to state strategies generally or even do away with master plans completely, and leave annual project formulation, budgeting, and institutional revisions to a competent organization or an ad hoc committee in charge. Similarly, regular overall planning such as five-year plans is still practiced in Malaysia, Thailand, China, and Vietnam but not in Japan, Singapore, Taiwan, or South Korea.

Mr. Vallop Tiasiri, the president of the Thailand Automotive Institute mentioned above, which drafts the automotive master plan, prefers the process-oriented approach in ensuring implementation. Although the first automotive master plan of Thailand (2002–2006) had a large action-plan matrix, the second automotive master plan (2007–2011) has only a small action summary table and relies heavily on continuous project-based implementation toward agreed goals. If in any given year greater financial resources and more projects are available, policy implementation is accelerated and vice versa. In the case of the Thai automotive industry, strong leadership and coordination exercised by Mr. Vallop and his institute and deep trust and information sharing among industry, government, and donors enable such an approach.[8]

4.5 Suggestions for Vietnam[9]

Finally, an example of country-specific advice in policy procedure and policy organization is presented for the case of Vietnam, a country whose policymaking has been studied by the author for nearly two decades. In order for Vietnam to carry out industrial policy effectively toward 2020, the year by which the country hopes to achieve the goals of *modernization* and *industrialization*, three concrete suggestions are in order.

4.5.1 Targeting a small number of priority issues

While many issues must be tackled in industrialization, Vietnam's knowledge, human capital, and financial resources are limited. For effective implementation, it is of utmost importance that key policy entry points be limited in number, perhaps up to four or five, for industrialization toward 2020. The Socio-Economic Development Strategy 2011–2020 (the so-called ten-year development plan) lists too many issues to be dealt with, which prevents proper budgeting, staffing, and planning. Too many priorities are equivalent to no priority. The Vietnamese government must select only a few industrial priority areas to be really worked on. Selectivity must be exercised by the top leaders of the country, because this is difficult to realize by a participatory bottom-up approach.

Development partners including Japan, Germany, Singapore, and the UNIDO have long supported industrial human-resource development and establishment of linkage between industry and training institutions in Vietnam. The Japan International Cooperation Agency has assisted creation of SME policy and training of related officials of the Ministry of Planning and Investment. Since 2008, Japan has also highlighted supporting industry promotion as one of the key policy entry points and jointly worked with the Vietnamese authorities to design action plans. Vietnam Competitiveness Report 2010, drafted jointly by the Central Institute for Economic Management and Singapore's Lee Kuan Yew School of Public Policy, proposes industrial cluster development as another possible policy entry point for industrialization (Ketels et al., 2010) although no major donor is supporting this effort yet[10] and the operational concept of industrial clusters needs to be clarified and narrowed down.

While the ultimate choice rests with the Vietnamese policy leaders, it is hoped that these areas—industrial human resource, SME promotion, supporting industries, and industrial clusters—will be given high attention. This is partly because they are universally important challenges in any newly industrializing country and partly because international cooperation is likely to be forthcoming for these purposes.

4.5.2 The Ministry of Industry and Trade (MOIT) and the Ministry of Planning and Investment (MPI)

SME promotion and supporting industry promotion have significant overlaps although the two are not exactly the same. In most countries the two policies are under the same ministry in charge of industry. In Vietnam, the former is taken up by MPI's Enterprise Development Agency (formerly the Agency for SME Development) and the latter is handled by the Supporting Industry Enterprise Development Center (SIDEC) of the Industrial Policy and Strategy Institute under MOIT. Both are young organizations, especially the latter, and their policy capabilities in knowledge, human resource, and financial means are not yet strong enough to carry out the designated tasks effectively.

Given this situation, it is proposed that MPI should continue to be the lead ministry for SME promotion and MOIT should be the lead ministry for supporting industry promotion for the moment. Each organization must be strengthened through more budgeting and staffing, learning international best practices, and additional international cooperation. This arrangement should work in the short run as long as each ministry makes a serious effort at improving its functions and policy coordination between the two ministries is secured.

In the long run, when Vietnam's policy capability rises sufficiently and policy scope needs to be expanded, the two functions should be merged under the same ministry. MOIT is perhaps the more suitable ministry for this purpose. At the same time, the internal structure of MOIT must be restructured by reducing direct policy intervention while enhancing its capabilities in assisting private-sector development through technology transfer, human-resource development, stakeholder coordination, information collection, and shock management.

4.5.3 Establishment of an inter-ministerial coordination mechanism

Many of the industrial strategies, including supporting industries, SME promotion, and industrial cluster development, are multi-sectoral issues. One lead ministry cannot cover a broad range over industry, trade, investment, technology, taxes and tariffs, budgeting, finance, industrial standards, education and training, labor, environment, logistics and connectivity, regional development, FDI and ODA, and so forth. MOIT, MPI, the Ministry of Finance, the Ministry of Education and Training, the Ministry of Labor, Invalids and Social Affairs, the Ministry of Science and Technology, the Ministry of Transport, the State Bank of Vietnam, etc. must be brought in. However, a lead ministry cannot direct or intervene in the affairs of other ministries horizontally. For multi-sectoral issues, a supervisory mechanism above all ministries must be created for facilitating inter-ministerial cooperation and solving any problems that may arise.

In Vietnam, one option is establishment of a national council headed by the prime minister (or the deputy prime minister in charge of industry) which supervises and coordinates several key industrial strategies as shown in Figure 4.12. Under the strong leadership and vision of the prime minister, policies should be supervised by the National Competitiveness Council (the precise name does not matter) supported by issue- and sector-based working groups. The Council and each of the working groups must appoint a responsible ministry which will serve as the secretariat. Members of the Council should include

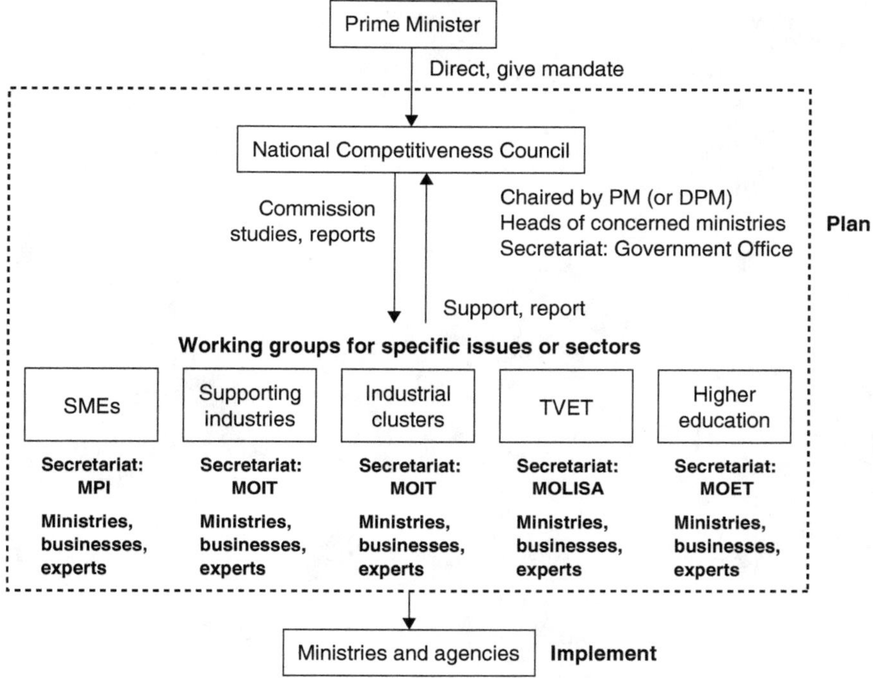

Figure 4.12 Vietnam: a proposal for the National Competitiveness Council

Note: This is a preliminary idea for initiating discussion; listed issues and ministries are suggestions only; everything is subject to addition, subtraction, or change.

heads of concerned ministries and agencies, business leaders and associations, and academics and experts. Ministries and agencies participate in this mechanism in two functions: participation in planning and as implementing agencies. Inter-ministerial issues and conflicts will be solved at the level of the Council with the ultimate decision resting with the prime minister. For example, coordination between MOIT and MPI, as discussed above, should be one of the tasks of this mechanism.

Five working groups shown in Figure 4.12 are for illustrations only. The Vietnamese government should select most appropriate working groups. However, the total number of such issue- or sector-specific working groups should not greatly exceed four or five.

In November 2010, a similar idea of the National Competitiveness Council was proposed for Vietnam by Professor Michael E. Porter of Harvard University in the launching seminar of Vietnam Competitiveness Report 2010 mentioned above (Ketels, et al., 2010).

Part II

Country studies

5 Meiji Japan

From feudalism to industrialization

5.1 Miracle in the late nineteenth century

From the late twelfth century to the middle of the nineteenth century, the samurai (swordsmen) class ruled Japan. The first period of samurai rule, up to the early seventeenth century, was an age of frequent wars among samurai lords over influence and territories. After the decisive Battle of Sekigahara in 1600 and the extinction of the rival Toyotomi Family in 1615, Tokugawa Ieyasu emerged as the final winner unifying and bringing peace to the country. Ieyasu and his posterity in the Tokugawa Family, 15 in all, ruled the country as *shogun* (supreme military leader) in the following two-and-half centuries. Although the emperor, residing in Kyoto, nominally gave the authority to rule to the head of the Tokugawa Family, who resided in Edo (now Tokyo), real power was exercised by the latter and not the former. The central military government in Edo was called *Bakufu* and the period of Tokugawa shogunate, from 1603 to 1867, was called the Edo period.

Japan during the Edo period was a feudal class society based on peasant agriculture. The samurai ruled the other three classes consisting of farmers, craftsmen, and merchants. Below them, there were also outcasts. The samurai class was organized into complex family standings and functional ranks. At the apex was the Tokugawa Family which directly ruled nearly a quarter of Japanese land, including principal cities and important mines, and monopolized foreign trade which was highly controlled and limited in volume. Other samurai lords, called *daimyo*, were given territorial domains to rule, called *han*, in exchange for total submission to the Tokugawa Family. The number of han fluctuated over time, and stood eventually at about 300 at the end of the Edo period. As long as han lords obeyed all orders and regulations imposed by the central government,[1] they were left free to conduct affairs within their han including determination of the rice tax rate, promotion of agriculture and industry, issuing local paper currency, education of samurai, and other social and economic measures. Under the conservative rule of the Bakufu bureaucracy, Japan spent two-and-half centuries of relative stability, seclusion from the rest of the world, and development of unique civil culture and local products.

However, in the middle of the nineteenth century, gradual internal evolution of Japanese society suddenly ended with the arrival of the Western powers with superior economic and military might. In 1853, an American military fleet (the "Black Ships") led by Commodore Matthew C. Perry appeared in the Bay of Edo to demand the opening of Japanese ports with a display of cannons. In the following year, the Bakufu was forced to sign "friendship" treaties with Western powers which permitted foreign ships to use designated Japanese ports. From this time onward, Japanese national goals had turned outward which included withstanding pressure from the powerful West and maintaining political independence, accelerating Westernization and modernization of Japanese society, and ultimately catching up with the West.

Japan achieved these self-set goals very well. In a period as short as half a century after the opening of ports, it vigorously imported Western systems and technology; turned itself into a "modern" society with Western-style constitution, laws, and government; achieved an industrial revolution around the 1890s in which mechanized factories became the leading mode of production; defeated China and Russia in regional wars (1894–95 and 1904–05, respectively); overtook the British textile industry in the global market by the early twentieth century; and was counted as one of the "Big Five" nations by the time World War I ended in 1918. Japan was the first non-Western country to modernize and join the club of "first-class" nations by a wide margin in comparison with other high-performing Asian economies which began to industrialize only after World War II. It should be added that Japan's industrialization in the Meiji period[2] (1868–1912) was carried out in the age of ruthless colonialism in which military occupation of "backward" countries was considered normal, and no grants, loans, and technical assistance were available to latecomer countries in international cooperation. How could Meiji Japan, an agricultural society with backward technology in the Far East, achieve a transformation from feudalism to industrial society so early and so quickly?

I hope to answer this difficult question by introducing three perspectives of history, politics, and concrete measures and actions. These perspectives are mutually related and should be combined to understand the Japanese miracle in the late nineteenth century. Enumeration of policy measures and enterprise actions adopted in the Meiji period to enhance domestic capability, as done in section 5.5, is not enough to explain the economic development of Japan unless historical and political backgrounds were simultaneously presented.

At the outset, it should be stated generally that Japan's remarkable industrial achievement in the late nineteenth century, as well as in the post-World War II period, was made possible by a happy blend of strong private dynamism and (mostly) appropriate industrial policy. In both periods, private dynamism was the main engine of growth without which rapid industrialization was impossible while policy played an important but supporting role. The natural question is: where did such strong private dynamism and relatively wise government come from? That is when the historical and political perspectives become crucial. The answer must be found in the periods leading up to the

Meiji period, not just in what the Meiji government did in technology absorption or human resource development. It will be shown that pre-conditions for the Japanese industrial revolution were unique both historically and politically. Our analysis will also explain why today's developing countries, lacking what Japan had one-and-half centuries ago, are advised not to directly copy the policy menu of Meiji Japan—not only because external conditions have changed greatly but also because internal capability has not been fostered in most of the latecomers today. The chapter may also indicate what Japan in the early twenty-first century has lost in comparison with Japan in the late nineteenth century.

5.2 Japanese history as a continuous merger of domestic and foreign systems

5.2.1 Translative adaptation

Evolution of any society in any age is interplay of internal and external forces. While relative weight of the two forces shifts over time, both are always there. Each society has its own logic and structure which do not mutate easily, and their internal dynamics drives history during the period of limited foreign contact. Except in rare occasions in which accumulated domestic tension explodes (i.e., a revolution), internally driven history is usually slow and continuous. However, once this society is exposed to powerful foreign influence, whether military, religious, or economic, internal equilibrium is broken and the society is thrown off the track on which it has been treading. If domestic response to external force is robust and appropriate, the society will absorb new elements productively and start a new growth path. But if domestic response is weak or disorderly, there is a risk of social tension and instability, and, in the worse case, disintegration of the society due to civil war or foreign intervention.

What is remarkable in world history after the Industrial Revolution is the fact that the term *development* no longer means socio-economic transformation produced mainly by gradual maturing of domestic factors as had often been seen from time immemorial. It now invariably means an engineered merger of two systems, domestic and foreign, which are in principle incompatible and with the foreign system always seeming more powerful than the domestic, through international integration. This merger normally calls for radical modification of domestic culture and institutions. Moreover, in our time, each society is advised (or forced) by international groups and organizations, backed by authority, money, and theory, to jump into the global system and accept its rules, rather than refusing to be integrated, as the only way toward prosperity. No country will be welcomed as a legitimate member of the international community unless it does so.

International integration is an extremely adventurous process experienced perhaps only once in the history of any latecomer country. The bad news is that the process does not always promise a happy ending. If poorly handled, opening of the country will bring economic crisis and civil strife. Only a small number of countries can manage this difficult process well and accomplish an economic take-off under the strong pressure of foreign products, firms, ideas, and systems. Although rules and players shift with time, this basic problem associated with latecomer integration remains the same. The challenge of forced integration experienced by Meiji Japan was fundamentally the same as what latecomer countries must overcome in the early twenty-first century (Chapter 1).

Forced merger of two systems must be managed rather than left to its own dynamics. Friction, hostility, and rejection generated by the merger must be controlled. That is why government is vital as an administrator of integration and protector of social cohesion. Government constitutes a part of the domestic society but it must also perform an important duty of deciding the way to cope with external force and directing its implementation. In other words, government is simultaneously the subject and object of social transformation, and its policy skill critically determines the destiny of a nation that goes through globalization.

As Maegawa (1994, 2000), cited in Chapter 1, notes, integration of a latecomer country should ideally proceed with the initiative and ownership of the country to be integrated rather than under sheer foreign pressure. Even if a latecomer country may look small and helpless before the dominant world, the former should somehow overcome this power imbalance and determine the terms, scope, and sequence of its integration process. It should also maintain social continuity as well as national pride and identity. Even though the society changes significantly as a result of importation of foreign elements, direction and speed of change must be set by the people and government of that country. Under such integration, foreign ideas and technology are accepted with modifications to fit the reality of domestic society rather than in their original forms. If integration is of this type, which Maegawa calls *translative adaptation*, the latecomer country undergoing social transformation is not really weak or passive. It is bravely and wisely using external stimuli to launch a new development path. According to Maegawa, Meiji Japan was the country that succeeded brilliantly in translative adaptation, and most observers tend to agree with him.

However, success must be judged in relative light. Although the achievements of Meiji Japan look great *ex post facto*, the people and government in the process were not so self-confident or comfortable. Serious debate, emotional oscillation, and trial-and-error were the order of the day. In his lecture "Development of Modern Japan" delivered in 1911, Natsume Soseki (1867–1916), perhaps the most popular Japanese novelist in the Meiji period, remarked as follows:

> Development in the West is endogenous, while Japan's development is exogenous. Here, endogenous means emerging naturally from within,

> like a bud blooms into a flower in an outward motion, and exogenous means being forced to take a certain form because of external influences . . . Overall, throughout history, Japan was developing more or less endogenously. Then suddenly, after two centuries of isolation, we opened up and encountered Western civilization. It was a big shock we never experienced before. Since then, the Japanese society began to evolve in a different direction . . .
>
> Western tides dominate our development. Since we are not Westerners, every time a new wave arrives from the West we feel uneasy like a person living in someone else's house. Even before we can grasp the nature of the previous wave, a new wave arrives. It is as if too many dishes are brought in and soon removed before we can start to eat. In such circumstances, people will inevitably become empty, frustrated, and worried . . . In summary, we can safely conclude that Japanese development is a superficial one . . . To put it politely, a part, perhaps the dominant part, of our development is superficial. But I am not saying that we should stop developing. The sad fact must be accepted. We must swallow our tears and continue to develop superficially . . . I have no good solution to offer to you. The only thing I can say is that we should try to develop as internally as possible so long as we can avoid a nervous breakdown.
>
> (Soseki's lecture in 1911 as cited in Miyoshi, 1986, p. 26 and pp. 33–34)

Irritation and anxiety in a latecomer country under globalization, as sarcastically illustrated by Soseki, are common to all countries in similar processes of integration. Although Soseki was quite pessimistic in this lecture, and Japanese people at that time did go through a psychological crackup, we must still stress the fact that Meiji Japan ended up in successfully marrying Japanese spirit with Western technology. Being unsure and upset is common to all such nations, but conducting effective integration despite such stress is a rare accomplishment. Knowing a large number of developmental experiences of other latecomer countries in the following century, we must but marvel at Meiji Japan as the first achiever of an almost impossible task.

5.2.2 The Umesao theory

The next question that must be addressed is how Japan could perform translative adaptation as early and as successfully as this. To answer this question, at least partially, the ecological theory of history advanced in 1957 by Umesao Tadao, a scholar in comparative civilization and the founder of the National Museum of Ethnology, is introduced (Umesao, 1986, 2003). His theory emphasizes a special geographical position shared by both Japan and Western Europe. Traditionally, we consider nineteenth-century Japan as a weak, backward country with pre-modern technology which was no match for the Western powers. However, according to Umesao, this view is fundamentally flawed. He sees no mystery in Japan's emergence as a non-Western industrial country.

Japan and Western Europe were situated at an appropriate distance—not too far, not too near—from the great civilizations of Eurasia, namely, China, India, and the Middle East (Islam)—see Figure 5.1. They could absorb the achievements of these civilizations while being protected against the fierce invasion and destruction of nomad people roaming in the central dry areas of the Eurasian continent. In particular, Japan and Britain were two island nations just across a strait from the continent. Ever since the Japanese ethnicity was established through migration from south, north, and west, Japan has never been invaded by foreign forces (excepting the post World War II American occupation in 1945–1951). The water between Japan and Korea blocked the Mongolian fleet twice in the late thirteenth century. As for Britain, its old base of the Celtic culture was transformed by a few mild interactions with its European brothers (Roman invasion, first century BC; Anglo-Saxon migration, fourth and fifth centuries AD; Norman Conquest, 1066). The delicate distance from the center, offering double advantages in absorption of advanced civilization and ease of national defense, permitted both societies to evolve cumulatively and organically. They were given enough time and control to mix domestic culture with foreign impact, without being wiped out and having to start over again from scratch.

The Great Wall of China could not stop the Mongolians from coming. Smaller countries on the Eurasian continent also faced the fate of being

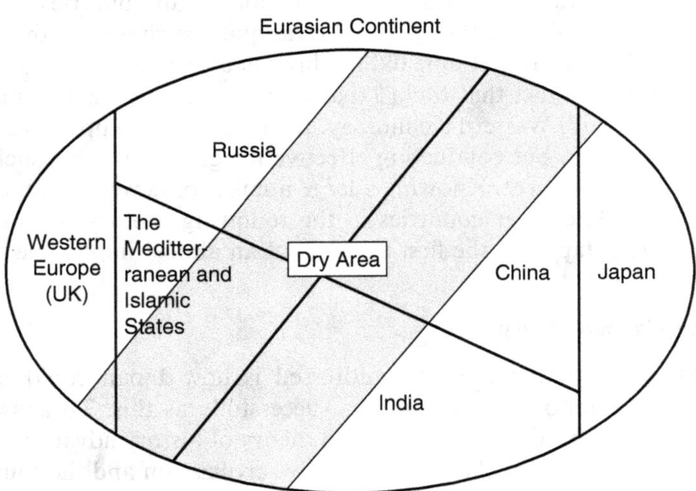

Figure 5.1 Umesao's view of the world

Source: Compiled by the author from Umesao (1986, 2003) with Dr. Umesao's additional advice.

plundered and invaded every few centuries. Under such circumstances, unbroken evolution of political, social, and economic systems was difficult. Chinese, Indian, and Islamic civilizations produced great cultural and scientific achievements, but their social structures were static; only empires and kingdoms (and later, colonialism) ruled. From one dynasty to another, there was no clear progress from the viewpoint of social, political, and economic systems. They adopted different economic, diplomatic, and ethnic policies but the pattern was more random than evolutionary. For thousands of years, emperors and kings looked basically the same although some were wiser and more powerful than others. On the other hand, in cultures far from the center—the Pacific islands, for example—social change tended to be very slow because they could not import advanced systems and other foreign stimuli to propel history.

Meanwhile, under similar locational conditions, Japan and Britain (or more generally, Western Europe) developed independently and in parallel. Their societies first established an ancient kingdom or empire, whose power gradually eroded over time. This was followed by decentralization and the rise of local powers. The fighting class (samurai or knights) with high spirituality emerged to defend land and manors. Feudalism, or the master–servant relationship based on the give-and-take of land-ruling rights, took root. While the word "feudalism" often connotes rigidity and backwardness, especially in Japanese language, it played a vital role in fostering local political and economic powers which had their own spheres of influence, and preparing social conditions for building modern industry with mechanized factories in the subsequent period. Japan in the nineteenth century was a typical example of a society that proceeded from feudalism to an industrial revolution.

If we look back on Japanese history from this perspective, we must but notice that Japanese society has a cumulative multi-layer structure as a result of frequent absorption of foreign elements and their gradual digestion without ever abandoning the former nature entirely. The original character of Japanese people must have been forged by the natural features of the Japanese archipelago situated in the Temperate Zone with four distinct seasons laced with both subtlety and violence, as well as complex geography, vegetation, and creatures. On top of this, imported elements such as rice cultivation (third century BC?), Buddhism (sixth century), Chinese culture and systems (from seventh to the early tenth century), guns and Christianity (sixteenth century), re-encounter with the West (mid-nineteenth century), and reforms under US occupation (mid-twentieth century), were added in repeated translative adaptation. Among these, modernization and industrialization of the Meiji period, which we are concerned with, was the biggest external shock.

Throughout constant transformation over the two millennia, the ethnic and cultural identity of Japanese people was maintained despite the fact that Japan today and Japan in the past are entirely different in their appearances. We may even say that the process of never-ending translative adaptation has been the core characteristic of Japanese society. In the minds of Japanese people, old and new elements co-exist flexibly and surface alternately depending on the circumstance. Sensitivity to nature, nostalgia for rice cultivation, optional allegiance to Shinto, Buddhism, and Christianity, and Western rationalism and frontline industrial technology are all part of Japanese characters. To put it positively, Japanese are flexible, generous, and pragmatic. But to put it critically, they are without principle, fidelity, or devotion. This is a unique feature of Japanese people not often seen in other cultures.

In sum, thanks to the right distance from the center, Japan could manage cumulative external shocks reasonably well and used them relatively effectively for its own transformation and growth throughout history in comparison with other non-Western countries. Repeated acceptance and digestion of foreign elements strengthened Japan's capability to respond strongly to such shocks. It is not really surprising, then, to see Japan in the mid-nineteenth century able to cope adequately with the powerful impact of the West.

5.3 Preparation for a take-off

5.3.1 The seven conditions

We now turn to the question of what concrete conditions were prepared by the feudalism of the Edo period (1603–1867), under relative seclusion from the rest of the world and gradual evolution of domestic society, which facilitated Japan's industrialization in the following Meiji period (1868–1912). Below is a list of seven such conditions, which are the summary of voluminous research and academic debates on this period and can be considered as the near-consensus view among Japanese economic historians:

(i) political unity and stability;
(ii) agricultural development in terms of both area and productivity;
(iii) development of transportation and the emergence of nationally unified markets;
(iv) the emergence of commerce, finance, and the wealthy merchant class;
(v) the broad-based rise of pre-modern manufacturing such as agro processing, handicrafts, and metalworking;
(vi) agricultural and industrial promotion by local (han) governments—which was sometimes successful but not always;
(vii) high level of education for both leaders and ordinary people.

The fact that political unity and stability (first condition) contributed to economic development should not be surprising. The four conditions from the second to the fifth can be restated as rising output and productivity; emergence of institutions, infrastructure, and social structure which supported it; and the resulting development and diversification of the private sector. The sixth and the seventh can be rephrased respectively as building of policy capability (of local governments) and human-resource development.

What is remarkable about these seven conditions of Edo Japan is the fact that very few developing countries satisfy them even today. Admittedly, this statement suffers from selection bias because societies equipped with these conditions have already industrialized and joined the rich country club. Even so, it is undeniable that many developing countries, receiving for a long time economic aid and trade privileges which were not available in the nineteenth century, still remain underdeveloped and without these conditions. Even among emerging economies in Southeast Asia such as Thailand, Vietnam, and Indonesia, few are equipped with all the seven conditions. In Sub-Saharan Africa, we suspect that some countries even lack all of these conditions. This shows the high level of socio-economic development attained by Edo Japan despite feudalism and pre-modern technology. It also warns us against transplanting policies adopted by Meiji Japan, as explained in section 5.5, to societies that are not in possession of these conditions.

The Edo society was agrarian, particularly at the beginning, with about 90 percent of the population being peasants although this ratio subsequently declined a little. The basic unit of production was the small family. In the previous centuries, one farming household often contained a large number of people with many families and their servants. But a series of official land surveys and registration (*kenchi*) conducted before and after the beginning of the Edo period dismantled the big family system into small farming units, with each family guaranteed (and obliged to cultivate) its portion of farmland. Villages were well organized and permitted autonomy as long as they paid rice taxes as stipulated by the Bakufu or local government. The rice tax was levied on villages, not on individual farmers. Village leaders, who were often themselves farmers, allocated the tax burden among villagers. In this sense, village leaders played the role of the lowest-level tax administration.

The agricultural sector grew in two phases. From the mid-fifteenth century to the late seventeenth century, which partly overlaps with the previous warring period, there was an enormous expansion of farmland. Large-scale water-management projects were carried out all over Japan by daimyos and influential farmers to control floods and use rivers for irrigation. As a result, the plains which had hitherto been uninhabitable marshlands were turned into productive paddy fields. The population increased rapidly in a way rarely seen in a pre-modern society. Oishi (1977), an Edo historian, calls this the "Great Age of Opening Fields." From the eighteenth century onward the area of cultivation and population remained relatively stable, but rice output continued to grow thanks to increased productivity.[3] Contributing factors included double cropping, new species of rice, fertilizer (dried fish was especially popular), and the introduction of new farming tools. Many guidebooks were published to teach farmers how to produce crops more effectively. Miyazaki Yasusada's *Nogyo Zensho* [Encyclopedia of Agriculture] in 11 volumes, published in 1679 and reprinted many times, was one of them.

At the start of the Edo period, peasants produced mainly for family consumption. From the middle Edo period, as productivity rose and agricultural surplus was generated, peasants began to sell their rice and other crops to the market which was often nationally integrated. Subsistence agriculture was gradually replaced by commercial agriculture. As rural income rose, many well-to-do farmers enjoyed village theaters and festivals, climbed Mt. Fuji, Mt. Tateyama, and other sacred mountains, and made a pilgrimage to Ise Shrine and other religious sites, nominally for worship, but actually for fun. Tanaka (2000), another Edo historian, argues that Edo farmers were dynamic and independent and they often rejected government officials and their unreasonable policies. The Bakufu repeatedly issued laws to regulate farmers' lives including prohibition of smoking tobacco and drinking tea and sake (rice wine) and an order to divorce a wife who liked trips and entertainment. But Kurushima (2003) asserts that these laws should be understood as the Bakufu's desperate but failed attempt to keep farmers frugal as a tax base against the reality of their enrichment, rather than a proof of Bakufu's strict control of their living conditions.

The Edo tax system was based on the transfer, storage, and cashing of rice. The economic size of han was measured and samurai's salaries were paid in physical quantities of rice. For this reason, the existence of a nationally integrated rice market with efficient transportation and settlement systems was required. The development of cash crops and handicrafts also stimulated domestic commerce. Osaka was the commercial center with a large number of wealthy merchant families, money changers, and lenders, while Edo was the political center with great demand for consumer goods. Naturally, a sea lane between the two cities was opened and developed. The Bakufu also designated five official highways and opened other sea lanes. But it was the private sector that provided such services as inns, restaurants, shippers, and baggage carriers. The obligatory bi-annual commuting of all han lords between Edo and their domains (see note 1) brought additional prosperity to service providers along the major highways and sea lanes.

With the expansion of economic activities, *gosho*, or rich merchant families, emerged. They included Konoike, Onogumi, Tennojiya, Hiranoya, Shimadaya, Kashimaya, and Yoneya. Many of them declined after Meiji, but two families, Mitsui and Sumitomo, survived the political change and expanded to form business conglomerates as pre-World War II *zaibatsu* and post-World War II *keiretsu*.[4] The Mitsui Family was originally a dealer in *kimono* (Japanese dress) and a money changer while the Sumitomo Family started as a copper mining and refining business. Development of domestic enterprises such as these, with large capital and extensive business networks, during the Edo period was a great advantage for Japan whose expertise and financial power could later be mobilized to absorb imported technology and compete with foreigners. In contrast, not many developing countries today have local companies that are strong enough to compete globally. Another point to be noted is the speed with which large business families and groups emerged and disappeared. According to a series of published lists of top business families analyzed by Miyamoto (1999), the survival rate of prominent businesses was fairly low. Among the top 231 business families in the list of 1849, only 44 percent also made the list of 1864. The same group's survival rates further fell to 15 percent by 1888 and only 9 percent by 1902. In this sense, Mitsui and Sumitomo, which have continued to thrive until today, were the exception rather than the rule. The rise and fall of individual enterprises is a hallmark of a dynamic market economy, which existed in Japan toward the end of the Edo period.

As agriculture and commerce grew, pre-modern manufacturing such as handicrafts and food processing also developed. Many specialized local products emerged and were marketed all over Japan. For example, tea, tobacco, wax, indigo, salt, knives, sword, pottery, lacquer ware, silk, cotton, soy sauce, sake, paper, cut stone, medicine, and dried fish were traded widely. In order to enrich the local population and increase the tax revenue, many han promoted local industries, and some even succeeded (Nishikawa and Amano, 1989). Tokushima Han's promotion of indigo farming, Takamatsu Han's sugar production from sugar beets with newly developed technology, Yonezawa Han's safflower and lacquer, Akita Han's silk and silk dress, Hizen Han's pottery and coal, and Higo Han's lumber and silk, are just a few examples. To be objective, however, we should not forget other han governments which were less successful and fell deeply into debt. They borrowed large sums of money from private merchants but never repaid.

The popularity of education in the Edo period is often cited as the cause of fast industrialization in the later periods. Education in the Edo period ranged from the recondite study of ancient Chinese philosophy and literature at public schools to children's basic education at private schools. Education fever was not just in such large cities as Edo, Osaka, and Kyoto but also a nationwide phenomenon.

Bakufu schools mainly taught Confucianism, an ancient Chinese philosophy started by Confucius in the sixth to fifth century BC and reinterpreted variously in later centuries. It emphasized social order, proper rituals, the way of good political leadership, and respect for the elderly and superiors. The Edo government promoted Confucianism as an ideology to legitimize and maintain the class society. How to modify this old foreign doctrine to fit the Japanese reality was one of the important theoretical questions. Han governments also established schools to educate their young samurais. The number of han schools were 230 at the end of the Edo period. The curriculums were basically the same as those of Bakufu schools, with Confucianism at the center of learning. Toward the end of the Edo period, these public schools started to teach practical skills such as military training and foreign language.

In the private sector, eminent scholars often set up their own schools and recruited students. Depending on the instructor, various subjects were taught ranging from Confucianism to *kokugaku* (research on ancient Japanese literature and history), Western languages (Dutch, later also English), medicine, science, technology, and so on. These schools accepted both samurai and non-samurai students. In the late Edo period, they often attracted talented and passionate young people with the desire to contribute to the country. Their eyes were opened to the international situation and Japan's precarious position in it. A large number of national leaders in the late Edo period and the early Meiji period came from such professional schools.

Terakoya (private primary schools) were run by local teachers to teach the "3Rs"—reading, writing and arithmetic (abacus)—to small children ranging from 7–8 up to 12–13 in age. It was a profit-making institution charging tuition fees, where normally one instructor taught a few dozen children with individual assignments. As the public realized the importance of studying letters and arithmetic, a large number of terakoya were established all over Japan contributing to high literacy among the general public. It is estimated that the number of terakoya at the end of the Edo period was in the order of 20,000 (Banno and Ohno, 2010).

This section has given only a glimpse of what Edo Japan achieved (for a fuller discussion, see Ohno (2006a) and Banno and Ohno (2010)). While Japan at that time was a pre-modern feudal society which discriminated people according to lineage and blood connection, its private-sector economy and supporting policies exhibited a high degree of maturity not often seen in developing countries. Would it be too much to say that Japan in the mid-nineteenth century was ready and even craving for the Western impact in order to begin a new growth path?

5.3.2 Centrifugal politics and centripetal nationalism

We now come to the two specific factors that emerged around the time of opening of ports in the 1850s which enabled Japan to get rid of the Bakufu–Han System along with its feudalism and class society. The amazing thing about this political-cum-social revolution was that it was achieved without splitting the country into pieces, spilling a large amount of blood, or being colonized by the Western powers. Admittedly, these judgments must be taken relatively; Japan did have divisions and it did experience a civil war between pro- and anti-Bakufu forces in 1868–69. But Japan's divisions and combats were minor compared with what the French, Russian, and Chinese revolutions went through. As Tokutomi Soho, a renowned journalist in the Meiji period, observed,

> The French people always shift from one extreme to the other as the Japanese people do. But on a closer inspection, we must but notice a significant difference between the two peoples. Although both go from one extreme to the other, our people do so within certain bounds while the French do so outside these bounds.
>
> (Tokutomi, 1889, p. 2)

About 10,000 deaths were estimated to have occurred in the Japanese civil war to topple the Tokugawa rule. Meanwhile, five million died in the French

Revolution and the Napoleonic Wars. Many internal conflicts in the post-World War II period, for example in Korea, Vietnam, Nigeria, Cambodia, Afghanistan, Mozambique, and Sudan, each killed in excess of one million. Why was Japan's transformation so "peaceful"? How could Japan accomplish a revolution with such a small human cost?

Two forces were at play in the critical years from 1853 (the arrival of the American gun ships) to 1867 (the collapse of the Bakufu). The one was centrifugal force unleashed by the decline of legitimacy of the Bakufu as a result of poor handling of external and internal affairs. The other was a spontaneous surge of private nationalism fostered by kokugaku, which was greatly stimulated by the appearance of foreign rivals. These two forces kept Japan's policy debates and military conflicts "within certain bounds" without exploding into an uncontrollable crisis and blood shedding. Leaders and fighters put national interests above the interests of specific han, classes, or groups, and were ready to cooperate for pragmatic purposes flexibly without harboring indelible enmity against each other.

The legitimacy of the Bakufu as a supreme ruler was supposedly derived from its capability to maintain internal peace and withstand foreign enemies with its military power. However, the appearance of the mighty West in the mid-nineteenth century destroyed the previously solid authority of the Bakufu. Furthermore, diplomatic, political, and economic blunders of the Bakufu in handling the foreign pressure, as explained below, created a movement that dared to defy the Bakufu's authority and challenge its policies. The Bakufu's legitimacy collapsed quickly during 1858–1863 until it became irreparable. Criticism against Bakufu leaders, collective demand by influential han lords to take part in national decision making, refusal to obey Bakufu orders, and even military action against the Bakufu, all of which were totally unthinkable before, became widespread. From around 1863, potential leaders contested to build a new political order on the premise that the Bakufu's days were over (Mitani, 1997).

When American Commodore Perry and his Black Ships entered deep into the Bay of Edo and fired warning shots from ship-mounted cannons in the summer of 1853, it became clear to everyone that the Bakufu was not in possession of military power to repel foreigners. In response, the Bakufu government hurriedly built coastal forts, implemented a military reform, placed an order to purchase military ships from the West, and tried to introduce shipbuilding and navigation training. At the same time, however, it had no true intention of fighting foreigners. From the beginning, the Bakufu's diplomatic stance was acceptance of foreign demand for Japan's international integration and coaxing or forcing various domestic groups into agreeing with this policy. While this seriously damaged the value of the Bakufu as a military government, it must be admitted that Japan had no other choice given the harsh international environment at that time. But in executing this diplomatic line, the Bakufu made several policy mistakes.

First, the commercial treaties concluded with the five Western powers in 1858 were defective in the sense that Japan did not have the right to determine its own tariff rates or judge foreign criminals in Japanese courts. It took Japan another half century to recover these rights through excruciating negotiations with the West. This was certainly a diplomatic blunder, but it must be recalled that such unilateral obligation was considered normal in commercial treaties between the West and "backward" countries in the late nineteenth century. It was difficult for Japan alone to reject such conditions when all other Asian countries, including China, were forced to accept them.

Second, these commercial treaties were signed at the command of Ii Naosuke (1815–1860), the supreme minister (*tairo*) of the Bakufu's executive office, without receiving the emperor's consent. As a matter of fact, Emperor Komei (1831–1866) was strongly opposed to these treaties. This revealed a serious schism between the emperor and the Bakufu, the two powers which were supposed to be in harmony, with the former willingly conferring the authority to rule to the latter. If the emperor and the Bakufu were in fact two competing powers with different policy orientations, new political dynamism could be unleashed in which diverse groups gathered around either pole to initiate real debates and even combats. Although the Bakufu tried to minimize this risk by launching *kobu gattai*, a strategy to unite the two authorities through marrying the emperor's younger sister to the shogun, proposing to close the Port of Yokohama (which was in reality impossible), and other face-saving measures, the effects were unstable and limited. It only accumulated dubious commitments between the two parties which wanted fundamentally different policy directions. The strategy finally collapsed with the passing of Emperor Komei in 1866.

Third, the Bakufu's despotic policymaking which first ignored and then cracked down on the opponents of opening ports severely marred its legitimacy. In particular, the Great Incarceration of Ansei (1858–1859), which punished and executed a large number of challengers to the Bakufu's authority, had the contrary effect of accelerating anti-Bakufu movements of all kind. The Bakufu's oppression invited demands from influential han lords to convene a feudal assembly for broader policy deliberation, on the one hand, and increased terrorist attacks from the "Respect the Emperor and Expel Foreigners" hardliners, on the other. Yet, the Bakufu continued to refuse to share power with others until the end. It was only in 1866 that the Bakufu finally acknowledged the power-sharing proposal, but it was after the *kobu gattai* strategy disintegrated completely, the Bakufu suffered a military defeat in the second campaign to punish rebellious Choshu Han, and Tokugawa Yoshinobu (1837–1913) assumed power as the new (and last) shogun. The formal return of ruling power to the emperor by Yoshinobu, in October 1867, was his last-ditch effort to avoid the termination of the Tokugawa Family while the anti-Bakufu forces were gathering to attack the Bakufu for a final military showdown. But Yoshinobu's political survival act failed within a few months as a coup staged by the opponents installed a direct rule of the emperor without the Bakufu, and the civil war started in Toba and Fushimi, near Kyoto, branding the Bakufu as the traitor to be eliminated by the imperial order.

Fourth, economic confusion caused by the opening of ports must be cited. The main problem was inflation, and its associated effects were shocks to existing industries brought by new trade opportunities and relative price changes. Around 1858, the prices of export commodities such as silk and silk products rose and the prices of import-competing goods such as cotton products fell. In 1859 and 1860, different conversion rates between gold and silver in Japan and abroad prompted an outflow of gold and associated inflation. After 1863, the explosion of Bakufu finance with a surge of military expense and debasement of gold coins accelerated inflation until it destroyed the monetary system of the Bakufu–Han system (Takeda, 2009). In the process, producers and merchants of silk and tea expanded strongly and enjoyed great profits in response to large foreign demand. As for import-competing cotton products, the market of white cloth with no product differentiation shrank but the markets of creased, striped, or splash-patterned cotton products requiring special technique were not hit hard and even expanded. These demand fluctuations were accompanied by the rise and fall of individual localities. Many traditional producing regions declined quickly while new regions, which had the cooperation of merchants who introduced the use of imported fiber and new rural markets, emerged. Change of players is an inevitable phenomenon under globalization, but the speed with which this occurred was very fast in the final years of the Edo period. In any country and age, inflation, bankruptcies, and unemployment make people hostile to the government. Japanese people at that time must have felt that the days of the Bakufu were coming to an end as it was totally incapable of controlling foreign pressure, domestic opponents, or economic chaos.

We now turn to the emergence of nationalism in the private sector, which was the second force that kept Japanese response to globalization shocks and the collapse of the Bakufu "within certain bounds." It must first be noted that political information traveled quickly and widely in the late Edo period and that there was strong demand among intellectuals for such information. The news that four Black Ships commanded by American Commodore Matthew C. Perry appeared at the mouth of the Bay of Edo, in 1853, spread across Japan instantaneously. This communication speed was an important factor that shaped the political development of this period.

National transport and communication infrastructure of the Edo period not only stimulated agriculture and industry and united markets nationally but also promoted human and information exchange for various purposes including academic, cultural, and political. Samurai from influential han were dispatched to major cities such as Edo, Kyoto, Osaka, and Nagasaki to gather information and make political allies. They communicated frequently through *hikyaku* (rapid-delivery service on foot or by horse) which carried letters, money, and bills of exchange within four to ten days between

Edo and Osaka, for example. According to Miyaji (1999), there were 128 hikyaku dispatchers organized by destinations in Kyoto in the 1830s, and 180 hikyaku dispatchers existed in Edo in the 1860s. From 1859 to 1868, 114 letters of Saigo Takamori, a political and military leader of Satsuma Han (section 5.4), addressed to his colleague Okubo Toshimichi who was serving his lord at home, remain. Given the speed of letter delivery at that time, this means that the two were in constant communication whenever they were in different locations. Frequent letter exchange was not unique to Saigo and Okubo but common among all intellectuals of this period as Banno and Ohno (2010a) prove.

Demand for swift and accurate political information rose dramatically after the arrival of Commodore Perry. The number of political records and newsletters compiled by intellectuals (samurai, rich farmers, doctors, scholars, etc.) increased, and cultural networks which previously composed Japanese and Chinese poems turned political. This was because nationalism which was gradually forming and developing through kokugaku and the Respect the Emperor ideology was suddenly and greatly activated by a direct contact with hostile Western powers. The acute sense of national crisis under foreign pressure bolstered the national identity of Japanese people, increased demand for political information and discussion, and politicized all intellectuals regardless of their classes.

The foundation of kokugaku was laid jointly by Keichu (1640–1701) and Kadano Azumamaro (1668–1736). The former criticized existing research that evaluated Japanese literature by foreign (Chinese) criteria and urged the analysis of internal structure of literary works from the perspective of ages and cultures that produced them. The latter established a new academic doctrine to examine Japanese literature, history, and laws independently from Confucianism or Buddhism, which were imported from China and India, to illuminate the Japanese Way. These ideas were put into practice and further developed by Kamono Mabuchi (1697–1769) who studied *Manyoshu*, the first recorded collection of Japanese poems, and Motoori Norinaga (1730–1801) who re-interpreted the Tale of Genji (the first long novel) and scrutinized *Kojiki* (Ancient Chronicle). Finally, Hirata Atsutane (1776–1843) turned this academic trend into a complex and bizarre theology, which provided a spiritual support to the "Respect the Emperor and Expel Foreigners" movement of the late Edo period.

What is important here is the fact that kokugaku was an evolutionary effort arising spontaneously from inside Japanese society to re-discover and admire Japan's spirituality and culture in the original and set it against Buddhism and Confucianism which dominated the minds of Japanese intellectuals for long. In the words of Natsume Soseki, it was an endogenous development of ideas rather than an exogenous one forced by foreign contact and pressure. But once established and developed, kokugaku began to change its nature from academic research to political ideology against the intention of its founders. In the late eighteenth century to the early nineteenth century, kokugaku and its vision spread widely among lower samurai, rich merchants, and rich farmers all over Japan. This caused popularization of Shinto (Japanese traditional religion) and, along with it, the trend in which people outside the ruling class freely discussed social issues and national policies without instruction and guidance from above, a situation never permitted previously. In Nagoya region, for example, kokugaku of Motoori Norinaga invaded and quickly replaced Suika Shinto, a religious doctrine officially sanctioned and taught by high-ranking noblemen.

Nationalism fostered by kokugaku and activated greatly by the arrival of the American fleet was not state-guided nationalism, which is often seen in developing countries today, as rulers impose an artificial sense of national unity across different ethnicities and regions to create an "imagined community." Rather, it was a nationalism born spontaneously from the private sector, exciting and infuriating intellectuals and ordinary people alike, and sometimes even going to violent extremes to constrain and upset the policies of government. Unguided nationalism triggered by external pressure is hardly unique to Edo Japan as it is a social phenomenon commonly observed in virtually all countries. Uncontrollable emotion expressed by Chinese citizens in electronic media at any foreign insult and criticism against China is a good example of this.

The last version of kokugaku, advocated by Hirata Atsutane, did instill political radicalism into its believers, especially rich farmers. It taught that, for example, dedicated service to the emperor even to one's death would be rewarded by Okuninushi no Mikoto, an ancient Japanese god, in the next world. It cannot be denied that this peculiar doctrine promoted terrorist acts among the "Respect the Emperor and Expel Foreigners" hardliners, and contributed also to the formation of other anti-foreigner movements such as the Late Mito Doctrine and the radical activism of Yoshida Shoin (1830–1859). However, it would be unfair to judge kokugaku only negatively just because it stimulated terrorism among some radical sects. We must also note that kokugaku firmly established the national identity of Japan and its people in the minds of a larger number of Japanese intellectuals who did not resort to terrorism. This nationalism enabled them to put national interests above interests of a particular han or class to which they belonged. The social ethos derived from kokugaku served as a centripetal force that drove Japanese leaders to think and act primarily for "Japanese nation" and "all people under the heaven" even they were on different sides, at the time of Western impact.

Let me sum up. The previously rock-solid legitimacy of the Tokugawa rule was seriously tarnished at the military impotence of the Bakufu by the appearance of the powerful West. Additional problems associated with the content and signing procedure of the commercial treaties with the West, despotic and unilateral decision making in coping with the external crisis, and inflation and other economic shocks generated by international trade further diminished the Bakufu's authority to govern. This created a social condition under which the Tokugawa's rule could be challenged and political competition for establishing a new government could be started without regard to old convention or class boundaries. However, political competition was fought under social psychology anchored by spontaneous nationalism which was broadly shared by lower samurai, rich farmers, rich merchants, and other intellectuals. This cemented the hearts of all leaders and fighters toward achieving the primary goal of maintaining national independence against foreign pressure. Centrifugal force was balanced by centripetal force to keep the movement "within certain bounds," which prevented a deep internal schism from emerging and gave no excuse for foreigners to intervene or invade.

5.4 The flexible structure of politics[5]

5.4.1 Politics of coping with globalization pressure

From the late Edo period to the early Meiji period—from 1858 to 1881 to be more precise—Japanese politics exhibited a pattern which we shall call the "flexible structure," a feature that was very unique in a latecomer country facing the enormous challenge of global integration. This was a critical period of Japanese transformation in which the nation had, in response to the Western impact, to re-organize the political regime, re-define national goals, and debate and decide on the contents, priorities, roadmaps, and implementers of these goals.

The year 1858, four years after the "friendship" treaties, was the year in which commercial treaties with the West—Americans, Dutch, Russians, British, and French—were concluded, and trade with these countries began in the following year. It was also the year that saw an embryonic formation of political and economic strategies to cope with the Western pressure, called *kogi yoron* (government by public deliberation) and *fukoku kyohei* (enrich the country, strengthen the military).[6] Thus, the year 1858 was the starting point of transformation from the viewpoint of global integration as well as the initiation of domestic response to it.

On the other hand, the year 1881 was the year of the "Political Incident of the Fourteenth Year of Meiji" (the ousting of Okuma Shigenobu (1838–1922), who proposed a radical plan to introduce a constitution and parliament, from the government) which resulted in an imperial edict that promised to establish a (conservative) constitution and a national assembly within nine years. It was also the year in which the policy of privatizing state-owned enterprises was announced, finally abandoning the idea of official management of business enterprises. Moreover, these events were followed immediately by Matsukata Deflation in which Finance Minister Matsukata Masayoshi launched fiscal austerity measures to end inflation and began a series of monetary and fiscal reforms that established the Bank of Japan in 1882. These measures, though painful, provided the necessary conditions for the private sector to grow—and it did begin to grow strongly from the late 1880s. Thus, it can be said that the long debate over what must be done for the transformation from a feudal to a "modern" society ended in 1881, as the government set the deadline for establishing a constitutional monarchy and industrialization strategy based on state-run industries was replaced by private-sector driven one. From then on, Japan entered the period of implementation toward these agreed goals, and indeed succeeded, within a decade or so, in promulgating the Meiji Constitution and founding a Western-style parliament as well as seeing the emergence of private joint-stock companies which initiated an industrial revolution.

According to the textbook account of Japanese history, *Taisei Hokan* (the return of governing authority from the Bakufu to the emperor) or subsequent *Ousei Fukko* (the restoration of the emperor's direct rule) in late 1867 divides the Meiji period from the previous Edo period. However, this is not a very meaningful period demarcation for our purpose. What happened from late 1867 to early 1868 was the exit of the Bakufu (the Tokugawa Family) as the leading political player as a result of military confrontation triggered by machination and provocation. This was a big event from the viewpoint of who ruled the country, but not from the viewpoint of the characteristics of the political process at that time. The content and pattern of political competition did not change appreciably before and after the Meiji Restoration. Moreover, political players other than the Bakufu remained basically unchanged. For this reason, from the perspective of the history of a latecomer country facing the pressure of globalization, it is more logical and convincing to regard the pre-1858 period as the pre-opening period, the period of 1858–1881 as the transformation period in response to the Western impact, and the subsequent period as the implementation period.

According to the popular view, the Meiji period (1868–1912) is regarded as the period of a despotic government monopolized by the former samurai of strong han (Satsuma, Choshu, Tosa, and Saga) which, elevating the emperor as the national symbol, engaged in an all-out effort in economic and military modernization while delaying the arrival of constitutional politics as much as possible. Some even argue that the Meiji regime was the first model of authoritarian developmentalism which was later adopted by other East Asian countries in the post-World War II period. However, our argument is that this view is at odds with the facts.

In the post-World War II period, an authoritarian state guided by a strong leader emerged in many East Asian economies to propel industrialization and bring the population out of poverty. A series of developmental policies were executed by the directives of top leaders to accelerate import substitution, export promotion, heavy industrialization, technology transfer, education and training, and the construction of infrastructure. Meanwhile, the introduction of democracy was significantly delayed or even denied. The most salient cases were the Park Chung-hee government in South Korea (1961–1979) and the Chiang Kai-shek government in Taiwan (1949–1975). Additionally, the Deng Xiaoping government in China (1976–1997), the Lee Kwan Yew government in Singapore (1965–1990), the Mahathir government in Malaysia (1981–2003), and the Sarit and Thanom governments in Thailand (1958–1973) can be cited as such political regimes (Watanabe 1995; Ohno and Sakurai 1997).

These authoritarian developmental states of East Asia exhibited the following features: (i) internal or external crisis as a catalyst to set up the regime; (ii) a powerful and often charismatic leader (all of whom happened to be male); (iii) a loyal and capable technocrat group to support him; (iv) prioritization of developmental ideology and postponement of political reform; (v) legitimization through economic performance and not by democratic procedure; and (vi) continuation of the regime for a few decades and internal social transformation caused by the success of its economic policies. However, the Meiji Revolution had only one common feature with these, namely, crisis as a catalyst for initiating the regime, and shared no other. The early Meiji period was not a period when a dictatorial regime with a simple, solid, and oppressive political structure lasted for decades. It did not have a charismatic leader who gave orders unilaterally, nor did it pursue economic modernization at the cost of all other goals. The legitimacy of the Meiji government was not derived solely from the authority of the emperor or economic performance. Surely, Emperor Meiji played an important political role as the symbol of national unity, and all Meiji leaders admired and respected him as one important source of political legitimacy, but he was not a political player with real power.

The Meiji Revolution was achieved by the flexible structure of politics, which permitted the competition of multiple goals (two goals of *fukoku kyohei* and *kogi yoron* in the late Edo period, or four goals of industrialization, foreign expedition, drafting a constitution, and establishing a national assembly in the early Meiji period) and continuous re-grouping of political leaders around these goals (Banno, 2006, 2007, 2008). Policy priorities shifted over the years, and neither winning coalitions nor losing ones stayed long in these positions. Political goals were not sacrificed for promoting economic goals. Despite occasional setbacks, dynamics derived from the flexible structure of politics resulted in the steady achievement of political and economic reforms in the long run without falling into chaos or national division. This was a very complex process with many phase shifts, far from the image of an authoritarian developmental state that single-mindedly pursued economic growth under a simple political structure and its linear evolution.

5.4.2 Three aspects of the flexible structure

The flexible structure of the Meiji Revolution can be decomposed into three aspects: (i) multiplicity and dynamism of national goals; (ii) constant re-formation of alliances; and (iii) variability and resilience of leaders and leader groups. These aspects are discussed in more detail below.

The first aspect of the flexible structure was the multiplicity and dynamism of national goals. Japan's national goals continued to evolve throughout the transformation period. The earliest reform goals which gathered support among influential han after the opening of ports, as noted above, were the political goal of *kogi yoron* (government by public deliberation) and the economic and military goals of *fukoku kyohei* (enriching the country, strengthening the military). Of these, *kogi yoron*, which started as the proposal of alliance among four or five intelligent han lords, evolved into the idea of a conference of all han totaling approximately 300, and even into the creation of the bicameral system consisting of the Upper House of han lords and the Lower House of lower-level samurai. As it turned out, the last plan among these which intended a peaceful transition of power was prepared but eventually overturned by the Boshin War that erupted in 1868–1869. This military conflict was caused partly by the refusal of the Bakufu to be downgraded to a minor power in the proposed political scheme and partly as a result of provocation by the opponents of the Bakufu.

After the Meiji government was established in 1868, Kido Takayoshi (1833–1877), who formerly belonged to Choshu Han, a number of leaders from former Tosa Han, and the students of Fukuzawa Yukichi (1834–1901), a renowned academic leader who established Keio University, upgraded the feudal assembly model based on the class society to the idea of establishing a modern constitution and a Western-style parliament. Political reformers were then split into the progressive group promoting a British-style party cabinet government and the conservative group advocating a German-style constitutional monarchy. Despite these differences in form or orientation, installation of a government by public deliberation of one sort or another was regarded as a key political requirement that would confer legitimacy to the Meiji Revolution and the new government established by it.

On the other hand, the goal of *fukoku kyohei* in the late Edo period was the idea that each han should set up a trading firm as external trade was resumed; procure highly demanded products from all over Japan for export; with proceeds purchase cannons, guns, and military ships from the West; and bolster its military capability to compete effectively with other han and the Bakufu. In reality, those han that successfully achieved this feat became the major powers that eventually toppled the Bakufu and occupied central places in the new government. However, after the Meiji Restoration in 1868 and especially after the Iwakura Mission to the West by high officials to study Western systems and technology in 1871–73, Okubo Toshimichi (1830–1878), a former Satsuma samurai and a top official in the Meiji government, became convinced that *fukoku* should not mean merely the mercantilist principle of buying and selling of local products for the profit of han but should be the developmental notion of industrialization, namely, building factories equipped with imported modern machinery under the central government's guidance to dramatically raise national output. As to *kyohei*, the revolutionary army (called, perhaps unjustly, *fuhei shizoku* or "former samurai with gripes"), which had nothing to do domestically after achieving the revolution, began to demand foreign campaigns and the budget for their execution. Because of this development, *fukoku* and *kyohei* became two separate goals that competed for the same budgetary resource. In this context, what Okubo, the leader of the industrialization group, tried to do was to avoid external conflicts by appeasing the foreign expedition group, and secure as much fiscal resource as possible to build factories.

The second aspect of the flexible structure of politics was the constant regrouping of political coalitions. As noted above, the two goals of *kogi yoron* and *fukoku kyohei* in the late Edo period split into the four goals of industrialization (led by Okubo Toshimichi), foreign expedition (led by Saigo Takamori, 1827–1877), establishment of a parliament (led by Itagaki Taisuke, 1837–1919), and drafting of a constitution (led by Kido Takayoshi), and supporters gathered around these leaders. Figure 5.2 illustrates coalition formation and re-formation among these four groups from Meiji Restoration (1868) to the end of the transformation period (1881).[7] What is important here is the fact that no one group yielded sufficient political power to carry out desired policies, and could pursue them only by forming a coalition with one or two other groups which entertained other policy objectives. Whether advocacy of a foreign expedition, demand for a popularly elected parliament, or industrial promotion, dominance of one group invited intervention from other groups, and the defeat of another group was compensated by assistance from others. Furthermore, this coalition re-formation with checks and balances hardly resulted in permanent grudges or vengeance against each other. Depending on circumstances, they could alternately become friends and enemies without generating irreconcilable hatred for mutual destruction. This process, which from outside seemed like an endless political battle, was surprisingly successful in avoiding chaos and achieving multiple national goals in the long run, albeit with many setbacks and through trial-and-error.

Why did such flexible re-formation of coalitions continue for decades? One reason was that, during the decade leading up to *Ousei Fukko* (restoration of the emperor's direct rule, 1867), interaction among influential han for pursuing commercial profits through feudal trading firms and contriving the plan to establish a feudal assembly became very active. This interaction generated mutual trust across different han and different policy lines, which naturally carried over to the post-Meiji Restoration period as continued coalition building based on former han groups. Another reason was shared ideologies, such as nationalism and the Respect for the Emperor, among leaders in the late Edo period as analyzed in section 5.3.2 above. These ideologies were suddenly and greatly activated at the contact with the powerful West. Such centripetal social ethos kept political fights within certain bounds without exploding into unstoppable mutual destruction.

The third aspect of the flexible structure of politics was the variability and resilience of leaders and leader groups. In the eyes of the posterity, Saigo is remembered as a military leader and a rebel, Okubo as a developmental

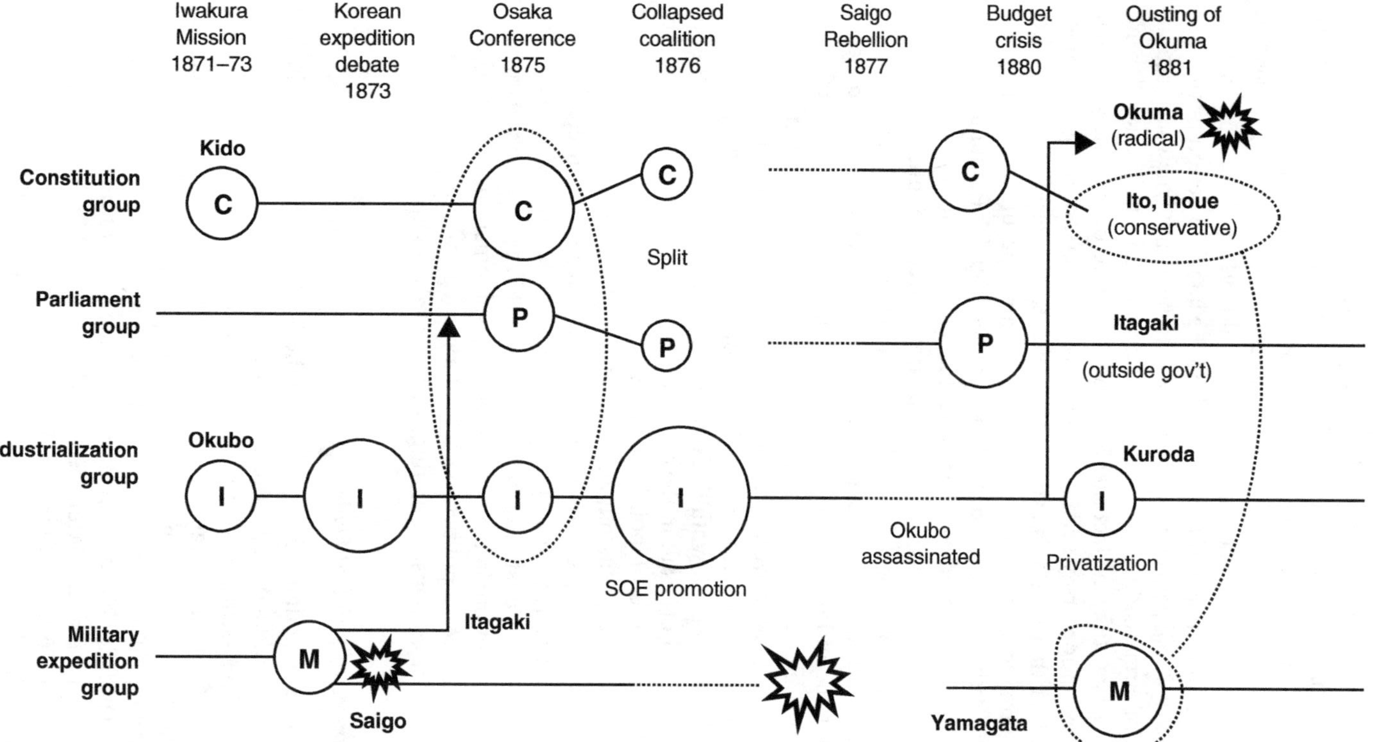

Figure 5.2 Coalition and competition among political leaders, 1868–1881

Source: Banno and Ohno (2010).

Notes: Circle size and solid and dotted lines roughly indicate the amount of influence yielded by each group. Dotted ovals show cooperative relationship. Lines with arrows are jumps across groups by individual leaders. Explosion marks show political defeat.

bureaucrat *par excellence*, and Itagaki as a campaigner for political freedom, people's rights, and the establishment of a parliament. However, none of these leaders pursued their respective goals single-mindedly from the outset. On the contrary, sharing goals and shifting allegiance were common among leaders in the late Edo to the early Meiji period. It could even be said that they all understood the importance of the two goals in the late Edo period or the four goals in the early Meiji period. It was through external stimuli, new inspiration, or the force of circumstance that they ended up specializing in one of them.

From this perspective, the fact that Saigo continued to be extremely popular among the revolution army even after he was expelled from the government in 1873, the fact that Okubo's eyes were opened to modern industry during the official mission to the West (1871–1873), and the unexpectedly great success of the Petition for the Establishment of the Popular Parliament (1874) which Itagaki co-authored after leaving the government, were crucial in deciding the path of each leader. Had they not shared the multiple goals at the root, it would have been unthinkable that Okubo would write a letter to convey his shock and excitement in visiting British factories to Saigo waiting in Japan, and it would be difficult to explain why Itagaki vacillated between demanding a parliament and proposing a foreign expedition while he was in the caretaker government waiting for the return of other ministers from the West. For the same reason, Meiji politics required no charismatic leader, and the death or downfall of one leader (such as the assassination of Okubo in 1878) did not result in the extinction of the group which he had led.

The flexible structure of politics exhibited by the Meiji leaders proved effective in the simultaneous pursuit of multiple goals, resilience to internal and external shocks, and durability of the political regime in comparison with the simple hard structure of politics which was the hallmark of developmental dictatorship of East Asia in the post-World War II period. Although political institutions were in the early stage of development in the early Meiji period, the substance of politics, such as the content of policy competition and the process of consensus building, were already highly mature.

5.4.3 The source of political leaders

Who were the people that led and executed the Meiji Revolution? In the late Edo and the early Meiji period, political leaders predominantly came from the samurai class. The Meiji Revolution was a revolution staged by samurai, and the social transformation triggered by the Western contact was carried out by the hands of samurai who had been the political leaders and the privileged class in the Bakufu–Han System of the preceding Edo period. Table 5.1 shows the dates, field of achievement, and original class of prominent leaders in the late Edo and the early Meiji period. They are listed in the order of birth year. Among the 56 leaders tabulated here, there are 44 han vassals (low-ranking samurai), six han lords, two *hatamoto* (samurai belonging to the Bakufu), two court nobles, one merchant, and one farmer.[8] Han vassals,

Table 5.1 Origins of political leaders in late Edo and early Meiji

	Name	*Years*	*Area of achievement*	*Original class*
1	Nakane Sekko	1807–1877	Political scientist	Han samurai (Fukui Han)
2	Shimazu Nariakira	1809–1858	Han lord	Han lord (Satsuma Han)
3	Yokoi Shonan	1809–1869	Confucianist, statesman	Han samurai (Higo Han)
4	Sakuma Shozan	1811–1864	Militarist, jurist, confucianist	Han samurai (Matsushiro Han)
5	Nabeshima Naomasa	1814–1871	Han lord	Han lord (Saga Han)
6	Uchida Masakaze	1815–1893	Bureucrat	Han samurai (Satsuma Han)
7	Yoshida Toyo	1816–1862	Statesman	Han samura (Tosa Han)
8	Shimazu Hisamitsu	1817–1887	Han top leader	Han lord in substance (Satsuma Han)
9	Okubo Tadahiro	1817–1888	Bakufu official, statesman	Bakufu samurai
10	Hasebe Jimbei	1818–1873	Bureaucrat	Han samurai (Fukui Han)
11	Date Munenari	1818–1892	Han lord, statesman	Han lord (Uwajima Han)
12	Nagai Uta	1819–1863	Advocate for open door policy	Han samurai (Choshu Han)
13	Murata Ujihisa	1821–1899	Statesman	Han samurai (Fukui Han)
14	Katsu Kaishu	1823–1899	Bakufu militarist, statesman	Bakufu samurai
15	Iwakura Tomomi	1825–1883	Statesman	Nobleman
16	Yamauchi Yodo	1827–1872	Han lord	Han lord (Tosa Han)
17	Saigo Takamori	1827–1877	Statesman (1 of 3 Ishin Heroes)	Han samurai (Satsuma Han)
18	Iwashita Michihira	1827–1900	Statesman	Han samurai (Satsuma Han)
19	Saisho Atsushi	1827–1910	Bureaucrat	Han samurai (Satsuma Han)
20	Ijichi Masaharu	1828–1886	Militarist	Han samurai (Satsuma Han)
21	Matsudaira Shungaku	1828–1890	Han lord	Han lord (Fukui Han)
22	Yoshii Tomozane	1828–1891	Bureaucrat	Han samurai (Satsuma Han)
23	Soejima Taneomi	1828–1905	Statesman	Han samurai (Saga Han)

Table 5.1 (cont'd)

	Name	*Years*	*Area of achievement*	*Original class*
24	Yuri Kosei	1829–1909	Statesman, businessman	Han samurai (Fukui Han)
25	Takechi Hampeita	1829–1865	Statesman	Han samurai (Tosa Han)
26	Yoshida Shoin	1830–1859	Thinker, teacher	Han samurai (Choshu Han)
27	Okubo Toshimichi	1830–1878	Statesman (1 of 3 Ishin Heroes)	Han samurai (Satsuma Han)
28	Oki Takato	1832–1892	Statesman	Han samurai (Saga Han)
29	Kaieda Nobuyoshi	1832–1902	Statesman	Han samurai (Satsuma Han)
30	Kido Takayoshi	1833–1877	Statesman (1 of 3 Ishin Heroes)	Han samurai (Choshu Han)
31	Mori Kyosuke	1834–?	Bureaucrat, statesman	Han samurai (Tosa Han)
32	Eto Shimpei	1834–1874	Statesman	Han samurai (Saga Han)
33	Iwasaki Yataro	1834–1885	Founder of Mitsubishi Zaibatsu	Unaffiliated samurai (Tosa Han)
34	Fukuzawa Yukichi	1834–1901	Philosopher, founder of Keio Univ.	Han samurai (Nakatsu Han)
35	Sakamoto Ryoma	1835–1867	Freelance patriot	Han samurai, absconded (Tosa Han)
36	Komatsu Tatewaki	1835–1870	Statesman	Han samurai (Satsuma Han)
37	Godai Tomoatsu	1835–1885	Business leader in Kansai area	Han samurai (Satsuma Han)
38	Inoue Kaoru	1835–1915	Statesman, businessman	Han samurai (Choshu Han)
39	Fukuoka Takachika	1835–1919	Statesman	Han samurai (Tosa Han)
40	Matsukata Masayoshi	1835–1924	Statesman	Han samurai (Satsuma Han)
41	Kawamura Sumiyoshi	1836–1904	Navy militarist, statesman	Han samurai (Satsuma Han)
42	Sanjo Sanetomi	1837–1891	Statesman	Nobleman
43	Tani Tateki	1837–1911	Army militarist, statesman	Han samurai (Tosa Han)
44	Itagaki Taisuke	1837–1919	Military leader, statesman	Han samurai (Tosa Han)

Table 5.1 (cont'd)

	Name	*Years*	*Area of achievement*	*Original class*
45	Kabayama Sukenori	1837–1922	Navy militarist, statesman	Han samurai (Satsuma Han)
46	Nakaoka Shintaro	1838–1867	Freelance patriot	Rural samurai (Tosa Han)
47	Goto Shojiro	1838–1897	Statesman	Han samurai (Tosa Han)
48	Okuma Shigenobu	1838–1922	Statesman, founder of Waseda Univ.	Han samurai (Saga Han)
49	Yamagata Aritomo	1838–1922	Statesman, army militarist	Han samurai (Choshu Han)
50	Komuro Shinobu	1839–1898	Statesman, businessman	Son of a rich merchant
51	Kuroda Kiyotaka	1840–1900	Statesman	Han samurai (Satsuma Han)
52	Shibusawa Eiichi	1840–1939	Business leader and coordinator	Son of a rich farmer
53	Ito Hirobumi	1841–1909	Statesman	Han samurai (Choshu Han, upgraded from peasantry)
54	Mutsu Munemitsu	1844–1897	Statesman, diplomat	Han samurai (Kishu Han)
55	Furusawa Uruu	1847–1911	Statesman, bureaucrat	Han samurai (Tosa Han)
56	Yano Fumio	1850–1931	Statesman, literary man	Han samurai (Saeki Han)

which accounted for 79 percent, were the dominant group. Among them, the four most powerful han of Satsuma, Choshu, Tosa, and Saga produced 35 leaders. The collective samurai class, which included han lords, han vassals, and hatamoto, counted 52, or 93 percent of all leaders of this period.[9]

Needless to say, the number of leaders was minuscule relative to the total population. Their precise number is impossible to pin down because of the ambiguity of the definition of leaders. One suggestion comes from *Who's Who of the Meiji Restoration*, compiled in 1981 by mobilizing 800 historians all over Japan to enumerate all VIPs in the period with which we are concerned, whether they were politically conservative, gradualist, or radical (Japan Historical Academy, 1981). The leaders contained in this volume are approximately 4,300 in number which are again dominated by the samurai class. If we tentatively assume this to be the number of active leaders in the late Edo and the early Meiji period, the leaders occupied about 1 percent of the samurai population (about 450,000) or 0.012 percent of the total population (about 35 million).

A question may arise as to why the samurai class forced a revolution which would destroy the feudal system and the class system on which their privileged position depended. The answer is that their initial intention was merely to reorganize the polity within the old regime to cope effectively with the foreign pressure rather than a radical transformation of the regime itself. For this purpose, samurai performed the assigned role of leadership with a sense of duty and pride. However, the movement unexpectedly proceeded to the denial of the old system because the establishment and defense of the new government required an action far beyond the original plan. This came about because of enlightenment by Western thoughts, political conflict with the Bakufu, the necessity of a strong central authority, and resistance from the conservative forces (court nobility and han lords) in the early years of Meiji. Thus, the movement that started as a political reform ended up in a social revolution.

In the late Edo to the early Meiji period, political contribution of the non-samurai groups belonging to the old regime, such as court nobility, Bakufu scholars, private scholars, rich merchants, and wealthy farmers, was limited although there were some exceptions.[10] Similarly, the newly emerging groups in the period following the opening of ports (1859) or the Meiji Restoration (1867), such as farmers and landlords enriched by the export of silk and tea, the Yokohama merchants,[11] *seisho* (politically connected businessmen) and *zaibatsu* (business conglomerates), and intellectuals of the *Meirokusha* (the Society of the Sixth Year of Meiji) or Fukuzawa's Keio Academy, were not the main political players although some had close contacts with government officials. As to the political participation of the general mass, it is hard to detect anything in this period. Apart from farmers' uprisings which carried little message for national politics and had been observed since the Edo period, it can be said that political participation of the general mass began with the Hibiya Riot in 1905, in which the urban mass protested against the small size of war compensation paid by Russia following Japanese victory in the Japan–Russia War (1904–1905). Modern popular movements and demonstrations demanding universal (male) suffrage, women's rights, and the liberation of the underclass arose in the Taisho Democracy period (from the mid-1900s to the end of the 1920s), much later than the early Meiji period with which we are currently concerned.

Three additional remarks are in order to supplement the discussion of the Meiji Restoration.

First, the Meiji Revolution was not a revolution by low-ranking samurai alone. The lords of the influential han were equal or even superior to their most capable vassals in knowledge, leadership, and agility. For example, Satsuma Han Lord Shimazu Nariakira (1809–1858), and his younger brother and successor Shimazu Hisamitsu (1817–1887), ordered Saigo Takamori, Okubo Toshimichi, Komatsu Tatewaki (1835–1870), Godai Tomoatsu (1835–1885), and other vassals to manage the feudal trading firm of the han, push the idea of a feudal assembly, and build coalitions with other han.

These lower samurai frequently reported to the han leader. Thus, the revolutionary movement of Satsuma Han was a joint product of the han leader and his samurai. The contribution and influence of han lords, who were naturally fewer than han vassals in number (Table 5.1), should not be underestimated. From another angle, it can also be stated that one peculiar feature of the Meiji Revolution was active participation of low-ranking samurai, who in normal times should be less visible than their lords.

The second point, related to the first, is that a clear division of labor between a few top leaders and a much greater number of supporting elites was not observable in the Meiji Revolution. Many countries in East Asia, such as South Korea, Taiwan, Singapore, and Malaysia, in the post-World War II period had a strong president or prime minister who led development effort, on the one hand, and a cohort of elite technocrats, often with PhDs from the West, who were mobilized to concretize the leader's vision, on the other. However, Japan in the late Edo to the early Meiji period did not have such a division. While samurai supplied most leaders, who would occupy the top position and who would serve him as supporters was not pre-determined. Had the "Upper House" of the feudal assembly come into being in a peaceful manner, intelligent han lords could have played an important role in the new political arrangement. But in reality top leaders of the Meiji government who emerged from the military conflict were former low-ranking samurai and not han lords. Moreover, leaders in the early Meiji period did not have to rely on a large number of technocrats or voter support to run the government, because the parliament and the election system had not yet been installed. In this sense, leaders and elites were undifferentiated and political support base for the government was neither present nor necessary.

Third, the role of han was vital as a unit that prepared the conditions for the flexible structure of politics to emerge within the samurai class. Vassals in powerful han accumulated domestic and foreign knowledge, negotiation skills, and commercial experience through contacts with similar samurai from other han and Bakufu officials as well as exposure to foreigners and information from Europe and America. This in turn led to the sharing of the national sense of crisis and nationalism among them. Low-ranking samurai of the influential han, trained in both theory and practice, continued to form and re-form groups into the early Meiji period with the former han as the basic unit. In this way, han in the late Edo period served as an incubator of human resource and network formation that enabled Japan to cast off the class-based feudal system and face squarely with the Western powers.

5.5 Technology transfer

Japan was the first non-Western country to successfully receive, modify, and internalize Western technology as early as in the late nineteenth century. This section will review concrete modes of technology transfer in the Meiji period. In so doing it relies heavily on the analysis provided by Uchida (1990). The process of technology transfer in this period can be classified into (i) early attempts in the late Edo period, (ii) foreign experts and turnkey projects, (iii) engineering education, and (iv) acquiring technology through machinery imports and foreign partnership. These modes were adopted sequentially from (i) to (iv) to gradually replace expensive foreign experts by Japanese professionals and engineers although there were significant overlaps among their periods. These various methods are examined one by one below.[12]

5.5.1 Early attempts

In 1854, the Bakufu made its first conscious effort to import pragmatic foreign technology when it adopted Western-style armaments for coastal defence against possible foreign invasion. Many han also tried to replicate foreign technology in the spirit of *fukoku kyohei* by building furnaces to smelt and process metals for casting cannons. Scholars of Dutch studies and traditional craftsmen designed and built these furnaces relying solely on descriptions in imported Dutch books which, however, were already outdated by the time they were translated. Haphazard copy production of steel and arms such as these generally failed, and there is no evidence that the cannons or bullets thus produced were effective in the battles that brought an end to the Tokugawa shogunate. Some han also test-produced Western-style ships and steam engines from Dutch texts, but the technology gap between the results and the foreign ships that actually visited Japan was so great that this effort had to be abandoned. Realizing the limits to imitating technology from books, the Bakufu and some powerful han changed their strategies and reverted to directly importing firearms manufactured abroad as soon as Japan opened its ports in 1859.

However, the results were not so dismal in some cases where technical knowledge was transmitted in the presence of foreign experts and their direct guidance. The construction of a Western-style wooden sailing ship at Heda port in the Izu Peninsula in 1854, where Japanese carpenters worked on designs by Russian naval officers and under instructions of Russian shipwrights to replace the storm-wrecked vessel to take Russians home, can be regarded as the first successful case of on-site technology transfer. The Japanese carpenters absorbed the technology so well they later became the first skilled workers at Japanese naval arsenals or privately-owned shipyards.

Another notable case was the Nagasaki Naval Training Center, established in 1855, that trained the crew of Japan's first Western-style battleship, the *Kanko-maru*, which was a gift from the Dutch government to the Bakufu. The center was a joint undertaking of the Dutch navy and the Bakufu with daily management entrusted to Dutch instructors. Five Dutch navy personnel trained 167 samurai who had been competitively selected by the Bakufu and various han. Courses focused on operational technologies such as navigation, artillery training, and the care and maintenance of steam engines, which were the standard curriculum for a battleship crew. The Japanese crew also received on-the-job training through exercise navigation to Kagoshima. Between 1860 and 1870, the Bakufu and a number of han imported a total of 166 ships from the West. It was the graduates of the Nagasaki Naval Training Center and other similar centers that the Bakufu subsequently set up in Edo and Hyogo who operated them. The importation of different types of ships enabled the Bakufu and han to compare and enrich their knowledge of warships, engines, and gunnery. In a similar way, the Bakufu army acquired technology both through the artillery it imported and the invitation of foreign military advisors to Japan who trained military students.

In addition, the Bakufu built the Nagasaki Steel Mill and Shipyard in 1857 and the Yokosuka Steel Mill in 1866 as ancillary facilities for the Nagasaki Naval Training Center. These two facilities, which later became Mitsubishi Nagasaki Shipyard and Yokosuka Naval Arsenal, replicated Western mechanized factory production and transferred technology to Japanese by the employment of foreign engineers and skilled workers. Kagoshima Spinning Mill, established in 1867 by Satsuma Han, also adopted a similar approach. After the Meiji Restoration, these early factories became a model for the new government's program to hire foreign advisors for concrete factory operation, as explained in section 5.5.3 below.

5.5.2 Foreign experts and turnkey projects

In the early years of Meiji, the new government hired foreign advisors to the tune of 300 to 600 in any year on a project contract basis, at considerable fiscal cost, to establish Western-style state-owned enterprises in the fields of railways, telegraphy, and silk reeling. Some foreign advisors received salaries higher than that of the Japanese prime minister. Some of the projects recruited a large number of foreigners of the same nationality with various functions and imported virtually all hardware to create an exact replica of a foreign model. These can be considered as turnkey projects with a foreign director supervising his fellow countrymen and Japanese workers, with the Japanese side eventually overtaking operation after the project completion.[13] Yokosuka Shipyard, the Tokyo–Yokohama Railway, the Imperial Mint, and Ikuno Silver Mine were such examples. There was also another type of foreign advisors hired not as a country team but as individual engineers and skilled workers filling specific technological needs of the project under Japanese management. Many offices for industry, mining, and agricultural businesses run by the Japanese Home Office as well as some businesses under the Hokkaido Settlement Agency were such examples. Comparing these two types of projects, the latter naturally required greater ownership and involvement on the Japanese side in technology transfer.

The turnkey projects were managed by foreign directors and advisors with hired Japanese employees performing only unskilled or auxiliary works. For example, the Imperial Mint was directed by William Thomas Kinder who was dispatched, along with other foreign experts, by the British Oriental Bank to manage the mint under a Japanese government contract. *Annual Reports of the President of the Imperial Mint* were published in the name of Kinder. In the case of Telegraphic Service of the Ministry of Industry, the official report was written in the name of the Japanese second-in-command. In its first few reports which were published in both English and Japanese, the Japanese version stated that the Japanese were working in cooperation with foreigners sharing the duties of construction engineers and maintenance staff, and requesting the foreigners' support as necessary. The English version, however, presented an entirely different picture in which the Japanese worked under the supervision of foreigners as telegraph operators, clerks, engineers, inspectors, and labourers. It is suspected that the latter was closer to the truth while the former story was made up to please the higher-ups in the ministry.

From the viewpoint of the Japanese government, the primary aim of establishing a mint, a telegraphic service, railways, and shipyards was to rapidly introduce modern industrial infrastructure comparable to Western models. Given the speed with which they had to be built, it is not surprising that these enterprises were run by a large number of foreigners who managed them in the same manner as the businesses they had managed at home. These early businesses did not always consciously aim at transferring technology to Japan.

At the same time, the Western countries which obtained trading rights with Japan also considered it highly desirable that Japan build the type of infrastructure described above as soon as possible. For the various foreign delegations, shipping lines, and merchants, Nagasaki and Yokosuka Steel Mills became indispensable facilities for the repair of foreign ships because Japan was at the end of long-distance sea routes that linked Europe with the Far East. Similarly, repairing foreign ships and replenishing fuel (charcoal) were the main purposes of creation of Nagasaki Kosuga Dock, managed by the trading company of British merchant Thomas B. Glover, and Takashima Coal Mine. The construction of lighthouses and the telegraph service was requested by the British consul general, Harry Smith Parkes, to the Meiji government shortly after the government's formation. By the end of 1874, British engineer R. H. Branton, who was commissioned for the task, had assembled a large team of British, Chinese, and Filipino workers, 88 men strong, who included builders, lighthouse keepers, and boat crews. While the Meiji government bore the full cost of building lighthouses, Branton and his team undertook both construction and maintenance. The lighthouses thus constructed ensured safe passage for foreign and Japanese ships alike.

In the area of telegraphy, the Bakufu signed an agreement with the French government to build a telegraph service in 1866. However, this decision was overturned by the Meiji government which chose, through the mediation of the British consul general, a domestic telegraphic service. Okita Telegraph Company, owned by the Danish, was awarded a contract for sole agency.

Behind these developments lay the completion of international telegraphic networks that had started from the construction of Anglo-French submarine transmission cables in 1851. By 1866, one telegraph network stretched from Europe to the Far East via an overland route that the Russian government had laid, reaching Vladivostok. Between 1869 and 1871, another submarine telegraphic network laid by private British companies connected Aden to Hong Kong and Shanghai via Bombay and Singapore. The Japanese telegraphic cables built by Okita Telegraph Company connected these two international networks at the end and extended them to Nagasaki and Yokohama, the two ports with a large foreign settlement. The construction of Tokyo–Yokohama and Tokyo–Nagasaki telegraphic lines enabled foreign delegations and merchants in Japan to have virtually instantaneous contact with home. From the beginning, telegraphic service handled messages in the Western alphabet as well as in Japanese characters. The fact that 10 percent of the initial messages were in the alphabet shows that the telegraph system proved useful to foreign residents as well as to the Japanese public and private sector. Solid establishment of modern seafaring and telegraphy in Japan enabled foreigners in Japan to conduct their diplomatic and commercial affairs efficiently.

Japan's heavy reliance on imported machinery, equipment, and materials in establishing these businesses brought handsome profits to foreign merchants, who were also the mediators of technology transfer. Jardine Matheson & Co. and the Oriental Bank competed over an order to build and equip the Imperial Mint. When the latter won the contract, it not only imported second-hand equipment from the Hong Kong Mint and sold gold and silver for minting but also provided Japan with management expertise by hiring a British team headed by Kinder as described earlier. For any such project, foreign merchants would act as middlemen for importing management and technology, providing Japanese government-run businesses with engineers and skilled workers from the home country.

International migration of Western engineers also reflected the situation on the supply side. It was not just a phenomenon observed in Japan or driven only by strong Japanese demand for such projects. As British industrial infrastructure was nearly completed by the 1850s, the pace of building railways, ports, and related facilities slowed down and there was a surplus of civil engineers in Britain. Needing work, many of them chose to pursue careers building railways and cities in the Continent, then in British colonies and foreign lands in the less developed world such as Canada, India, Australia, South Africa, and South America. Machinery and equipment makers also turned their eyes to overseas markets. For British railway contractors, it was customary for a supervisor who received an overseas order to first secure the materials needed such as train tracks and locomotives from foundries and manufacturers at home, hire subcontractors and a team of skilled workers, then travel with them to his destination. In the case of Argentina, 160 Britons, including engineers, came to build its railway in 1857. It is not surprising then to see a similar team coming to Japan 13 years later to lay its first railway between Shimbashi and Yokohama. Japan's adoption of the narrow gauge of 3 feet 6 inches is often thought to be a policy mistake, but all railways built in Australia and South Africa around 1860 were of the same gauge.

Hiring foreign experts and workers through turnkey contracts did not intend or require systematic technology transfer, but the method did have the merit of providing a training ground for Japanese workers in the work practices of advanced countries. It created groups of skilled workers that were new to Japan including machine operators, steam-engine drivers, steel-workers, and electricians. They often migrated from state-owned enterprises to the private sector or set up their own, spreading Western technology that they had acquired and paving the way for the Western-style management of industry by the Japanese from the 1880s onwards.

From around 1875 state-owned enterprises stopped hiring large foreign teams, and by 1880 foreign engineers and skilled workers had disappeared from all but a few workplaces. Factories and facilities that had been created by turnkey projects and management contracts were now permanent businesses under Japanese management and operation which no longer needed foreign supervision. Foreign advisors were retained only in those areas where technology transfer was considered inadequate. This shift resulted partly from a policy change of the Meiji government which could no longer afford to hire expensive foreigners. It was also the natural consequence of fixed-term contracts which foreign experts did not expect to renew. But what is truly amazing was the fact that the Japanese government and businesses did not feel the need for continued foreign help in operating the modern and complex Western-style machinery and equipment which Japan imported for the first time only a decade or so ago. There were already Japanese managers who could take over the role of foreign supervisors and trained Japanese technicians who were ready to replace foreign engineers.

5.5.3 Engineering education

After the departure of foreign advisors, Japanese engineers assumed the role of internalizing and diffusing Western technologies in Japan. They understood the fundamentals of Western technology and could put this knowledge to practical use. They collected and digested technical information from abroad and instructed appropriate technologies to purchasing missions dispatched to foreign manufacturers. Once a factory was built, they supervised its operation. The smooth transfer of Western technology owed much to the fact that Meiji Japan trained a large number of local engineers to an exceptionally high standard in a short period. World history tells us that few latecomer countries can do this. The deeper reason why this was possible was hinted in the sections we have already traversed: political, social, and economic conditions engendered in Japan by repeated translative adaptations prior to the encounter with the powerful West.

Turnkey projects managed by foreigners, described in the previous section, were an important channel for industrial human training, but it was not the only one. Japanese engineers and skilled workers were also produced by sending students to Europe and America as well as through establishing institutions for technical education and training at home.

Early Meiji-era engineers were those who had studied Western technology before Japan had established a formal university and technical education system. The group can be divided into three types. First, there were the scholars of Dutch studies from the late Edo period who had taught themselves from imported technical books and journals. They worked for Western-style businesses owned by the Bakufu or various han, and were later recognized as engineers by the Meiji government. Oshima Takato, who built the first blast furnace in Japan, Takeda Ayasaburo, who built the star-shaped fort in Hakodate, and Utsunomiya Saburo, who became Japan's first cement manufacturer, were among them.

Second, there were graduates from schools and centers managed and taught by foreigners. They included the Nagasaki Naval Training Center (1855), the Yokosuka Shipyard School (1870), the Telegraphic Service Technical Training College (1871), the Imperial Japanese Naval Academy's Institute for Maritime Studies (1873), and the Railway Engineer Training Center (1877). At these schools, foreign engineers taught Japanese trainees the engineering knowledge required for the functions they performed. The graduates later worked as foremen or junior technicians throughout Japan's modern army as well as in the telegraphic service, railways, and shipbuilding during their infant stages. The education offered at these institutions was limited to foreign-language training and the knowledge necessary to run the business at hand. But this was sufficient to ensure that these businesses could go on normally even after foreign management left. For instance, graduates from the Railway Engineer Training Center supervised and successfully completed the construction of a railway line from Kyoto and Otsu, which included tunnelling through Osaka Mountain, in 1878–1880.

The third group of early Meiji-era engineers were those who were selected and sent abroad to study by the government. Normally, the Ministry of Education or the military selected best achievers among graduates of Japanese education or training institutions for continued study abroad although some engineers chose foreign education by their own will. By the Western educational standards of the time, they were extremely good students despite the meagre stipends provided by the Japanese government. On their return to Japan, they usually worked as senior technical experts for the government[14] or for the private sector. The very first overseas students were seven men sent to the Netherlands by the Bakufu to learn Western navigation in 1862. Some students even went abroad without official permission, including master engineers Yamao Yozo and Inoue Masaru who previously served Satsuma and Choshu Han, respectively, and became senior bureaucrats in the Ministry of Industry after the Meiji Restoration. In the early years of

Meiji, students from all over Japan traveled abroad to study, including Dan Takuma who later became the director of Mitsui Mining. The navy also sent many trainees from the Yokosuka Shipyard School and the Naval Academy abroad to master technologies for shipbuilding and arms manufacture, as did *Kaisei Gakko*, the precursor to the University of Tokyo. By the end of the 1880s, Japan had sent around 80 students abroad to be trained as engineers as far as records remain.

By the field of study, 21 Japanese overseas students studied shipbuilding, 17 studied mechanical engineering, 13 studied civil engineering, ten studied mining and metallurgy, six studied arms manufacture, and four studied chemistry. By destination, 28 were sent to Britain, 20 to the US, 14 to France, nine to Germany, and eight to the Netherlands (excluding unknowns, based on Uchida 1990). They not only studied at universities but also went to various recognized technical schools, received on-the-job training, or had private lessons.[15] It should be noted that not many Western universities at that time acknowledged or offered pragmatic technical education. In Great Britain, only universities in Scotland and London established mechanical and civil engineering chairs before the 1840s. It was customary for a British engineer to be trained on site, first working as an apprentice and then as an assistant. Many of the British engineers who migrated abroad had been trained in this manner. In France, there were some notable technical institutions such as *École Polytechnique*, *École d'Application*, and *École Centrale*. In Germany, each state boasted a number of technical and vocational schools, including the mining school of Freiberg established in 1765. In the US, there were few technical education institutions until the first half of the nineteenth century. Boston Tech, which later developed into Massachusetts Institute of Technology, was founded in the 1860s, just before the Meiji Restoration and at around the same time that Columbia and Cornell universities first offered civil, mechanical, and mining and materials engineering courses. However, these technical institutions were still considered a rank below universities until the end of the nineteenth century. This being said, it can be concluded that the first wave of Japanese overseas students were sent to appropriate institutions for the purpose of absorbing pragmatic technical knowledge and received an education on par with engineers of the first rank in Europe and the US. It is no surprise that on their return, these engineers were able to assume the responsibilities and positions previously occupied by foreign technical advisors and engineers.

Japan accepted engineering, along with medicine and law, as one of the new subjects to be studied vigorously in order to absorb useful imported knowledge. Unlike Western Europe, it did not have the mindset to look down on engineering as an inferior subject to be treated with less academic respect. The early establishment of faculties of engineering at Japanese universities became a distinctive feature that contributed greatly to the country's technological advance. It may be said that Meiji Japan quickly and selectively imported the components of engineering education abroad which the West had just established through a century of trial-and-error and combined them for the best results. This new tradition was started with the founding of Kobu Daigakko (Institute of Technology) in 1871[16] and the courses in applied science and civil and mechanical engineering offered at the University of Science.

The Institute of Technology was created by the Ministry of Industry to train a cadre of engineers for its bureaus of mining, railways, telegraphy, and construction. As the ministry did not possess the technical know-how to teach engineering students, it hired a British engineer, Henry Dyer, to run the Institute under a management contract. As the principal and professor of engineering of the Institute, Dyer was in a fortunate position to be able to design an ideal institution from scratch that integrated both theory and practice, a feature that British engineering education lacked. The six-year program of the Institute included basic education in English and mathematics in the first two years, classroom instructions in science and engineering in the next two years, and internship at various bureaus of the Ministry of Industry under the supervision of foreign engineers in the final two years. On graduating, the engineers were expected to assume positions within the Ministry of Industry. On the other hand, a smaller number of students who took engineering courses at the University of Science found employment in the Home Ministry, the Imperial Mint, and so on. The two institutions were merged to become the Faculty of Engineering at Tokyo Imperial University in 1885. By the end of the Meiji period, each of the other imperial universities founded in Kyoto, Tohoku, and Kyushu possessed a faculty of engineering from the very beginning.

These faculties of engineering at Meiji-era imperial universities were not research-oriented. They were dedicated solely to transmitting Western engineering knowledge. The textbooks used were all from abroad, and many of the lectures and the examinations were conducted in a foreign language (English or German). The journals published by the Societies of Industrial, Mechanical, and Electrical Engineering devoted many of their pages to overseas mission reports or excerpts from foreign journals. The science education offered by high schools in preparation for university entrance, too, devoted a considerable amount of time to teaching English and German as well as mathematics.

The technical and vocational schools that trained middle-rank engineers also contributed greatly to Japan's industrialization together with the faculties of engineering at imperial universities. In 1881, the Tokyo Shokko Gakko (Tokyo Workers School) was established to train worksite foremen and engineers. In 1897 under the Technical Schools Act, it became a technical high school along with Osaka Technical High School, which had been established a few years earlier. By the end of the Meiji period, additional technical high schools were created in Nagoya, Kumamoto, Sendai, and Kyoto. Subsequently, an even greater number of technical high schools were created during the Taisho period (1912–1926).

Table 5.2 Number of engineers by type of education

Employer	*Category of Engineer*	*Year*				
		1880	*1890*	*1900*	*1910*	*1920*
Government departments and agencies	Early Meiji-era engineers	61	72	–	–	–
	University graduates	25	183	474	1,075	1,795
	Technical college graduates	–	45	263	1,160	1,999
	SUBTOTAL:	86	300	737	2,235	3,794
Private organizations	Early Meiji-era engineers	–	17	54	34	–
	University graduates	–	131	385	846	3,230
	Technical college graduates	–	34	389	1,963	7,138
	SUBTOTAL:	–	182	828	2,843	10,368
TOTAL	Early Meiji-era engineers	61	89	54	34	–
	University graduates	25	314	859	1,921	5,025
	Technical college graduates	–	79	652	3,123	9,137
	GRAND TOTAL:	86	482	1,565	5,078	14,162

Source: Uchida (1990), p. 281.

The education offered at technical high schools was more limited in scope than that offered at the faculties of engineering at universities, but the quality of the students was outstanding. They attracted good students who could not afford university education for financial reasons. While graduates from the faculties of engineering at universities usually assumed official or academic positions, technical high-school graduates became core engineers on the factory floor. Early technical high schools also offered special courses on how Western technologies could be adapted to upgrade indigenous Japanese industries like textiles, ceramics, and brewing. In the late Meiji period, technical high-school graduates overtook university engineering graduates in number and began to produce the majority of Japanese engineers with pragmatic industrial knowledge. Tables 5.2 and 5.3 show the number of Japanese

Table 5.3 Number of engineers by sector

	Year				
	1880	*1890*	*1900*	*1910*	*1920*
Private sector					
Railways		34	153	149	496
Maritime transport		3	15	28	85
Construction		16	10	23	131
Commerce		2	34	186	745
Mining		46	177	513	1,779
Metallurgy		–	8	47	635
Shipbuilding		16	69	250	1,071
Machinery		6	38	106	554
Electric nachinery			23	104	770
Electric power generation & gas		20	34	231	861
Ceramics		11	24	90	302
Chemicals			12	93	570
Paper		1	14	68	207
Food		–	17	149	180
Textiles		18	77	300	1,103
Other		9	123	506	879
SUBTOTAL:		182	828	2,843	10,368
Public Sector					
Home Ministry	8	39	64	61	206
Local government offices	3	33	89	295	624
Hokkaido Settlement Agency	–	–	23	160	179
Ministry of Finance	6	18	43	169	208
Schools	–	53	169	349	594
Army	6	14	9	98	163
Navy	14	54	90	248	418
Ministry of Agriculture & Commerce	–	31	83	198	400
Ministry of Communications	49	13	57	120	222
Japanese National Railways		39	105	514	751
Other	–	6	5	23	29
SUBTOTAL:	86	300	737	2,235	3,794
GRAND TOTAL:	86	482	1,565	5,078	14,162

Source: Uchida (1990), p. 281.

engineers by type of education and by sector from 1880 to 1920 (Uchida, 1990). In the early years of Meiji, the total number of engineers was fewer than one hundred causing a scarcity of people who could comprehend and adopt Western technologies. Subsequently, the number of university-educated engineers and graduates from technical high schools rose, which greatly increased the supply of capable domestic engineers. By the turn of the century, engineers employed in the private sector outnumbered those in government offices. The sectoral distribution of engineers indicates the leading industries of Japan in the late nineteenth and the early twentieth centuries.

5.5.4 Import of machinery and foreign partnership

From 1880 onwards, new industries such as cotton spinning, paper, sugar, shipbuilding, telephony, electric power generation, and electrical machinery grew from technologies transferred from the West. This was initially done by analyzing and absorbing the technology embodied in imported machinery and equipment. From the 1900s, Japan began to employ another method of technology transfer by way of technical cooperation agreements with Western firms. Contracts were drawn with foreign companies that offered instructors and know-how as well as machinery and equipment. Needless to say, these two methods of technology transfer became possible by the existence of a growing number of Japanese engineers, described above, who could absorb technical information, select technologies, and assimilate them. Concrete examples are given below.

When the Ministry of Communications, which took over the Telegraphic Service from the Ministry of Industry, set up a telephone network, a group of engineers, including Oi Saitaro, a graduate of the Institute of Technology, collected publicly available technical information; visited Britain, the US, and Germany to study their telephone systems; and negotiated with telephone equipment makers and selected the kind of system suitable for Japan. Advanced products and equipment such as telephones and telephone exchanges were imported, but Japanese engineers and workers, without any foreign assistance, laid the lines and managed operations. Compared to the time when Japan created a telegraph service (section 5.5.2), its capacity as a receiver of foreign technology had improved remarkably.

In the navy, early Meiji-era engineers trained in Britain and France, along with shipbuilding and armaments engineers who graduated from naval technical high schools, were key figures in designing plans to reinforce and expand the naval fleet. Throughout the Meiji period principal battleships were imported chiefly from Britain. Japanese naval shipbuilding and armaments engineers made it a custom to stay in Britain as observers while the ordered state-of-the-art battleships were being built and readied for delivery. This provided them with ample opportunity to learn about ship design and construction from the British Navy and shipyards. Their knowledge proved invaluable to the domestic production of arms and support vessels by Japanese naval arsenals. And with time, Japan became able to build even principal ships. Privately-owned shipyards also gradually improved their ability to construct steel-hulled ships through importing machinery and equipment. These enterprises relied on importing steel materials and parts that could not be produced domestically. Sometimes they also procured designs from Britain.

In the textile industry, the government imported ten large-scale sets of spinning machinery equipped with 2,000 spindles from Britain. After installing and test running the equipment at state-owned mills in Aichi, the government sold these concerns off to the private sector as ten equipped cotton mills. Engineers and skilled workers from the Ministry of Agriculture and Commerce assisted

Table 5.4 Machinery imports in the Meiji period (unit: 1,000 yen)

	1878–1882	*1883–1887*	*1888–1892*	*1893–1897*	*1898–1902*	*1903–1907*	*1908–1912*
Telegraphic & telephone equipment	11.8	19.3	35.8	43.1	65.1	113.5	78.0
Railway carriages	–	29.0	355.8	518.5	1,045.6	1,771.7	2,336.0
Locomotives	–	72.2	408.2	1,505.4	1,963.5	1,705.8	1,156.8
Steamships	81.9	718.5	841.7	4,744.5	3,562.2	4,692.1	2,215.6
Steam engines	–	81.7	329.1	586.2	759.8	1,208.8	797.2
Internal combustion engines	–	–	–	–	102.5	262.2	873.9
Dynamos & electric motors	–	–	–	–	322.6	1,546.0	2,275.4
Machine tools	–	3.0	4.5	106.1	649.1	2,404.2	2,687.9
Spinning machines	–	71.9	784.5	3,012.1	1,330.3	1,840.8	3,608.0
Looms	–	25.6	99.0	206.1	199.8	391.5	1,060.8
TOTAL	1219.2	12,066.4	5,755.0	16,427.7	19,145.1	30,354.8	37,381.6

Source: *Nihon Boeki Seiran* (Japanese Statistics of International Trade), Toyo Keizai Shimposha (1935).

Note: Import of steam engines for 1883–1887 does not include the value for 1883.

commercialization of these factories. Meanwhile, graduates of the Institute of Technology, employed as master engineers, built and managed Owaribo and Miebo, the two dominant mills of that early period. In the next phase of development, the large-scale private cotton mills of Osakabo, Amagasakibo, and Kanebo were built. For this, university-educated engineers designed the factory plans and imported the spinning machinery, and travelled to Britain to purchase machinery and acquire the necessary practical skills and technology.

As these examples show, technology transfer from the middle of the Meiji period onwards occurred mainly through importing machinery or the transfer of know-how that accompanied imported products. As Table 5.4 shows, the value of machinery imported for communications, transport, and automotive industries as well as for equipping factories increased significantly throughout the Meiji period. It may be added that imported machinery entered Japan with a uniform low tariff of 5 percent which was imposed by the "unequal" commercial treaties with the West until Japan regained tariff rights in 1910.

Along with machinery imports, domestic production of machinery had also emerged. Not surprisingly, the design and quality of Japanese machinery in the Meiji period were less sophisticated than those of the West. Moreover, in design, nearly all of the machinery manufactured in Japan was copied from imports. Such copy production, which accompanied increased machinery imports, was the means by which Japanese producers—gradually, arduously, and through trial-and-error—acquired technology that could serve as the basis for commercially viable domestic production.

The early days of electric equipment production provide an example of such trial-and-error. Tokyo Light Company, a buyer of imported electrical machinery, tried to support the domestic production of dynamos and light bulbs which it was procuring. The company's Senju Power Plant purchased dynamos from Ishikawajima Shipyard that were designed and copy produced from a catalogue under an instruction of a certain professor, but the heat they generated distorted their shape. Similarly, Miyoshi Electric Machine, a pioneer firm in electrical machinery, supplied dynamos to Kobe Light Company and tram motors to the Municipality of Kyoto. In both instances the products were returned as defective. Through such experiences, Japanese industries learned that they could not rely on amateurish copy production of domestic machine manufacturers. Thus, imports of machinery that embodied latest Western technology continued to increase, and technology they contained had to be learned more systematically and analytically through repeated copy production before Japan could finally absorb and internalize it.

It is also important to underline the role of the importer who mediated technology transfer during the Meiji period. There were two kinds of importers: foreign traders which acted as agents for foreign machinery manufacturers and domestic general trading companies such as Mitsui, Takada, and Okura. These trading companies were not only middlemen but also providers of information and technical services to domestic producers. A large number of graduating engineers from technical institutions were employed by private trading companies. For example, in 1910, Mitsui recruited 42 young engineers, Takada recruited 36, and Okura recruited 12. Many of these engineers either were assigned in Europe and the US or traveled there frequently on business. These engineers interacted with manufacturers in the West to keep abreast of new trends, circulated manufacturer catalogues at home, and assisted Japanese companies by helping to draw up business plans and selecting and installing mechanical equipment.

In the 1890s, when spinning mills were established in large numbers in Japan, Mitsui, as the Japanese agent for Britain's Platt Bros & Co., provided most of the equipment. In the case of electrical machinery, Bagnal Hills, an American trading company, was the agent in Japan for General Electric, and Britain's Healing & Co. represented British manufacturers. Okura was the agent for Allgemeine Elektricitäts-Gesellschaft (AEG) and Takada was the agent for Westinghouse. Siemens had its own branch office in Tokyo. Mitsui competed with the other agents over electrical equipment sales to the Japanese market and eventually became an agent for procurement of Shibaura Seisakusho (Shibaura Engineering Works). Japanese trading companies also facilitated the building of new hydroelectric power plants all over the country at the end of the Meiji period. Agents actively provided domestic entrepreneurs with basic knowledge needed for the electricity generation business, helped choose locations, and set up imported machinery and equipment.

From the 1900s, technical cooperation agreements offered a new model for the transfer of relatively new technology between large foreign firms of various nationalities. In some cases, such as Japan Steel Works, Nippon Electric Company (NEC), Tokyo Electric, and Shibaura Engineering Works, these contracts were accompanied by the establishment of joint-stock companies between Japanese owners and the foreign firm.

Let us first look at the case of steam turbine technology. The steam turbine was a new technology invented in Britain in 1884 by Charles Parsons. Within a decade, this technology had become the basis for ship engines and thermal power plants throughout the West. Navy yards and private shipyards in Japan were producing their own reciprocating steam engines and boilers. However, in 1905 the Japanese navy learned that the British navy planned to adopt steam turbines in their principal ships for increased speed. This news prompted the Japanese navy to import Curtis turbines from the US and install them on the *Ibuki* and *Aki*, battleships that were under construction at the time. Furthermore, the navy acquired the patent for turbine technology from Curtis and encouraged Mitsubishi Shipyard to acquire the Japanese patent for Parson's turbines. Thereafter, Mitsubishi and the Japanese navy began their own turbine production for future ships while continuing to import turbines for ships under construction. This was a complex way of technology transfer combining learning from imported products, the rights to patent execution, and copy production.

Steelmaking is an area in which the Ministry of Industry had difficulties in transferring technology to Japan during the 1870s and 1880s. State-owned steel works at the Kamaishi Iron Mines with the assistance of hired foreign engineers, which was later privatized, did produce pig iron and steel but the quality was not up to the standards in shipbuilding, arms manufacture, railways, and civil engineering projects. By that time, technology in the US and Germany had improved greatly; open-hearth furnaces and basic oxygen furnace led to the construction of large-scale mills integrating ironmaking, steelmaking, and rolling processes. Under the circumstances, strong petitioning from the Japanese military led the government to import a complete set of integrated steel mill. In 1901, the state-owned Yawata Ironworks, with technology from Germany's Gutehoffnungshütte, opened for business. This transfer of technology was a turnkey contract which consisted of confidential mill design, imported machinery and equipment, and the provision of German engineers and skilled workers. However, unlike the turnkey projects in the early Meiji period, metallurgy engineers were Japanese. Moreover, the Japanese side chose the factory location and the type of technology to be adopted, and made the decision to procure raw materials from China. When initial operations using the German technology failed, it was Japanese engineers who adjusted the technology to local conditions and allowed the mill to operate successfully.

The creation in 1907 of Japan Steel Works, a joint-stock company owned by Mitsui and two British companies, Armstrong and Vickers, also originated from a request by the Japanese military for domestic production of armor plating and large-caliber guns for its lead ships. In this case, equipment and know-how were entirely British, but the Japanese engineers and skilled workers, who came mostly from naval munitions factories, quickly learned and assimilated the technology transferred.

With regard to electrical machinery, the following historical circumstances led to the establishment of joint ventures with American firms. On the Japanese side, the revision of commercial treaties with the West around 1900, based on the principle of equal treatment between domestic and foreign nationals, for the first time permitted foreign direct investment in Japan. Furthermore, as the modified Japanese law upheld the patent rights of foreigners, Japanese manufacturers were no longer allowed to copy-produce the latest imported goods for free. On the American side, major electrical machinery manufacturers that had invested in technological development adopted a corporate strategy of manufacturing new products in overseas subsidiaries.

In 1896 the Japanese government had decided to adopt the American Telephone & Telegraph (AT&T) system under its First National Plan to Expand Telephony. As the government intended to produce telephone equipment domestically, Western Electric, which was the manufacturing department of AT&T, first tried to form a joint venture in Japan by acquiring the stock of Oki Electric Industry. However, negotiations with Oki Electric failed, which prompted Western Electric to establish Nippon Electric Company (NEC) in 1899, which became the first subsidiary of a foreign firm in Japan, by holding 54 percent of the shares. Western Electric and NEC were bound by a technical cooperation agreement that gave NEC the right of sole agency in Japan and a monopoly on the patent re-execution rights in the future. Western Electric offered technical guidance to NEC, for which the latter paid roughly 2 percent of its sales revenue. NEC initially sold imported telephones, then built a manufacturing plant with imported designs and equipment from Western Electric and produced telephones by using materials and processes satisfying international standards under the supervision of an American foreman. All internal documents were written in English. Thus, the products and production methods of NEC were identical to those in the United States.

In 1905 General Electric (GE), another American electrical machinery company, concluded a technical cooperation agreement with Tokyo Electric that was similar to the one between Western Electric and NEC, with GE acquiring 51 percent of Tokyo Electric's shares. The latter had evolved from Hakunetsusha, a light-bulb manufacturer established in 1890. As the company was unable to establish a viable production technology or compete with imported light bulbs from Germany in terms of quality or price, it sought management assistance from GE, a world leader of that industry in scale and technology. GE's policy to allow its subsidiaries to produce light bulbs under their own patents was another reason why Tokyo Electric selected GE as a business partner. Equipment and materials were imported from GE, and GE engineers came to Japan to teach manufacturing methods. Under the agreement, Tokyo Electric engineers were well placed and quite able to quickly master any new technology developed by GE. Unlike NEC which was newly founded, Tokyo Electric was an existing company acquired by GE as an overseas factory. But the method of technology transfer of the two cases was basically the same.

Business collaboration between GE and Shibaura Engineering Works in 1907 was different from the above two cases and was more incremental and partial. GE acquired only 24 percent of Shibaura's shares while the remainder was held by Mitsui & Co. Technical assistance was conducted through patent-licensing agreements supplemented by sharing of R&D results, exchange of engineers, and access to the blueprints for production equipment. In return, Shibaura paid royalties amounting to 1 percent of its sales revenue. Mitsui opted for this technical cooperation in order to catch up with rapid technological advances abroad under the constraint of the Universal Patent Convention that now protected the patents of foreign manufacturers in Japan. Through this business collaboration, Shibaura was able to design heavy electrical equipment by executing its rights on the GE patent and obtain new technical information through the exchange of engineers. But this did not introduce discontinuous and revolutionary technology to Shibaura unlike the cases of NEC and Tokyo Electric. GE's technology was added to the existing technology of Shibaura without fundamentally changing the character of the latter. Large-size dynamos continued to be imported from GE which competed with the Shibaura products. This was a case of a patent-licensing agreement supplemented by a purchase contract of machinery and know-how.

The ten cases described above were examples of how the latest Western technology was introduced to Japan in the late Meiji period. Whether technical cooperation agreements were accompanied by an acquisition of shares by foreigners depended largely on the corporate strategy of the foreign company. Some transfers of technology were selective and partial while others were guided by foreigners in every aspect of the project. In this sense, the latter may look like a repetition of wholesale purchase of Western technology practiced in the early Meiji period, but there were important differences. First, at the end of the Meiji period, Japan imported frontline technologies which were simultaneously developed and adopted in the West rather than buying common and mature technologies as a latecomer country as in the early Meiji period. Second, the existence of domestic engineers and skilled workers meant that Japan was now able to take a significant lead in selecting, adjusting, and internalizing imported technologies instead of remaining a passive student. Excellence of Japanese workers was one of the reasons why Tokyo Electric was chosen by GE as a business partner. As mentioned earlier, Japanese engineers at Yawata Ironworks were competent enough to adapt German technology to local conditions. When the first steam turbine was developed in Britain, Japanese engineers were quick to comprehend its potential from publicly available information. Based on the reported test results, they could select the most appropriate foreign partner and the appropriate timing to acquire this technology for application to the construction of naval ships.

5.6 Concluding remarks

This chapter is longer than others because it has explained not only how Meiji Japan digested Western industrial technology from the mid-nineteenth century to the early twentieth century but also why that was possible. The historical perspective given in sections 5.2 and 5.3 and the political perspective provided by section 5.4 were the necessary background for understanding why Japanese engineers, workers, and policymakers were so able, devoted, and unified in learning and assimilating foreign technology and systems. On the surface, we can conclude that the private sector of Japan, which was already highly dynamic and flexible, was assisted by mostly appropriate policies of the government to produce a miraculous transformation of a agriculture-based feudal society into a modern industrialized economy within a space of half century. The use of foreign experts, turnkey projects, engineering education, machinery import, and foreign partnership were highlighted as principal methods for this feat together with concrete examples. But the methods themselves were nothing novel; they were and are adopted by many other latecomer countries. The true wonder of Meiji Japan was the existence of a thick layer of human capital that could mobilize these methods effectively to a successful completion.

This naturally leads to a deeper question: can a developing country that lacks the historical and political conditions of Meiji Japan accomplish similar feat in industrialization and modernization? What if short-terminism, dependency culture, and social division ruled instead of high aspiration, penchant for learning, and patriotic dedication? This issue is largely beyond the scope of this book. The only thing that can safely be said is that there should be more than one path to development in response to different initial conditions of each society as well as shifting global situations. The idea that industrialization will take place only under certain rigid historical conditions and nowhere else is hardly credible. There is no need for today's developing countries to imitate Meiji Japan, but laissez-faire policy will not solve the problem of unprepared society, either. To identify—and modify—the unique domestic conditions that hinder the development of any latecomer country would require more serious analysis and harder policy learning than commonly practiced today.

6 Singapore

National productivity movement

6.1 Obsessed with productivity

Singapore is a city-state on an island situated near the equator with the population of five million including both permanent residents and non-residents. Its ethnic composition is dominated by Chinese (74 percent) followed by Malay (13 percent) and Indians and others (13 percent). It was a former British colony which was subsequently occupied by the Japanese military during 1942–45. After World War II, Singapore reverted to British rule with increasing self-autonomy. In 1963, Singapore merged with the Federation of Malaya to form Malaysia. However, this merger proved unsuccessful leading to social unrest and political division between the two parts of the federation. In August 1965, Singapore separated from Malaysia and became an independent republic (Lee, 2000). Ever since, the People's Action Party has ruled Singapore without interruption. Meanwhile, as far as policy capability is concerned, the government of Singapore is reputed to be among the most able governments in the world. The state machinery is staffed with highly competent bureaucrats producing complex policies which normally fail dismally in other countries. This "wise" government regulates all aspects of civil life, including how to walk the streets and who should get married and produce children, which to some people is too intrusive.

Singapore has been extremely successful in economic development. After the turmoil of the 1965 separation and independence was overcome, the immediate economic challenge was a severe shortage of jobs and housing. Singapore embarked on a modernization program featuring labor-intensive manufacturing, public-housing projects, and heavy state investment and involvement in education and training. With no natural resources and without farmland, the only resource this small city-state could rely on other than its strategic location was human capital. The government has consistently emphasized human-resource development and made serious efforts to enhance labor productivity and international competitiveness. Since independence, the Singaporean economy has grown on average about 9 percent per year. Its per capita income rose from US$533 in 1965 to US$40,920 in 2010 (World Bank GNI data). Industrial structure shifted steadily from labor-intensive in the 1960s to skills-intensive in the 1970s, technology-intensive in the 1980s, innovation-intensive in the 1990s, and to knowledge-intensive in the 2000s (Chan, 2008). The country has grown from its traditional role as a regional port and distribution center to an international manufacturing and knowledge-intensive technical services center (Lee et al., 2008). Today Singapore is the most business-friendly country (World Bank and IFC, 2010), among the top three most competitive countries (World Economic Forum 2010), and one of the most prosperous economies in the world. This affluence is generated by skills, knowledge, and technology of Singaporean people rather than a lucky endowment of extractive resources or geopolitical advantages.

Singapore's obsession with productivity dates back to the early days of independence, or even before. The first step toward this was the creation of the Productivity Unit within the Economic Development Board, an implementation agency of state-led development, in 1964 and declaration of the Charter for Industrial Progress in 1965. The latter was a joint agreement by employer groups and labor unions to work together to increase productivity under the Productivity Code of Practice, which was witnessed by the Ministers for Finance and for Labor. The Charter also proposed establishment of the Singapore Productivity Center. In 1972, the Center was upgraded to the National Productivity Board, a state agency. Separately, the Singapore Productivity Association was set up in 1973 as an affiliated body of the Board for promoting active involvement of companies and individuals in the productivity movement and spreading related ideas and techniques among them. The quest for productivity went into a high gear in the 1980s when a new national productivity movement was launched by the strong leadership of Prime Minister Lee Kuan Yew accompanied by Japanese support (section 6.3). After a few years of adjustments and mutual learning,[1] Singapore and Japan cooperated successfully to internalize, scale up, and institutionalize the productivity movement in Singapore, contributing significantly to its economic miracle. By the 1990s Singapore mastered productivity concepts and techniques so well it started to teach other countries.

Singapore presents a case of a state-led national productivity movement unlike Japan's in the 1950s and 1960s where the private sector-led kaizen movement was the central force in improving industrial productivity with public policy playing second fiddle. Singapore's top-down productivity enhancement, discussed in detail below, had the following features that contributed to its success. First, it was pursued as a broad-based national movement for mindset change rather than a one-time event or project. Second, there was an unwavering high-level political commitment by Prime Minister Lee Kuan Yew. Third, institutionally, a national productivity organization was set up as a core agency charged with productivity issues whose authority and functions were adjusted over time to respond to changing needs and private-sector situations. Political mechanisms were also there to embrace government, industry, and labor unions in tripartite cooperation. Fourth, a massive campaign was organized to first raise awareness and then promote concrete actions. Fifth, private-sector management consultants were produced by mobilizing those trained under Japanese assistance, giving them proper institutional design and incentives.

In Singapore, the productivity movement has always been supported by mutual commitment and active participation of government, employers, and labor which comprise the holy trinity of economic development in this nation.[2] All industries and public organizations regardless of size are strongly encouraged to cooperate for the national goal. According to the National Productivity Board, the goal of the productivity movement was to improve national welfare through economic progress based on the following three guiding principles: (i) improvements in productivity would increase employment in the long run; (ii) government, employers, and labor must work together to implement measures to improve productivity; and (iii) fruits of improved productivity must be distributed fairly among management, labor, and consumers. It should be added that these guiding principles were drawn from those of the Japan Productivity Center in 1955 at the time of its establishment.

6.2 Policymaking in Singapore

The Singaporean government is staffed with young, casual, and clean officials who compete fiercely for excellence and rotate frequently across functions and sections. Policy formulation is flexible with good inter-ministerial coordination. Singapore does not produce national development plans at regular intervals (there was only one Five-Year Development Plan in the 1960s which was discontinued subsequently). Structured planning at regular intervals is too rigid and slow for Singaporean leaders and officials. Instead, they do long-term vision formation and strategic planning through ad hoc or task-based committees and councils such as the Economic Strategies Committee and the National Productivity and Continuing Education Council which will be discussed in detail in section 6.6, and scenario planning by "Future Divisions" as explained below. Being an open city-state, Singapore considers it vital to maintain agility in policymaking to respond quickly to changing global environment. Flexible strategic planning is possible thanks to high institutional capacity of civil servants who can translate leaders' visions and policies into actions. The small size of Singapore and its unique politics in the absence of rural and farming interests may also facilitate information sharing and consensus building among stakeholders without political capture or serious conflicts of interest.

The policy process in Singapore is characterized by a multi-functional approach involving all relevant government ministries and agencies in close collaboration. Regarding industrial policy, the Singaporean government takes both broad-based and targeted (sectoral) approaches. General supports available to all industries and enterprises are supplemented by negotiations and promotion for individual sectors or even specific firms. The government offers various incentives and subsidies to encourage enterprises and individuals to improve and compete better through (policy-guided) price signals rather than through quantitative bans, quotas, or legal regulations. Two examples are given below to illustrate Singapore's unique policymaking.

The first example is establishment of Future Divisions in key government organs such as the Prime Minister's Office, the Ministry of Finance, and the Ministry of Trade and Industry. The Future Division (or a similar team of officials with a different name) is a unit detached from daily administrative works of the ministry to conduct long-term scenario planning from national and global perspectives and analyze chances and risks that may affect Singapore's future. Exercises and reports it produces go to ministers and national leaders as inputs to setting broad policy directions and determining Singapore's future positioning. Future Divisions work closely with research institutes, universities, and other stakeholders to collect information and facilitate vision-sharing. In some countries national vision is produced by a top leader and his personal advisors. In others vision making is outsourced to research institutes or special committees of experts and business leaders. In Singapore, production of visions is institutionalized within the government. While external advice is sought, at least some government officials are not burdened by daily works and have time to think about the nation's future. My team once visited the Center for Strategic Futures in the Strategic Policy Office of the Prime Minister's Office. Although our visit was without appointment, 15 minutes before the lunch break, and just suggested by other officials we met in the same building, the head and an economist of the Center were more than happy to receive us, exchange business cards, and explain what their Center did succinctly in the staff tea room before adjourning for lunch. In many other countries it would require a formal letter of request and a long wait to meet officials engaged in strategic planning. Bureaucratic formalism is not a problem with the Singaporean government.

Another example is Singapore's strategic FDI policy which shows how the country combines general promotion and targeted attraction. For industrial development, the Industry Division of the Ministry of Trade and Industry is responsible for policy formulation while the Economic Development Board is in charge of implementation. The two work closely to attract FDI, foster "industry verticals" (suppliers of parts and components), and enhance business environment. The Economic Development Board, despite its solemn name, is a business-friendly one-stop agency for domestic and foreign investors. It is also designated as the hub of industrial development in transport engineering, electronics, precision engineering, chemicals, biomedical sciences, logistics, healthcare services, education services, infocomm and media, professional services, and consumer businesses as well as new areas of growth such as clean energy, environmental technologies, bio-technology, and digital media. In attracting FDI in these priority sectors, the Economic Development Board uses both broad-based approaches and targeted approaches. It continuously improves business environment generally, which is always at or near the top of global ranking. For instance, Singapore has consistently held the first position among more than 180 countries in the World Bank's Doing Business Reports from 2007 to 2011. At the same time, the Board also engages in individual negotiations with foreign companies in priority sectors to offer company-specific support and incentives in what is called the "Queen Bee" approach. It is an approach in which inviting the queen bee (an anchor firm with global reputation and large-scale production) automatically brings a large number of other bees into the country. A good example is the attraction of world-class aerospace firms such as Rolls-Royce, Pratt & Whitney, and ST Aerospace to Seletar Aerospace Park, an industrial estate with an area of over 300 hectares which was converted for this purpose from a secondary airport, prompting arrival of related maintenance and repair services.[3]

6.3 Productivity Movement of the 1980s[4]

6.3.1 The beginning

By the late 1970s, there were signs of strain in the Singaporean labor market. An increasingly tight labor market had driven up wages. The state of management–labor relations was fragile and often confrontational, leading to many industrial disputes. Companies realized that, to compete successfully, they must introduce better management systems with more favorable management–labor relations and better teamwork. Despite one and a half decades of effort to enhance productivity since independence, the leaders of Singapore felt that the country remained far behind the rival countries in productivity development. "Workers here are not as proud of or as skilled in their jobs compared to the Japanese or the Germans" were the words of Prime Minister Lee Kuan Yew in his speech delivered in 1979.

Foreign manufacturing companies operating in Singapore served as benchmarks for assessing Singapore's productivity level. In early 1981, the prime minister met Japanese company executives in Singapore to discuss practices, work attitudes, and productivity in Japan. Additionally, the Committee of Productivity was formed to study Japan's productivity movement and examine related issues. Prime Minister Lee met Mr. Kohei Goshi, chairman of the Japan Productivity Center, in June 1981 and was deeply convinced of the need for a new national productivity movement. The Committee of Productivity issued a report which emphasized the importance of "human aspects" and mindset change, and proposed the establishment of a high-level council to review productivity effort and outline future strategy.

The National Productivity Council was established in September 1981 as an oversight and policy coordination body for productivity enhancement. The Council was chaired by the State Minister of Labor (from 1986, by the State Minister of Trade and Industry) with high-level representation from government, employer groups, labor unions, and academia. The first action of the Council was to officially launch the Productivity Movement designating the National Productivity Board, established earlier in 1972, as the primary implementing agency. As the new movement is launched, this Board was re-structured and expanded to inculcate the concept of productivity in every man, woman, and child in Singapore (National Productivity Board 1987).

In parallel, the Singaporean government requested technical cooperation from the Japanese government. The Productivity Development Project, a program supported by the Japan International Cooperation Agency (JICA) mobilizing a large number of Japanese experts, was implemented from 1983 to 1990 in support of this nationally owned movement.

6.3.2 The awareness stage, 1981–85

The Productivity Movement initiated in the 1980s went through three stages as shown in Figure 6.1: (i) awareness stage (1981–85); (ii) action stage (1986–88); and (iii) ownership stage (1989–90s).

The awareness stage worked on the mindset of managers and workers to create widespread consciousness of the importance of productivity. The main objectives included promotion of positive attitudes, teamwork spirit, and recognition for excellent companies and individuals. Actions taken by the National Productivity Board were as follows.

- (i) public education—launching of the Productivity Movement, publication of productivity data, media support, amendments in the curriculums of educational institutions, etc.;
- (ii) information dissemination and training—courses that emphasize human relations, a library of local case studies on good management practices, a registry of courses on productivity and management, etc.;
- (iii) company-level incentives—payment of variable bonuses, awards for long-serving employees, house unions, privileged use of support facilities for employees of good companies, etc.;

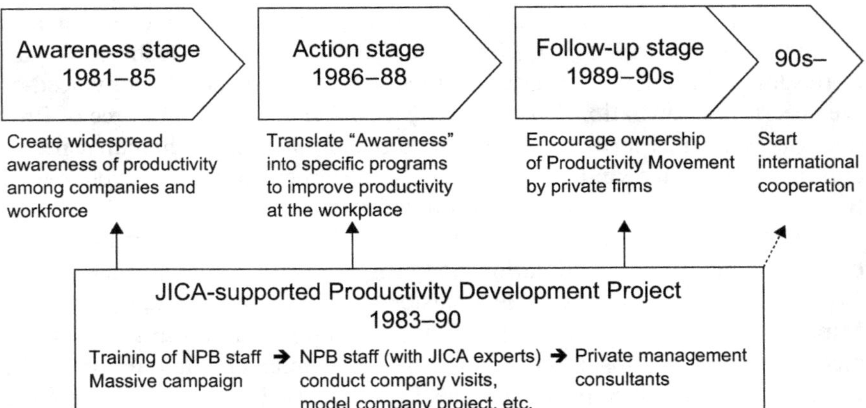

Figure 6.1 Evolution of Singapore's productivity movement

Note: JICA is the Japan International Cooperation Agency; NPB is the National Productivity Board.

(iv) promotion of management–labor consultation—work excellence committees, quality control circles, etc.;
(v) public-sector improvements—productivity campaign in the public sector, work-improvement teams, Productivity Working Committee, etc.

Throughout the awareness—and subsequent action—stages, strong commitment and leadership of Prime Minister Lee Kuan Yew was critical. Productivity campaigns were launched at both national and company levels. November was designated as "Productivity Month," as in Japan, in which Lee Kuan Yew delivered a speech on productivity every year from 1981 to 1987.

To disseminate the spirit of productivity to the public, the National Productivity Board created a mascot named Teamy, which was a cute bee character. Teamy Bee symbolized hard work, teamwork, and efficiency. Slogans and posters were created in 1982 around the key message of "Together We Work Better." This message had clear political connotations. Productivity improvement often invites worker resistance because employees fear that efficiency might be pursued through shedding labor and cutting wages. Mindful of such resistance, the official message deliberately highlighted a virtuous cycle formed by productivity-generated growth leading to more income and demand for products, which in turn increased employment and benefited all workers.

Unlike Japan where the productivity drive was driven by and confined to the business community, Singapore introduced the Productivity Movement to both the business and the public sector. This had a remarkable impact on popular mindset. As noted above, work-improvement teams were implemented in the civil service. They were a Singaporean adaptation of the concept of Japanese-style quality control circle (QCC) implemented in the public sector as part of the civil service reform program. Worker involvement, participation, and bottom-up management were emphasized, and team members worked together to solve problems in their common work areas. The Productivity Working Committee was established jointly by management and labor. By the mid-1980s, high awareness of productivity among the Singaporeans was achieved until even taxi drivers started to talk about productivity.

6.3.3 The action stage, 1986–88

In the next stage, the focus shifted from national promotion of the idea of productivity to company-level implementation on the ground. The objective of this stage was to translate "awareness" into specific action at the workplace through a participatory program. It aimed at upgrading the skills of management and workers as well as operational efficiency of companies. In 1986, the concept of total approach to productivity (TAP), which emphasized productive interaction of humans, machines, and systems at the workplace, was introduced (National Productivity Board and JICA, 1990).

In 1986, the National Productivity Board established the Management Guidance Center to provide management consultancy programs for local companies. Programs and activities implemented by the Center were as follows:

(i) the model company project;
(ii) the management consultancy referral scheme;
(iii) the associate consultants scheme;
(iv) the industry-based consultancy assistance scheme;
(v) training of workforce through the Skills Development Fund.

The model company project was implemented jointly by Japanese experts and local counterparts at the National Productivity Board, providing assistance to companies for productivity improvement. Observing the concrete work of Japanese experts in factories in effect served as on-the-job training of Board staff for acquiring relevant consultation skills. Together with training sessions, workshops, and other company-related productivity improvement programs, Japanese experts transferred consultation skills to local counterparts under the JICA's Productivity Development Project (see below). The management-consultancy referral scheme and the associate consultants scheme were the systems to mobilize those trained under Japanese cooperation as qualified private management consultants. The National Productivity Board allowed private-sector participation in the training fellowship in Japan, and such private trainees became National Productivity Board associate or referral consultants. A pool of over 200 associate and referral consultants was produced to supplement the Board officials' effort in reaching out to industries (National Productivity Board and JICA, 1990). Furthermore, the Board introduced the industry-based assistance scheme in 1986. The scheme was designed to raise productivity in priority sectors and assist companies on an industry-wide basis for visible impact on national economic development. Food manufacturing, restaurant, hotel, retail, textiles and garment, and finance were the six priority sectors targeted for assistance under the scheme.

Through the Management Guidance Center, the National Productivity Board assisted companies, especially small and medium ones, in improving their business efficiency and productivity management. Successful companies were selected to serve as models for others. The Board also promoted the growth of management consultancy services for SMEs. More than 100 local companies have benefited from assistance rendered by Board consultants and Japanese experts, as well as associate and referral consultants (National Productivity Board and JICA, 1990).

Besides consultancy, in-company training was given to equip the workforce with relevant skills to increase productivity. The National Productivity Board teamed up with reputable companies such as Singapore Airlines (Service Quality Center), Philips Singapore (Industrial Engineering Training Center), and Seiko Instruments (OJT Project) to develop national training programs in specific areas for managers and workers.

Moreover, extensive training for upgrading workforce skills was conducted with the support of the Skills Development Fund. The Skills Development Fund was founded in 1978 under the Ministry of Labor as an employer-based funding that provided financial incentives for staff training. From 1986 it came under the responsibility of the National Productivity Board. In Singapore, all employers must pay a Skills Development Levy for each worker they employ for up to the first S$4,500 of gross monthly remuneration at a levy rate of 0.25 percent, or S$2 per worker, whichever is higher. The government then provides subsidies to employers who invest in upgrading the skills of their employees. Currently, employers can receive course fee subsidies of up to 90 percent with the amount of subsidies varying with each course. The Central Provident Fund, rather than the National Productivity Board, now collects the levy on behalf of the Workforce Development Agency which is subsequently channeled into the Skills Development Fund.

6.3.4 The ownership stage, 1989–90s

By 1989, many companies and individuals had become actively involved in the Productivity Movement. Hence, keeping up this enthusiasm became the focus of the ownership stage. This was critical to internalize the Productivity Movement as a permanent and integrated feature of the Singaporean work ethic rather than a one-time event orchestrated by the government. Private and public organizations as well as individuals were encouraged to actively lead the Productivity Movement instead of passively following it. The National Productivity Board urged the private sector to take initiative and own annual productivity campaigns. Employer groups were asked to chair the Campaign Steering Committee. The Singapore Quality Award was introduced in 1994 and the Productivity Activist Scheme was launched in 1996. The latter scheme in particular aimed to develop productivity champions among company staff. Key activists from the public and private sectors were selected to lead, organize, and influence other members of the workforce in various productivity-enhancing activities. A network was formed to enable members to benchmark their productivity against partners and improve their skills and techniques. Resources were pooled for an effective exchange of information in support of productivity improvement.

These activities certainly had the aspect of "spontaneity imposed from above," but they apparently worked superbly in Singapore, judged from continued high growth and emergence of a new service industry that teaches productivity to other countries. A top-down movement eventually became a part of Singaporean culture accepted by all stakeholders. In this regard, the following words of Mah Bow Tan, former chairman of the National Productivity Board, in 1981, are noteworthy: "To have a successful Productivity Movement, we must have a critical mass of organizations and individuals who know that they will benefit from it, are proud to be part of it, and are willing and ready to make it succeed."

6.4 The institutional framework

To implement the Productivity Movement, Singapore established a strong organizational structure. As already noted, political alliance was forged among the public sector, labor unions, and employers to ensure that productivity gains were shared among all Singaporeans without creating winners and losers. A centralized oversight and coordination mechanism was created, and the existing national productivity organization was reinforced to implement public campaigns, training, consulting, research, measurement, and industrial relations. These institutional factors contributed significantly to the successful awareness raising and scaling-up of the Productivity Movement.

6.4.1 The core organizations

As noted earlier, the core productivity organization has evolved with the stages of development and the shifting needs of the Singaporean economy (Table 6.1). In 1964, one year prior to independence, Singapore created a small unit specializing in productivity under the Economic Development Board. In 1967, the National Productivity Center was established, also under the Economic Development Board, by building on the existing unit. In 1972, the Center was upgraded to the National Productivity Board, a statutory body which, as discussed above, played a principal role in executing the Productivity Movement starting from 1981. In 1996, the National Productivity Board

Table 6.1 History of core organizations for productivity improvement

Period	*Core organization*	*Events*
1964–1967	Productivity Unit under Economic Development Board (EDB)	Charter for Industrial Progress, and Productivity Code of Practice (1965)
1967–1972	National Productivity Center, an autonomous division under EDB	Tripartite Interim Management Committee for preparing NPB (1971)
1972–1995	National Productivity Board (NPB), a statutory body initially affiliated with the Ministry of Labor and later with the Ministry of Trade and Industry (MTI)	Establishment of Singapore Productivity Association (1973) Productivity Movement: 1981–85: Awareness stage 1986–88: Action stage 1989–90s: Ownership stage
1996–2001	Productivity Standard Board, a statutory body affiliated with MTI	
2002–present	Standards, Productivity and Innovation Board (SPRING), a statutory body affiliated with MTI	Renewed productivity movement targeting aged and foreign workers (2010–)

Source: Japan Productivity Center (1990).

was merged with the Singapore Institute of Standards and Industrial Research to become the Productivity Standard Board. In 2002, productivity-related functions of this Board were transferred to the Standards, Productivity and Innovation Board (SPRING).

Figure 6.2 shows the institutional setup for policy coordination among key stakeholders and organizations in the Productivity Movement of the 1980s. Participation of policymakers, economic groups, professionals, and service providers facilitated the initiation and scaling-up of the movement. Because Singapore is a city-state, there was no need for a mechanism to coordinate central- and local-level decision making.

In 1981, the National Productivity Council was established as a high-level oversight and policy coordination body for the Productivity Movement. The Council had a tripartite composition, initially chaired by the State Minister of Labor and after 1986 by the State Minister of Trade and Industry with the participation of about 20 members from government, employer groups, labor unions, and academia. The National Productivity Council annually reviewed productivity programs and outlined future strategies, ensuring national consensus.

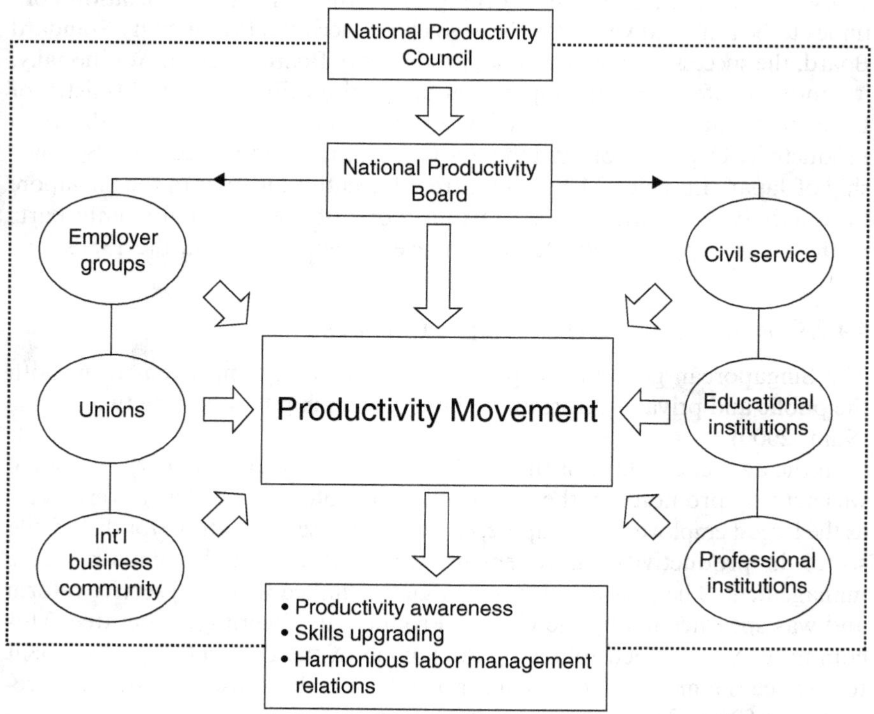

Figure 6.2 Stakeholders of the productivity movement, 1980s

Source: Information provided by Mr. Lo Hock Meng to the GRIPS Development Forum mission in September 2010.

The National Productivity Board was the secretariat of the National Productivity Council as well as the operational arm in spearheading productivity campaigns in both the public and private sectors throughout the three stages of the Productivity Movement. Under the oversight of the Council, the Board implemented and coordinated the activities of the Productivity Movement as explained above. The Board was also a service provider in such areas as training, management consultancy, promoting quality control (QC) circles, and disseminating the concept of productivity. Additionally, it administered the Skills Development Fund which provided financial incentives to companies that sent their staff to productivity-related training.

The Singapore Productivity Association, established in 1973 as an affiliated body of the National Productivity Board, also played an important role in broadening the Productivity Movement. It promoted active involvement of organizations and individuals in the Movement and expedited its diffusion and learning of productivity techniques. It still plays an important role in Singapore's current productivity drive as explained below. The Association charges fees to individual and institutional members for participation in courses, seminars, company visits, study tours, and so on, which are organized to enhance and update their knowledge and skills. The members also have access to information and networking opportunities. The Association continues to be affiliated with SPRING which replaced the Productivity Standard Board, the successor of the National Productivity Board, in 2002. Additionally, it conducts international cooperation in collaboration with the Ministry of Foreign Affairs, the Ministry of Trade and Industry, SPRING, the Asia Productivity Organization, and the Association for Overseas Technical Scholarship of Japan. Lo Hock Meng, the current Executive Director of the Singapore Productivity Association, was previously one of the principal counterparts of the JICA-supported Productivity Development Project in the 1980s.

6.4.2 Channels of awareness raising and scaling-up

The Singaporean government promoted productivity improvement in both the public and private sectors and built a partnership between the two sectors (Sum, 2000).

In the awareness stage of the 1980s movement, the productivity campaign was actively promoted in the public sector as noted above. The government, as the largest employer in Singapore, endeavored to set an example for the private sector in productivity improvement, work attitude, and human-resource management. The productivity campaign was linked with civil service reform and was spearheaded by the Central Productivity Steering Committee. This committee was formed following the launch of the Productivity Movement to oversee the movement in civil service. Its members also included a representative from civil service unions. An annual civil service campaign was launched in conjunction with the national productivity campaign. Work-improvement teams, which were small groups of civil servants of different ranks from the same work units, were formed in all ministries to make up plans to promote teamwork spirit and productivity. This "voluntary" groups met regularly to identify improvements that could be achieved and formulate ways to attain them (Sum, 2000).

Particularly noteworthy in this conjunction was the productivity drive launched by the Ministry of Defense and the Armed Forces in 1981. Since all young Singaporean males aged 18–21 were obligated to enroll in national service (which included the Singapore Armed Force, the Singapore Police Force, and the Singapore Civil Defense Force) for 24 months, this proved to be an excellent way of instilling the concept of productivity into the minds of young males.[5]

Regarding labor unions, the National Trade Union Congress led the productivity campaign and created the Productivity Promotion Council. The campaign aimed to inculcate productivity and quality consciousness in the workplace. Regarding employer groups, the Singapore National Employers' Federation and the Singapore Manufacturers' Federation backed the Productivity Movement. Both unions and employer groups supported workforce training with financial incentives from the aforementioned Skills Development Fund. Furthermore, productivity-related programs were promoted at many educational institutions, including polytechnics (see below), to raise productivity awareness in future workers.

6.4.3 Japanese assistance

The JICA-supported Productivity Development Project was a crucial part of the Productivity Movement. The project was fully integrated into Singapore's national initiative and contributed to (i) upgrading the skills of National Productivity Board officials; (ii) developing manuals and promotion materials; (iii) developing a pool of private-sector management consultants; and (iv) raising productivity in key industries. A total of over 200 long-term and short-term experts were dispatched from Japan to help improve the capabilities of the Board and local industries. Furthermore, the project also helped transform the National Productivity Board into an international cooperation organization by providing the Board with an opportunity to consolidate acquired management consulting skills and share them with other Southeast Asian countries through regional training programs.

Figure 6.3 shows the JICA-supported Productivity Development Project which emphasized training of trainers and upgrading of Board staff as two major pillars. Various methods were used including practical guidance, development of training materials, model company and pilot company projects, seminars and workshops, papers and reports, and training in Japan (PDP fellowship). The project emphasized human aspects, transfer of Japanese experience, and the importance of quality, cost, and delivery (QCD).

The Productivity Development Project continued for seven years with four phases: (i) preparatory phase, from June 1983 to March 1985; (ii)

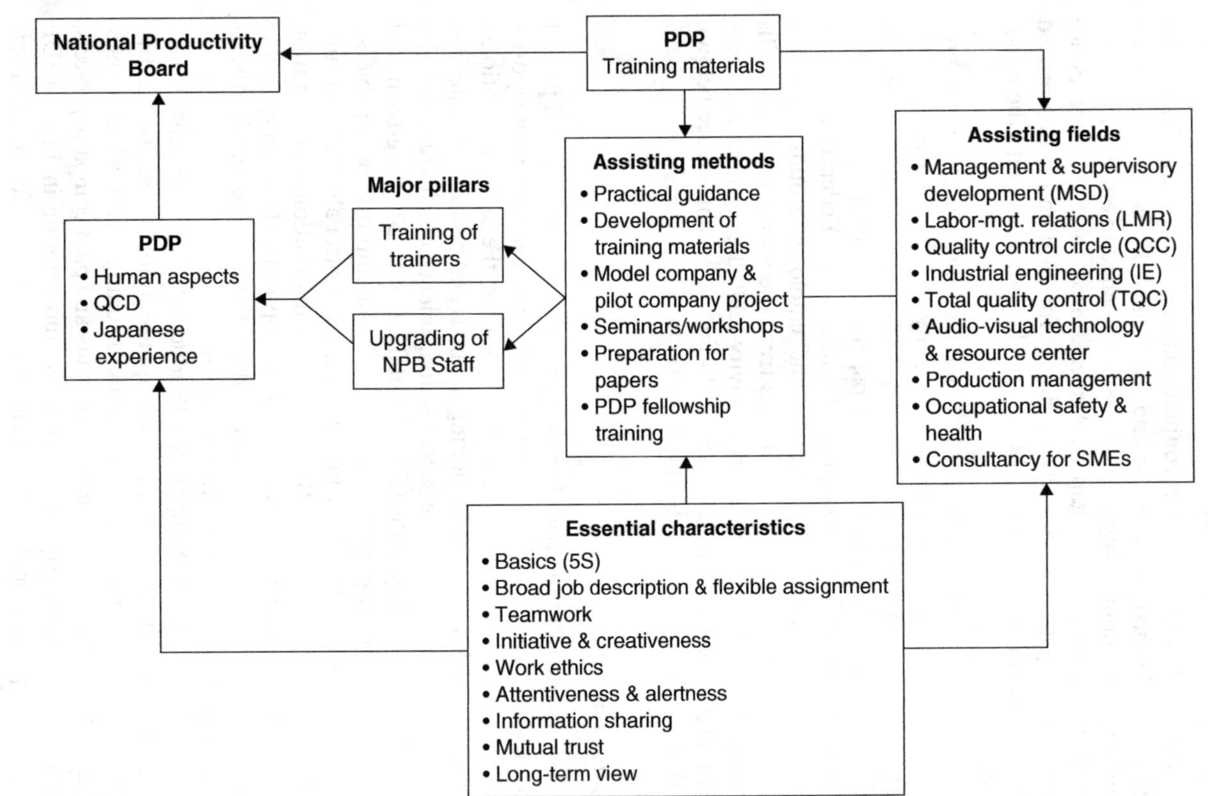

Figure 6.3 JICA-supported productivity development project (after restructuring).

Source: Japan Productivity Center (1990).

restructuring phase, from April 1985 to October 1986; (iii) implementing phase, from November 1986 to June 1988; and (iv) follow-up or consolidation phase, from June 1988 to June 1990 (National Productivity Board and JICA 1990).

Because this was the first experience for Japan to transfer comprehensive knowledge and technology of productivity enhancement to another country through a technical cooperation scheme, the initial years (preparatory phase) of the Productivity Development Project encountered some difficulties. Japanese experts, assuming that the same steps should be taken in Singapore as in Japan, started by instilling basic concepts and principles in their Singaporean counterparts. They believed that this step was necessary to form a solid mindset among students before teaching concrete methods of productivity improvement (Ueda, 2009). However, Singaporeans demanded quick and tangible results such as the transfer and application of production management techniques on the ground. This was partly because the management of the National Productivity Board was under strong pressure from the prime minister who personally monitored the progress of the project. Based on subsequent discussions between JICA and the Board, the modality of Japanese assistance was modified. In addition to classroom instructions, on-the-job training was provided so that the Singaporean counterparts could learn the works practiced by Japanese experts and take them over in the future (Ueda, 2009).

During the restructuring phase, a technology transfer plan was developed to build up expertise within the National Productivity Board to directly assist industries in improving productivity without the help of Japanese experts.

The implementation phase saw the dispatch of long-term JICA experts specializing in management consultancy for SMEs. This was in line with the Board's focus on providing management guidance services for local companies. During this phase, the experts' role shifted from that of leaders to advisors vis-à-vis the Board staff who by then were sufficiently equipped to lead industry project teams. Also, for the first time, Japan's fellowship program which provided training in Japan for government officials was extended to private sector managers and consultants. Upon their return, several of them were appointed as National Productivity Board associate consultants to supplement the expertise of the Board in providing consultancy services to industry.

The follow-up or consolidation phase, which lasted two years, was devoted to upgrading management consultancy skills of the Board staff through practical on-the-job training and the launching of a two-month Japan-Association of Southeast Asian Nations (ASEAN) Regional Training Program on Management Consultancy where the National Productivity Board took prime responsibility for sharing acquired skills with other ASEAN countries.[6] By the end of the Productivity Development Project, fundamental productivity practices such as 5S and QC circles were firmly entrenched in Singaporean manufacturing industries while attention was also given to service industries with Japanese experts providing advice on upgrading customer service.

6.5 International cooperation

Singapore was such a good student in productivity that, by the early 1990s, it felt confident enough to teach others what it had learned from Japan. In 1992, the government established the Singapore Technical Cooperation Program (SCP) to share the country's development experience and public-sector expertise with developing countries. SCP is administered by the Technical Cooperation Directorate of the Ministry of Foreign Affairs which is responsible for planning and organizing training courses, seminars, workshops, and study visits in collaboration with domestic agencies and foreign partners. In FY2009, about 300 such activities were organized, and the number of SCP participants reached a record 6,729. SCP is implemented in various channels including (i) bilateral training programs, (ii) joint training programs or third-country training programs, (iii) Initiatives for ASEAN Integration (IAI) Centers, and (iv) small island developing states technical cooperation programs.

Bilateral training programs in the areas where Singapore has strength are offered directly by Singapore to developing countries on a government-to-government basis. Examples of such training courses during FY2010 included the private-sector growth and FDI attraction course taught by Civil Service College, and technical and vocational education and training (TVET) programs for principals and instructors executed by ITE Education Services. In addition, JICA, together with the Singaporean Ministry of Foreign Affairs, in 1997 organized the Japan–Singapore Partnership Program for the Twenty-first Century (JSPP21) which conducted a joint training program on productivity management in the Southern African Development Community (SADC) countries in 1997–2004.

Apart from SCP, which offers assistance to developing countries free of charge, the Singapore Cooperation Enterprise (SCE) provides fee-based technical cooperation. SCE was formed jointly by the Ministry of Trade and Industry and the Ministry of Foreign Affairs in 2006 to respond to growing foreign demand for Singapore's development skills and knowledge. It mobilizes expertise accumulated in the country's public agencies as well as retired civil servants and politicians on a project basis. SCE does not receive financial support from the government and instead charges fees for technical cooperation on a cost-recovery, non-profit basis.

The Singaporean government sees complementarity between ODA-based SCP and commercially-oriented SCE and uses them strategically. On a government-to-government basis, SCP is used as an entry point to share Singapore's development experience with developing countries in general, which can lead to demand for more specific country-tailored cooperation projects conducted by SCE. SCE can work with both government and non-government clients in developing countries. A good example is the cooperation with Rwanda, a small landlocked country in Africa. President Kagame of Rwanda has a strong desire to learn from Singapore, an equally small and resource-poor country which, despite these handicaps, achieved impressive economic growth by building human capability. Cooperation started with SPC-managed bilateral training programs, which subsequently developed into various projects supported by SCE such as workforce development and public-sector capacity building and social security fund reform. At present, SCE has expanded its cooperation projects to China as well as the rest of Asia, Middle East, and Africa.

The Singapore Productivity Association also provided cooperation in productivity improvement to Botswana for about ten years from 1991 at the request of President Ketumile Masire of Botswana to then Singaporean Prime Minister Goh Chok Tong. Based on the experience of the JICA-supported Productivity Development Project, the Association assisted Botswana with (i) promotion of tripartite cooperation among government, labor, and industry, (ii) staff training for the Botswana National Productivity Center, and (iii) implementation of pilot projects for model companies. In the public sector, a twinning arrangement was made between the Botswana Institute of Administration and Commerce and Singapore's Civil Service Training Institute which introduced work improvement teams to Botswana's civil service (World Bank, 1996).

6.6 The renewed productivity movement

6.6.1 The report of the Economic Strategies Committee

Even though the JICA-supported Productivity Development Project was completed years ago with impressive results, Singapore continues to work on productivity. As Mah Bow Tan, the former Minister of State, Trade and Industry, and Communications and Information as well as the Chairman of the National Productivity Board, stated, "The Productivity Movement has been compared to a marathon with no finish line" (National Productivity Board and JICA 1990).[7] In recent years, productivity has been resurrected as a high-priority national agenda.

As Singapore came out of the global financial crisis triggered by the Lehman Shock which broke out in 2008, the government saw the need as well as an opportunity to restructure the Singaporean economy and maximize growth capability in the post-crisis era which was characterized by the emergence of new economic powers such as China and India. The government formed the high-level Economic Strategies Committee in May 2009, chaired by Finance Minister Tharman Shanmugaratnam, with 25 members coming from government, labor unions, and businesses. This committee was one of the many ad hoc mechanisms routinely used by the Singaporean government for solving specific problems. Under the committee, eight subcommittees co-chaired by representatives of the public and private sectors as well as several working groups were formed.

The Economic Strategies Committee submitted the final report to Prime Minister Lee Hsien Loong in January 2010. While the Singaporean economy grew by an average 5 percent per annum over the past decade, productivity gains have declined in recent years. According to the report, the country's productivity levels in manufacturing and services are only 55–65 percent of comparable sectors in Japan and the US. In the construction sector, the productivity level is only one-third and one-half of Japan and the US, respectively. This apparent inefficiency in a country renowned for well-educated people and excellent policies can be explained by the existence of low-skill foreign workers and the old generation of Singaporeans who received little education in their youth, both of whom bring down average productivity. In terms of sectors, low productivity is observed in construction, SMEs, and a number of services such as retails, restaurants, and tourism.

Over the past decade, Singapore has become increasingly dependent on foreign workers, including both highly skilled professionals and low-skill workers, which now account for about one-third (or one million) of the entire workforce. Low-skill foreign workers compete with relatively less educated Singaporeans in the job market. The report pointed to the need to manage (i.e., gradually reduce) the country's dependence on low-skill foreign labor and support continuous education and training of low-wage Singaporean workers. The report also emphasized the importance of productivity growth to sustain high wages and high living standards which Singaporeans have come to enjoy, and urged the government to encourage enterprise innovation, investment in technology, and training to create more high-paying jobs.

Envisioning "high-skilled people, innovative economy, distinctive global city," the report recommended a shift from factor-based growth to productivity-driven growth with the targeted annual productivity growth of 2–3 percent and GDP growth of 3–5 percent on average in the next ten years. It also presented seven key strategies to achieve this goal. The main thrust of the report was endorsed by the prime minister and reflected in the budgetary allocation for FY2010 (starting from April 1, 2010).

In Singapore, productivity primarily means labor productivity (value-added per worker), reflecting the government's deep concern with sustaining high wages and high living standards for its citizens. As such, it is affected by technology, capital accumulation, efficiency and waste reduction, systemic innovation, and training adopted by companies. Concerns about Singapore's recent slowdown in productivity have been also pointed out in Singapore Competitiveness Report 2009 (with a foreword by Michael E. Porter) produced by the Asia Competitiveness Institute of Lee Kuan Yew School of Public Policy. It also recommends the government's effort to move towards an innovation-driven economy.

6.6.2 The National Productivity and Continuing Education Council

One of the key strategies proposed by the Economic Strategies Committee Report was "growing through skills and innovation." To implement revived national effort to boost productivity and skills upgrading, the government established the National Productivity and Continuing Education Council (NPCEC) in April 2010. NPCEC is chaired by Deputy Prime Minister Teo Chee Hean, which signifies high priority accorded to the productivity issue, with members coming from the usual tripartite of government, business community, and labor unions. The Ministry of Trade and Industry and the Ministry of Manpower jointly act as the secretariat for the Council. Below NPCEC are two layers of executing organizations: (i) the Working Committee for Productivity and Continuing Education (WCPCE) led by the permanent secretaries of the two ministries, and (ii) 12 sector working groups and horizontal thematic working groups coordinated by various government agencies (for the institutional mechanism of the current productivity drive, see Figure 4.5 in Chapter 4).

Twelve priority sectors were selected by the criteria of contribution to employment and GDP and high potential for productivity gain. Each working group must formulate a productivity roadmap (a development plan) for the sector for the next ten years which is reviewed by WCPCE and submitted to NCPEC for final approval. A ministry or an agency is assigned to oversee each priority sector. For example, the Economic Development Board is responsible for electronics, precision engineering, transport engineering, and logistics and storage; while SPRING is responsible for general manufacturing, food and beverages, and retail. In addition, horizontal working groups are created to cover cross-cutting issues such as low-wage workers, research and benchmarking, and infocomm and logistics. Government, businesses, and labor unions participate in all of the sectoral and thematic working groups.

6.6.3 Policy measures

Beginning in FY2010, the government has committed to a total of S$5.5 billion over the next ten years to support productivity initiatives. This includes S$3 billion for the Productivity and Innovation Credit and the National Productivity Fund and S$2.5 billion for Continuing Education and Training. The Productivity and Innovation Credit is a broad-based tax benefit scheme that provides financial incentive for any enterprise in any sector that invests in productivity enhancement or innovation. Specifically, enterprises are entitled to a deduction of 250 percent of eligible expenditures from their taxable income with a cap of S$300,000 per activity. Meanwhile, the National Productivity Fund is a targeted support which provides funding for productivity initiatives in specific industries or enterprises only. Under the priorities and guidelines established by NPCEC, sector working groups propose a list of productivity initiatives to be supported which is reviewed by WCPCE.

Regarding Continuing Education and Training, the previous system has been expanded to upgrade workforce skills and competitiveness at all levels, by providing multiple skills-based progression paths to complement the academic path, and by reaching out to more professionals, managers, executives, and technicians. Furthermore, the government now encourages companies to retain and train workers, especially low-wage workers and older workers, by introducing the Workfare Training Scheme and enhancing the Workfare Income Supplement Scheme. Companies can also receive financial support for employee training from two additional sources: the Skills Development Fund, mentioned earlier, and the Lifelong Endowment Fund. Until 2008, the Skills Development Fund targeted only low-wage workforce, but more recently the Skills Development Levy was broadened to cover the entire workforce. The Lifelong Endowment Fund was established in 2001 with an initial capital of S$500 million and with the current total capital of S$2 billion. Interest earned from this fund can be used to support various lifelong learning initiatives. While all workers have access to the Continuing Education and Training scheme, subsidies from the Skills Development Fund and the Lifelong Endowment Fund are currently limited to Singaporean workers only.

Another important policy area for the purpose of enhancing productivity is SME promotion. There are over 116,000 local SMEs in Singapore accounting for 50 percent of value-added and 60 percent of employment of the nation.[8] Responsibility for SME development rests with the Enterprise Division of the Ministry of Trade and Industry for policy formulation and SPRING for implementation. The Singaporean government adopts both broad-based and targeted approaches to SME promotion. Broad-based approaches are implemented on a scheme base in collaboration with business chambers and associations. There are five Enterprise Development Centers located at business associations and chambers, where a team of business advisors give face-to-face advice to SMEs on government assistance schemes applicable to SMEs, finance, management, human resources, operations, and so on. As part of this advisory service, the Financial Facilitator Program has experts composed of ex-bankers, financial consultants, and advisors who help SMEs to gain access to financing. Targeted approaches are tailored to individual enterprises which are usually medium enterprises rather than micro and small ones. Managers of SMEs can contact designated SPRING officers to seek advisory services and resolve problems.

Singapore does not have the equivalent of Japan's Shindan system (SME Management Consultants System), an institutionalized and state-backed system for training, certifying, registering, and renewing certified SME consultants (shindanshi) who advise on management of SMEs and facilitate their financial access. In Japan, shindanshi reports are regularly used by Japanese banks to evaluate loan applications submitted by SMEs. In Singapore, banks and business consultants work more independently, and banks' loan officers have the responsibility to assess and approve loan applications. Instead of the Shindan system, Singapore has the Practising Management Consultant Certification Scheme, modeled after the British Certified Management Consultant System, in which SPRING, the Workforce Development Agency, and International Enterprise Singapore give formal endorsement on the quality of management consultants. As of 2010, about 200 consultants were qualified by the Certification Board. This scheme focuses mostly on abilities in project management, finance, laws, and applications for government incentives and less on production management on the factory floor, which is a topic covered by Japan's shindanshi.

In Singapore, manpower policy is formulated jointly by concerned official bodies and educational institutions. The National Manpower Council, a ministerial council headed by the Minister of Manpower, identifies the country's human resource needs in the medium to long run and maps out strategies to meet these needs. Various government ministries and agencies, including the Ministry of Trade and Industry, the Ministry of Education, and the Economic Development Board, participate in the Council. Based on workforce demand projection and skills mapping, the Council sets numerical targets for specific skills required by the country and decides on the number and type of students to be graduated from universities and polytechnics over the next four to five years. The Ministry of Education provides funding to educational institutions for establishing new courses if that is judged necessary. The Economic Development Board may also provide additional funds to relevant industries for upgrading their workforce. For instance, the aerospace industry was recently targeted for such sector-specific workforce development.

Polytechnics have played a significant role in enhancing the skills of Singaporean workers. There are five state-run polytechnics in Singapore, among which Nanyang Polytechnic is the largest and most prominent. It was established in 1992 and now boasts about 78,000 students, providing both pre-employment training for regular students and Continuing Education and Training for current workers. Regarding pre-employment training, seven schools of Nanyang Polytechnic offer 47 full-time courses for three-year diploma in engineering, IT, business management, interactive and digital media, design, chemical and life sciences, and health sciences. As for Continuing Education and Training, the polytechnic has formal diploma courses, customized courses, and degree programs with overseas universities. The government provides full funding for administration and operation of Nanyang Polytechnic (except for the part covered by tuition fees). Additional revenues of the school coming from services rendered to industry, as explained below, can be used freely for any purpose by the polytechnic.

Industry has seats in the Board and Advisory Committees of Nanyang Polytechnic and participates in its course development and review. The polytechnic also has many other channels to work with industry such as (i) education of suitably trained graduates to meet the manpower needs of industry as stipulated by the national policy; (ii) practice- and application-oriented training; (iii) "industry attachment" (internship) for students; and (iv) collaboration with industry and development agencies such as SPRING and Infocomm Development Authority. It carries out a large number of industrial projects on a commercial basis in R&D, product design and development, and innovative solutions for industry, as well as teaming up with the Economic Development Board to support start-up "technopreneurs." Such collaboration creates a "win–win" situation for both industry and the polytechnic because the former can benefit from reduced cost and risk for R&D and start-up investment and because the latter can have ample opportunities for staff and student training in frontline technology in addition to earning money. Reputation of Nanyang Polytechnic is solid and long standing among Singaporean manufacturers. It is unable to accept all cooperation proposals from industry because it receives too many. The school is also active in international cooperation. Nanyang Polytechnic International provides consultancy services to a World Bank project in TVET reform and cooperation with the Suzhou Industrial Park Institute of Vocational Technology, both in China. It also conducts training programs for management staff and specialists of TVET institutions around the world.

6.7 Concluding remarks

Singapore's success with the Productivity Movement can teach many lessons to countries that are striving to introduce similar government-led national movements to strengthen and invigorate the private sector. In concluding this chapter, I will reiterate such lessons.

First, a nationwide productivity drive requires a paradigm shift and a mindset change. It is not just a one-time event or a project but a movement with no finishing line. It requires establishment of an attitude by which all people strive for and acquire the habit of improvement as well as systems and practices that translate such an attitude into action. A new way of thinking, living, and working must be firmly built in the minds and actions of all leaders and actors.

Second, in addition to a mindset change, productivity enhancement needs political commitment from the top. In Singapore, unwavering concern and resolve of Prime Minister Lee Kuan Yew was critical to making the Productivity Movement widespread and entrenched in the society.

Third, productivity enhancement requires strong organizational backup. Singapore established a high-level tripartite council for policy coordination and a national productivity organization as an implementation body. These organizations had to be linked with all key stakeholders such as government, businesses and its related organizations, labor, and academia enabling them to collectively disseminate productivity awareness and translate awareness into action in workplaces and training and educational institutions. Linkage between workplaces and training and educational institutions was equally important for matching graduating engineers and workers with the manpower needs of industry and promoting collaboration between industry and academia.

Fourth, the three stages of the Productivity Movement—awareness, action, and ownership—are a useful reference for national movements. Attitudinal change and internalization of productivity actions require time, and they must be achieved through proper sequencing to generate understanding, conviction, and action. Before introducing QC circles at workplaces in full force, Singapore spent some years in annual productivity campaigns; public education, seminars and publication campaigns; national awards; and dissemination of best practices.

Fifth, to sustain the Productivity Movement, a cadre of private management consultants must be fostered to take over the main responsibility in productivity improvement in the future. The JICA-supported project in Singapore trained not only official counterparts but also private experts. Under the Management Consultancy Referral Scheme and the Associate Consultants Scheme, trained private experts became National Productivity Board associate or referral consultants and were mobilized for subsequent productivity programs. While government officials may teach companies at first, the task of diagnostic and advisory services must eventually be carried out by private agents with government receding to concentrate on policy formulation.

7 Taiwan

Policy drive for innovation

7.1 From "Banana Republic" to "Silicon Island"

Taiwan, a small island off mainland China with a total area of approximately 36,000 km^2 and a current population of 23 million, started development in the post-World War II period from the position of a poor agrarian economy exporting rice, sugar, oolong tea, bananas, and pineapples. By the end of the twenty century it had attained a high income backed by world-class technology-based manufacturing. This chapter examines how today's Taiwan, as one of the highly industrialized economies in the world, promotes innovation to continue to climb the technological ladder and secure its place in global competition. Our focus is not only on what policies are used for this purpose but also on how and by whom they are formulated and executed. We will see that, since 2010, Taiwan's key industrial policy instruments have consisted of a uniformly low corporate tax, competitive and strictly monitored "technology development programs," research institutes that support policy formulation and implementation, various industrial parks, and promotion of SMEs. Taiwan no longer uses a complex set of incentives for targeted industries or products or discriminates firms based on their nationalities.

Looking back, the island was a Japanese colony from 1895 to 1945. After Japan was defeated in World War II and expelled from Taiwan in 1945, fighting over the control of Mainland China continued between the Communists and the Kuomintang (Nationalist Party). With the final victory of the Communists and establishment of the People's Republic of China in 1949, defeated Kuomintang leaders and supporters, including Chiang Kai Shek, his elite followers, and about 1.5 million bureaucrats, military officers, entrepreneurs and their families, fled to Taiwan. The declared policy of Communist China to "liberate" Taiwan and escalation of the Cold War into hot wars in Korea and Indochina put Taiwan under a strong external threat and pervasive sense of crisis. As a matter of top national priority, rapid economic growth had to be engineered to secure the material basis of national security. To accomplish this, a strong authoritarian developmental state was installed in the Republic of China (Watanabe, 1995; Ohno and Sakurai, 1997).

Kuomintang leaders realized their policy mistakes that caused the military loss of the mainland. According to Ezra Vogel,

> In their analysis of why they lost the mainland, Kuomintang leaders acknowledged that public support had eroded because of their failure to stop corruption and to provide for the common people's livelihood. Above all, they concluded, they should have done more to control inflation and implement land reform. They were determined to do better on Taiwan. They resolved to be strict with corruption, to expand the role of government enterprise in a way not susceptible to private influence, and to create a greater distance between the government and the private sector.
>
> (Vogel, 1991, p. 18)

The Kuomintang government relocated in Taiwan devoted its skills and passion to economic development. A group of able and highly-educated technocrats who had practical policy experience on the mainland took charge of nation-building and economic strategy making. Some of them managed state-owned enterprises which laid the foundation of Taiwan's initial industrialization. Economic construction plans were formulated and executed. Land reform was implemented successfully in 1951. As the international political support shifted from the Republic of China (Taiwan) to the People's Republic of China (mainland) in the 1960s and the 1970s, the authoritarian developmental state in Taiwan was further convinced that rapid economic development was the only way to survive in international isolation and enhance bargaining power against the mainland. Economic growth was sustained by a state-led drive for heavy and chemical industrialization known as the "Ten Major Development Projects" as well as strong growth of labor-intensive exports by competitive local SMEs.

As a result of over 60 years of continued effort at industrialization, with shifting phases, Taiwan's economic structure has been transformed enormously, creating a miracle island that dominates the world in the manufacturing of ICT hardware. Taiwan's industrial policy goals and key industries shifted steadily over the years as follows:

1950s: Import substitution with a focus on the food industry
1960s: Export expansion with a focus on the textile and garment industry
1970s: Enhancement of industrial infrastructure with a focus on the petrochemical industry
1980s: Economic liberalization with a focus on the information technology (IT) industry
1990s: Industrial upgrading with a focus on the integrated circuit (IC) industry
2000s: Global deployment with a focus on the liquid crystal display (LCD) industry

In 2010, Taiwan's per capita GDP was US$19,046, which stood among the richest economies of the world. It should be stressed that, as in the case of Singapore, this income was generated by technology and hard work rather than a lucky endowment of natural resources or inflows of external capital and aid. Adjusted for differences in price levels, Taiwan's real income is now equivalent to Japan's.[1] Taiwan is the leading global supplier of a large number of parts and components in ICT such as mask ROM (94 percent), IC foundry (66 percent), blank optical disk (63 percent), IC package (44 percent), electronic glass fabric (39 percent), IC design (27 percent), and DRAM (22 percent). But this is counting products made in Taiwan only. If overseas production by Taiwanese firms is also considered, the list of "made by Taiwan" products with dominant global shares becomes longer. It includes such ICT hardware as motherboard (96 percent), notebook computer (95 percent), server (89 percent), wireless LAN device (81 percent), cable modem (79 percent), portable navigation device (77 percent), and LCD monitor (72 percent). The numbers in parentheses are the global market share in 2009 as reported by the Taiwanese government.

As industrial structure steadily deepened and the private sector strengthened competitiveness, the policy mechanism that promoted Taiwan's industrialization also changed. Up to the mid-1980s, the remarkable structural transformation was directed by a powerful bureaucracy, the Ministry of Economic Affairs (MoEA), and a handful of key elite figures that constituted an authoritarian developmental state model which Robert Wade described as "Governing the Market" (Wade, 1990). At that time, principal policy instruments included SME finance, market entry regulation (to protect SMEs from large firms), trade promotion agency, credit facilities and insurance, industrial estates, and technical assistance by officially created research institutions. SMEs in Taiwan were dynamic and could respond strongly to these policy initiatives. In those days, SMEs were Taiwan's main exporters while large corporations such as Formosa Plastic (private) and China Steel (state-owned) supplied to the domestic market.

After the mid-1980s, a number of structural shifts occurred. First, the private sector became more powerful relative to the government as a result of economic development. Second, within the private sector, large local firms emerged while the relative share of SMEs in output, export, and employment all declined. Third, economic liberalization, increasing economic interaction with mainland China, and accession to the WTO in 2002 exerted international competitive pressure. Currently Taiwan's largest firms include TSMC (semi-conductor), UMC (semi-conductor), AU Optronics (LCD), Foxconn (electronics manufacturing service), Acer (computer), Asus (computer), Yulon Motor (automotive), San Yang Motors (motorcycle), and Kwang Yang Motor (motorcycle). Old giants such as Formosa Plastic and China Steel are also moving into new fields such as artificial fiber in the case of the former and high-quality steel for auto, electronics, and machinery in the case of the latter. With the growth of vibrant domestic

Table 7.1 Taiwan: key economic indicators

	Population (mil)	GDP (US$ bil)	Per capita GDP (US$)	Production structure (%)			Employment structure (%)			Export structure (%)				R&D (%GDP)	Gini coef.
				Agr.	Ind.	Serv.	Agr.	Ind.	Serv.	(US$ bil)	Agr.	Light ind.	Heavy ind.		
1952	8.1	1.7	213	32.2	19.7	48.1	56.1	16.9	27.0	0.1					
1955	9.1	2.0	220	29.1	23.2	47.7	53.6	18.0	28.3	0.1					
1960	10.8	1.8	164	28.5	26.9	44.6	50.2	20.5	29.3	0.2					
1965	12.7	2.9	229	23.6	30.2	46.2	46.5	22.3	31.3	0.5					
1970	14.8	5.7	393	15.5	36.8	47.7	36.7	27.9	35.3	1.5					0.29
1975	16.2	15.7	978	12.7	39.9	47.4	30.4	34.9	34.6	5.4					0.31
1980	17.9	42.2	2,385	7.7	45.8	46.6	19.5	42.5	38.0	19.9					0.28
1985	19.3	63.1	3,290	5.7	44.6	49.7	17.5	41.6	41.0	30.8	6.1	60.0	33.9	1.03	0.29
1990	20.4	164.7	8,124	4.1	38.9	57.0	12.8	40.8	46.3	67.4	4.5	49.6	45.9	1.62	0.31
1995	21.4	274.7	12,918	3.3	33.1	63.5	10.5	38.7	50.7	113.3	3.8	37.6	58.6	1.72	0.32
2000	22.3	326.2	14,704	2.0	30.5	67.5	7.8	37.2	55.0	151.9	1.4	26.8	71.8	1.94	0.33
2005	22.8	364.8	16,051	1.7	31.3	67.1	5.9	36.4	57.7	198.4	1.3	18.5	80.2	2.39	0.34
2010	23.2	430.1	18,588	1.6	31.3	67.1	5.2	35.9	58.8	274.6	1.1	15.6	83.3	2.94*	0.34*

Source: Council for Economic Planning and Development (CEPD), *Taiwan Statistical Data Book*, 2011. Production structure data from 1952 to 1980 are from CEPD, *Taiwan Statistical Data Book*, 1991. Export structure prior to 1980 cannot be traced due to statistical discontinuity in 1981. Data with asterisk are for 2009.

firms, Taiwan's industrialization no longer depends very much on FDI or foreign technology.

Even today, Taiwanese SMEs are highly active by international standards and remain more autonomous (not constrained by a hierarchical order like Japanese keiretsu or Korean chaebols) and have a high start-up ratio of 7.1 percent, which shows how many new firms are established every year relative to the number of existing firms. However, as integration deepens and corporate size becomes increasingly important in global competition, large firms have began to dominate even in Taiwan and the relative role of SMEs in industrialization has shrunk. Moreover, even large Taiwanese firms feel that they are too small compared with Japanese or South Korean giants and want to grow more and create brand-name products. Taiwan has succeeded greatly in industrialization by specializing in contracted hardware manufacturing for foreign brand-name electronic products. However, this type of manufacturing, which includes original equipment manufacturing (OEM), original design manufacturing (ODM) and electronics manufacturing service (EMS), does not necessarily capture the highest value-creating segment of the value chain. Taiwan feels that contracted hardware manufacturing has already reached a plateau and that it needs a new business model to grow into the future.

Given these trends, the industrial policy of the MoEA is also changing. In Taiwan, the industrial policy statute is the most important legal document governing industrialization. The first such law, the Statute for Encouragement of Investment (effective 1960–1990), and its successor, the Statute for Upgrading Industries (effective 1991–2010), guided past industrial policies. The Statute for Industrial Innovation, approved by the National Assembly in May 2010, is the current law which sets future directions for Taiwan's industries. Three features of the new statute are particularly noteworthy. First, it expands policy scope from the previous manufacturing-only focus to agro and biotech industries, industrial services, and high-value services which would additionally require coordination among a number of ministries other than the MoEA. Second, it replaces the previous system of multiple incentives by a uniform corporate income tax rate of 17 percent (lowered from the previous 25 percent)[2] and elimination of all tax incentives except for R&D. This change was made to simplify the incentive structure while at the same time retaining tax advantage against neighboring countries.[3] Third, it aims to shift Taiwan from a hardware manufacturer to a soft power economy with strong national brands and a regional logistic and transport hub. Like many other high-income economies, Taiwan wants to become an innovation-driven economy as it graduates from the successful factor- and efficiency-driven growth of the past.

Taiwan's current industrial policy has two pillars: creation of soft power and improving cross-strait relations. The soft power drive has three subcomponents: (i) supply of industrial professionals; (ii) promoting emerging industries; and (iii) upgrading conventional industries including ICT, garment, and footwear. Regarding emerging industries, the six "major emerging industries" are biotechnology, precision agriculture, green energy, medical and healthcare, tourism, and cultural innovation industries. The four "emerging intelligent industries" are invention and patent commercialization, cloud computing, electric intelligent cars, and intelligent green construction industries. Besides these, ten service industries which are outside the mandate of the MoEA are also targeted. Even with streamlined tax incentives, the MoEA can promote targeted sectors and activities through technology development projects commissioned by the Department of Industrial Technology and other agencies, as explained below.

Regarding cross-strait relations, restrictions on China-bound investment were relaxed in August 2008 when permissible ratios and value ceilings for Taiwanese corporate and individual investors in China were raised. Meetings, seminars, and industrial collaboration with mainland China have also been activated. The Taiwanese markets have also been opening to Chinese investors since June 2009, though gradually and based on careful monitoring of actual performance. The recently signed cross-strait Economic Cooperation Framework Agreement (ECFA), effective from January 2011, is expected to have further impacts on cross-strait relations. ECFA is modeled after the ASEAN–China Free Trade Agreement which features "early harvest" trade items in goods and services.

With the exception of carefully watched economic relations with mainland China, Taiwan does not care about the nationality of investors whether they are domestic, foreign, or joint venture. Taiwan accepts FDI in any sector except in national defense. As noted above, Taiwan's FDI attraction policy is based on the low and universal corporate income tax and transparent incentives for R&D only. Unlike Singapore, Taiwan does not engage in customized negotiation to attract targeted individual foreign investors. Industrial policy is mainly directed to local firms which are the major industrial players in Taiwan.

7.2 The making of industrial policy

7.2.1 The Industrial Development Bureau

The most important policymaking body for Taiwan's industrialization is the Industrial Development Bureau (IDB) of the MoEA. Although its influence has waned over the decades, it still yields substantial power in guiding the private sector. The IDB currently has 240 permanent staff mainly with engineering backgrounds as recruitment of economists into the IDB is only a recent phenomenon. Temporary staff are also hired to cope with its heavy work load. Many components of policy drafting and consultations are outsourced to government-created semi-official think tanks, especially the Taiwan Institute of Economic Research (TIER) and the Chung-Hua Institution for Economic Research (CIER), which are discussed below. In addition,

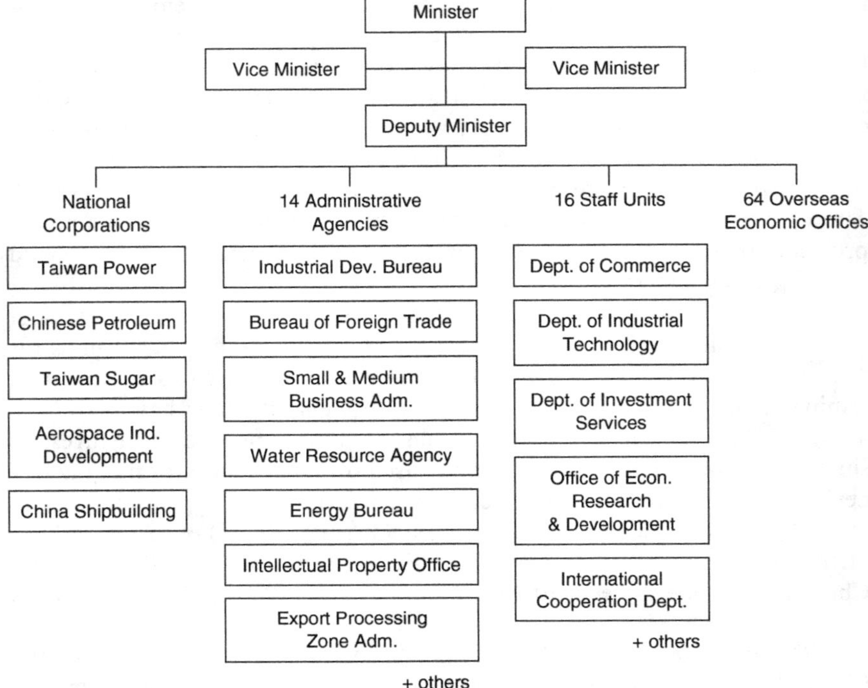

Figure 7.1 Organizational structure of the Ministry of Economic Affairs

"committees" are used for consensus building between ministries and experts, and "seminars" are organized extensively for interacting with the private sector. In Taiwan, think tanks, committees, and seminars are not just means of information exchange and policy discussion but integral parts of action-oriented policy formulation and implementation. Their reputation and funding depend directly on their contribution to the policy process.

The IDB has three sectoral divisions (metal and mechanical, IT, and consumer goods and chemicals) and four functional divisions (industrial policy, knowledge services, sustainable development, and industrial parks). Besides these, a number of task forces and offices for sectoral promotion are placed under the IDB. Restructuring of the MoEA is expected for the implementation of the new industrial statute which has a wider sectoral scope than the previous one.

7.2.2 Principal policy instruments

Taiwan's industrial policy aims at commercial application of technological innovation. Public support is provided on a competitive and conditional basis to research institutes, private firms, and universities that conduct and

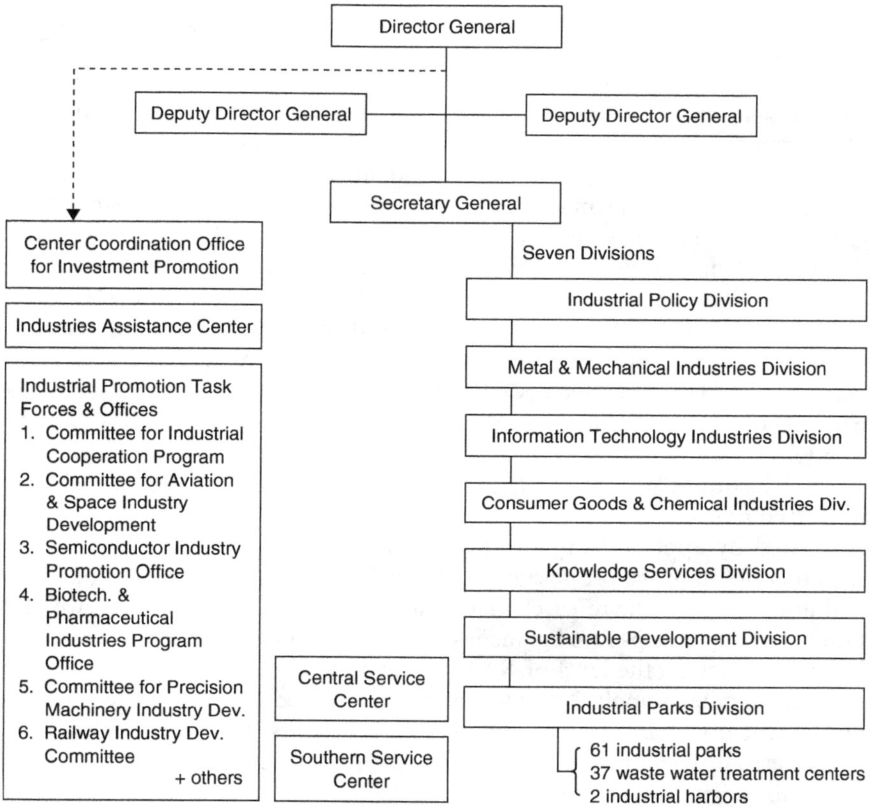

Director General

Deputy Director General

Deputy Director General

Secretary General

Center Coordination Office for Investment Promotion

Industries Assistance Center

Industrial Promotion Task Forces & Offices
1. Committee for Industrial Cooperation Program
2. Committee for Aviation & Space Industry Development
3. Semiconductor Industry Promotion Office
4. Biotech. & Pharmaceutical Industries Program Office
5. Committee for Precision Machinery Industry Dev.
6. Railway Industry Dev. Committee

+ others

Central Service Center

Southern Service Center

Seven Divisions

Industrial Policy Division

Metal & Mechanical Industries Division

Information Technology Industries Division

Consumer Goods & Chemical Industries Div.

Knowledge Services Division

Sustainable Development Division

Industrial Parks Division

61 industrial parks
37 waste water treatment centers
2 industrial harbors

Figure 7.2 Organizational structure of the Industrial Development Bureau, MoEA

commercialize R&D with results being closely monitored and evaluated. At present, technology development programs and industrial zones (especially science parks) are the two principal instruments for promoting innovation. Sector- or activity-specific incentives are no longer a major policy instrument under the current industrial statute which eliminated all incentive schemes except for R&D.

Regarding technology development projects (TDPs), the Department of Industrial Technology (DoIT) of the MoEA is responsible for identifying, screening, and financing projects that directly enhance technology of the private sector.[4] TDPs are classified into three types: organization TDPs that are provided to research institutes for commercializing their R&D activities and assisting enterprises (since 1979), industrial TDPs that offer direct grants to private enterprises engaged in R&D and innovation (since 1997), and academic TDPs that encourage universities to utilize their R&D facilities and resources to develop new industrial technologies (since 2001). Viewed from the budget allocation in 2010, organization TDPs are by far the largest part of DoIT programs occupying 75.3 percent while the share of industrial TDPs was 20.6 percent and that of academic TDPs was 4.1 percent. Within organization TDPs, the electronics, information, communication, and opto-electronics sector receives the largest amount (23.7 percent of organization TDP budget) followed by machinery and transportation (20.6 percent), innovative and advanced R&D (15.1 percent), biotechnology and pharmaceutics (13.2 percent), material and chemical engineering (12.3 percent), and others. How organization TDPs are administered will be explained in detail below for the case of metal engineering.

In 2010, the national budget for science and technology totaling NT$94.2 billion (about US$2.9 billion) was allocated among the National Science Council (43.0 percent), the MoEA (30.8 percent), and Academia Sinica (11.0 percent). The DoIT received NT$19.9 billion which was the lion's share (69 percent) of this fund allocated to the MoEA amounting to NT$29.0 billion. The DoIT uses this fund to finance three types of TDPs described above by research institutes, private organizations, and universities that support national industrial policy. Funding is allocated competitively by evaluating proposals submitted by applicant organizations. The DoIT sometimes works closely with them to improve proposals. TDPs aim at industrial application of R&D and not pure scientific research. The results of these projects are reviewed by DoIT advisory groups for alignment with national policy and key performance indicators such as the level of R&D relative to GDP or corporate revenue; numbers of patents applied, granted, and filed; revenue derived from technology and patent transfers; and private-sector investments stimulated by TDPs.

As for industrial estates, there are three types of centrally managed industrial estates with different overseeing authorities: 13 science parks under the National Science Council, eight export processing zones under the Export Processing Zone (EPZ) Administration of the MoEA, and 61 industrial parks under the IDB of the MoEA. There are different technology requirements for tenant firms in these zones with the required level of innovation and R&D being highest in science parks and lowest in industrial parks. The National Science Council, through its Science Park Administration, supervises 13 science-based parks. Among them, Hsinchu Science Park (HSP), established in 1980, was the first and most successful. It has become the central location for Taiwan's ICT industry with high international reputation. EPZs, first established in Kaohsiung in 1966, have been home to Taiwan's vibrant industrial activities and contributed greatly to its export drive. Reflecting Taiwan's economic transformation, the sectoral distribution of tenant firms in EPZs shifted overtime from low-tech labor-intensive manufacturing to high-end OEM and high-tech electronics. Meanwhile, industrial parks focus on light industry, basic consumer goods, petrochemical, and so on, with regional specialization and local regulatory differences. Unlike science parks and EPZs which only rent land and factories, industrial parks can sell land to investors. However, industrial parks are not required to provide one-stop investor service as others. There is a plan to merge the administration of

EPZs with industrial parks. Besides centrally managed industrial estates, Taiwan also has 18 industrial parks developed by local governments and 93 industrial parks developed by the private sector as of 2010.

7.2.3 Drafting of the industrial statute

Taiwan's industrial policy is strongly guided by the MoEA. A think tank provides supporting functions such as providing secretariat service, conducting studies and reports, running a related center, and organizing committees, seminars, and hearings. Consultation with concerned ministries and the private sector is an important component of the policymaking process. However, the traditionally strong leadership of the MoEA and the passive attitudes of other ministries and organizations makes this process somewhat unilateral and lopsided. Another unique aspect of Taiwan is intervention by the powerful legislature which may upset the picture painted by technocrats. Interest groups often lobby the legislature to influence policy outcome.

As an example, let us examine the drafting process of the Statute for Industrial Innovation of 2010 mentioned above. In anticipation of expiration of the previous industrial law, a task force was created by the IDB under the MoEA three years in advance to draft a new law. MoEA Minister Yen-Shiang Shih led brainstorming sessions and provided the vision and key ideas for this law. These sessions were conducted by the Chung-Hua Institution for Economic Research, a think tank chosen for supporting the MoEA in drafting the new law. The proposed vision and ideas were conveyed to the private sector through public hearing meetings with six sectoral business associations representing steel, IT, and so on. The main purpose of these meetings was for the ministry to persuade the private sector and make it agree with its policy direction rather than receiving substantive comments for revision. Sometimes private firms had divided opinions.

In addition, a small number of inter-ministerial meetings were also held with the MoEA minister presiding and ministers of other related ministries attending. Interventions by other ministries were few and no objections were raised against the MoEA's visions and ideas. While the MoEA has historically dominated industrial promotion, other ministries in charge of services, agriculture, health care, education, culture, etc., which are now included as targeted sectors, are unfamiliar with industrial promotion measures and remained passive on the listening side. After these consultations, the Industrial Policy Division of the IDB drafted the law with the support of law firms for wording.

However, the draft law prepared by the MoEA was substantially revised in the legislative process. Taiwan's National Assembly is powerful and therefore attracts lobbying by interest groups. The law drafted by technocrats originally proposed lowering the corporate income tax from 25 percent to 20 percent and kept four incentive schemes for R&D, branding, human-resource training, and attracting headquarters of foreign multinational corporations to Taiwan. The National Assembly, backed by the industrial and SME lobby, slashed the proposed corporate income tax rate further to 17 percent despite the fact that the Ministry of Finance was concerned about revenue loss, and eliminated all incentive measures except for R&D. According to one industrial expert, this legislative action was too aggressive but must be accepted as a compromise in democracy. Finally, an "island tour" was conducted in the North, Middle, and South of Taiwan to disseminate the new law.

It is worth noting that the consultative policymaking procedure as described above was established in the late 1980s when the previous industrial statute was formulated. Prior to that, policymaking was dominated by a few elite leaders and technocrats who drafted policies with limited help of research institutes that produced internal studies without public review and comments.

Regarding this policymaking process, there are different voices among local experts outside government. According to one expert, private firms often complain that government does too much R&D which competes with and crowds out private R&D. However, another expert argued that government must be more proactive than before in pushing innovation in the twenty-first century. One expert said that private firms, especially SMEs, are still willing to listen to and follow government because government-backed R&D and technology transfer greatly benefit them. One scholar stated that "embedded autonomy," or government with close interaction with businesses without being hijacked by vested interests, was possible in Taiwan because of such historical factors as social mobility, fair competition without class discrimination, and leadership paranoia over external threats (previously from Communism and now from integration pressure). While most experts appreciate proactive policy guidance, some express mild doubts about the prospects and effectiveness of the current innovation drive. For example, the biotech industry targeted by government is slow to emerge and grow.[5]

7.3 Research institutes

In Taiwan there are 19 research institutes created by the MoEA which play vital roles in designing and implementing national industrial and technology policy. Some of them received seed money at establishment but they now all operate as NPOs competing for funds for TDPs commissioned by government and industrial services and projects requested by private firms without receiving any regular budget allocation from the state. Taiwan's research institutes can be classified into policy think tanks which assist policy drafting and technology support institutes which play key roles in policy implementation. We will describe the functions of four of them, two from each category.

7.3.1 Policy research institutes

Among policy research institutes, the Taiwan Institute of Economic Research (TIER) and the Chung-Hua Institution for Economic Research (CIER) are the two applied economic research think tanks strongly supporting the policy-making of the MoEA. With overlapping research capabilities and support functions, they are also competitors in bidding for government research projects.

TIER was founded in 1976 with private funding. It boasts over 100 scholars, maintains a databank of Taiwanese industries, conducts domestic and global economic forecasts, and acts as a secretariat to the Industrial Development Advisory Council as well as several cross-strait economic cooperation projects. It also conducted the impact study of the Economic Cooperation Framework Agreement (ECFA, for increased trade with mainland China). TIER has seven research divisions, several service providing centers, the Tokyo office, and other departments and committees. Its revenue comes from undertaking government projects (about 70 percent) and private-sector projects (about 30 percent). The Industrial Development Advisory Council, to which TIER serves as secretariat, is a platform for interaction among government, businesses, and academics which was established in 1984 following the Japanese model of MITI's Industrial Structure Council. The MoEA uses the Council to fathom the impact of its policies and hear the requests and problems of the business community. The Council holds 15 meetings per year, two of which are organized by the IDB of the MoEA and others by other bureaus of the MoEA.

CIER, established in 1982 with a (mostly official) endowment of NT$1 billion, is located on the premises of the National Taiwan University. Like TIER, it conducts commissioned projects for the president, the Executive Yuan (Taiwan's executive branch), and government ministries and agencies. It has three research divisions that conduct applied research on mainland China, international issues, and domestic issues respectively. CIER also produces economic forecasts and operates the WTO Center as well as other ad hoc centers. CIER was the secretariat to the formulation of the 2010 industrial statute as explained above, ECFA, and Taiwan's WTO entry. For ECFA, for example, CIER spent two to three years for research and produced a report on the costs and benefits of increased economic interaction with mainland China which was circulated to the public and academia for critical review. The report was then discussed among concerned ministries and agencies, businesses (through "seminars"), and finally with legislators before it was sent to the Legislative Yuan (national assembly). CIER feels that about 70–80 percent of what it proposes in its report makes to the final stage.

7.3.2 Technology research institutes

Among the 11 technology support institutes, the Industrial Technology Research Institute (ITRI), founded in 1973, is Taiwan's largest R&D organization in support of technology transfer and commercialization. Its supervising agency is the MoEA. ITRI has 5,800 employees in its large building complex in Hsinchu County, of which 80 percent are engaged in R&D and 1,200 hold doctoral degrees. At ITRI there are three ways to disseminate R&D—technology licensing; spinning off a research team to form a start-up company; and forming a joint venture to become a new section in an existing company ("spin-in"). Taiwan Semiconductor Manufacturing Company (TSMC) and United Microelectronics Corporation (UMC), the two world largest IC foundries, are ITRI's most famous spin-offs. In total ITRI has produced 65 ventures and 19,589 ITRI alumni. ITRI also offers open labs where domestic and foreign companies can send staff to do joint research with ITRI researchers using ITRI facilities. About half of ITRI's revenue comes from fees charged to domestic and foreign firms for industrial services such as system planning, product design, intellectual property licensing, and intellectual assets and the other half from state-funded research projects on a competitive bidding basis. ITRI is commissioned to plan, train, and formulate policies mainly for the MoEA but it also provides services to other ministries. Its location in Hsinchu, in proximity to science parks and two technology universities, allows active cooperation with private firms and academia although ITRI also works with industrial and academic partners all over Taiwan. Many graduates from the two science and technology universities nearby join ITRI for several years to learn industrial application and accumulate practical experience, then start migrating between industry and ITRI. In this way, ITRI is the largest focal point for industry–government–academia cooperation as well as for carrying out the MoEA's technology development programs.

ITRI is also a focal point for industrial network formation. Concrete ITRI-aided achievements in this area include enhancement of global competitiveness of the Taiwanese bicycle industry by the two leading bicycle producers, Giant and Merida, forming an organization ("A-Team") with 11 bicycle-parts makers that adopted the Toyota Production System; horizontal integration of machine tools companies to apply core technology to upgrade overall industry capability; R&D alliance among research institutes, academia, and industry that integrated and strengthened 12 local companies that produced flexible panel display manufacturing equipment; and the creation of a national brand saxophone, "Saxhome," in the musical instrument cluster in Howli Township, Taichung.

ITRI College, a new addition to ITRI, is a training provider for ITRI staff at all levels as well as for industry. It offers courses lasting from one day to three months on five innovation competencies and six technological domains.[6] It also offers customized training programs for enterprises. ITRI College issues certificates but no degrees because its courses are strictly for actual use by industry to create value and not for academic merits. Of particular interest are its need-based programs for government officials and researchers from developing countries in such topics as national innovation system, human resource development system, SME promotion, science park development, and intellectual property management. In 2010, for example, ITRI College received official delegations from Vietnam and Philippines (about 25 persons each) as well as India and Poland (2 persons each) for customized policy training. However, Taiwan is not conducting knowledge sharing with developing countries as a national project, and the size of its intellectual assistance remains small compared with similar programs by Japan or South Korea. Political concern vis-à-vis mainland China is one reason for Taiwan to remain low-key in its international assistance activities.

The Metal Industries Research and Development Center (MIRDC), established in 1963, is one of the sectoral technology institutes under the MoEA. It is headquartered in Kaohsiung with seven branches and centers across Taiwan. It supports the metal industry and industries of metal-related technologies including automation. MIRDC has 612 employees, of which 51 are doctoral degree holders and 325 possess master's degrees. Main specializations of the professional staff are mechanical engineering (38 percent), material and chemical science (11 percent), and electrical, opto-electronic, and info-tech areas (8 percent). Its annual staff turnover is 10 percent and the average working period is ten years (at ITRI, they are 20 percent and six years respectively). MIRDC also hires staff on a contract base. It has five focused industries for support: metal material and fabricated metal products, mold and die and micro parts, automotive technology, opto-electronics and energy equipment, and medical devices and care. MIRDC has over 50 R&D labs and can provide services to private firms through industrial TDPs, transfer of technology project achievements, patent sale, application for governmental resources, as well as in management, e-automation, market survey, and industrial training.

Specifically, commercial applications of MIRDC-assisted R&D include the industrial innovative transformation and cluster value-added promotion program which supported 48 industrial clusters consisting of 230 companies leading to 117 product pilot developments; application of super thin slice motor technology to the production of micro heat dissipating fans, water cooling heat dissipating pumps, automobile internal air monitors, mobile phone vibration motors, and medical cosmetic products; and development of an integrated dental implant system that upgraded ten producers and created one spin-off company that replaced traditional OEM and entered the global market with a brand name.

The annual revenue of MIRDC, amounting to NT$2 billion, comes from industrial services (25 percent directly from private sector and 35 percent commissioned by government) and from government's technology development programs discussed earlier (40 percent). A team is formed for each project undertaken. Teams may last for four to five years for big projects and three to six months for small ones. For a large DoIT-funded project, for example, about two years are spent for sounding local industry needs and working out a proposal jointly with the DoIT. After approval, implementation and monitoring will usually take three to four years. As with other research institutes, MIRDC must bid competitively for government projects and their performance is reviewed closely by such indicators as the number

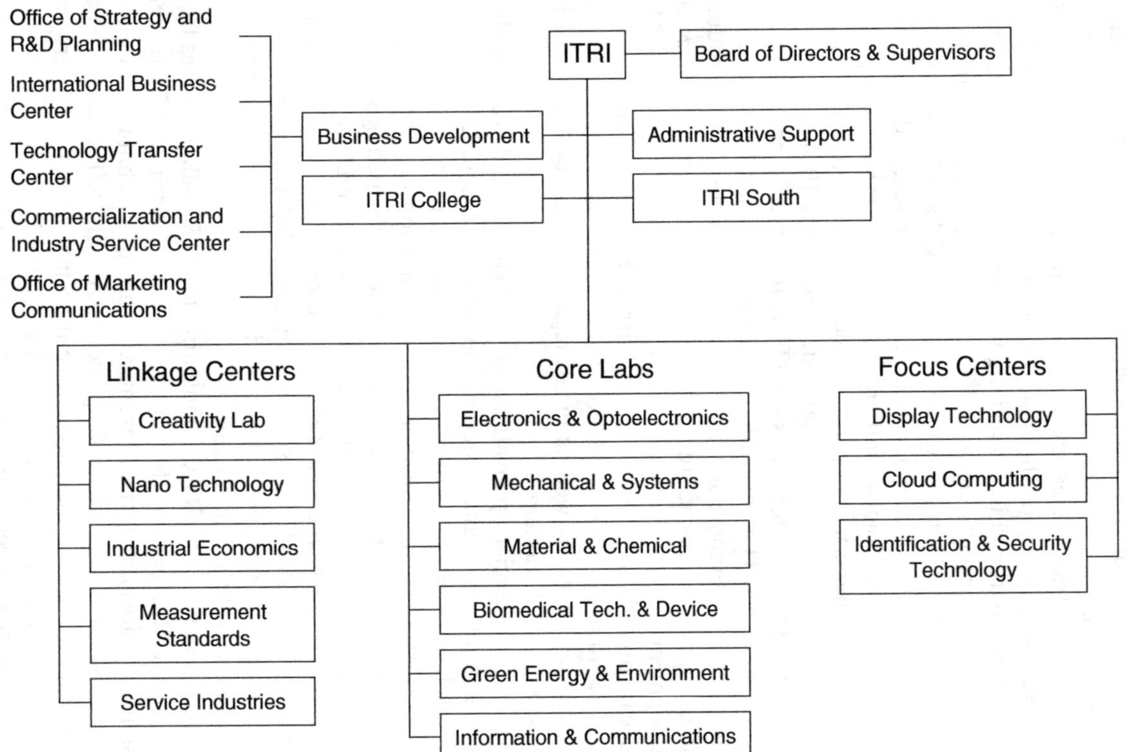

Figure 7.3 Organizational structure of the Industrial Technology Research Institute

of patents or companies assisted, new investments and technology applications generated, and so on.

7.4 Hsinchu Science Park

As noted above, there are three types of state-managed industrial estates in Taiwan, among which science parks, under the direct control of the National Science Council, are most demanding in the requirement of R&D and its commercialization. Hsinchu Science Park (HSP), established in December 1980 in Hsinchu City in Northern Taiwan, was the first such science park that contributed greatly to the development of Taiwan's ICT industry. This location was chosen due to its proximity to ITRI and two engineering universities, Chiao Tung University and Tsing Hua University, that could provide necessary technology support and human resource to the science park. The government additionally established several labs at HSP including the National Center for High-performance Computing, the National Chip Implementation Center, and the National Nano Device Laboratories. Interacting with Silicon Valley in California, USA, industry structure, entrepreneurship, R&D mechanism, and venture systems of HSP were built up. HSP currently generates 4.5 percent of Taiwan's GDP, and many of the high-tech products dominating the global market mentioned earlier originate in this park. Its enormous success attracts about 1,000 study missions annually from around the world that hope to learn how high-tech industrial parks such as this can be created and managed.

The number of tenant companies, their revenues, and park employees grew steadily and significantly over the years. At the end of 2010, they stood at 449 companies, US$40.9 billion, and 139,416 employees respectively. Park employees were predominantly Taiwanese but they also included 4,134 foreigners of which 1,074 were highly skilled. In the period of 1989–2008, the average R&D-to-sales ratio of tenant firms at HSP was 6.0 percent against the national manufacturing average of 1.1 percent. Land in HSP is state-owned and leased out on a 20-year contract at subsidized rates to domestic and foreign firms with no intervention in corporate activities. 400 standard rental factories with the size of 700–1,000 m^2 are also available (a firm may rent more than one unit). The monthly rent is NT$53/$m^2$ for land and NT$98–126/$m^2$ for rental factory. As expected of a top-notch industrial estate of world fame, one-stop service, good infrastructure, and comfortable living conditions are all guaranteed. The average income per household in Hsinchu City is second highest in Taiwan, after Taipei.

Measured by company revenues which recorded a total of US$40.9 billion in 2010, the largest industry by far at HSP is integrated circuits (67.5 percent) followed by opto-electronics (20.7 percent), computers and peripherals (6.4 percent), telecom (2.7 percent), and precision machinery (1.8 percent). Some of the park's renowned tenants include TSMC, UMC, Acer, Foxconn, AUO, Logitech, Du Pont, Hoya, Shin Etsu, and DNP. While 90 percent of the tenants are Taiwanese, HSP is also host to 44 foreign firms, of which 17 are American and ten are Japanese. 95 companies were set up by overseas Chinese.

More than 30 years after establishment, HSP is still growing. Although HSP's land of 653 ha has no plan for future expansion, there is a relatively high turnover of tenant companies whose number is continuously increasing. Instead of enlarging the physical boundaries of HSP, five satellite parks such as Jhunan Science Park and Longtan Science Park are created to accommodate more firms. At HSP, about 30 companies move in and a considerable but fluctuating number of companies move out every year with the result that the number of park tenants is increasing and average space per factory is becoming smaller over time, which is the intended policy of the Science Park Administration. HSP is an attractive location for high-tech companies because of its accumulated talent, technology, and knowledge networks as well as subsidized rents and high reputation. There are about 60 companies waiting to enter HSP as of early 2011. Applicant companies are screened for their R&D activities, capital, environmental concern, and so on. Meanwhile, tenant firms which fail to spend at least 2.28 percent (twice the national average) of sales revenue on R&D, or those which miss monthly payments twice, are asked to leave HSP.

Since its establishment, HSP has received state investments by the Science Park Administration amounting to NT$86 billion. In addition, HSP's income is supplemented by the collection of management fees and rental and operational revenues. HSP began to make profit around 2000 and currently enjoys stable revenue. Because HSP is the leading science park in Taiwan, it financially assists other science parks, including those in Taichung and Tainan, and monitors their operational performance.

7.5 Export processing zones

Export processing zones (EPZs), together with the strong SME sector backed by appropriate policy support, discussed in the following section, were the two main drivers of Taiwan's industrial growth in the past which were emulated by many other countries. Nowadays they have become standard policy tools for latecomer industrialization around the world. As Taiwan's industrialization moved into the age of innovation and soft power, they no longer play the primary role in policy formulation as in the previous decades although they are still well-functioning and important for securing robust and shared growth. A great deal can be learned from the management of these two crucial policy instruments, from which Taiwan has realized so much economic and social gains, by developing countries of the twenty-first century which have not yet installed them successfully.

EPZs have a longer history than science parks. Combining the functions of free trade zone and industrial park, Taiwan established an EPZ at Kaohsiung Port in the Southern part of the island in December 1966.

Administrative procedures were streamlined, one-stop service was installed, and tax incentives were provided. The Kaohsiung EPZ was the world's first successful EPZ that became the model for other countries to follow.[7] Since its space next to the harbor were quickly occupied by manufacturers of radios and garments, two more such zones, the Taichung and Nantze EPZs, were subsequently added in 1969 and 1971, respectively. As demand for superior industrial land continued to outstrip the supply of space, the government began in 1997 to further develop the Linkuang, Chungkang and Pingtung EPZs and the Chengkung Logistics Park. The Software-based Technology Park was recently added to the list to stimulate development of the software industry in Southern Taiwan. The EPZ Administration of the MoEA, located in Kaohsiung, oversees these EPZs and parks in Central and Southern Taiwan. The total area of these estates is 532 hectares, which includes Kaohsiung EPZ (72.4 hectares), Nantze EPZ (97.8 hectares), and Taichung EPZ (26.2 hectares), which are the original three.

Unlike science parks which were established for the pursuit of high technology from the beginning, industrial focus of EPZs shifted over time to trace the structural transformation of Taiwan, from clothing and hair dryers to cameras and sewing machines and finally to integrated circuits (ICs) and liquid crystal displays (LCDs). This transition is visually displayed in a small museum housed in the EPZ Administration. By the suggestion of Kuo-Ding Lee, the Commissioner of the International Economic Cooperation Council, the Taiwanese government adopted the "labor-intensive light industry development first" strategy to promote export in the early 1960s. Initially, the four objectives of the EPZs were attraction of industrial investment, development of international trade, transfer of new technologies, and creation of employment. From 1966 to 1976, tenant firms of EPZs were engaged mainly in traditional manufacturing as well as low-end original equipment manufacturing (OEM, or contract manufacturing for foreign brand products) of general consumer electronics and components such as black-and-white TVs, transistor radios, calculators, and audio devices (56.7 percent); garment such as trousers, jackets, leather coats, and knitwear (16.4 percent); plastic products (5.9 percent); and other miscellaneous goods (21.0 percent). From 1977 to 1986, production in the EPZs gradually moved up to mid-end and high-end OEM of consumer electronics and components such as color TVs, car audio system, IC, variable resistors, memories, and fluorescent displays (65.0 percent); garments (11.4 percent); precision products such as camera lens (5.7 percent); and others (17.9 percent). In these early days, foreign firms had high representation in the EPZs. Workers in the zones were predominantly female. Young women commuting on bicycles to EPZs was a common sight in the 1970s. All products made in EPZs had to be exported initially, a requirement that was subsequently relaxed in 1986 and eventually abandoned in 1997.

From 1987 to 1996, industries in EPZs shifted further to high-tech and capital- and technology-intensive industries while mid- and high-range OEM also continued. The product mix became dominated by electronic components such as IC packaging, LCDs, single-layer printed circuit boards, and so forth (75.3 percent) followed by high-end garment (6.2 percent), precision products (5.0 percent), and others (13.5 percent). The trend continued in 1997–2004 while trading and warehousing industries and original design manufacturing (ODM) were added. Products continued to climb up the technological scale as follows: mid- and high-level electronic components (81.0 percent), precision products (7.0 percent); international trade (4.4 percent); and others (7.6 percent). In 2005, the industrial cluster development strategy was launched by the government.

The current focus industries at the EPZs include IC testing and packaging (Nantze EPZ), LCD modules (Kaohsiung EPZ), and opto-electronics (Taichung EPZ). Gauged by distribution of corporate revenues which totaled US$8.66 billion in 2009, the currently dominant sector is electronic parts and components (64.2 percent) followed by non-metallic mineral products (8.8 percent), and computer, electronic, and optical products (8.6 percent). In 2009, new investments in the EPZs were made mainly by domestic firms (42.1 percent) and joint ventures (45.8 percent) whereas the share of 100 percent foreign investors was small (12.2 percent). Back in 1991, the latter had an investment share of 38.2 percent.

Institutions and services offered by the EPZ Administration also changed as industrial competitiveness and structure were upgraded. As noted above, the requirement that all goods produced in the zones must be exported was dropped partially in 1986 and completely in 1997. As a result, about two-thirds of the products are currently exported and the remaining one-third are sold domestically. Investor categories were also expanded from manufacturing only to trading and logistics. For efficiency, the door management system of cargo handling was replaced by the account management system, and 24-hour automated customs clearance which takes only 30 minutes from customs to port or airport was introduced. Trade permits were abolished, except for restricted high-tech products, in accordance with WTO rules.

In absolute numbers, corporate revenues, investments and trade at EPZs have increased significantly over the decades. In the first 35 years, EPZ tenant firms have generated about US$50 billion in foreign exchange. In relative terms, the zones' contribution to Taiwan's exports peaked in 1974 when they accounted for 9 percent of Taiwan's total exports of US$5.6 billion in that year. Their share of exports has shrunk steadily since then to stand at around 3.5 percent at present. In 2010, the number of tenant companies was 456 which collectively recorded NT$380 billion in corporate revenue, NT$56 billion in investment, and US$19.2 billion in export.

As factors of long-term successful operation, the EPZ Administration cited the right timing of establishment in the post-World War II high-growth period; excellent location in dynamic Asia with a deep sea port and an international airport; the perfect legal system to encourage and assure investors; a single contact window; good infrastructure and industrial services with favorable living conditions; availability of skilled workers; and successful absorption of foreign technology and qualified tenant companies.[8] In fact, these are common requirements for successful industrial estates anywhere in the world, which must be fulfilled from the viewpoint of tenant companies, but only a small number of industrial zones, high-tech parks, and special economic zones in the world can actually provide them. Since 1966, there have been 19 countries that requested planning, and 13 countries that requested evaluation, consultancy, and field study, of their EPZs with the assistance of Taiwanese experts. For example, the Tan Thuan EPZ in Ho Chi Minh City, which is the first and most successful EPZ in Vietnam, was established and managed by a team of Taiwanese experts who earlier created the Kaohsiung EPZ.

Compared with science parks which require high R&D-to-sales ratios for entry and subsequent stay, EPZs are for more downstream manufacturing which does not necessarily require constant development of new technology with heavy capital investment. For firms that wish to manufacture advanced products with a large and stable pool of skilled and well-educated workers rather than a few scientists and engineers with advanced degrees and high turnovers, EPZs may be an ideal location that can offer logistic efficiency, reliable workers, and continued availability of good and cheap industrial land. Among the tenants of the EPZs are Advanced Semiconductor Engineering, the world's largest IC tester and packager which has 12 factories in the Nantze EPZ; Taiflex Scientific, a spin-off company of ITRI that produces high-tech components for photo-voltaic modules; Emerging Display Technologies, an LCD company in the Linkuang EPZ; Arima Display, a maker of small- and medium-size flat panel displays for mobile phones in the Linkuang EPZ; and Taiwan Brother Industries, a high-end sewing machine manufacturer in the Nantze EPZ.

From around 2005, the EPZ Administration began to mediate industry–university linkage. The program consists of human exchange such as student internship and visiting professors at factories as well as research cooperation for technology transfer and commercialization. The EPZ Administration offers matching services, one-stop window, and database for the use of universities. Based on company needs, a team of students led by a professor is to conduct joint R&D—as is actively done at Nanyang Polytechnic in Singapore (Chapter 6). While formation of such industry–university collaboration was the very reason for the establishment of science parks such as HSP, it is a policy measure introduced relatively recently at EPZs.

7.6 Promotion of small and medium enterprises

Historically, Taiwan has been an SME-driven economy par excellence. Unlike most developing countries where SME promotion is always planned but continues to remain on paper, Taiwan's dynamic SMEs were the true driving force of catch-up industrialization. Together with export processing zones, Taiwan's SME-led industrialization has become a standard model referenced by many countries in the world. Although the remarkable structural transformation spearheaded by local semi-conductor giants in recent years makes SMEs look less important, decline is only relative and not absolute. Taiwan's SME sector remains very strong by international standards and continues to play key roles in generating output, employment, investment, and export. Under globalization and rapidly changing markets, challenges faced by Taiwanese SMEs are basically the same as those for large companies or foreign competitors. They must grow out of their traditional mode of operation and transform themselves for international competitiveness. New business strategies must be adopted to improve productivity, accelerate innovation, conduct R&D, and explore new products, markets, and partners. Collaboration among industry, government, universities, and research institutes is also important for the survival and prosperity of SMEs in the future.

In the manufacturing, construction, mining, and quarrying sector, SMEs are defined as establishments with less than NT$80 million (US$2.5 million) in paid-in capital or less than 200 persons. In the service and commerce sector, they are establishments with less than NT$100 million (US$3.2 million) in paid-in capital or less than 100 persons. Micro businesses are defined as establishments with less than five persons for all sectors. In 2010, the number of SMEs in Taiwan was 1.24 million, or 97.77 percent of all enterprises. The SME sector accounts for 76.7 percent of total employment, 29.8 percent of total sales, and 17.9 percent of total export.[9] The number of start-up companies is 88,531 annually, amounting to 7.1 percent of total SMEs.

Promotion of SMEs is the responsibility of the SME Administration under the MoEA. It has five divisions which are policy planning, management consulting, business start-up and incubation, information technology, and financing. Taiwan's SME service network consists of the SME Administration headquarters in Taipei which houses a one-stop service center, two regional offices in Central and Southern Taiwan, and 24 local service centers. The SME Administration also cooperates with the National Association of SMEs, the China Youth Career Development Association, and 23 industrial associations and 24 chambers of commerce at central and municipal levels. SMEs located in industrial estates can receive services from zone administrations.

Taiwan's SME promotion is composed of many programs covering a wide ground (Table 7.2). Support is organized in three layers according to existing management and technological capabilities of SMEs. The "award strategy" is adopted for top SMEs (1–3 percent of all SMEs in number) by which national, rising star, and R&D awards are given. The "guidance strategy" is used for the middle layer of SMEs (27–34 percent of total) where 11 guidance systems are available which are industrial safety, R&D, pollution prevention, production technology, marketing, management, finance, quality upgrading, information management, business start-up and incubation, and mutual assistance and collaboration. For the remainder of SMEs which are called

Table 7.2 Components of small and medium enterprise policies

I Enhancing business management	
1. e-services	Promoting digital applications and bridging divital divice
	Industry-specific e-commerce business
	e-Service Corp Project
	Supply chain connectivity and competitiveness
	Knowledge management and competitiveness
	Value chain information for manufacturing
	Value-added ICT for traditional manufacturing
	Quality of business services, healthy business development
	Logistics niche and supply chain management
	Intelligent display shelf sales service and brand competitiveness
	RFID technology
2. Quality and management	SME clusters with innovation and integration
	Quality management and new quality image
	Quality and competitiveness for high-value industries
	New image via the promotion of Qualia
	System supply chain collaboration
	International green supply chain
	Energy conservation and reduced carbon emissions
	Manufacturing sector energy conservation and carbon reduction
	Sustainable development under international environmental standards
	Knowledge-intensive service-oriented clusters
	Improving working environment
3. Technology upgrading	Real-time technology
	Traceability in food processing industry
	Business innovation and internet development for new markets
4. R&D capabilities	Small Business Innovation Research Program (SBIR)
	Industrial Technology Development Program (ITDP)
	Innovative Technology Application and Service (ITAS)
	Conventional Industry Technology Development (CITD)
	Leading Product Development Guidance Project
	Technology development in service sector
5. Business management	Assessing intellectual property innovation value
	Brand blueprints for innovative products and service values
	Training for management consultant capabilities
	SME awards and recognition events
II. Strengthening financing and investment capabilities	
1. SME finance diagnostic guidance	SME Financing Service Contact Windows
	SME Troubleshooting Centers
	Financing Services Team
	Assistance to help obtain working capital
	Using intellectual property to obtain financing
2. SME financing and credit guarantees	SME Financing Service Platform
	Policy loans for special projects
	Increasing loans to SMEs by domestic banks
	Credit guarantees with 25 types of guarantees

Table 7.2 (cont'd)

3. SMEs affected by natural disasters	Reconstruction & financial assistance after Typhoon Morakot Assistance after the 2010 Kaohsiung Earthquake
4. Investment	SME Development Corporations SME Start-up Investment Trust Account National Development Fund's plan for promoting SME investment
III. Start-up capabilities and business incubation	
1. Start-up Guidance Plan	One-stop guidance integrating existing sub-plans SME Entrepreneurship and Innovation Service Centers
2. Industry–university incubation network	Support and direct operation of incubation centers Industry-specific incubation networks Resource integration platform for industry-university collaboration SME innovative service certification subsidies and grants Assistance to SME technology development by universities
3. Environment conducive to start-ups	Commercialization of award-winning start-up projects Information and consulting services SME Entrepreneurship and Innovation College Entrepreneur Lab Business start-up awards
4. Female entrepreneurial activity	Free consulting service & resources handbook Training, awards, subsidies, Flying Goose Program, Phoenix Plan, etc. Mutual assistance networks Information exchange platforms Financing support
IV. Local economies and new business opportunities	
1. Stregthening local industries	One Town One Product (OTOP) with innovation and marketing Guidance for regional/thematic cultural industries The ICT747 Plan to revitalize regional economies Local industrial cluster development Creative Lifestyle Industry Development Plan Local Industry Innovation Engine Plan Local Small Business Innovation Research (Local SBIR) Plan Local Business District Branding Development Plan
2. Local Industry Development Fund	Individual funding support Integrated funding support Central government inter-regional subsidy Local industry service teams
3. i-Care Plan (proactive service for local SMEs)	Needs survey through local concern hotline, on-site interviews, etc. SME service network
4. New opportunities and markets	Assisting market development with 14 sub-programs Assisting brand development with 5 sub-programs

Table 7.2 (*cont'd*)

V. International relations and other resources	
1. International SME meetings and events	OECD, APEC, ICSB, GEM, bilateral exchanges
2. Manpower training	Digital learning, business incubation, technology training R&D and management technology talent training Professional training for specific industries Fostering international trade and business talent Entrepreneurial incubation for women
3. Legal rights adaptation	Survey, analysis and amendments of SME legal rights adaptation Improving SME knowledge of regulations Analysis of SME-related laws and regulations

Source: The author's summary from Small and Medium Enterprise Administration, *White Paper on Small and Medium Enterprises in Taiwan*, 2010.

foundation SMEs (65–70 percent of total), the "grouping strategy" comprising mutual cooperation, industry clusters, local cultural industry, and financing programs is offered. The SME Administration works closely with IDB, DoIT, the Bureau of Foreign Trade, and the Department of Commerce, all under the MoEA, to provide integrated support. Four pillars of SME promotion policy are described in more detail below. Under each policy pillar there are numerous programs and mechanisms to support that pillar.

The first policy pillar is management and technical support. SMEs are provided with courses, enterprise consultancy (which is connected to bank loans), technology, and linkage. The support topics include guidance on e-service; guidance in quality and management; technology upgrading services; R&D capabilities; and guidance on business management. A large number of programs, up to 34, are available according to the White Paper on SMEs in 2010. Providers of SME consultation service are private firms and individual consultants selected through open bidding for government procurement. Unlike Malaysia today or Thailand in the past, Taiwanese SME consultants are all private agents with no government officials involved in direct provision of services. SMEs receive consultation free of charge. However, if new investment or additional training becomes necessary, that must be financed by SMEs themselves. Japanese terms such as kaizen and shindan are not well known although standard productivity tools such as 5S and QCC are widely recognized and used.

The second policy pillar is finance and investment. Under this pillar, diagnostic guidance, SME financing and credit guarantees, support for SMEs affected by natural disasters, and investment promotion are offered in 16 different programs. The SME Administration has arranged for the establishment of SME Financing Service Contact Windows in the branches of 34 major financial institutions where SMEs can obtain comprehensive financial information including low-interest loans available from the government. The SME Administration also has SME Troubleshooting Centers with consulting services in financial and loan matters. Resources for SME loans are provided by the SME Development Fund and the National Development Fund. These funds are on-lent by commercial banks to SMEs and start-up companies. In addition, 15 percent of funding from the SME Development Fund goes to target companies through SME investment companies. Separately, the SME Credit Guarantee Fund guarantees 80–90 percent of commercial bank loans to SMEs and offers a large number of credit guarantee programs. The Incubation Fund Account and various official rewards given to excellent SMEs are additional facilitators of SME finance. These government-funded financial measures are expected to pump-prime greater SME finance by private funds, capital markets, and venture capital.

The third policy pillar is strengthening of business start-up capabilities. In 2009, the SME Administration launched a newly enhanced approach called the Start-up Guidance Plan which integrated 16 sub-plans to improve the start-up incubation environment, build start-up knowledge information platforms, and help new businesses to obtain funding. It set the goal of cultivating 800 core innovation-oriented SMEs in 2009–2011. The Plan is implemented through the SME Entrepreneurship and Innovation Service Centers located in Northern, Central, Southern, and Eastern Taiwan. These centers serve as one-stop service windows for guiding potential and existing new entrepreneurs through the entire process toward becoming innovative SMEs. For this purpose, the sub-plans include incubation centers, industry-specific incubation networks, resource integration platform for industry–university collaborative research, Business Start-up Awards, commercialization of award-winning projects, information and consulting services, SME Entrepreneurship and Innovation College, Entrepreneur Lab, various mechanisms for providing services to female entrepreneurs, and many others.

The fourth policy pillar supports local economies and establishment of local cultural industries. It aims to leverage distinctive features of Taiwan's local communities and help rural areas upgrade and transform themselves. The most important tool for this pillar is the Taiwan One Town One Product (OTOP) program, adopted from Japan's One Village One Product Movement,[10] which aims to develop local specialty industries with township or city as units and targeting both domestic and tourism markets. Starting from 1989, the SME Administration has supported local SMEs with management, design, packaging, technology, space arrangement, and so on; participation in exhibitions and training courses; and creation of publications, websites, and Taiwan OTOP shops. Specialist guidance teams are organized to collaborate with business enterprises in identified potential local industries. Two important supplementary programs to OTOP are the ICT747 Plan that uses information and communications technology to upgrade traditional industries and the Creative Lifestyle Industry Development Plan that promotes local tourism, innovation, and new business models. Through these programs a total of 96 featured towns have successfully generated their distinctive local products (information as of August 2011 on the OTOP website).

This concludes our brief tour of "Silicon Island." Overall, it can be said that Taiwan's industrial capability and supporting policies are highly advanced. Industrial policy has a relatively simple structure and its objectives are clearly defined in a law while each of the policy instruments has developed into a comprehensive and elaborate system which cannot be easily imitated by developing countries with low policy capability and at a lower stage of industrialization. Obviously, policy learning from Taiwan must start with selecting, simplifying, and modifying the lessons to fit the local capabilities and needs of student countries.

8 Malaysia

Trapped in upper middle income

Malaysia is a country in Southeast Asia comprising Peninsula Malaysia and the northern part of Borneo Island. By Asian standards, it has a relatively small population of 28.3 million that breaks down to three main ethnic groups: the indigenous Malays who are dominant (two-thirds of the population) and Islamic, the Chinese, and the Indians. The latter two are migrants or the posterity of former migrants to Malaysia. Maintaining peace among ethnicities and promoting economic prosperity are two overarching, intertwined, and sometimes conflicting goals of Malaysia to which all policies must contribute. Striking an appropriate balance between the two goals is a great challenge for the country, with each administration adjusting its position on this delicate question.

From the end of the eighteenth century to the nineteenth century, Britain occupied and controlled Malaysia in steps viewing it as a strategic sea route as well as a supplier of primary commodities. After British Malaya was established in 1874, Chinese labor was imported to engage in commerce and tin mining while Indian labor was imported to work on rubber plantations. Dependence on natural resources and ethnic division of labor in productive sectors were the characteristics of Malaysia inherited from the days of British rule.

Since independence in 1957, Malaysia has successfully transformed its economic structure from a resource-based to a manufacture-based one. In 1960 the export share of primary commodities such as rubber, tin, timber, palm oil, and crude oil was as high as 80 percent. Through the 40 years of industrialization effort that followed, the share of manufactured exports rose steadily from 25.4 percent in 1970 to 27.2 percent in 1980, 53.6 percent in 1990, and 77.4 percent in 2000 although it then declined to 64.8 percent in 2009 (Department of Statistics data). In the late twentieth century Malaysia emerged as one of the world's largest exporters of consumer and industrial electronic products which still dominate its manufactured exports. In 2010, Malaysia's per capita GDP stood at US$7,900 (World Bank Atlas method) which puts the country comfortably in the upper-middle-income group. However, despite brilliant structural transformation in the past and reasonably competent policies and bureaucrats, the country feels entrapped in average achievement without reaching high income. This chapter explores the nature and possible causes of Malaysia's accomplishments and woes.

8.1 Policy evolution

As with other high-performing economies in East Asia, the industrial policy of Malaysia has gone through several stages as illustrated in Figure 8.1. In the early years of independence the main objective was diversification of economic structure to escape from heavy reliance on a small number of traditional primary commodities. In its 1955 report on the economic development of Malaysia, the World Bank advised diversification through the development of additional primary commodities and new industrial products. To carry out this strategy, *pioneer industries status* was invented in 1958, which exempted corporate income taxes for two to five years for eligible firms. Most of the approved pioneer industry firms at that time belonged to the import-substituting consumer goods sector. During this early period, the free-market principle was upheld with little official intervention into private-sector activities.

In the 1970s two major changes were made in economic policy. First, policy focus shifted from import substitution, which was deemed unsuccessful due to the limited size of the domestic market, to export orientation based on attraction of manufacturing FDI which engaged in assembly and processing for export. A series of laws were promulgated to expertise this policy, such as the Investment Incentive Act (1968), which gave the pioneer status and other incentives to export-oriented industries, and the Free Trade Zone Act (1971), which exempted tariffs on imported inputs and allowed ten-year tax breaks (12 years for electronics) for firms in free trade zones exporting 80 percent or more of their products. In addition, the Licensed Manufacturing Warehouse system was introduced by which these privileges were extended even to companies located outside free trade zones. Armed with these incentives, Penang Island on the western coast of Malay Peninsula started to attract global semi-conductor giant firms while Klang Valley in the vicinity of Kuala Lumpur, the capital city, saw the arrival of foreign electronics firms many of which were Japanese. The high-wage policy of nearby Singapore also pushed labor-intensive foreign manufacturers to relocate to Malaysia.

The second important policy shift of the 1970s was triggered by the May 1969 ethnic riot between the economically powerful Chinese and the poorer but more populous Malays. A national election that increased the seats of Chinese resident-friendly parties prompted a victory march of elated Chinese citizens and a counter-march of Malay youths, which ended up in a bloody crash. This was a big shock to Malaysia, shaking the foundation of the multiracial society and forcing the national leaders to give up laissez-faire policy for more engineered social equity. The Bumiputra (indigenous residents) policy, previously in place, was greatly strengthened and formalized by setting administrative quotas for public positions, business ownership and management, and worker employment in favor of ethnic Malays. The second Malaysia Plan 1971–1975 (equivalent to the five-year plan), which was also called the New Economic Policy (NEP), proclaimed these racial affirmative actions.

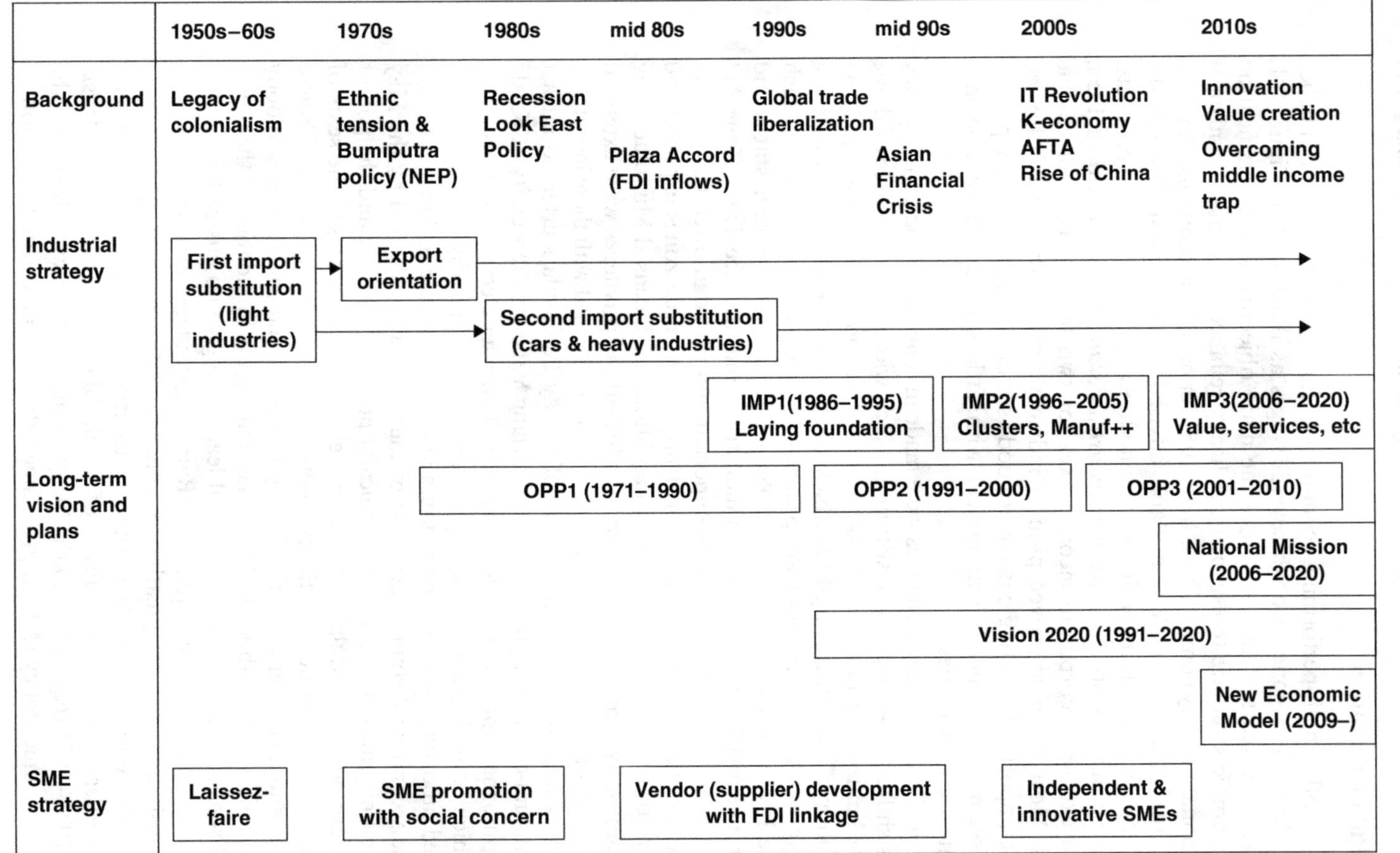

Figure 8.1 Malaysia: evolution of industrial policy

Source: Ide (2004) with revisions and updates by the author.

In the 1980s, under the leadership of Mahathir bin Mohamad, who served as prime minister from 1981 to 2003, heavy industrialization was initiated along with continued export orientation. Look East Policy (learning from Japan and South Korea) was also launched. Heavy industrialization was carried out with strong official intervention. The Heavy Industries Corporation of Malaysia (HICOM), a state-owned conglomerate, was established in 1980. Proton, a national car maker, was set up as a joint venture with Japan's Mitsubishi group in 1983 (section 8.5). The company began to produce Saga, modeled after Mitsubishi Lancer, in 1985. Establishment of a national car company was driven by the economic motive of creating a broad industrial base as well as a social motive of assisting Malay workers and Bumiputra firms. National car production was heavily protected with import tariffs of 140–300 percent for passenger cars, 42–200 percent for commercial vehicles, 42–80 percent for complete knockdown passenger cars, and 5–40 percent for complete knockdown commercial vehicles. In 1988, the Proton Component Scheme was introduced to increase parts procurement from Bumiputra supplier firms, which later developed into the Vendor Development Program. A mandatory local procurement program was installed in 1991 (which, however, had to be abolished by 2004 in the process of WTO trade liberalization negotiation).

The First Industrial Master Plan (IMP1) 1986–1995 recognized the weaknesses of Malaysian industries such as excessive reliance on foreign semi-conductor giants for export and the lack of linkage between FDI and local firms. The key thrusts of IMP1 included outward-looking industrialization which targeted exports, modernization of "ancillary firms" (part and component suppliers, also called "supporting industries"), and strengthening of industrial linkages. A number of liberalization measures were undertaken such as allowance of 100 percent foreign ownership to enterprises exporting at least 50 percent of products (instead of previous 80 percent) or hiring at least 350 regular employees. Sales to free trade zones and licensed manufactured warehouses were now counted as exports. Meanwhile, a sharp appreciation of the Japanese yen starting in 1985 pushed up production costs in Japan and drove Japanese manufacturing FDI to come to Southeast Asia to build new factories, an incident which greatly expanded the industrial base of Malaysia. The number of Japanese firms operating in Malaysia increased from 477 in 1986 to 1,070 in 2005. Among them, Japanese firms in the electronics sector increased from 30 to 244. In this way, heavy state intervention, practiced mainly in the automobile sector, and economic liberalization for absorbing FDI, adopted mainly in the electronics sector, proceeded in parallel.

In 1991, Prime Minister Mahathir announced Vision 2020, an aspiration to become a fully-developed country by 2020 based on nine broad principles such as democracy and prosperity.[1] Ever since, Vision 2020 has become the supreme national goal of Malaysia for which all policies and actions must strive. In ethnic balance policy, a new objective was added for the creation of the Bumiputra Commercial and Industrial Community, a concept that the Malays should become creators of value rather than passive receivers of privileges. As in previous years, promotion of supporting industries, especially local automobile component suppliers, was pursued with two purposes: as a means of expanding industrial capability and as a component of Bumiputra policy to strengthen Malay suppliers.

The Second Industrial Master Plan (IMP2) 1996–2005 was guided by two overruling ideas of *cluster-based industrial development* and *manufacturing plus plus*. The first broadened the concept of an industry to include not just supporting industries (physical inputs) but also supporting services, R&D, human skills, infrastructure, institutions, and other elements that collectively support the development of any industrial sector. The second expressed the desire to enhance capability of industries both horizontally and vertically, i.e., encompassing more processes, both upstream and downstream, and improving productivity of each process—hence two *pluses*—along the value chain as shown in Figure 8.2. These two ideas were uniformly applied to eight target sectors which are electronics and electrical, textiles and apparel, chemicals, resource-based industries, food processing, transport equipment, materials, and machinery and equipment. The fact that the background paper of IMP2 was drafted by a researcher at the Malaysian Institute of Economic Research, a prominent policy think tank, gave it a lucid style and mechanical consistency throughout the plan document unlike IMP1 or IMP3, which were bottom-up collections of writings of various expert groups without central instruction (Ohno 2006b).

Since the late 1990s, several internal and external developments have occurred. The rise of China, and later Vietnam, India, and Indonesia, as

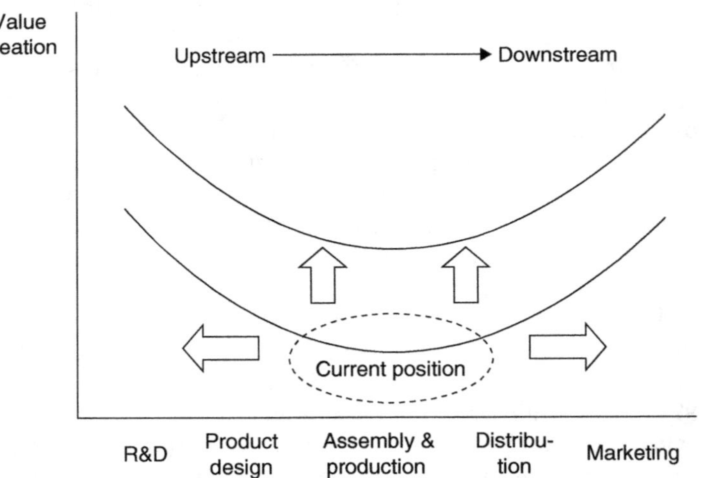

Figure 8.2 Manufacturing plus plus

Source: Drafted by the author based on the Second Industrial Master Plan 1996–2005, an interview with Malaysian industrial planning officials in 2006, and the website of the Ministry of International Trade and Industry of Malaysia.

regional competitors in manufactured export and FDI attraction called for policy re-consideration. Malaysia also had to cope with economic downturns associated with the Asian financial crisis of 1997–1998, the global semiconductor recession around 2001, and the severe global recessions caused by the Lehman shock of 2008–2009 and the Euro shock of 2011–2012. The electronics sector dominated by foreign giants continued to be the largest exporter of Malaysia whereas the results of two-pronged value creation and development of broad-based industrial clusters, as envisioned in IMP2, were not very successful. As global and regional integration deepened, the protected automobile sector faced an increasing challenge from foreign competitors while its domestic market remained small (section 8.5).

Meanwhile, policy interest in absorbing a large amount of manufacturing FDI to form the nation's industrial base, strengthening supporting industries, and forging links between local and FDI firms, a strategy vigorously pursued in the late 1980s and the 1990s, has waned. Although the electronics and automobile sectors remain the largest manufacturing activities in Malaysia, they are no longer the main concern of the Malaysian government. The policy objective has shifted to the creation of innovative local SMEs which can operate competitively and independently from multi-national corporations or government-linked companies. Instead of upgrading manufacturing skills and management for automobile part suppliers, terms like K-economy, ICT, e-commerce, bio-tech, and branding began to proliferate in policy documents.

The Third Industrial Master Plan (IMP3) 2006–2020 seeks holistic development. Services, especially high-value services and industry-supporting services, have been added to the policy menu along with traditional manufacturing. Emphasis is placed on value-added, technology, knowledge, human resources, and other cross-cutting functions. Unlike the previous IMP2 which lacked an effective review mechanism, IMP3 is equipped with explicit annual monitoring and evaluation targets and procedure. The policy scope of IMP3, which is the last industrial policy document that will take the nation to Vision 2020, is longer (15 years) and broader (25 chapters over 247 pages) than IMP2. It targets six non-resource based manufacturing industries, six resource-based manufacturing industries, eight service sub-sectors, the halal industry, and eight functional issues.[2]

I led an international research team on a visit to Kuala Lumpur in 2006 and again in 2010 to discuss industrial policy formulation with Malaysian industrial officials. On both occasions we raised a question about the lack of policy focus as IMP2, and IMP3 even more so, seemed to cover virtually every industrial sector and aspect that could be thought of in Malaysia. While these plans look comprehensive and professionally prepared as far as policy documents go, policy outcome is less than assured. This is the fundamental Malaysian dilemma, with a sharp contrast between constant progress in policy sophistication versus lagging private-sector response, that will be examined more fully in subsequent sections.

8.2 Tackling the middle-income trap

In 2009, the World Bank published a report on the Malaysian economy, prepared by Philip Schellekens, that warned that the country seemed trapped in mediocre performance.

> The overriding medium-term challenge is for the Malaysian economy to join the select group of high-income countries. Malaysia has experienced solid growth over the last decades, but has relied on an economic model predominantly based on capital accumulation . . . In spite of these past successes, Malaysia's growth performance has lagged behind that of other regional economies. The economy seems to be caught in a middle-income trap—unable to remain competitive as a high-volume, low-cost producer, yet unable to move up the value chain and achieve rapid growth by breaking into fast growing markets for knowledge- and innovation-based products and services.
>
> (World Bank, 2009, pp. 52–53)

Prime Minister Najib Tun Razak, who assumed power in April 2009, takes this warning very seriously. He regards the overcoming of the middle-income trap as the most important economic goal of his government and initiated a series of policy action for this purpose. Mr. Najib's economic management stresses value creation backed by liberalization and open competition. Although Bumiputra policy, as one of the principal pillars of Malaysia's national development, will certainly not be dismantled any time soon, emphasis is shifting from administrative quotas to market-guided equal opportunities among all ethnicities.

To specify necessary actions, he formed the National Economic Advisory Board headed by Amirsham A. Aziz in May 2009 to draft the New Economic Model, an ad hoc strategy that spelled out Mr. Najib's policy concerns and solutions. In its mandate, the Council was required to "provide a fresh, independent perspective in transforming Malaysia from a middle income economy to a high income economy by Year 2020." The New Economic Model was published in two parts, in March 2010 and December 2010, with the first part setting strategic directions and the second (concluding) part proposing additional policy measures. With the official completion of the Council's mandate in May 2011, responsibility to execute its recommendations was passed on to relevant ministries and agencies under the coordination of the Prime Minister's Department.

The New Economic Model echoes the pessimism and urgency of action expressed in the World Bank report.

> [T]he progress we have made over the past half-century has slowed and economic growth prospects have weakened considerably. We are caught in a middle income trap—we are not amongst the top performing global

> economies. We urgently need a radical change in our approach to economic development which will be sustainable over the long-term, will reach everyone in the country and will enable Malaysia to reach high income status.
>
> (New Economic Model, executive summary, pp. 3–4)

Malaysia's shortcomings that prevent the overcoming of the middle-income trap, as portrayed by the New Economic Model, are as follows:

- Malaysia is a small open economy susceptible to external shocks and losing competitiveness; its place in the Global Competitiveness Index dropped from the previous 21st to 24th in 2010.
- Productivity grows too slowly and innovation is insufficient; slow growth is eroding Malaysia's position among regional economies.
- The education system is inadequate; not enough high-wage jobs are created and talent is leaving the country.
- Investment as a share of GDP is declining and private investment is particularly stagnant.
- Exports are still strong but do not generate much value added.
- The rich and poor gap is widening; ethnic-based economic policy worked but implementation issues raised the cost of doing business.
- Price control and subsidies have resulted in resource misallocations and focus on short-term profits.

At the same time, the drafters of the Model notes that Malaysia also have some advantages, such as good infrastructure, a world-class manufacturing base centered on electronics and electrical, strategic location at the heart of a vibrant region, and a model of cultural, ethnic, and biological diversity.

To take the country to high income by 2020, New Economic Model Part 1 proposes to ensure benefits to all citizens and businesses as a matter of principle, prepare "enabling actions" consisting of strong political leadership and the citizens' support for deep seated changes, then presents eight Strategic Reform Initiatives (SRIs) as main required actions which further break down to 38 policy purposes and 144 possible policy measures (see below). In New Economic Model Part 2, relationship among this model and other initiatives of the government is clarified and five "recommendations on key focused and integrated policy actions" are advanced which overlap but are somewhat different from the eight SRIs, namely, (i) transformation through reinvigorating the private sector, (ii) enhancing innovation, (iii) public sector transformation, (iv) intensifying human capital development, and (v) narrowing disparities. These recommendations subdivide into 16 policy measures and 45 sub-measures, some of which are given more details and sub-divisions.[3]

Actually, Prime Minister Najib's national transformation strategy is much larger than just the New Economic Model. It specifies Vision 2020 fairly concretely, proclaims a three-part national slogan, and presents two new programs that cover economic and government reforms which are supplemented by the five-year plans. The New Economic Model is the main component of economic reform. Additionally, a mechanism is created to implement and monitor the progress of this strategy. The logical structure of Malaysia's transformation strategy, completed in 2010, is quite complex and difficult to grasp. Citing numerous official tables and diagrams, which contain a number of parallel explanations, linkages, re-wordings, and re-groupings, may confuse the reader as it did me. The structure shown in Figure 8.3 and the ensuing explanation are my interpretation with certain simplifications and rephrases which may differ from the full official version.

In this framework, the economic elements of Vision 2020 are explained more concretely in a diagram that explains ultimate goals and another list of desired national characteristics. The triple-oval diagram in the upper panel of Figure 8.3 declares that (i) Malaysia wants to attain high-income status with per capita income of US$15,000–17,000 by 2020; (ii) growth should be inclusive and strike a balance between the special position of Bumiputra and legitimate interests of other groups; and (iii) economic and environmental sustainability must be assured. All these goals must be attained, with no one goal to be achieved at the expense of the others. It is also stressed that the ultimate beneficiaries of this strategy must be all *Rakyat* (ordinary citizens) and all businesses. Separately, the kind of country that Malaysia aspires to be by 2020 is presented in five adjective phrases: market led, well-governed, regionally integrated, entrepreneurial, and innovative.

To achieve these goals, four pillars of national transformation are put forth. The first pillar is a slogan, "1Malaysia—People First, Performance Now," which must be uttered together and in this order, and written with no space between numeral one and Malaysia.

The second pillar is the Economic Transformation Program (ETP) that comprises the New Economic Model with its eight SRIs, mentioned above, and the 12 National Key Economic Areas. The eight Strategic Reform Initiatives (SRIs) are (i) re-energizing the private sector, (ii) creating a competitive domestic economy, (iii) building the knowledge base infrastructure, (iv) ensuring sustainability of growth, (v) enhancing the sources of growth, (vi) developing a quality workforce and reducing dependency on foreign labor, (vii) strengthening of the public sector and fiscal sustainability, and (viii) transparent and market friendly affirmative action. These are grouped into four "thrusts," namely, creating a competitive investment environment (combining (i)–(v)), developing quality workforce (vi), transforming government (vii), and narrowing disparity (viii).[4] Separately, the 12 National Key Economic Areas (NKEAs), which include 11 sectors and one region, were launched by the government in October 2010 as engines of future growth that are expected to contribute to the achievement of high income. They are oil, gas and energy; palm oil; financial services; tourism; business services; electronics and electrical; wholesale and retail; education; healthcare; communications, content, and infrastructure; agriculture; and the Greater Kuala Lumpur and Klang Valley. These specify

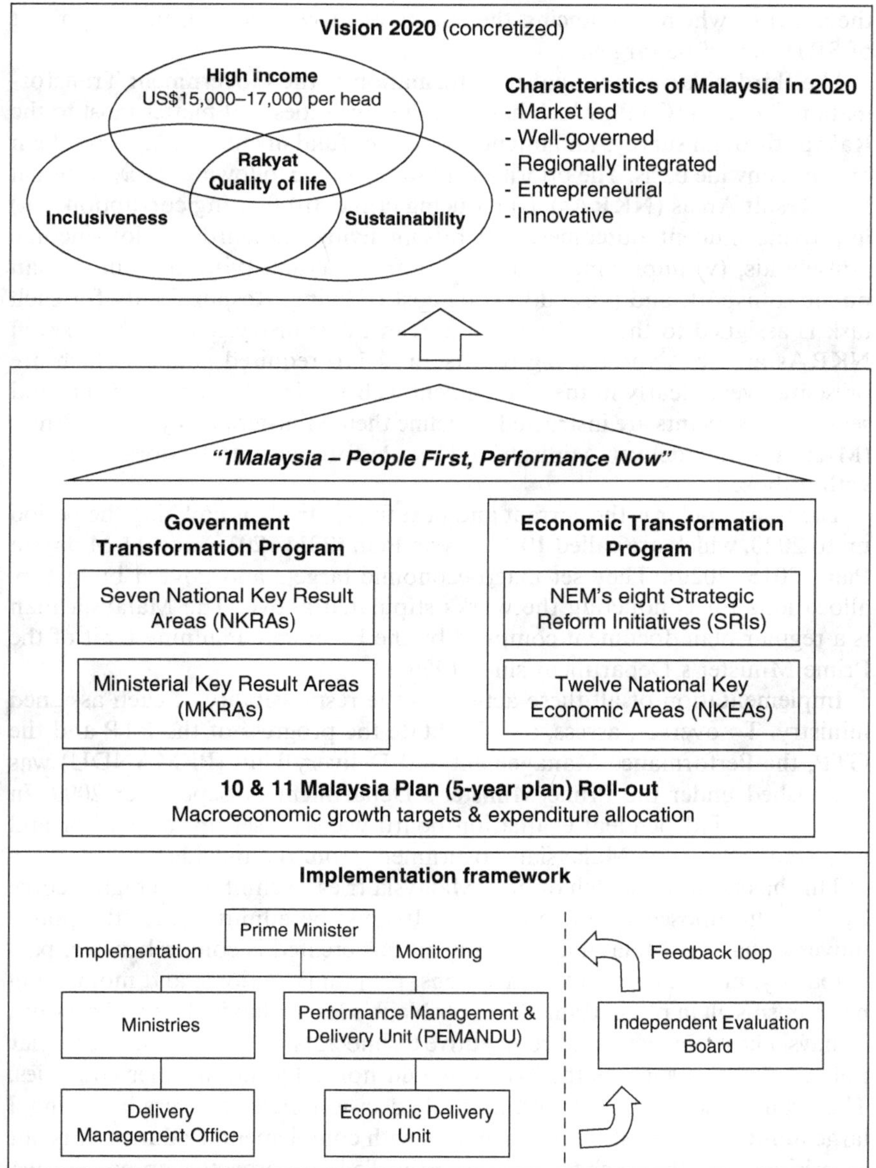

Figure 8.3 Malaysia: a summary of national transformation strategy

Note: Rakyat means ordinary citizens. See the main text for the definitions of the eight SRIs, the twelve NKEAs, and the seven NKRAs.

the areas to which "enhancing the source of growth" (the fifth component of SRI) should be targeted.

The third pillar of national transformation is the Government Transformation Program (GTP), which has identified priorities that matter most to the Rakyat through surveys and intends to deliver fundamental changes on them on a nationwide basis. The priorities are stated in the following seven National Key Result Areas (NKRAs): (i) reducing crime, (ii) fighting corruption, (iii) improving student outcomes, (iv) raising living standards of low-income households, (v) improving rural basic infrastructure, (vi) improving urban public transport, and (vii) addressing cost of living. Responsibility for each task is assigned to the minister of the relevant ministry. Under these seven NKRAs are 28 "expected big results" and 110 required actions which are presented very clearly in the government website. In addition, ministers and senior civil servants are instructed to define their Ministerial Key Result Areas (MKRAs) and deliver Ministerial Key Performance Indicators (MKPIs) within those areas.

The fourth pillar is the current and next five-year plans covering the period up to 2020, which are called 10 Malaysia Plan (2011–2015) and 11 Malaysia Plan (2016–2020). They set macroeconomic targets and govern budgetary allocations for conducting the works stipulated above. The Malaysia Plan is a regular plan document compiled by the Economic Planning Unit of the Prime Minister's Department since 1956.

Implementation of all these actions is the responsibility of each assigned ministry. To oversee, assess, and facilitate the progress of the ETP and the GTP, the Performance Management and Delivery Unit (PEMANDU) was established under the Prime Minister's Department in September 2009. In addition, an independent evaluation board was also set up to monitor and give feedback to the Malaysian government from the outside.

This has been the sketch of how Malaysia tries to climb up to high income by the self-imposed deadline of 2020. It must be admitted that the policy universe that the Malaysian government has created is comprehensive, participatory, and transparent with visions, programs, actions, and monitoring mechanisms all in place. Prime Minister Najib's leadership is clear and decisive. Malaysia has competent and competitive technocrats who can manage complex policy processes such as this which would normally fail in other countries. They can work effectively with multiple decision-making layers involving a large number of ministries and agencies with complementary duties. It is not surprising, then, that such technocrats, propelled by a proactive prime minister, have produced an elaborate policy system with a large number of internal linkages and key performance indicators. Documents they produce are colorful and easy to follow, and their websites are interactive and user friendly. Malaysian policies are not only well designed but actually implemented. They definitely have the quality to which any professor in public policy would be inclined to give an A+ if they were a term paper in Policy Design and Implementation in Developing Countries. Malaysia has mastered the art of policymaking to near perfection. Its policy documents can make good textbooks for other countries that want to follow.

However, if the reader still feels uneasy with the Malaysian approach, he or she is not alone. There is something fundamentally missing in this sophisticated policy package. The main reason why Malaysia is stuck in middle income is not because policy quality is low, but because private-sector response to good policy remains weak. Improving policy to perfection, driven by a natural instinct of intelligent government officials, will not solve the problem and even run the risk of policy improvements becoming an end in itself with an increasing gap between the aspiration of the government and the behaviors of local businesses and individuals. Transforming a sleepy private sector requires an entirely different set of policies which are less intricate but closer to the heart of the public (Chapter 3). Countries like Japan, Taiwan, and Thailand did not have a system of elaborate targets or key performance indicators in the past but could still achieve sustained high growth. In Japan, "think while running" (starting action without detailed plans and create and adjust them as you go) is practiced commonly. Similarly in Thailand, policy-making has been much simpler and more flexible without spending too much time in designing details in advance or reviewing past results. To overcome a middle-income trap and realize Vision 2020, Malaysia may need an entirely different approach than the present technocratic one with lots of acronyms and inflation of performance indicators.

8.3 Small and medium enterprise promotion

Nevertheless, the following two sections will examine good policy practices of Malaysia which should receive due credit. They take up SME promotion and FDI attraction as examples. Both policies are well developed and can be used as models for other countries to study and (selectively) follow.

SME promotion is a policy adopted in almost all countries, but its effectiveness varies greatly from one country to another. In some countries promotion exists only on paper. In others it is only partially and imperfectly practiced. It is also an area covering a wide range of issues such as industry, agriculture, trade, infrastructure, finance, taxes and subsidies, education and training, and science and technology, and it therefore requires strong coordination among ministries and agencies, which is a difficult assignment for countries with weak policy capability. Malaysia has established, over the years, a mechanism and a set of tools which are comprehensive and systematic for carrying out SME promotion. In recent years, the development of SMEs is an increasingly important national agenda as the hub of Malaysia's Economic Transformation Program that aims "to facilitate a quantum leap in SME growth and to achieve the aspirations of high income nation status by 2020" (National SME Development Council, 2011, p. 36).

In 1996, the Small and Medium Industries Development Corporation (SMIDEC) was established by upgrading the Small Industries Department of the Ministry of International Trade and Industry to serve as a central coordinating agency for SME policy as well as a provider of grants and soft loans to eligible SMEs. A new policy instrument created at that time for SMIDEC was the Industrial Linkage Program to facilitate cooperation between FDI and local firms. The Small and Medium Industries Development Plan 2001–2005 was prepared by SMIDEC as the first five-year plan document with clear focus on SME promotion. However, policy implementation continued to be fragmented across 16 agencies, including SMIDEC, with significant overlaps.

To further integrate SME policy and provide holistic support with strong political backing, the National SME Development Council chaired by the prime minister was established in 2004 as the highest body to direct Malaysia's SME policy. Fifteen ministries and 60 government agencies were brought under this Council. Initially serving as the secretariat to the Council, Bank Negara Malaysia (central bank) set three strategic thrusts (main policy areas), which were enabling infrastructure, capacity building, and access to financing. SMIDEC was elevated to become SME Corporation Malaysia (SME Corp for short) in 2009, providing central coordinating functions with greater authority, and also taking over the role of secretariat to the Council from Bank Negara (see Figure 4.6, in Chapter 4, for Malaysia's SME policy organization). Under the new arrangement, the Annual SME Integrated Plan of Action became the key policy document and the Council's Annual Report served as the vehicle for information dissemination. The common SME definition was adopted across the country and improvements were made in SME information services which consisted of the National SME Database, SMEinfo Portal, technology road mapping, and the SME Competitiveness Rating for Enhancement (SCORE).

In April and November 2011, the National SME Development Council endorsed the SME Masterplan 2012–2020 in two phases, with the first phase approving the framework and the second deciding on initiatives and programs. The Masterplan's vision is to create globally competitive SMEs that enhance wealth creation and contribute to the social well-being of the nation. Malaysia will develop not only national champions but also micro enterprises in rural areas. From 2010 to 2020, macro targets are set to (i) increase the contribution of SMEs to GDP from 32 percent to 41 percent, (ii) increase the employment share of SMEs from 59 percent to 62 percent; and (iii) increase the export share of SMEs from 19 percent to 25 percent. Additional numerical targets include business formation (6 percent per annum), the growth of high growth and innovative firms (10 percent per annum), labor productivity of SMEs (from RM47,000 to RM91,000), and formalization of the informal sector (informal establishments to be reduced from 31 percent to 15 percent). To achieve these targets, 32 key initiatives, which include six High Impact Programs (HIPs), are determined.[5] The National SME Development Council noted that growth of value added by SMEs was annual 6.8 percent during 2004–2010, exceeding that of the overall economy at annual 4.9 percent. The Council also decided to establish a National Steering Committee for Incubation Programs and annual SME Week, beginning in 2012.

As indicated above, SME support is directed to three policy areas—enabling infrastructure, capacity building, and access to financing—which is programmed and reported each year. According to SME Annual Report 2010/11, the total number of SME development programs in 2010 was 226 at the cost of RM7.1 billion (about US$2.3 billion) benefiting a total of 614,242 SMEs. As in previous years, the majority of programs in terms of number, as many as 165, were for capacity building of SMEs at the cost of RM718 million. This had four sub-areas: entrepreneur development, human capital development, marketing and promotion, and product development. Another 38 programs provided access to financing with the biggest budget allocation of RM6.3 billion. The remaining 23 programs were for strengthening the enabling infrastructure at the cost of RM180 million (National SME Development Council, 2011, p. 38).

Among the government agencies, several agencies under the Ministry of International Trade and Industry deserve special mention. They provide various functions for industrialization in general and SME promotion in particular:

SME Corporation Malaysia (SME Corp)—one stop service for SME policy as mentioned above;
Malaysian Investment Development Authority (MIDA)—investment promotion;
Malaysia Productivity Corporation (MPC)—training, consultation, research, etc.;
SME Bank—SME finance and training;
Malaysian Industrial Development Finance (MIDF)—policy finance;
Malaysia External Trade Development Corporation (MATRADE)—trade promotion.

Although SME policy organizations have been restructured for effectiveness, the system is still complex and overlapping functions among implementing agencies remain. However, All Malaysian agencies we interviewed stated that cooperation among them was close and that any service desired by customers but not offered by a particular agency would immediately be arranged and provided by others to minimize the customers' trouble and delay. MIDA (see section 8.4), for example, boasts to be a one-stop center for investors as it has in-house officials dispatched from six other agencies (immigration, customs, environment, energy, telecom, and labor) and has close service providing relations with eight more agencies. Similarly, SME Bank, whose vision is to become an SME Hub, not only offers finance, training, consultation, and rental factories but also collaborates tightly with other strategic partners (public agencies, commercial banks, and academic institutions) to provide comprehensive support to SME customers. If this system works as it is claimed, any agency could serve as a one-stop center and SMEs could approach any of them to get full information and support. Overlapping functions would then pose no problem as functions would be collectively filled by one or other of the agencies in the promotion system.

Regarding capacity building, a variety of training and consultation is offered by SME supporting agencies. For SME participants in training, grants that cover 80 percent of the tuition fee are provided. There are 41 skills training centers belonging to SME Corp and many others run by other ministries and agencies. At SME Corp, training courses are given by registered training providers (private consultancy or training companies) on such standard subjects as management, computer, technical skills, and accounting. As of 2010, SME Corp were using 41 training providers whose list is constantly revised. Prime Minister Najib instructs streamlining of programs and projects as well as outcome-based awards rather than unmonitored grants.

Among public-sector training organizations, the Malaysia Productivity Corporation (MPC) under the Ministry of International Trade and Industry is the leading institution providing productivity and quality short-term training and consultancy, as well as related services such as research, databanks, country ranking, systems development, best practices, and promotion. It was established in 1962 and has nearly 200 management and professional staff. Training at MPC is centered on management rather than specialized technical skills. In 2009, MPC trained 20,836 participants who came from the public sector (43 percent), SMEs (33 percent), other local firms (15 percent), and multinational companies (9 percent). In that year, 155 short-term courses lasting one to three days were offered at its headquarters in Petaling Jaya and four regional offices. Unlike SME Corp's courses, MPC's courses are basically taught by its own staff. The strategic focus of MPC expanded over time with the country's development, starting from the core mission on management, training, and advisory services (1960s) to include research and systems development (1990s), productivity and efficiency (mid-1990s), benchmarking and best practices (2000s), and competitiveness and innovation (present). In productivity and quality management systems development, MPC offers a broad menu of consultation ranging from ISO to 5S (called "Quality Environment"), QC circles (called "Innovative and Creative Circle"), TQM, benchmarking, balanced scorecard, productivity measurement, productivity-linked wage system, customer satisfaction measurement, and employee satisfaction measurement. It is also the only institution in Malaysia that officially certifies 5S practices at companies.

Another public organization that actively offers advisory services to SMEs is SME Bank, established in 2005 by merging two banks. It is 100 percent state owned and has over 1,000 employees and 19 branches all over the country. Its SME Bank Advisory Center is a platform to deliver structured and integrated programs with seven modules—performance and growth, human management, market development, business planning and financial management, resource planning and operations, branding and promotion, and customer management. These modules are taught by a network of service providers including SME Bank's in-house professionals, partners, and third-party experts (business consultants). The Center also provides business planning, information services, business matching, and other services. One of the remarkable things about Malaysia is that there seems to be an unknown but fairly large number of competent experts ("financial planners" and "business counselors") in both public and private sectors who can offer business consultation or management courses to SMEs.

Regarding finance, a variety of financial resources are available to SMEs in Malaysia, from both private and public sectors. Total financing resources outstanding to SMEs stood at RM164.5 billion (US$53.4 billion) at the end of 2010. By far the largest suppliers of funds to SMEs were banking institutions (78.1 percent), followed by government funds and schemes (12.0 percent), development financial institutions (7.8 percent), venture capital (2.1 percent), and factoring and leasing (0.06 percent). Development financial institutions, which are specialized state-owned financial institutions to support strategic sectors, include SME Bank mentioned above, Malaysia Industrial Development Finance, Agro Bank, and many others. SME Bank in particular provides financing and advisory support to SMEs in manufacturing, services, and construction sectors with emphasis on the development of the Bumiputra Commercial and Industrial Community. It offers five categories of loan which are "start-ups," "professional," "franchise," "procurement" (for component suppliers), and "global" covering both conventional and Islamic loans as well as equity and investment. Its funds come from various government and Bank Negara sources as well as foreign assistance; it does not accept deposits or go to commercial markets. It also provides business assessments, business matching, SME Advisory Center mentioned above, and entrepreneurial training. In its Factory Scheme, over 400 rental factories are made available to Bumiputra SMEs across the country with subsidized rent and comprehensive business support.

The central bank and the government are also directly involved in SME finance. Bank Negara has a number of special funds including New Entrepreneur Fund, Fund for Small and Medium Industries, Fund for Food, Bumiputra Entrepreneur Project Fund, and Micro Enterprise Fund. Separately, the government operates a large number of funds and schemes for SMEs which include grants, equity, soft loans, venture capital, etc. for encouraging innovation, technology upgrading, marketing, and strategy making (economic purposes) as well as development of Bumiputra SMEs and providing jobs for the youth and new graduates (social purposes). Other financial institutions and programs include the Credit Guarantee Corporation established in 1972, the Small Debt Resolution Scheme established in 2003, the SME Credit Bureau established in 2008, the Microfinancing Scheme, government crisis funds, and venture capital funds. The landscape of SME financing in Malaysia is comprehensive and always expanding.

8.4 FDI policy

Another exemplary policy of the Malaysian government is FDI attraction and related services. The Malaysian Investment Development Authority (MIDA), established in 1967 under the Ministry of International Trade and

Industry and renamed from the Malaysian Industrial Development Authority in 2010, is a federal agency responsible for issuing investment licenses and providing investment incentives. It is also an agency that effectively conveys Malaysia's country image and information to potential investors and offers one-stop trouble-free services to investors who have already come or decided to come. In recent years, besides receiving manufacturing FDI, its mandate was expanded to promotion of services (other than finance and utilities which belong to other agencies) as well as "cross-border investments" (outward FDI) by Malaysian companies. With rising wages and the government's orientation toward innovation and high skills, MIDA wants traditional labor-intensive industries such as garment to leave the country and become global. Instead, Malaysia wishes to attract targeted high-tech FDI.

The main incentive schemes of MIDA are (i) pioneer status, which provides corporate income tax exemption ranging from 70 to 100 percent of statutory income for five to ten years, (ii) investment tax allowance, which offsets 60 to 100 percent of qualifying capital expenditure against 70 to 100 percent of the statutory income for five to ten years, and (iii) reinvestment allowance, which offsets 60 percent of qualifying capital expenditure against 70 to 100 percent of the statutory income. Initial investors can choose either (i) or (ii), which are the main incentives offered by MIDA, but not both. In addition, import duty and sales tax exemptions are available for imported raw materials, components, and machinery and equipment vis-à-vis manufacturing firms but not for trading ones. In addition, MIDA can offer "pre-packaged incentives" (customized deals) to attract targeted individual FDI firms.

Except for such special deals, incentives are given to domestic and foreign firms without discrimination. After the Asian financial crisis in 1997–98, Malaysia decided to accept 100 percent foreign-owned projects regardless of how much the company exports. Regionally, two levels of incentive are given, the one for the developed areas of Kuala Lumpur, Johor Baru, and Penang, and the more generous one for the rest of the country. MIDA approves all FDI projects coming to Malaysia and provides various post-investment services. Tax and tariff incentives are centrally administered by MIDA, but 13 states (local governments) can offer other incentives related to location, rent, lease, water, and so on. If any problem arises between a company and a local authority, MIDA can intervene to solve it.

MIDA's investment incentives are given by the combination of the published eligibility list and case-by-case organizational judgment. To receive any incentive, activities or products must not only be included in the list but also be approved by MIDA's weekly committee. As for the eligibility list, MIDA publishes and updates it in its website as well as in the investment promotion package in five languages (English, Japanese, Chinese, Arabic, and Malay). The list is long and multiple, and eligible items are quite diverse. For example, the list published in January 2011 of promoted activities and products in the manufacturing sector consists of five parts: (i) general, (ii) manufacturing related activities, (iii) high technology companies, (iv) industrial linkage program, and (v) small scale companies. Among these, the list of "general" is subdivided into 26 groups with 256 promoted activities and products, many of which are further subdivided. When new products or components emerge, or when existing products and components become obsolete, MIDA adds or deletes them from the eligibility list through announcement in the official gazette.

As for organizational judgment, manufacturing industry applications seeking tax incentives are first reviewed by MIDA's relevant industrial divisions,[6] whose results are reported to MIDA's weekly Action Committee on Industry headed by the director general for deliberation and decision on a case-by-case basis. The approval is not automatic as the Committee places importance on whether the applicant is truly engaged in manufacturing and not just trading, whether the activity creates value, and whether it promotes technology or industrial linkage. Licenses and tax incentives for manufacturers are issued by this Committee while import licenses and service licenses are handled by other MIDA committees.

MIDA works closely and effectively with concerned bodies such as the Ministry of Finance (MOF), the Department of Statistics, several sister agencies under the Ministry of International Trade and Industry, and foreign chambers of commerce. Every Thursday, MIDA holds meetings to approve projects and incentives. A representative from MOF sits in these meetings and can approve proposed tax incentives on the spot. If there is any doubt, the proposal is reported to the higher level of MOF and the issue is resolved in the following week. Such quick decision making among economic ministries is unimaginable in countries with poor inter-ministerial coordination. Another proof of MIDA's competence comes from the opinion of foreign organizations. Our research mission asked the representative of the Japan External Trade Organization (JETRO) Kuala Lumpur to list main constraints for Japanese investors in Malaysia. He paused, and replied that he could not think of any as far as administrative obstacles were concerned. In a normal developing country, such an organization would have a long list of gripes against the host government.

8.5 Proton, the national car company

Proton, or Perusahaan Otomobil Nasional, is Malaysia's national car company. It was established in 1983 and started production in 1985. Its head office is located in Shah Alam in the western suburb of Kuala Lumpur. Its initial shareholders were Khazanah Nasional (government investment fund, 38.3 percent), the Employees Provident Fund (12.0 percent), Petronas (state-run oil and gas company, 7.9 percent), and other local and foreign investors (41.8 percent) which included Japan's Mitsubishi group. Propelled by Prime Minister Mahathir's passion for creating a Malaysian car, the project became the most important instrument for heavy industrialization policy. Production began with Proton Saga, a four-door sedan modeled after

Mitsubishi Lancer. The company at first had a close relationship with Japan's Mitsubishi Motors though capital ownership and technical cooperation but subsequently sought a more independent path. It gradually internalized capability in styling and design, platforms, engines, logistics, marketing, and so on. Cumulative car sales reached one million in 1996 and three million in 2008.

Unlike neighboring countries, Malaysia took a go-it-alone approach to automobile manufacturing. It hoped to build core capability and compete squarely in the world market instead of attracting foreign giants to form an automotive industrial base as done in most other developing countries. The Second Industrial Master Plan 1996–2005 targeted the automobile industry as a vital sector in which internal development of technology and engineering know-how was top priority. The government instructed Proton to adopt global orientation, enhance capacity, add value, create brand-name recognition, and improve management and skills. Acquisition of a controlling stake of Lotus, a British car maker, in 1996 also added to Proton's engineering capabilities. The national car project has enjoyed generous incentives and supports including preferential tax and duty treatment, high tariff barriers on foreign competitors, and technical assistance for its suppliers. The existence of Proton as a hub of domestic car production enabled the development of local part and component makers through the Vendor Development Program. By the end of 2005, there were 4,865 automobile parts and components produced locally, and 286 suppliers in Malaysia producing parts and components for Proton. Many key engine parts are locally produced and a full range of R&D is conducted in Malaysia while other Southeast Asian countries focus only on basic casting, machining, stamping, and final assembly—or at least this was the description given by a company official in our interview in 2006.

In 2001, Proton's share in the domestic car market was 53 percent, followed by Perodua,[7] another local company, with the share of 28 percent, and the rest of the domestic market supplied by foreign-brand manufacturers such as Toyota, Honda, Nissan, and Ford. Given its once strong domestic share, the quality of Proton cars seems acceptable to Malaysian consumers, at least as popular vehicles. By 2011, however, Proton's domestic market share shrank to 27 percent, with Perodua maintaining 29 percent and foreign brands supplying 44 percent. The company frequently suffers from losses, and the weak financial performance of Lotus, which it acquired earlier, has not helped to improve its profitability. As of early 2012, it is reported that Khazanah Nasional, the top shareholder of Proton, plans to sell its entire stake (43 percent) to DRB-Hicom, a Malaysian conglomerate.

Proton's effort at internalizing core automotive capability was admirable but not good enough to compete with global giants. As trade barriers fall and the average income of the citizens rises, it is losing domestic customers to foreign car makers while penetration into large export markets seems as remote as ever. The company blames the small domestic market, about 500,000–600,000 units per year, and the lack of brand recognition abroad for lackluster performance. But the deeper cause of hardship must lie in the inability of Proton and its local suppliers to fully internalize and develop core technology. In the global car market where fierce competition reigns, moderate achievement in technology is tantamount to nothing. Malaysia's approach was sufficient to sell cars in the heavily protected domestic market, but as protection is lifted, the fate of the company that does not possess cutting-edge technology is sealed. Although Proton boasts R&D and high engineering technology, its local suppliers continue to learn "basic processes" through Japanese technical assistance nearly 30 years after Proton's establishment.[8]

For survival, Proton desperately needs strategic alliance with one of the big-name foreign producers. Under such alliance, products should be re-targeted to specific components or car models to supply to particular markets, with the company becoming a crucial link in the global production network. However, negotiations for cooperation with Volkswagen, and then with GM, broke up in 2007, showing the difficulty for Proton to reconcile aspiration for national car production with the prospect of foreign dominance and intervention in management.

Meanwhile, the Malaysian government announced National Automotive Policy in 2006 which was revised and further elaborated in 2009. It sets Malaysia's automobile strategy to cope with the limited size of the domestic market, deepening globalization and regional integration, and insufficient competitiveness. Key policy directions are: (i) striving for volume by reducing the number of models and platform portfolio; (ii) restriction of new entry; (iii) preservation of Proton brand name and financial support for Bumiputra suppliers; (iv) conditional FDI policy in which foreign entry is welcome only if it contributes to the national policy objective; (v) an array of administrative measures, incentives, and penalties; (vi) strengthened regulations on prices, standards, automobile life, etc.; and (vii) continued commitment to global and regional integration. These measures, except the last, collectively show Malaysia's resolve to upgrade the automobile industry through a strong hand of the state instead of a market-guided approach. Questions may arise regarding weak private and foreign response to such interventionist policy, and wisdom of restricting the numbers of car models, component suppliers, and foreign firms by administrative means at a time when liberalization of the market and introduction of more competition are required to achieve scale and efficiency.

In this regard, a sharp contrast is seen in the basic thrust of automobile industry policy between Malaysia and Thailand. Thailand fully embraces market and globalization, tries to build an open and liberal business environment, welcomes foreign multinational corporations to form the industrial base, and does not entertain a desire to create national brand cars. The automobile industry is the leading manufacturing sector in Thailand, and Thailand is the largest automobile producer in Southeast Asia. Thai automobile production and sales faced serious setbacks through the Asian financial crisis of

1997–1998, global recessions of 2008–2009 and 2011–2012, and local flooding of 2011. But each time production recovered strongly and relatively quickly. In 2010, production of passenger cars and trucks was 1.64 million units of which domestic sales were 0.80 million units and exports were 0.84 million units. In the same year, the country exported automobiles and their components worth 584 billion baht (US$18.4 billion).

At the end of 2009, Thailand had 17 car-assembly companies (foreign and joint venture), 648 first-tier component suppliers (both foreign and local), and 1,641 second- and third-tier component suppliers (local). With this strong development of automobile supporting industries, Thailand is now regarded as not only an export base of passenger cars and pickup trucks but also a global production base of parts and components. The Thai Ministry of Industry continues to support the industry strongly, bolstering competitiveness in general and strengthening and broadening the supporting industries in particular. Unlike Malaysia where policy interest has moved to fostering new and independent SMEs with innovative capability, Thailand is still learning the Japanese production model, promoting automotive technical education and training, expanding technical consultancy, and strengthening linkage with FDI firms. Policy interest in engineering capacity in die and mold, machining, welding, and other "basic processes" is still alive and well among Thai industrial officials and local companies.

Malaysia developed the automobile industry by internalizing core capability quickly with strong official support and protection. But it has hit a thick wall due to limited scale and severe international competition. Thailand created a free business environment for foreign car makers to achieve scale, quality, and even exports. Its problem, however, is the slow pace of domestic capacity building and continued dominance of foreign design and technology. Both paths are fraught with difficulties, but the key question is which path is more likely, under appropriate policy, to establish a competitive automobile industry with sufficient domestic value creation in the long run. The fact that discriminatory measures are no longer permitted under WTO, FTAs, and EPAs must also be take into account when a nation decides on a basic orientation of its automobile industry policy.

8.6 Concluding remarks

To conclude the chapter on Malaysia, three related thoughts can be raised for future contemplation.

First, Malaysia's economic success in the future depends not so much on policy quality, which is already high, but on whether domestic investors and producers, especially Bumiputra ones, respond strongly to good policy in the globalization age. Without conjuring up private dynamism, there is a risk of policy perfection becoming an end in itself with a broadening gap between what policymakers want and what the private sector can deliver. What is required is not a more elaborate system of SME, FDI, or innovation policies but a new strategy to wake up Malaysian businesses which are quite inactive by East Asian standards. This is a problem of an entirely different dimension from policy inadequacy. For this purpose, a simple, down-to-earth approach is perhaps more appropriate than a sophisticated but mechanical approach which is logically consistent but fails to win the heart of the Ryakiat. A solution calls for a breakthrough in spiritual dimension through hope, pride, and excitement. The difficulties of individual local firms must be felt and understood by sharing their experiences on the ground—at farms and on factory floors—rather than just producing procedural frameworks such as key performance indicators, results-based awards, independent review, and the like.

Second, there may arise a tension between the government's desire to continue to guide the market, on the one hand, and increasing emphasis on innovation, SMEs, private investment, and globalization on the other. True, the Najib government is more friendly to market forces than its predecessors. Even so, the country remains more interventionist than its regional neighbors such as Thailand, especially in the automobile sector. This does not mean that the government should revert to a laissez-faire stance. But it must reconsider the scope and means of policy intervention so that it supports rather than irritates private investors. The high policy capability of Malaysia should be re-directed to building solid, productive, and arm's-length partnership with local and foreign entrepreneurs instead of pursuing internal consistency and transparency in policy documents. Proactive industrial policy is a very subtle thing that must be designed and implemented with utmost care, balance, and sensitivity.

Third, the leapfrogging approach, where entirely new industries, products, and actors are targeted rather than building on the existing industrial base, is risky because the possibility of success for each project starting from scratch is usually slim and the gestation period is long even if it is successful. In this regard, it is worrisome that Malaysia no longer pays special attention to its large export base of electronics and electrical and treats it equally with all other sectors. The bulk of current policy attention is directed to the creation of innovative and independent local entrepreneurs who can carry national brands. As far as policy documents are concerned, large foreign electronics manufacturers already belong to the past and serious intention to create industrial linkages between FDI and local firms or build supporting industries has evaporated. A more balanced approach would be to pursue two tracks by expending a sufficient amount of the nation's wisdom and resources on the existing industrial base for enhanced competitiveness while promoting and experimenting on new industries. If Malaysia does not succeed in creating new engines of growth as rapidly as the old industries shrink, it will face the danger of de-industrialization and falling income. The Second Industrial Master Plan 1996–2005 did not produce spectacular results in value creation of the targeted eight industrial clusters which included electronics and electrical and automobiles. Malaysia should not abandon this path entirely but continue to try again with different and better approaches.

9 Vietnam

Growth without quality

9.1 A latecomer in East Asia

Despite an ideal location in the heart of dynamic East Asia, a long coastline, and hard-working people, Vietnam's industrialization was significantly delayed in comparison with its neighbors due to prolonged wars and legacies of planning. Although independence was declared by President Ho Chi Minh in September 1945, it took nearly a decade of fighting to drive out the French colonialists in the decisive battle of Dien Bien Phu in 1954. Despite this military victory, Vietnam was split into the communist north and the capitalist south. The north was aided by China and, later, the Soviet Union, and the south was supported by the US which regarded it as a fortress against communist advances. In the 1960s, the Cold War turned hot in Vietnam. In 1960, the National Liberation Front (Viet Cong) was formed in the south to initiate a guerrilla war against the southern government. In 1965, the US marines landed in Danang, in the central coast of the country, and the US started bombing northern cities and industries which gradually escalated. The northern government and Viet Cong fought back with surprise attacks and sudden offensives. The US sprayed dioxin-laden "orange agent" extensively to destroy forests in which enemies hid, causing serious health and genetic effects on humans even to this date. This devastating war was in progress while many other East Asian economies were graduating from the initial import substitution phase to the export orientation phase or even trying heavy industrialization. Eventually, the rise of anti-war feeling in the US and the world, withdrawal of US troops following the 1973 Paris Agreement, and the weak and unpopular southern government led to the Fall of Saigon in the face of communist onslaught from the north, in April 1975. In the following year, Vietnam was reunited and Saigon was renamed Ho Chi Minh City.

After reunification, the communist government in the north imposed socialist planning in the south and harsh persecution and "re-education" of southern officials and intellectuals, which generated a flow of 560,000 "boat people" fleeing the country. The direct and immediate consequence of this suppression was a collapse of the Vietnamese economy. Collectivized farmers lost incentive to produce and private merchants were replaced by price controls, state subsidies, and rationing. The problem associated with planning was recognized early but it took many years to officially revise the policy, and the market mechanism was restored only gradually and in steps. Beginning in the late 1970s, partial and secret liberalization of agriculture, price system, and trade was attempted at local levels. By the early 1980s, many technocrats were supportive of the idea of introducing market incentives. Finally, *Doi Moi* (renovation) policy that affirmed the market mechanism was promulgated in December 1986 at the Sixth Congress of the Communist Party. However, the immediate economic challenge of the late 1980s was macroeconomic crisis centering on hyperinflation. Macroeconomic control was restored around 1989, private enterprises were legalized in 1990, and prices were significantly liberalized in the early 1990s (Tran Van Tho, 2010). Policies and institutions supporting the market mechanism, such as the dismantling of collective farms, introduction of land use rights, state-owned enterprise reform, financial sector reform, and global integration, were also started in the 1990s. Many of them are still underway into the twenty-first century.

After the disappearance of the Soviet Union and its aid for communist allies in 1991, Vietnam turned decisively to the West.[1] Around 1993, Vietnam opened its doors to the global market economy through trade, investment, and ODA which began to transform the Vietnamese society and economy enormously. After many years of fighting and economic mismanagement, Vietnam finally reached a point where serious effort for economic development, which most other developing countries had been expending for decades, could be initiated. Surrounded by its dynamic neighbors, Vietnam found itself a low-income agrarian country with outdated technology and infrastructure. Driven by nationalism and the shame of backwardness, the Vietnamese government turned to the task of economic development under globalization and systemic transition with the slogan of "Industrialization and Modernization" by the year 2020. With basically the same governing structure as before, namely the power monopoly of the Communist Party supported by the old administrative machinery, Vietnam belatedly introduced policies to train people, build infrastructure, and create new industries from around the mid-1990s.

9.2 Remarkable results

The first two decades of Vietnam's industrialization and modernization, under the pressure of systemic transition and globalization, brought high and relatively stable growth to Vietnam. Starting from a very low level, the Vietnamese economy grew rapidly with the average growth rate of 7.4 percent during 1991–2010. In 1990, Vietnam was among the world's poorest countries with GDP per capita of US$98 (Asian Development Bank data, in current dollars). By 2008, Vietnam reached the income threshold of US$1,000 per capita and joined the rank of lower-middle-income countries by the World Bank classification method.[2] Average foreign visitors to Vietnam are stunned at chaotic dynamism generated by an incredible number of motorcycles jamming the streets of Hanoi and Ho Chi Minh City. The growth up to the recent past was broad-based, touching virtually everyone and generating profound social changes in the entire country. Vietnam's shared growth was impressive and quite different from the historical experiences of many countries in Latin America, the Middle East, or Sub-Saharan Africa, where growth occurred in limited sectors and benefited only few people while poor farmers and ethnic minorities saw little improvement in their livelihood.

Vietnam is one of the early achievers of the Millennium Development Goals, a set of social goals to be achieved by 2015 by all low-income countries.[3] Population below the poverty line, as defined by the General Statistics Office and the World Bank, fell dramatically from 58.1 percent in 1993 to 14.5 percent in 2008. Pockets of poverty still remain for three groups, namely poor households in the coastal regions of the Red River Delta and the Mekong Delta; minority households in the northern mountains, central highlands, and other remote areas; and urban poor with low education and low skill (Ketels et al., 2010). But even for these groups, living conditions have gradually improved thanks to labor migration, public support in health, education, and disaster relief, affirmative actions for minority people, and activities of aid donors and NGOs. According to the United Nations Human Development Indicator 2010 which covers income, health, and education, Vietnam's ranking in overall "quality of life" was the 113th which was above India, Laos, Cambodia, and Bangladesh but below China, Thailand, Philippines, and Indonesia. Vietnam scored relatively high in the health component but relatively low in the education component, which does not auger well for human-capital accumulation. As for the rich–poor gap, which sometimes emerges with rapid economic growth, the same United Nations data, for 2007, show that Vietnam's level of income inequality is lower than those of China, Thailand, Philippines, Malaysia, and Cambodia and on a par with those of Indonesia and Laos (however, see the next section for rising inequality).

Structural transformation has also been observed. The share of manufacturing in GDP rose from 12 percent in 1990 to 19 percent in 2000 then hovered around 20–21 percent throughout the 2000s. The ratio of manufacturing exports to total merchandise exports was 18 percent in 1991 (Asian Development Bank data), rising to 44 percent in 1997 and continuing to rise to 55 percent in 2008 (World Bank data). Much of this apparent structural shift was attributable more to the large inflow of FDI than the dynamism of domestic enterprises. In Vietnam, FDI is an important source of capital accounting for 24.1 percent of gross capital formation in 2008 with a cumulative stock of US$164 billion with about 11,000 projects (UNCTAD data). FDI is also a bringer of foreign management, technology, brands, markets, and industrial inputs, though production linkage with local firms is weak and technology transfer is limited and far from automatic—which is the general case with almost all developing countries. It should also be noted that manufacturing FDI, which is the main driver of structural transformation, is only 30 percent of implemented capital during 1988–2007. The rest of implemented

Table 9.1 Vietnam: key economic indicators

	Population (million)	*GDP (US$ billion)*	*GDP per capita (US$)*	*Real GDP growth (%)*	*Economic size relative to ASEAN4*	*Consumer price inflation (%)*	*Fiscal balance (%GDP)*	*Current account (%GDP)*	*M2 stock (%GDP)*
1990	66.0	6.5	98	5.1	2.2%	67.1	–7.2	–4.0	27.1
1991	67.2	7.6	114	5.8	2.4%	67.5	–0.7	–1.7	26.5
1992	68.5	9.9	144	8.7	2.7%	17.5	–0.8	–0.1	24.6
1993	69.6	13.2	189	8.1	3.3%	5.2	–3.4	–5.8	23.0
1994	70.8	16.3	230	8.8	3.5%	14.4	–2.2	–7.2	24.1
1995	72.0	20.7	288	9.5	3.9%	12.7	–1.3	–9.0	23.0
1996	73.2	24.7	337	9.3	4.2%	4.5	–0.9	–8.2	23.8
1997	74.3	26.8	361	8.2	4.9%	3.6	–3.9	–5.7	26.0
1998	75.5	27.2	361	5.8	7.9%	9.2	–1.6	–3.9	28.4
1999	76.6	28.7	374	4.8	6.9%	0.1	–3.3	4.1	35.7
2000	77.6	31.2	402	6.8	6.8%	–0.6	–4.3	3.6	50.5
2001	78.6	32.7	416	6.9	7.4%	0.8	–3.5	2.1	58.1
2002	79.5	35.1	441	7.1	7.0%	4.0	–2.3	–1.7	61.4
2003	80.5	39.6	492	7.3	7.0%	3.0	–2.2	–4.9	67.0
2004	81.4	45.4	558	7.8	7.2%	9.5	0.2	–2.1	74.4
2005	82.4	52.9	642	8.4	7.6%	8.4	–1.1	–1.1	82.3
2006	83.3	60.9	731	8.2	7.2%	6.6	1.3	–0.3	94.7
2007	84.2	71.0	843	8.5	7.0%	12.6	–1.0	–10.0	117.9
2008	85.1	91.1	1,070	6.3	7.6%	23.1	–1.9	–11.8	109.2
2009	86.0	97.2	1,130	5.3	8.1%	6.9	–7.7	–7.7	126.2
2010	86.5	106.3	1,230	6.8	7.3%	11.8	–6.2	–4.0	140.8

Sources: General Statistics Office and Asian Development Bank Key Indicators (2010); ASEAN4 means Malaysia, Thailand, Indonesia, and the Philippines.

FDI is mostly in the service and real-estate sectors. With the volume of FDI already high, the Vietnamese government no longer welcomes FDI unconditionally and wholeheartedly; it is worried about low technological content, the low implementation rate of 30–40 percent, and negative impacts of real estate FDI such as the loss of agricultural land and property bubbles (see below). Additionally, concentration of FDI projects that hire a large number of unskilled workers is creating labor shortage, wage pressure, labor migration, and labor disputes in certain localities such as Dong Nai, near Ho Chi Minh City, a trend which is spreading to the rest of the country.

Domestic savings have risen gradually from a dismally low 2.9 percent of GDP in 1990 to about 30 percent of GDP in recent years, a level which is normal for a rapidly growing economy in East Asia. However, gross capital formation is always higher than domestic savings with the result that the savings–investment gap averaging 7–8 percent of GDP but widening to over 10 percent of GDP more recently must be filled by capital imports. Foreign savings are supplied in the forms of ODA, FDI, private remittances, and portfolio investment. This has enabled Vietnam to invest in private businesses and public infrastructure beyond its own means. The supply of infrastructure services has greatly increased since the early 1990s but their quality and quantity are still insufficient to support rapidly expanding industrial activities and compete with regional rivals. In 1996, the road connecting Hanoi to the port city of Haiphong was in disrepair requiring cars to queue up to cross a river one by one on an old railroad bridge when trains were not visible. Existing hydraulic and coal-fired power plants could not guarantee enough electricity for incoming FDI. By now the situation has improved greatly with ODA-built highways connecting major cities with ODA-aided ports. New power generation and transmission capability has been installed nationwide, similarly with foreign assistance. But these improvements can hardly catch up with strong infrastructural demand generated by an even faster pace of industrialization. Shortages in infrastructure continue to be among the top concerns of foreign investors interested in Vietnam.

Institutional reforms have progressed albeit at a slower speed than expected by some donors and businesses. Many laws and regulations have been revised to conform to international standards. Among them, revisions of the enterprise law, especially in 2000, prompted formation of new private firms and registration of informal business operations and created a more level playing field for all businesses regardless of size and nationality. Previously common discrimination between domestic and foreign businesses and between state-owned and private enterprises has largely vanished, at least on paper. It can safely be said that Vietnam today is a far more business-friendly place than 20 years ago although it is not yet as business-friendly as competitor countries in the region. Vigorously pursued integration through accession to the WTO, regional free trade agreements (FTAs), and bilateral FTAs and economic partnership agreements (EPAs) were certainly behind Vietnam's unwavering commitment to liberalization and conformity to global standards in principle.

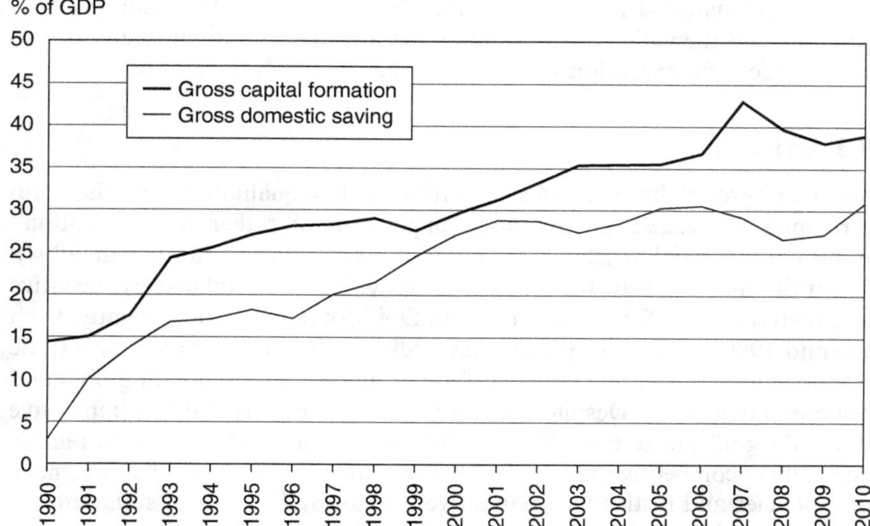

Figure 9.1 Savings and investment balance

Source: Asian Development Bank, *Key Indicators*, 2010.

However, one area in which progress seems to have stalled or even reversed is state-owned enterprise (SOE) reform. Equitization (privatization) of small SOEs has largely been accomplished, but that of the remaining large SOEs is behind schedule. Not only that, recent years have seen large SOE groups ("conglomerates") backed by official loans and guarantees expand into non-core business areas such as finance, insurance, telecom, and real estate brokerage which in some cases ended up in severe financial difficulties with mounting bad debt. Nevertheless, generally and overall, Vietnam's institutional reforms from plan to market have been slow but steady. Progress has been substantial although the road ahead is still long and winding.

These more or less exemplary achievements were generated by a growth model based on low labor cost and intensive capital investment rather than on productivity and competitiveness (Ketels et al., 2010, p. 16). Growth impetus came from the restoration of suppressed domestic private activities to a normal level and introduction of powerful foreign influences. To sustain this model, no sophisticated industrial policy was required beyond liberalizing and opening markets carefully and gradually, adopting international rules and standards, and coping with the problems that might arise on the way. It was essentially reactive adaptation to the new reality rather than proactive creation of new value and industries. Such a strategy was appropriate for a country starting from devastation of war and planning and without strong administrative capacity. Compared with other developing countries, it can even be said that Vietnam was better positioned to realize such initial gain due to its good location, unskilled but diligent workers, and political stability. But the validity of this model has already been diminished because of the successful execution of the first stage of industrialization.

9.3 Arrival of a new era

Vietnam's growth has been more quantitative than qualitative—or what Paul Krugman once called "growth based on perspiration rather than inspiration" in his controversial article on the myth of Asia's Miracle (Krugman, 1994). From the mid-1980s to the mid-1990s, growth was stimulated by incentive and re-allocation effects associated with Doi Moi reform. Subsequently, from the mid-1990s to present, growth has additionally been driven by new trade opportunities and large inflows of foreign funds associated with global and regional integration. Despite impressive growth records and less impressive but still significant reform efforts in the last two decades, local firms remain generally uncompetitive, much of manufacturing value is created by foreigners, and policies and institutions remain very weak by East Asian standards.

What is critically important for the purpose of this book in general and for the next step of Vietnamese policymakers in particular is the fact that institutional reforms undertaken in the past, centering on the judicious management of economic liberalization and opening, were adequate for systemic transition from plan to market but not sufficient as the basis of a growth strategy for creating internal value and overcoming a developmental trap. Now that Vietnam is nearing the final stage of systemic transition and global and regional integration, productivity breakthrough is needed to climb further. Future growth must be fueled by skill and technology rather than a mere injection of purchasing power or capital accumulation.

In the 1990s, external competitive pressure on Vietnam was still partial and indirect. By the early 2000s, however, global and regional integration began to bite with Vietnam's accession to the WTO in 2007 as well as substantive steps that had to be taken to fulfill the obligations of the ASEAN Free Trade Area (AFTA), the ASEAN–China Free Trade Agreement (ACFTA), and other FTAs and EPAs. Protection of weak domestic industries behind high walls of tariffs and non-tariff barriers was no longer allowed, and policies to enhance competitiveness were called for. Freer transaction in international remittances and direct and indirect investments generated large inflows of foreign funds relative to GDP and brought new instabilities such as inflation, property bubbles, and a gaping asset gap between haves and have-nots to the Vietnamese economy. The lack of progress in political and administrative reform resulted in slow response to these policy challenges, emergence of large public corporation groups, environmental and social problems generated by fast growth, and a continuing culture of corruption and insider trading.

It is now evident that Vietnam needs a fundamentally different growth model from the previous one, appropriate for its current development stage, in order to continue to grow and reach a higher level of prosperity in the future. This view is already widely shared by Vietnamese leaders and government officials as a result of extensive policy debate in recent years. A large number of studies have been undertaken by Vietnamese researchers and research institutions on the quality and sources of growth. Comprehensive hearings of domestic and foreign experts were conducted prior to the drafting of the Five-year Socio-economic Development Plan 2011–2015 and the Ten-year Socio-economic Development Strategy 2011–2020. Domestic and foreign experts generally speak in one voice. Ohno (2009a) warned of a future middle-income trap unless Vietnam's policy formulation was radically improved. The World Bank (2010) also studied the possibility of a middle-income trap in Vietnam and recommended a six-step solution crafted by its chief economist, Justin Lin. A joint report on Vietnam's competitiveness by the Central Institute for Economic Management of Vietnam and the Asia Competitiveness Institute of Lee Kuan Yew School of Public Policy, Singapore, supervised by Michael Porter and the Harvard Business School, states that

> the economic logic behind this [old] growth model ultimately has limited potential ... Vietnam's future growth has to move beyond providing access to and leveraging existing economic fundamentals. It needs to be based on a consistent upgrading of these fundamentals and creating new advantages.
>
> (Ketels, et al., 2010, p. 19)

Tran Van Tho (2010), a Vietnamese economist who teaches at Waseda University, Tokyo, shows that Vietnamese industrialization is still at a low level and argues for the creation of new and higher-quality institutions, which he terms as "New Doi Moi," that can stimulate and sustain internal sources of growth.

Some argue that a middle-income trap is still a remote risk for a country like Vietnam which just recently graduated from the status of a low-income country and joined the lower-middle-income group. However, the concept of middle-income trap is used in Vietnam as a political device to alarm its government and businesses, which are prone to complacency due to high growth in the past, into hard thinking about the future. Although it will be some years before Vietnam's developmental trap becomes a reality, as encountered in Malaysia, local officials and researchers are already fully aware of this risk. General awareness is already attained, but what is lacking is the government's ability to design and implement concrete strategies and action plans to avoid this risk. Policy learning in this direction has barely started.

Starting in the early 2000s, many signs of ending initial prosperity and emerging new challenges have appeared. One worry is absence of statistical evidence that Vietnam's productivity and competitiveness are improving. True, labor productivity has risen but this is the natural result of capital deepening (increase in machinery and equipment) which does not reflect overall efficiency. Structural transformation is proceeding rapidly but the main drivers of manufacturing exports are large foreign-affiliated firms with little participation of local companies. Although the products of Intel and Canon operating in Vietnam may be "high-tech," most value is created by foreigners, including product design, brand name, and marketing, while Vietnam, which offers cheap labor and industrial land, contributes relatively little to the value chains of these products. Surveys of foreign firms continue to reveal the severe shortage of managers and engineers with needed skills and experience. The lack of internal value creation in FDI-led industrialization is now widely recognized as a serious problem among Vietnamese policymakers.

Two indicators frequently cited to underscore this problem are total factor productivity (TFP) and the incremental capital–output ratio (ICOR). TFP is a measure of overall efficiency which is calculated as residual growth after increases in factor inputs such as labor and capital are accounted for. ICOR is a measure of capital efficiency computed as the ratio of the investment rate (investment in percentage of GDP) to the real GDP growth rate. It shows how much physical capital has to be invested to produce an additional 1 percent growth. While results differ somewhat due to data inaccuracy prevalent in developing countries and according to each researcher, general trends are unmistakable (Figure 9.2). Until the mid-1990s, ICOR was low

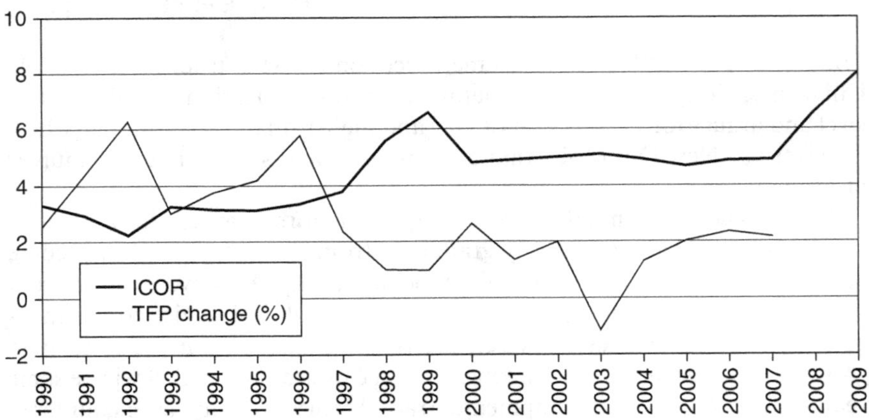

Figure 9.2 Investment-driven growth without productivity increase

Source: The incremental capital–output ratio (ICOR) was computed by the author using General Statistical Office (GSO) data. For TFP, Tran Tho Dat et al. (2005) for 1990–2004 and unofficial calculation by GSO's SNA Department for 2005–2007 were used. Continuity between the two is not guaranteed.

Note: ICOR is computed as investment ratio (I/Y) divided by real growth (ΔY/Y). The higher the ICOR, the more capital formation is required for growth (i.e., investment is inefficient). Total factor productivity (TFP) is a broad definition of productivity calculated as residual growth after the increases in factor inputs such as labor and capital are accounted for.

and the contribution of TFP to growth was high, which indicates that growth was achieved through improved efficiency without much investment—albeit from a very low level under planning and market suppression. In the more recent period, however, ICOR rose and TFP's contribution to growth declined as capital's contribution increased significantly. This is a clear sign of investment-driven growth with low efficiency in capital use.

The same problem can be stated from another angle as the problem of wage increase which is faster than the increase in labor productivity. If a large number of labor-intensive foreign manufacturers pour into Vietnam by the attraction of low wages, the labor market for unskilled workers will tighten as demand for such workers outstrips supply. Because Vietnam is much smaller than China in population size, such tightening can occur much faster in Vietnam than in China—as already seen in acute labor shortage and wage pressure in and around Ho Chi Minh City and Hanoi. When this happens, labor-intensive manufacturers will leave Vietnam for another country with even cheaper labor while no skill- or technology-intensive foreign firms will come to replace them if competent managers, engineers, and operators are hard to find. De-industrialization will proceed as old industries shrink and no new industries emerge. The country will be stuck in a developmental trap. Among Japanese manufacturers, Sony and Daihatsu have already left Vietnam and decided to supply their products through imports rather than local production. As tariff barriers and logistic costs decline, it becomes more efficient for multi-national corporations to produce any product in one location with scale merit and distribute it throughout the world rather than producing it in every country.

Put in still another way, Vietnam's challenge is whether it can take advantage of "demographic bonus" to climb further (United Nations Population Fund, 2010). Demographic bonus is a situation where the working population aged 15 to 64 is at least double the size of the dependent population aged 0 to 14 or 65 and above. Vietnam's demographic bonus has just begun around 2010 and is expected to last about three decades. During this period, Vietnam will have a large supply of workers entering the labor market as a basis of industrialization and supporters of the young and the old. If everyone has good access to education and training whose quality is greatly improved and closely linked with shifting industrial needs, Vietnam will enjoy a golden age of human-capital accumulation and rapid improvement in income and welfare. If industrialization fails, however, few managers, engineers, and high-skill workers will be demanded, and opportunities will turn to threats as the problems of unemployment, lost generation, wasted education and training, and social instability will arise.

Another phenomenon heralding a new era of Vietnam's development is sharply increased macroeconomic instabilities as a result of deepening international integration. Until the end of the 1990s, macroeconomic crises were mostly home-grown and caused by excessive fiscal deficits and monetary issue in the face of weak supply response. Hyperinflation and the collapse of the Vietnamese dong in the late 1980s were such cases. After successful macroeconomic stabilization, economic performance throughout the 1990s was characterized by high growth coupled with low inflation. In those days Vietnam was largely detached from global economic cycles. Even the Asian financial crisis of 1997–1998, which wrecked the economies of neighboring countries, touched Vietnam relatively lightly thanks to the low degree of financial integration of the Vietnamese economy. Real growth declined only moderately to 5.8 percent in 1998 and 4.8 percent in 1999. The Vietnamese dong was not targeted by currency speculators, and most shocks were felt indirectly through reduced demand for Vietnamese goods and less investment into Vietnam by crisis-hit countries.

However, the situation changed significantly around the turn of the millennium. In the 2000s, FDI inflows became much larger to the tune of US$6–9 billion rather than US$1–2 billion as before (actual implementation basis). Private remittances from overseas Vietnamese, including permanent residents ("boat people") and temporary workers, also increased to about US$7 billion per year. Meanwhile, ODA grants are about US$0.5 billion annually. Furthermore, new financial inflows were generated as the Vietnamese stock exchanges, established in 2000, started to grow and attract foreign investors. However, such investments are highly unstable and speculative. Portfolio capital inflows rose from virtually zero in the early 2000s to US$6.2 billion in 2007 as the Vietnamese stock market soared. But when the market declined subsequently a net outflow of US$0.6 billion was recorded in 2008. Other capital inflows, which include ODA loans as well as private property investments, are a few to several billion dollars per year. All this was happening in a country with GDP growing from US$50 billion to US$100 billion in the late 2000s. The macroeconomic impact of the combined inflow of foreign funds was overwhelming.

With greater trade and financial integration, the Vietnamese economy is more synchronized with global boom–bust cycles. In the periods of 2007–2008 and 2010–2011 (intervened by the Lehman shock), the world experienced commodity inflation and high capital mobility in search of speculative gain. In both periods, Vietnam experienced highest inflation in East Asia with consumer price inflation peaking at 23.1 percent in 2008 and 18.1 percent in 2011. Inflation was accompanied by urban property bubbles in both periods and a stock market bubble in the first instance. Vietnam was not alone to suffer from overheating caused by excessive inflows of purchasing power in these periods. Countries such as Russia, Kazakhstan, Mongolia, Nigeria, Zambia, South Africa, Botswana, Mauritania, and Angola also experienced economic booms as export earnings from extractive resources shot up in a classical phenomenon known as "Dutch Disease." But overheating can also occur by other inflows as experienced by Vietnam (FDI, ODA, remittances, and portfolio money), China (export earnings and FDI), the United Arab Emirates (portfolio and construction money), and the United Kingdom (oil export and portfolio money). Whatever the cause, the consequences are similar: consumption and construction booms, asset bubbles, inflation, trade deficits, and currency overvaluation.

In Vietnam, a large portion of incoming funds amounting to 20–30 percent of GDP feeds asset bubbles, especially urban property inflation, which further accelerates booms in the real sector. This asset amplifier mechanism creates a perverse situation where Hanoi's properties are as expensive as those in the suburbs of Tokyo despite the fact that Vietnam's per capita income is less than 3 percent of Japan's. Asset speculation has become the main mover of purchasing power in Vietnam, not corporate profits or workers' wages. Naturally, the best minds are attracted to short-term real estate transactions rather than long-term investment in technology, skills, and management. This is hardly an ideal situation to promote accumulation of industrial human capital.

Vietnam is rapidly becoming unequal. Vietnam's Gini coefficient, an index of inequality in income and expenditure, has long been stable at about 0.35–0.40 and lower (more equal) than China's which is about 0.5 and rising. In 2010, the General Statistics Office reported a Gini coefficient of 0.43 with a moderate widening of the income gap between richest and poorest groups. However, these data do not capture the greatest cause of the rich–poor gap in Vietnam which lies in asset markets rather than in the annual flows of income. Disparity is most visible—though statistically not yet captured—between haves and have-nots in urban areas. If you happen to own a house or land in Hanoi or Ho Chi Minh City, you are a winner. You can buy an expensive car, open a business, or send your sons and daughters abroad to study. Meanwhile, people without appreciating assets, including urban renters and migrant workers from rural areas, are losers. Their rents and living and education costs are skyrocketing and their real income is falling sharply. Vietnamese large cities now have these two very different groups living side-by-side. This is a political time bomb that may someday explode as hope for better future is dashed for the majority of people and their children.

In fast-growing Asia, some economies such as Japan, Taiwan, and South Korea succeeded in raising everyone's income during the high-growth era. But other countries such as China, Thailand, and the Philippines were unable to narrow huge income and wealth gaps as they grew fast. After many happy years of shared growth, Vietnam is standing at a crossroads. Policy must quickly catch up with the reality and begin to solve this problem. First, relevant income and asset statistics must be collected and analyzed. Second, new taxes must be introduced in reasonable steps to narrow the asset gap, including property tax, real estate transaction tax, and inheritance tax as some Chinese cities are trying to do. Third, there must be a continued battle against corruption, non-transparency, and insider trading in asset transactions. Finally and most important, industrial policies must be improved greatly to strengthen the competitiveness of Vietnamese companies and improve education and training for students and workers so that the general public can participate in growth through higher skills and better jobs. Otherwise, Vietnam may be stuck at middle income with an aging population and rising political instability.

9.4 The glass ceiling in East Asia

Vietnam's growth pattern has basically followed the past experiences of East Asian neighbors whose features include acceptance of openness and regional integration as an initiator of growth; deepening intra-regional trade and FDI; high savings and investment; dynamic transformation of industrial structure; urbanization and rural–urban migration; and growth-generated problems such as income and wealth gaps, congestion, pollution, and financial bubbles which became highly visible around 2008. At the same time, unique features of Vietnam, such as much delayed but faster global and regional integration than the neighboring countries, must be acknowledged. Within this dynamic East Asian context, Vietnam must successfully conduct three crucial policies to sustain growth, namely: (i) generation of internal value; (ii) coping with new social problems caused by rapid growth; and (iii) effective macroeconomic management under financial integration. The first produces sources of growth while the second and the third ensure political stability and social support without which industrialization and modernization cannot be sustained. Capability to manage industrialization in this broad sense must be acquired or the industrialization process may stall (Murakami 1992, 1994).

A low-income country just out of war, political mayhem, ethnic conflict, or severe economic mismanagement is often characterized by a fragile economic structure. It relies heavily on extractive resources, monoculture export, subsistence agriculture, or foreign aid. Productivity is low and innovation hardly occurs. Internal value created by traditional industries such as mining and agriculture is small, but the absence of a vibrant manufacturing sector makes them loom large in output and export structure. This is stage zero on a long road to industrialization.

Economic take-off in East Asian countries starts typically with the arrival of a critical mass of manufacturing FDI performing simple assembly or processing of light industry products for export such as garment, footwear, foodstuff, and other household goods. Electronic devices and components may also be produced in this way. In this early stage of industrialization (stage one), management, design, technology, production, and marketing are all directed by foreigners, key materials and parts are imported, and the country contributes only unskilled labor and industrial land. While this generates jobs and income for the poor, internal value remains small as value created by foreigners dominates. Vietnam's industrialization up to now is basically characterized by this situation. Myanmar may be entering this stage from the status of international isolation.

In the second stage, as FDI accumulates and industrial output expands, domestic supply of parts and components begins to increase. This is realized partly by the inflow of foreign suppliers and partly by the emergence of local suppliers. As quicker and cheaper supply of local parts and components is realized, assembly firms become more competitive and a virtuous circle between assemblers and suppliers sets in. The industry grows quantitatively and internal value creation rises moderately, but production basically remains under foreign management and guidance. Obviously, local wage and income cannot rise very much if important tasks that contribute greatly to value creation continue to be performed by foreign hands. Thailand and Malaysia have already reached this stage.

The next challenge is to internalize knowledge, skills, and technology by accumulating industrial human capital. Localization must expand from hardware to software of production processes. Locals must replace foreigners in all areas of production including management, product design, factory operation, quality control, logistics, and marketing. As foreign dependence is reduced, internal value rises dramatically. The country emerges as a dynamic exporter of high-quality manufactured products challenging more advanced competitors and re-shaping the global industrial landscape. South Korea and Taiwan are such producers trying to join the most advanced group.

In the final stage, the country acquires the capability to create new products and lead global market trends, not just copying frontline technology developed by others to produce new products faster and more cheaply. Japan, the United States, and a number of European countries have been such industrial innovators.

However, progress is not guaranteed for all. A large number of countries that receive too little manufacturing FDI stay at stage zero. Low-income countries may receive FDI in mining, telecom, power, tourism, or property development. While such projects based on locational advantages are lucrative for investors, can generate jobs for the poor, and provide basic infrastructure for the nation, these alone cannot put the country on a dynamic path of structural transformation as manufacturing does.

Even after reaching the first stage, climbing up the ladders becomes increasingly difficult. Another group of countries are stuck in the second stage because they fail to upgrade human capital. It is noteworthy that none of the ASEAN4 countries (Malaysia, Thailand, Indonesia, and the Philippines) which began industrialization before Vietnam has succeeded in breaking through the invisible "glass ceiling" in manufacturing between the second and the third stage. This phenomenon is essentially the same as what we called a developmental trap in general and a middle-income trap in particular, in Chapter 1.

Starting from a very low level, Vietnam is currently in the first stage of industrialization trying to reach the second in Figure 9.3. Large FDI inflows, a necessary condition for this transition, have already happened and are continuing to the extent that neighboring ASEAN countries even fret about losing FDI to Vietnam. While Vietnam's short-term goal is attainment of physical expansion of the industrial base (stage 2), it should also simultaneously prepare to avoid a middle-income trap and continue to proceed to the

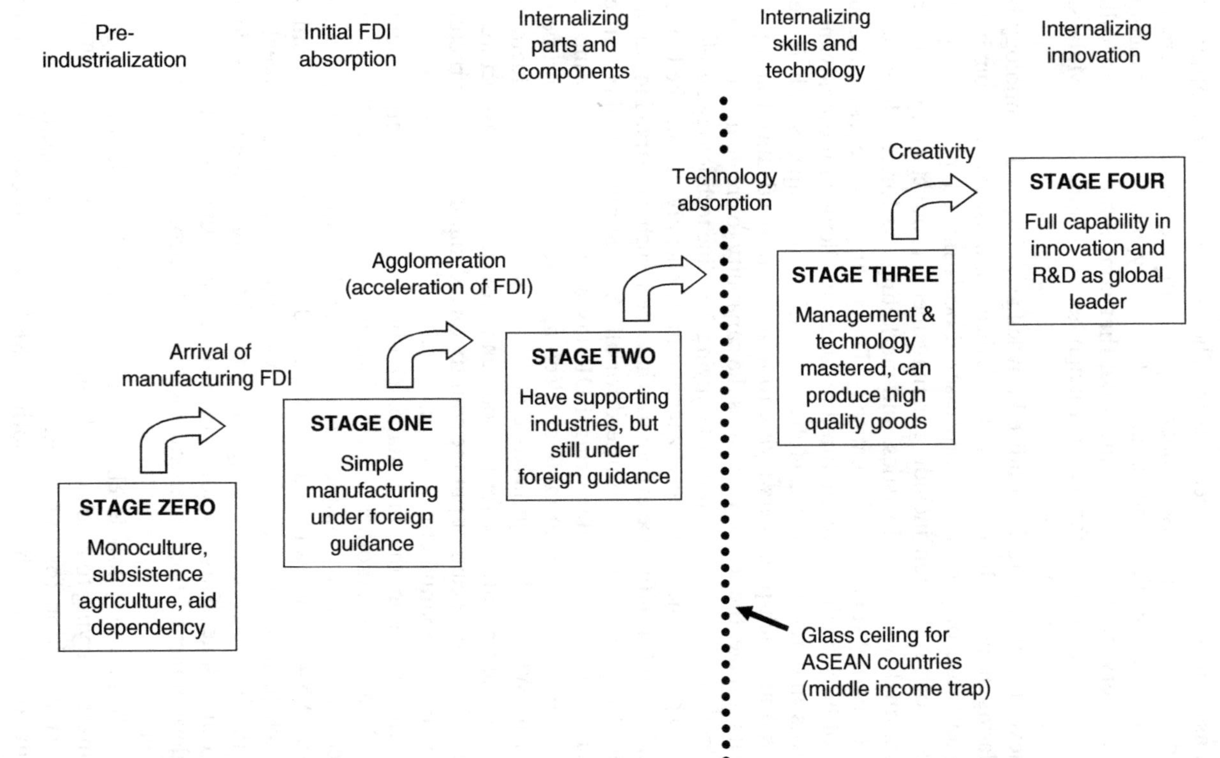

Figure 9.3 Stages of catching-up industrialization

next stage (stage 3). For this, front-loaded and well-targeted policy action for upgrading industrial human resources is the key.

Even without policy effort, Vietnam is likely to continue to grow at reasonable speed and can reach the per capita income of US$4,000 by around 2025—this is a Goldman Sachs forecast with which Tran Van Tho (2010) agrees. However, Tran Van Tho warns of two risks associated with such a scenario. The first is the problem of low quality of growth regarding capital efficiency, social justice, and environment. The second is the possibility of being trapped in middle income without soaring to high income in the long run. According to Tran Van Tho, solution of the latter problem depends on whether Vietnam can overcome two barriers, the one associated with the Lewisian "turning point" of moving from a labor-surplus to a labor-shortage economy and the other associated with transition from growth driven by factor inputs to TFP-based growth. Tran Van Tho emphasizes five necessary ingredients of New Doi Moi, which are: (i) restraint on state-owned enterprises and promotion of private enterprises; (ii) efficient use of investment funds; (iii) strengthening of industrial competitiveness; (iv) improving education; and (v) democratization and establishment of the rule of law.

9.5 Policymaking procedure and organization

Proposing a solution is one thing. Carrying it out is quite another. This caution is particularly relevant in the case of Vietnam where failure to produce effective industrial strategies comes mainly from structural weaknesses in the policymaking process rather than not knowing which way to go. Vietnam does not follow the standard policymaking process discussed in Chapter 4. Its policy formulation is saddled with the legacies of planning days and cannot cope effectively with problems in the age of global competition. Vietnam has reached the point where further progress towards higher income is increasingly difficult without a radical reform in policy formulation procedure and organization.

The problems associated with Vietnam's industrial policymaking are many. However, instead of presenting a long list of problems, I will highlight two procedural problems and two organizational problems which are interrelated and constitute the main sources of formalism and the general lack of creativity and responsiveness in policymaking. These four problems are unique to Vietnam in the sense that they are not observable in East Asia's other high-performing economies.

The two serious procedural problems are the *lack of involvement of the business community* and the *lack of inter-ministerial coordination* in designing and executing industrial strategies and action plans, which together render approved policies ineffective and unimplementable. In any developing country, policy implementation is a big challenge due to shortages of funds, human resources, and proper mechanisms for execution and monitoring. However, the proportion of unimplemented policies in Vietnam is exceptionally high not only in industrial areas but also in all other areas. It can even be said that very few policies are actually implemented as stipulated in Vietnam because of delays in preparing implementation details; non-provision of necessary budget, staffing, or equipment; the lack of support from the business community; and the lack of ability or interest among responsible ministries to solve these problems. On one occasion, an official who drafted an industrial master plan and faced angry protestation by FDI firms regarding certain parts of it reassured them that there was no need to worry because master plans in Vietnam were not implemented.

The policymaking process in Vietnam is largely closed within government with little substantive involvement of other stakeholders. Within each ministry, the order to draft a master plan is handed down to a drafting team, which normally consists of a few experts headed by a middle-ranking official. The team collects internal data and data from other ministries, and may commission additional analyses to experts in other ministries or government research institutes. The structure of chapters of all master plans is standardized by a circular issued by the Ministry of Planning and Investment.[4] The budgets for different types of master plan are also fixed by an inter-ministerial circular and used mainly for obtaining external data and analyses as well as conducting domestic travel, interviews, and hearings. A master plan drafted by the ministerial team is submitted to the minister or vice minister for internal review. After that, it is circulated among relevant ministries for comment (which is usually cosmetic) and submitted to the prime minister for final approval. Significant delay may occur at any stage of review and approval. Demand for revision is also common. The drafting team is routinely overworked with a large number of master plans to finish each year, which does not allow sufficient time (or money) to think creatively, interact with non-government stakeholders, or publicize the final result. Approved master plans are neither translated into English nor uploaded or printed for dissemination although executive summaries edited for the prime minister's approval, in the Vietnamese original, are usually available on the web.

If an enterprise wants to raise its voice, it must invent its own way since the current procedure does not allow meaningful involvement of the business community. Although enterprise hearings are becoming more popular, sufficient details of the master plan draft are not revealed at such hearings and enterprises therefore can only make general requests. If a firm later finds certain points in the master plan objectionable, it needs to seek special meetings with responsible ministries, use symposiums and media to protest, or write a letter to the prime minister to request a change in the already approved policy. This is in sharp contrast to Malaysia where private sector participation is institutionalized in the steering committee and task forces that draft the Industrial Master Plan; Thailand where automobile producers decide targets and action plans and the government merely accepts them; Taiwan where committees and seminars are routinely organized for public hearing (Chapter 7); or Japan where business decisions are basically left to individual firms and government provides only support functions such as trade negotiation and setting standards for quality, safety, environment, and industrial property (Ohno, 2006b).

Another procedural problem is the absence of inter-ministerial coordination on policy substance as well as budgeting, staffing, and other implementation details, which in turn comes from the lack of mechanism to force different ministries to work together. Compartmentalization of the government along ministerial lines is a common problem around the world, but most governments manage to somehow ameliorate it (Chapter 4). One solution is to have a strong top leader with a good economic mindset who directs various ministries and becomes the hub of policymaking. As a result, policy components become mutually consistent even though ministries still fail to talk to each other (Thailand under Thaksin Shinawatra, 2001–06; Ethiopia under Meles Zenawi, 1991–). Another way is to establish a powerful technocrat team directly serving the top leader and making key decisions while ministries become executing agents of plans emanating from this team (South Korea's Economic Planning Board, 1961–1994; also see below). Still another way is to let a super ministry, with sufficient policy authority and instruments at its disposal, lead industrial policymaking and be responsible for it (Japan's Ministry of International Trade and Industry in the 1960s; Taiwan's Ministry of Economic Affairs). Finally, it is also possible to install a mechanism to guarantee representation of all relevant ministries and non-government stakeholders in the official drafting process as well as in informal exchange (Malaysia's drafting of the Industrial Master Plan). In Vietnam, while every policy document specifies a leading ministry and a list of related ministries, a mechanism to make them work as one is entirely missing.

We can go deeper to see why it is difficult to ensure involvement of non-government stakeholders and inter-ministerial coordination. Behind these problems lie fundamental issues in policymaking organization. The most serious ones in this regard are the *lack of clear directives from the top* and the *distorted incentive mechanism among government officials that causes brain drain.*

It is well known that Vietnam's decision making is consensus-based. Checks and balances are in place horizontally (across ministries and departments), vertically (between central and local levels), and regionally (north, south, middle, large cities, and remote areas). There are three top leaders—party general secretary, president, and prime minister—and the Communist Party and the government interact in a complex manner. This system can produce stability and continuity but it is not suitable for staging bold reforms or responding quickly to the changing world. Policies remain mostly reactive rather than proactive. Development effort centered on a clear roadmap towards a national vision with concrete strategies and action plans, which is the hallmark of East Asian industrialization, is entirely missing in the Vietnamese policy process.

The Vietnamese government copes with urgent issues—be it inflation or traffic jam—in a bottom-up fashion and without a clear focal point of leadership or responsibility. When a serious problem is identified, an inter-ministerial committee is called and its chair is appointed. Each ministry proposes solutions from its perspective, which are collected into general policy recommendations without execution details. Bureaucracy can supply broad ideas touching every aspect of the problem, but it is not very good at prioritization or selectivity for real action. It is said that there are more than 1,000 research institutes attached to various ministries and levels of the government in Vietnam producing mediocre reports and proposals. This diffused approach must be replaced by a focal person or organization that decides on a shortlist of actions and measures and is responsible for it. There should be interaction between high and implementing levels of the government to produce policies which are both realistic and sharply focused.

Another problem which is common in many countries and also becoming increasingly serious in Vietnam is the decline of quality and morale of government officials, which prompts an exodus of talented people to other sectors. Vietnam's public service faces cumulative problems of overstaffing, low salary, prevalence of second and third jobs, formalism, rigidity, nepotism, corruption, relation-based promotion, and aid-related benefits such as foreign travel, free training opportunities, and other personal gains associated with supervising or participating in ODA projects. These were the legacies of the subsidy system existing up to the late 1980s, where the public sector was the guarantor of jobs, minimum income, and social security for all and where no alternative employment opportunities were available in the private or foreign sectors with far more attractive salaries and rewarding duties. Under the present circumstance of open market and global integration, however, the public sector only attracts people who want stability, people who genuinely believe in public service despite low salary, or people who want to take advantage of official privileges to study abroad or receive training as a stepping stone to a better-paying job in the future. As a result, highly-qualified and motivated people are becoming difficult to recruit or retain. Donor-funded training programs of government officials may only worsen the brain drain without raising the average quality of public service.

This problem cannot be solved by minor repairs or ad hoc adjustments. To reverse the exodus of talent from the Vietnamese government, far-reaching reforms to remake the public administration is needed as soon as possible. This should encompass, among others, a significant downsizing of the public sector through organizational reform; forced retirement and outsourcing of non-essential services; a competitive and transparent recruitment system; a higher and performance-based salary scale and promotion linked to objective personnel evaluation; and clear rules regarding the conduct of public servants and their interaction with citizens, businesses, and service providers. Obviously, these are not easy because of the magnitude of required tasks and political resistance. But they are also absolutely necessary for Vietnam to move forward. No East Asian country has overcome a middle-income trap without installing an effective public administration. It should also be reminded that initiative for such reforms must come from the top rather than the bottom. No bureaucracy can transform itself radically without an order from a strong leader.

9.6 How to break a solidified system

According to comparative institutional analysis, a branch of institutional economics that relies heavily on evolutionary game theory, a society may get stuck in bad equilibrium owing to institutional complementarity, strategic complementarity, and path dependence (Aoki 1995a, 2001a, 2001b). Institutional complementarity means that any social system has resilience to shocks because its institutional components enhance each other. For example, Vietnam's education, recruitment, salary, and promotion systems are mutually complementary to produce relation-based rent sharing. Strategic complementarity means that individuals in such an institutionally solidified society are under strong pressure to follow the existing rules and have little incentive to deviate from them. Finally, path dependence stresses the importance of the beginning. Once installed by chance or design, any social system requires a large amount of political and social energy to change it. Together, these concepts point to institutional inertia and difficulty of reforming any established system.

Policy impasse arises when an ineffective method of policy formulation is set up and then solidified, and institutional components and people's attitude to support it have formed. Removing one person or reforming one organization does not improve the situation because of institutional and strategic complementarities mentioned above. Changing policy formulation in a fundamental way in Vietnam, as proposed in this chapter, will surely require enormous energy and meet fierce resistance.

However, this does not mean that there is no way out. There are times when a social system jumps to another social system despite enormous inertia. Comparative institutional analysis suggests the following occasions and agents of change:

(i) *Collective mutation*: a large number of people residing in a society may mutate simultaneously, as if their genes have transformed. If only a few people behave differently, they are simply called "crazy" or "silly" and the system remains unchanged. But a sufficiently large mass begin to behave differently, institutional and strategic complementarities of the old type stop working and rules and customs start to change. This is a spontaneous and internally driven movement, which may occur when the majority of people feel suppressed or victimized under the existing system. In a rapidly growing economy, this may also happen when a generation with new values and behavioral patterns grow up, or when people begin to have new demands and expectations from the government as a result of high income brought by successful development. A small incident may trigger a large social movement by letting accumulated public discontent or demand to come to the open. In recent years the use of personal digital communication devices may have increased the odds of spontaneous popular movement.

(ii) *Foreign influence*: foreign governments, firms, and individuals follow different systems and are not bound by the dominant behavioral code of the domestic society. They bring and sometimes even force new elements, which cause friction, resistance, and inconsistency with the indigenous system. In low-income countries, bilateral donors and international organizations often exercise powerful influence. Foreign firms and investors as well as international migration and other human exchange may also produce foreign pressure on a society. If this prompts a change in a direction that generates healthy development, such pressure is highly welcome. However, not all foreign influences are good from the viewpoint of social evolution or economic development. For this reason, the government must guide and coordinate foreign pressure to prevent undesirable results.

(iii) *Policy*: even without domestic or foreign pressure, the government as *deus ex machina* (detached commander)[5] can start a change from inside the system by introducing policies that upset existing calculations and complementarities. Here the key question is who will activate such policies. Government itself is submerged in existing connections. As noted before, it is also extremely difficult for lower bureaucrats to initiate a fundamental reform. Their power within the government is minuscule compared with enormous institutional and strategic inertia they face. Drastic policy breaks are usually introduced when a strong top leader comes to power and a new government is formed. Leadership equipped with strong will and economic literacy is crucial for this to succeed. When such leadership skillfully and strategically aligns with foreign partners who want to go in the same direction and offer necessary technical and financial assistance, even a very bold reform becomes possible.

Following these theoretical considerations, let us identify three players that may make institutional reforms possible in the Vietnamese context. They are leadership, a technocrat team combined with a national council, and foreign partnership.

9.6.1 Leadership

The crucial importance of leadership is made sufficiently clear in the discussions above as well as in Chapter 4. Leadership is the prime force of social change while other necessary conditions can be created or reshaped by the leader if they do not already exist. In countries with advanced political systems, policy initiative can also emerge from various domestic groups such as civil society organizations, intellectuals, interest groups, and political parties because legal mechanisms to capture and reflect their opinions are firmly in place. However, in developing countries where political systems are less well developed, only a few channels of effective participation are available. For all practical purposes, initiative for bold change in these circumstances must come from the top leader. When such leadership is combined constructively with the aspiration of domestic groups and foreign support, reform becomes possible. For the leader to play a proper role in development, it is not always necessary to change the existing political regime or expending social energy to change it. Vietnam's political regime at present is flexible enough to allow a strong leader with political savvy to emerge and orchestrate policies.

However, this point is often disputed by domestic analysts. Many young Vietnamese officials have confessed to me that they saw little possibility of change in their government. It is argued that Vietnamese politics is based on collective decision-making rather than charismatic leadership. Non-government stakeholders are weak while there are many powerful persons and groups in the Communist Party, parliament, government, military, state-owned businesses, municipalities, and regions, hidden from the eyes of the general public, who can block any initiative and make trouble for any leader. Anyone, even those at the top, wanting to start a new initiative must consult and convince all others in the governing mechanism, which is nearly impossible. As a result, leaders often play defensive and pursue only obvious goals and well-established policies without launching new ones that may rock the boat in the ocean of complex political interests. In most countries, it is customary that a person just elected (or selected) as the head of the state would announce a new policy initiative to distinguish his or her administration from the previous one and take full advantage of the honeymoon period to re-set policies. However, such an announcement is rarely heard in recent Vietnam. The prime minister's hands are tied from day one.

Be that as it may, we can still debate how permanent the current political arrangement is and whether it completely shuts out the possibility of effective developmental leadership or it just takes more charisma, skills, and patience than in other countries to make a difference in Vietnam. It should be recalled that Doi Moi reform in the 1980s was realized only after a long preparation period and its implementation also took many years. Launching New Doi Moi in the twenty-first century may equally take a long time. At any rate, action to break the impasse and change history ultimately belongs to the will and choice of the Vietnamese leaders and people, not foreign officials or academics.

9.6.2 A technocrat team and a national council

In high-performing economies of East Asia, a technocrat team directly under the top leader has frequently played a crucial role (Chapter 4). The team is summoned from the brightest officials from various ministries as well as the smartest returnees who have studied, taught, or ran businesses abroad. Prominent domestic business leaders with strong policy mindset may also be mobilized. The team receives full confidence and responsibility from the top leader to concretize the policies that this leader envisions. It also acts as the command post for all ministries which are obliged to implement the policies that this team drafts. It is the nation's brain for development without which even excellent leaders cannot function. The Economic Planning Board in South Korea, the Kuomintang technocrats in Taiwan, the Economic Planning Unit (EPU) in Malaysia, the National Economic and Social Development Board (NESDB) in Thailand, the so-called Berkeley Mafia in Indonesia, the National Economic Development Authority (NEDA) in the Philippines, and the Planning Commission in India all aimed to fill this need at certain critical points in their economic development with varying degrees of success. Japan's Ministry of International Trade and Industry (MITI), although being one ministry among many, had broad functions and operated effectively to strengthen the competitiveness of Japanese manufacturing industries in the high-growth period of the late 1950s and the 1960s. The Ministry of Economic Affairs in Taiwan also functions this way.

Vietnam also had the Prime Minister's Research Commission (PMRC) in the past, but it was an advisory group rather than a central policymaking body entrusted with the power to lead the entire government. Its responsibility was too weak and its members were experienced but perhaps too old. A new advisory team for the prime minister with younger economists and officials was formed in 2011, but it is still without authority to make policies. Nor does Vietnam have a super-ministry such as Japan's MITI or Malaysia's EPU to centrally coordinate development effort. The Ministry of Planning and Investment is not strong enough in terms of authority, capability, and policy instruments to undertake this task. It is urgently suggested that Vietnam create a new dynamic technocrat team within the government as a focal point of policymaking authority and responsibility. Vietnam needs such a team at least for the next few decades to climb to higher income and cope with growth-generated problems and instabilities along the way.

Besides the technocrat team, Vietnam could also adopt the national council model, which is a standard mechanism in many developed and developing countries (Chapter 4). Many industrial policies, such as the fostering of SMEs and supporting industries, formation of industrial clusters, and linking of technical training with industrial needs, are mutually related and require coordinated promotion. They must also be supported by various policy tools that belong to different ministries and agencies. Assigning one ministry to lead and other ministries to follow, as is regularly stipulated in Vietnamese policy documents, cannot work in reality because no one ministry can instruct or overrule others which have equal standing in the government. For multi-ministerial policies to work, an overarching mechanism, above all ministries and agencies and headed by a person with appropriate clout, is necessary to supervise and coordinate different policy components. A national competitiveness council chaired by the prime minister, which meets monthly or quarterly, to monitor the progress of key industrial policies, identify problems that may arise, and assign relevant ministers to solve them and report the results, should be seriously considered for this purpose.[6]

The problem with Vietnam is that there are already too many ad hoc government committees and councils. Most of them meet one or two times and are forgotten or continue to exist only formally without producing substantive results. They cannot function well because sufficient and consistent policy attention is not given from the top. These meetings are often chaired by the minister of a designated ministry rather than the prime minister or deputy prime minister, with an inability to solve issues touching more than one ministry. These councils and committees should be merged into a small number of more powerful and permanent mechanisms covering, for example industrial and trade issues and macroeconomic management respectively. Top leaders should use these mechanisms effectively and intensively to concretize policy visions, accelerate implementation, and remove obstacles (see section 4.5 in Chapter 4 for a more concrete proposal for a national competitiveness council in Vietnam).

Establishment of a technocratic team and a national competitiveness council is an issue where policy learning based on international best policy practices is very effective because East Asia abounds in such practices. Experiences of other countries should be referenced in designing their functions and structure, with necessary modifications as usual.

9.6.3 Foreign partnership

Vietnam's foreign policy shifted dramatically in the early 1990s when close ties with the Soviet bloc were replaced by multi-directional diplomatic relations and re-integration into the global (Western) economy. Since then, interaction with foreign actors has exerted indirect and subtle influences on Vietnam's development orientation although the Vietnamese government never allows foreigners to take the driver's seat in policy formulation (Izumi Ohno, 2005). Bilateral and multilateral donors have registered their desire to see faster reforms and more administrative transparency and efficiency on such occasions as the semi-annual consultative group meetings, comments on the five-year plan and the ten-year strategy, and policy dialogue associated with the Comprehensive Poverty Reduction and Growth Strategy (CPRGS) and the Poverty Reduction Support Credit (PRSC) led by the World Bank. Foreign businesses also have pressed the Vietnamese government to improve the legal and policy framework, tax and import duty system, and other business-related matters through the Vietnam Business Forum, government–business dialogue, and numerous trade fairs and symposiums.

Among leading economies in East Asia, Japan in particular has contributed significantly to Vietnam's development since the early 1990s through trade, investment, aid, and human exchange. The Japanese business and official communities are greatly interested in bolstering Vietnam's industrial competitiveness, and have implemented a large number of bilateral programs to this end. They include the building of physical infrastructure (especially in power and transportation), education and training of industrial human resources, and a series of bilateral policy dialogues as shown in Table 9.2.

Table 9.2 Vietnam–Japan bilateral policy dialogue for industrial competitiveness

Program	*Period*	*Principal actor(s)*	*Content*
Ishikawa Project (Study on the Economic Development Policy in the Transition toward a Market-oriented Economy in Vietnam)	1995–2001 (3.5 phases)	MPI–JICA	Joint research on macroeconomy, fiscal and financial issues, agriculture, industry, integration, currency crisis, SOE reform, and PSD; based on the principle of country ownership and mutual respect, with emphasis on long-term real sector development.
New Miyazawa Initiative (Economic Reform Support Loan)	1999–2000	JBIC	Quick disbursing loan of 20 billion yen with conditionalities in PSD, SOE auditing, and tariffication of non-tariff barriers. Action plans in PSD were monitored and evaluated.
JICA–NEU Joint Research on Vietnam's Industrialization Strategy	2001–2003	JICA–NEU with Japanese researchers	Bilateral policy research by university researchers on selected industrial issues and sectors: AFTA, WTO, FDI, motorcycles, steel, textile and garment, footwear, electronics, and software.
Vietnam–Japan Joint Initiative to Improve Business Environment with a View to Strengthen Vietnam's Competitiveness	2003–	MPI–4J	Two-year cycle agreement and implementation of dozens of concrete action plans which were monitored and reported to high-level, with initial focus on removal of business impediments and added emphasis on strengthening of local industrial capabilities.
Joint Work between Vietnam and Japan to Strengthen the Competitiveness of Vietnamese Industries	2004	MPI–4J	Analyses by Vietnamese and Japanese experts as inputs to the drafting of the Five-year Plan 2006–2010, with attention on industrial policy formulation and competitiveness of individual industries (automobile, electronics, supporting industries, etc).

Joint drafting of Motorcycle Master Plan under MOI and VJJI2	2006–2007	Joint Working Group (MOI, VDF, producers, experts)	Drafting of master plan following new content and method, with active participation of large motorcycle assemblers and interaction with other stakeholders; VDF serving as facilitator. Master plan, after significant editing, was approved in August 2007.
Drafting and implementation of supporting industry development action plan	2008–	3J, MOIT, MPI	To implement supporting industry development master plan of 2007, action plan with clear time schedule and executing agents, together with proposed Japanese assistance, was proposed. Agreement with Vietnam was not reached but Japanese assistance projects began to be executed and monitored.
Vietnam's Industrialization Strategy	2011–	METI, 3J, CIEM	Based on past and current industrial studies, a small number of industries and/or regions are to be chosen to receive concentrated policy effort and Japanese cooperation to produce new industries in Vietnam.

Abbreviations: 3J (Japanese embassy, JICA, JETRO), 4J (Japanese embassy, JICA, JBIC, JETRO), JICA (Japan International Cooperation Agency), JETRO (Japan External Trade Organization), JBIC (Japan Bank for International Cooperation), METI (Ministry of Economy, Trade and Industry), MPI (Ministry of Planning and Investment), MOI (Ministry of Industry), VJJI2 (Vietnam–Japan Joint Initiative Phase 2), CIEM (Central Institute for Economic Management), GRIPS (National Graduate Institute for Policy Studies), NEU (National Economics University), VDF (Vietnam Development Forum), PSD (private sector development), and SOE (state-owned enterprise). MOI was merged with the Ministry of Trade to become the Ministry of Industry and Trade (MOIT) in 2007. JICA and part of JBIC were merged to become new JICA in 2008.

Japan is the largest foreign partner that engages in bilateral industrial policy dialogue with Vietnam.

These programs aim to improve Vietnamese policies in the areas where Japan has strong business concerns or comparative advantage. There is no denying that they are used to pursue Japan's national interests. At the same time, they have the additional purpose of institutionally correcting the weaknesses of Vietnam's policy formulation by introducing new procedures and organizations as well as jointly drafting and implementing industrial actions. Japanese officials and businesses are well aware of the structural shortcomings of Vietnam's policymaking. They are willing to invest time and resources to work with the Vietnamese side to solve them, without which they know their dialogue will not lead to meaningful results.

The objectives and contents of bilateral industrial policy dialogue have evolved over time. Initial programs emphasized joint study by Vietnamese and Japanese researchers, which greatly contributed to academic exchange and mutual learning, but lacked the mechanism to put what was recommended into policy action (Ishikawa Project, JICA–NEU Joint Research, and Joint Work). In order to overcome this problem, a formal and transparent mechanism for implementing and monitoring agreed actions was introduced, which gradually but greatly improved Vietnam's overall business climate by repealing or revising undesirable laws and procedures one by one (New Miyazawa Initiative and consecutive phases of Vietnam–Japan Joint Initiative). For example, under the Vietnam–Japan Joint Initiative, concrete action plans were bilaterally agreed and rigorously monitored in two-year cycles. Inter-ministerial cooperation was enforced by making the Ministry of Planning and Investment responsible for the participation of all other ministries. This can be considered as an institutional device, with the participation of a foreign partner, to ensure positive results even before the government of a developing country learns effective policymaking.

Subsequently, Japan started more difficult cooperation of improving Vietnam's policy capability by jointly drafting policies, but so far with limited success (joint drafting of motorcycle master plan, and drafting and implementation of supporting industry development action plan). For example, with the motorcycle master plan, strong involvement of non-government stakeholders (especially major FDI manufacturers) was secured throughout the joint drafting process—perhaps for the first time in the history of Vietnam's master plan drafting. However, policy learning of the Vietnamese government was harder to induce than expected and slower than other countries in the region such as Singapore, Taiwan, South Korea, and Thailand. Even so, the Japanese government decided to carry out proposed actions on the Japanese side without waiting for the Vietnamese side to fulfill their requirements. The latest bilateral policy initiative (Vietnam Industrialization Strategy) goes to the heart of industrial policy, namely policy-aided creation of new industrial clusters with selective and intensive promotion, by stressing speed and effective public–private partnership in the hope that the

Vietnamese government will pick up some ideas from the concrete demonstration of how this is done.

9.7 Concluding remarks

While Vietnam's past achievements as a developing and transition country are great and many, this chapter has focused on current problems and future challenges. With reference to policy methods and industrial achievements of neighboring high-performing countries, it offered candid assessment and advice so that Vietnam might develop its industrial potential to the fullest extent. It is evident that the Vietnamese people and government are not satisfied with merely achieving the Millennium Development Goals or stopping at middle income. Their aspiration is high, which is to ultimately join the rich-country club with continued industrialization and modernization beyond 2020. This should be attainable if the nation clearly recognizes its present shortcomings, sets ambitious but realistic goals, and overcomes institutional barriers through persistent and systematic policy learning. The key message of this chapter can be summed up as follows.

Vietnam has reached the point where further progress towards higher income is possible only if internal value creation is enhanced. This calls for proactive government action, rather than laissez-faire, to guide and complement private dynamism and avoid being caught in a middle-income trap. To improve policy quality, Vietnam needs to overhaul its policy-formulation process. This in turn requires a radical organizational change in the public administration system. The task is daunting but it must be done to avoid stagnation. Enlightened and strong leadership, establishment and effective use of a technocrat team and a national competitive council, and strategic partnership with foreigners are proposed as appropriate entry points for this national endeavor.

10 Ethiopia

The Growth and Transformation Plan

10.1 A poor country with strong resolve

Ethiopia is one of the poorest countries in the world with a per capita income of US$390 in 2010 (World Bank Atlas method). Recently it has also been one of the world's fastest-growing economies with the average growth rate of 11.0 percent in the five-year plan period of 2005/06–2009/10. Historically, Ethiopia is host to one of the oldest civilizations of the world. With the population of over 80 million, it is also the second most populous country in Sub-Saharan Africa after Nigeria.

Ethiopia has long struggled with a series of hardships including famines and hunger, suppression under a communist regime, civil war and war of separation, and regional instability. However, it is not accurate to describe the country today as a destitute aid-receiver with little hope of development. Ethiopia largely overcame these internal and external difficulties and turned seriously to the task of economic development around 2003. While structural fragilities and the risk of instabilities remain, policy focus is no longer famine relief or controlling insurgents. Ethiopia's current policy attention is directed to enhancement of productivity and competitiveness by spreading good practices in agriculture, promoting micro and small enterprises, and strengthening eight designated industrial sectors.

Ethiopia is also unique in other ways among low-income countries. The federal government, led by Prime Minister Meles Zenawi for over 20 years, is strong and action-oriented. The country has established a developmental vision and related strategies which are embodied in the concepts of Democratic Developmentalism (DD) and Agricultural Development Led Industrialization (ADLI), with the following characteristics.

First, there is a very strong policy ownership. Despite the fact that Ethiopia is a country heavily dependent on foreign aid and having only a small traditional export base,[1] the Ethiopian government has a clear development strategy which is homemade. Unlike many other "donors' darling" countries in Africa, Ethiopia does not allow bilateral donors or international organizations to dictate its policy affairs through aid harmonization, general budget support, loan conditionalities, or imposition of "international best practices" from the West. Division of labor among donors is managed by the Ethiopian government, not by donors themselves. ODA and FDI are welcomed only when they align closely with the national development plan. Donors and investors interested in industrial or infrastructure projects are requested to transfer technology, provide training, and increase local procurement as much as reasonably possible. WTO accession is being sought, but only on the condition that its membership would leave sufficient policy room for Ethiopia to catch up rapidly as a latecomer country. From the East Asian perspective, these strong attitudes toward development and international cooperation are highly commendable in a latecomer country without which industrial catch-up can hardly be started. Strong policy ownership is a necessary—though not sufficient—condition for sustained economic growth. It may be added that Ethiopia's strong policy ownership hinges heavily on the governing style and intellectual ability of its top leader, Meles Zenawi.[2] Maintaining strong policy ownership into the future will require institutionalization of good policy practices which make them less dependent on the quality of a top leader.

Second, a strong state is to guide the private sector. The Ethiopian government rejects neo-liberal economic philosophy from Washington and vigorously studies policy methods from East Asian high-performing economies. While the Industrial Development Strategy of 2002 states that it is private firms, not state-owned enterprises, which must be the main engine of production and investment, it also contends that the state must use its power to guide private firms away from rent seeking and toward productive investment, technology acquisition, and global competition. The Ethiopian government does not believe that the free market, left to its own, will spontaneously raise productivity or learn technology. It also asserts that, if the state's capability is initially weak, it must be enhanced to fulfill its assigned role in guiding and supervising the market. According to this view, the state should not form an unconditional alliance with "capitalists" who may or may not behave productively. The Ethiopian government wants to maintain arm's length relations with both local and foreign enterprises by preparing both carrots and sticks for different behaviors.

Third, internalization of skills and technology is top priority. This is of course highly welcome and appropriate for a country determined to catch up economically from a very low level. Ethiopian leaders admit that natural resource-based growth is unsustainable and that knowledge, skills, and technology to upgrade agriculture and industry must be the central concern. The requirement of training, technology transfer, and maximum local procurement to foreign contractors of industrial and infrastructure projects is similarly motivated. Keen interest in building engineering universities in large numbers, urgent expansion of the technical and vocational education and training (TVET) system, and proposed institutionalization of kaizen (factory improvement methods developed in Japan—see section 3.4.1) is also manifestations of the same orientation. This policy focus seems to come partly from the proactive attitude of the current administration and partly from the fact that Ethiopia is poorly endowed with natural resources relative to its large population.

Fourth, policy scope expands as policy learning proceeds. Several years ago when Ethiopia began to seriously implement economic development policies, the government had little practical knowledge or experience of industrial policy formulation and had to start with a simple strategy of giving generous incentives and disproportionate policy attention to a few selected export-oriented sectors including leather and leather products, textile and garment, and agro products (floriculture was later added as the private sector discovered its potential). Donor support for industry was also concentrated in these sectors. At the same time, Ethiopia learned East Asian policy methods by studying literature, sending young officials to South Korea, and conducting policy dialogue with Japan, among other means. It also learned from other donors that provided industrial support such as Germany, Italy, and UNIDO. By around 2010, the government felt ready to move on to the next phase of policy formulation with the knowledge accumulated in the implementation of previous development plans. The current industrial policy features promotion of import-substituting industries in addition to export-oriented ones, institutionalization of kaizen as a new productivity tool to supplement benchmarking and institutional twinning, promotion of micro and small enterprises, expansion of the TVET system, creation of new industrial zones, and general speeding up of industrialization.

While Ethiopia's industrial policy is still primitive and its private sector is very weak by the standards of East Asian high-performing economies, emerging correlation between policy learning and policy scope expansion is an encouraging sign that gives hope for further progress. To realize its development vision, the Ethiopian government is trying to absorb and mix any useful ideas and tools from around the world. Nevertheless, it is evident that main policy inspiration comes from the East rather than the West.

10.2 Steps toward development policy formulation

Recognizing that predatory states and rent seeking culture have been the major obstacles to African development, the Ethiopian leaders are determined to build a developmental state—a state that promotes skills, technology, and productive investment for all citizens and businesses in place of patronage and benefits for a few—and has taken a number of steps for its realization ever since the present government assumed power in 1991.

The Ethiopian attempt to build a developmental state in the current form dates back to the early 1990s when an interim regime of the Ethiopian People's Revolutionary Democratic Front (EPRDF) was established after ousting the previous socialist dictatorship by military force. The EPRDF was an association of ethnic political groups led by the Tigray People's Liberation Front (TPLF) which spearheaded the anti-government fight from 1975 onward (Ishihara, 2001). With the coming of the interim government in July 1991, Ethiopia abandoned economic planning and adopted a market-oriented economic system. The national economy at that time was on the verge of collapse. The radical shift in policy orientation was necessary because of the failure of the previous socialist government to realize economic growth and improve living standards; the need to secure finance and cooperation from donors and international financial institutions; and pressing economic issues in transiting from civil war to peace. This policy shift opened the door for the private sector to play an important role as opposed to the previous hostile environment that kept the private sector and market forces at bay and in a very rudimentary state.

During the transition period from 1991 to 1995, new policies were adopted and incorporated into key policy documents. The policy thrust of the interim government was proclaimed in Economic Policy for the Transitional Period in 1992 which contained a shift toward market orientation, removal of most restrictions on private-sector activities, and liberalization and reforms in sectoral, investment, and public enterprise laws. Meanwhile, the interim government retained some features of the previous regime such as the state ownership of land and development centered on agriculture and rural areas. Between 1992 and 1994 the idea of Agricultural Development Led Industrialization (ADLI) took its concrete shape as an overarching economic strategy. An Economic Development Strategy for Ethiopia in February 1994 highlighted the concept of ADLI and defined its strategic direction. On the political front, the Charter of the Interim Government in July 1991 upheld peace and democracy as guiding principles and introduced federalism based on ethnic autonomy. The Communist Military Junta (Derg) of the previous regime was replaced by a multi-party political system. These changes were incorporated in the new constitution which established the Federal Democratic Republic of Ethiopia in August 1995. Additionally, the first phase of the structural adjustment program of the international financial institutions was also put in place during the transition period.

The motivation behind ADLI was the recognition that Ethiopia was an agrarian society in which the bulk of the population (84 percent in the 2007 census) resided in rural areas earning a livelihood from land. Agriculture had long dominated the economy in terms of output, employment, and export earnings. The government emphasized that structural transformation should be initiated through robust agricultural growth, and that peasants and pastoralists should be the main agents of agricultural transformation and economic growth. It was argued that labor and land were the main—and most abundant—factors of production in Ethiopia and that their effective use should generate rapid and sustainable development. These arguments were contained in An Economic Development Strategy for Ethiopia of 1994 mentioned above.

Beginning in 1995, the concept of ADLI was incorporated in the first and the second national development plans which were published only in Amharic. The subsequent development plan, the Sustainable Development and Poverty Reduction Program (SDPRP) 2002/03–2004/05, which further concretized the ADLI strategy, was prepared in both Amharic and English and took the form of a poverty reduction strategy paper in order to solicit cooperation of the international community. SDPRP promoted agricultural development and poverty reduction in rural areas by: (i) strengthening agricultural extension services; (ii) training of extension agents at TVET institutions; (iii) training of farmers at Farmers Training Centers; (iv) water harvesting and irrigation; (v) improved marketing opportunities; (vi) restructuring peasant cooperatives; and (vii) supporting micro-finance institutions.

The initial application of ADLI targeted smallholder farmers, especially crop producers, so as to achieve rapid growth in agricultural production, raise income for rural households, attain national food self-sufficiency, and produce surpluses which could be marketed to urban or industrial sectors. A rise in agricultural output was expected to stimulate industrial production by providing food and industrial materials, thus establishing a link between the rural and urban sector. The industrial sector, in turn, could produce inputs to agriculture such as fertilizers and farming tools and equipment as well as consumer goods for rural households. Such dynamic linkage, which can be called *Core ADLI* (see below), was supposed to ignite the first stage of industrialization until the economy moved into a higher stage.

However, policymakers gradually came to realize the limitations of SDPRP during its implementation. By the time the following national development plan, A Plan for Accelerated and Sustained Development to End Poverty (PASDEP) 2005/06–2009/10, was prepared, there was sufficient recognition of the problems associated with an agricultural development strategy exclusively targeted to smallholder agriculture in rural areas. The productivity of the agricultural sector did not show significant improvement and output remained volatile due to heavy dependency on the amount and timing of rainfall. In the 2002/03 season, the output of the crop sub-sector contracted by 16.5 percent following the decline of 3.7 percent in 2001/02. It was only in 2003/04 that growth in the agricultural sector in general and the crop sub-sector in particular started to recover significantly. From a long-term perspective, however, labor productivity in agriculture has been on a declining trend (World Bank, 2007). Although agriculture has shown strong performance in recent years thanks to favorable weather, this did not herald a significant structural change such as crop diversification or productivity breakthrough.

PASDEP 2005/06–2009/10 broadened the policy scope from smallholder agriculture to other sectors, especially industry and the urban sector. In what may be called *Enhanced ADLI*, strong emphasis was placed on growth acceleration which was to be attained through commercialization of agriculture and private-sector development (PASDEP, English, p. 46). In the first three years of the PASDEP period of 2005/06–2009/10, good performance was recorded in agricultural and industrial production as well as export. Subsequently, however, the Ethiopian economy experienced a slowdown accompanied by inflation, balance-of-payments pressure, and a severe shortage of foreign exchange. Several causes were cited for this boom-and-bust cycle such as expansionary fiscal and monetary policy, an excessive inflow of foreign funds (including aid) relative to economic size, unfavorable weather, speculation and hoarding, and external shocks such as commodity inflation and global financial crisis.

Performance of the productive sector, such as agriculture and industry, is dependent on long-term trends in productivity and economic structure as well as external shocks in the global economy. The three-year boom starting around 2005 and the less spectacular results in the remaining two years of PASDEP seem to have reflected short-term disturbances rather than long-term trends produced by policy effort or private dynamism. The sign of significant structural change was not yet visible. The share of industry in GDP stagnated at 13–14 percent and export continued to be dominated by unprocessed commodities (Table 10.1). Although exports of leather products and cut flowers have shown remarkable growth, they are still tiny and without a clear breakthrough in competitiveness and productivity (Table 10.2).

10.3 Democratic Developmentalism[3]

Ethiopia intends to radically transform the state-management paradigm from the system in which rent seeking is the dominant behavioral pattern to the system in which value creation is central. This drive comes from Ethiopian leaders' deep disappointment with the two paradigms which have ruled in Africa: the paradigm of predatory state which was the root cause of rent seeking and the neo-liberal paradigm introduced in the 1980s and 1990s from the West for the purpose of eradicating rent seeking but, according to Ethiopian leaders, failed miserably in that attempt. To replace these paradigms, an alternative state-management paradigm consistent with multi-party democracy, market-orientation, and international integration is proposed.

Ethiopia's Democratic Developmentalism can be defined as "a political regime in which a developmental party remains in power for a long time by consecutively winning multi-party elections, under which policies that punish rent seeking and encourage productive investment and technology absorption are implemented under strong state guidance." This is a political regime which Ethiopia is trying to build rather than an already established and well-functioning regime. It is a model different from East Asia's authoritarian developmentalism which postponed democracy for the sake of development (see below) or the Western-style "good governance" that forces adoption of advanced governing principles in latecomer countries. As such, it is a new political model for low-income countries that has not been tested by history. It contains many potential problems associated with state leadership, fragile democracy, and formation of political coalition with farmers that must be overcome before the Ethiopian developmental vision is realized. These issues will be discussed in turn below.

The first issue is concerned with the merits and demerits of a strong state. As discussed in the Vietnamese context in the previous chapter, comparative

Table 10.1 Ethiopia: basic data

	1998/99	*1999/00*	*2000/01*	*2001/02*	*2002/03*	*2003/04*	*2004/05*	*2005/06*	*2006/07*	*2007/08*
Real GDP growth (%)	5.2	6.1	8.3	1.5	–2.2	13.6	11.8	10.8	11.1	11.3
Nominal GDP (million Birr)	58,789	66,648	68,027	66,557	73,432	86,661	106,473	131,641	171,834	245,585
Nominal GDP (million US$)	7,828	8,188	9,167	7,794	8,559	10,042	12,306	15,164	19,539	27,939
Per capita GDP (US$)	129	131	127	118	126	143	171	205	257	357
Sectoral share of GDP (%)										
Agriculture	51.2	49.8	50.9	49.1	44.9	47.0	47.4	47.1	46.3	44.6
Industry	12.4	12.4	12.1	12.9	14.0	14.0	13.6	13.4	13.3	13.1
Services	37.2	38.7	38.0	38.6	41.7	39.7	39.7	40.4	41.4	43.4
External relations (% of GDP)										
Export	11.6	12.0	12.0	12.6	13.3	14.9	15.1	13.8	12.7	11.8
Import	24.0	23.9	23.7	26.6	27.4	31.6	35.5	36.5	32.1	26.9
Trade balance (export – import)	–12.4	–11.9	–11.7	–14.0	–14.1	–16.7	–20.4	–22.7	–19.4	–15.1
Total trade (export + import)	35.6	35.9	35.7	39.2	40.7	46.5	50.6	50.3	44.8	38.7
FDI (approval, million Birr)	1,080	1,627	2,923	1,474	3,369	7,205	15,405	19,980	46,949	92,249
(approval, % of GDP)	1.8	2.4	4.3	2.2	4.6	8.3	14.5	15.2	27.3	37.6
Population (million)	60.8	62.9	64.4	66.3	68.2	70.1	72.1	74.1	76.1	78.2
Population in rural area (%)	85.5	85.3	85.1	84.9	84.7	84.4	84.2	84.0	83.8	82.9
Population in poverty (%)	–	41.9	–	–	–	–	38.7	–	–	–
Birr/US$ (annual average)	7.51	8.14	8.33	8.54	8.58	8.63	8.65	8.68	8.79	8.79

Sources: Ministry of Finance, Economy and Development, the Ethiopian National Bank, and the Ethiopian Investment Agency.

Note: Numbers do not add up to 100 percent due to estimation errors of intermediary margins of financial institutions (services sector).

Table 10.2 Export performance of targeted industrial products (unit: million US$)

	2003/04	*2004/05*	*2005/06*	*2006/07*	*2007/08*	*2008/09*
Total export	597	819	1,008	1,185	1,481	1,450
Leather and leather products	43	67	75	89	101	76
Semi-finished leather	42	56	58	49	67	...
Finished leather	–	3	8	27	12	...
Leather shoes	0.8	0.8	2	6	10	...
Agro products	20	34	36	43	52	48
Textile and garment	9	7	11	13	15	14
Cut flowers	12	21	63	111	130	...
(Memorandum items)						
Sum of above four (% of total export)	14.1%	15.8%	18.4%	21.6%	20.1%	...
Sum of above four (% of GDP)	0.8%	1.0%	1.2%	1.3%	1.1%	...

Source: Ministry of Trade and Industry.

institutional analysis shows that it is not easy to transform a "system" (a collection of institutions) which has already solidified (Aoki, 1995a, 2001a, 2001b). Different types of inertia work to defend the existing system such as institutional complementarity (mutual dependence of institutions in which removal of only one institution hardly changes the system), strategic complementarity (strong incentive for individuals to follow the existing rules and play the existing game), and path dependency (difficulty of deviating from the system which was chosen first and subsequently solidified). On the other hand, there are configurations of forces that can lead to systemic transformation despite such inertia. They include collective mutation of internal agents (for example, revolt of disgruntled citizens), policy launched by the government who acts as a destroyer of an old regime, foreign pressure, and a combination of the above three.

Using this framework, Democratic Developmentalism can be interpreted as appointing government as the primary driver for installing developmentalism (i.e., replacement of rent seeking with value creation) and additionally soliciting foreign investors, bilateral donors, and international organizations to enhance this effort through technology transfer and financial resources. This endeavor must eliminate patronage, zero-sum games, and dependency culture associated with the old system and at the same time create new institutions, human resources, and incentive structure to support the coming system. Either effort will require enormous social energy to surmount political resistance. That is why a strong government is needed. Laissez-faire policy that lets the market operate freely is unlikely to generate such social energy.[4]

According to the Ethiopian leaders, the neo-liberal paradigm failed to uproot the rent seeking system because it denied the role of government as a leading agent of systemic change. The naïve view of "market is good, government is bad" could hardly prepare a systemic change in a latecomer country. The Ethiopian government contends that the policy mix of liberalization, privatization, decentralization, and global integration generates a horde of new rent seekers such as mining companies, foreign investors, NGOs, and ODA consultants who rally for budgets and subsidies without contributing to a systemic change. More generally, the strategy of giving power to people and local communities has not succeeded in installing developmentalism in Africa, either.

In Ethiopia, a government led by a strong leader allocates incentives and punishments to steer economic actors such as farmers, workers, merchants, entrepreneurs, and foreign investors away from rent seeking and toward value creation. The strategy to combine carrots and sticks is most clearly seen in the leather and leather product industry. The goal of this industry set by the government is to supply finished leather or leather products for export and domestic sales by improving management and technology to process what has hitherto been sold as raw or semi-finished leather. For sticks, the ban on raw-material export and the high tax on semi-finished leather have been introduced. For carrots, a large number of supporting measures have been offered to the industry including (i) establishment of the Leather Industry Development Institute (LIDI) that provides training, technical support, testing, and some production processes; (ii) donor assistance, foreign advisors, and twinning with an Indian textile institute to strengthen LIDI; (iii) privilege in land allocation, bank finance, and foreign-currency allocation; (iv) business matching between domestic leather shoe producers and European buyers; and (v) monthly government–business meetings to monitor export performance and solve any problems that may arise.

What will guarantee that Democratic Developmentalism will not repeat the same mistake as the neo-liberal paradigm—that it will not become a new playground for rent seekers? Experiences of other developing countries show that strong states are not immune to patronage and collusion among politicians, bureaucrats, and businesses. At present, Ethiopia is led by a strong and intelligent leader who is determined to avoid such political capture. This is a source of strength for the moment but may become a source of weakness when the time for power transition arrives.

The second issue related to Democratic Developmentalism is the effectiveness of democracy in low-income countries. Why should a country in an early stage of economic development adopt democracy instead of authoritarianism? One reason is for enjoying the inherent and universal value of democracy itself, such as freedom, human rights, empowerment, and participation. Another reason, from the perspective of the ruling authority, would be to use democratic procedure to secure legitimacy, maintain national unity, and gain popular support for developmental policies. Additionally, it must be noted that no country at present, regardless of its development stage, can be accepted as a valid member of the international community and receive aid and cooperation unless it embraces a democratic form of government.

This is an international environment sharply different from the one in which, for instance, Taiwan or South Korea faced during the Cold War era.

However, the kind of democracy that can be introduced in a poor country with a limited popular mindset and institutional set-up is not an ideal type equipped with full conditions and features. It must be a variation of democracy which is relatively simple, manageable, and consistent with the developmental goals of a low-income country that faces many constraints and problems. The core elements of this democracy are an election-based transition mechanism in the presence of opposition parties and protection of most basic human rights. These are formal requirements that must be adopted by all developing countries of today. But even this limited version of democracy is subject to many challenges which prevent its smooth operation. The true spirit and substance of democratic rule—acceptance of diverse views and interests, majority rule, tolerance, compromise, and solution of disputes through non-violent means—may be harder to come by.

Based on extensive qualitative research, Paul Collier concludes that democracy has not produced accountable and legitimate governments and has rather increased political violence in many developing countries, especially in the societies of the "Bottom Billion" (Collier, 2009). This is because governing rules are yet to be institutionalized and authority has not been firmly established and universally accepted. If there is no consensus regarding how democratic procedure should be applied in practice and in detail, the incumbent government can exercise much discretion in handling election, human rights, budgetary allocation, and relationship with the parliament. Equally, opposition groups can readily criticize and challenge any action by the government. Election itself becomes a complicated political game, and victory in it can hardly confer full legitimacy. Vendetta politics is repeated as former leaders are prosecuted and their policies are reversed by incoming governments. Arrests and bombs are preferred weapons rather than telecast debates and peaceful demonstrations. Irregularities such as these are fairly common in developing countries that have accepted the form of democracy. In Ethiopia, the violence following the 2005 national election showed that the country was also not free from the risks associated with developing country politics. In the 2010 national election, however, the ruling party won a landslide victory and regained urban votes without major violence.

Under Democratic Developmentalism, a legal procedure for election-based political transition must be in place while the ruling party is determined to stay in power for a long time. This may be regarded as contradictory requirements. If the possibility of power change is real, it is highly unthinkable that one party will consecutively win elections for a number of decades. Every time a new government comes into power, previous policies are repealed or at least greatly modified, damaging credibility and time consistency of policies which are considered necessary for sustained growth. On the other hand, if there is a hidden mechanism which prevents the opposition from winning elections, there is no true democracy or political competition. The only way for the EPRDF to stay very long in power legitimately is to consistently produce high growth and distribute its fruits to everyone so that people will happily vote for it even without coercion or election gimmicks. This is a real challenge for any government, especially those in developing countries.

Third, there is the question of political support base of a democratic developmental state. In the past national elections the EPRDF enjoyed solid support from poor farmers in rural areas who are recognized as the political coalition partner of the ruling party. It is natural that a political party intending to win an election every five years chooses small farmers, which occupy 80 percent of the population, as its support base. In addition, the ruling party also counts on the future support of micro and small entrepreneurs in urban areas although their number is still small. The current five-year plan targets micro and small enterprises as the generator of income and employment for poverty eradication as well as a new political support base for the incumbent government.

Generally speaking, poor farmers on subsistence living are characterized by conservatism, low levels of education and knowledge, and submissiveness to authority. They are often passive followers rather than mature and independent forgers of national politics. The situation is not very different in Ethiopia where farmers live a meager and highly unstable life. In Central Highlands where the majority of the Ethiopians reside, small farmers are scattered across vast mountainous terrains with difficult road access. They live on what they produce with little external sale or purchase. The supply of electricity, drinking water, and hygiene is severely limited. Agriculture basically depends on the whims of rainfall, the use of fertilizer is inadequate, and the arable plot of each family is very small and being further subdivided under population pressure. Eastern Tigray, Eastern Amhara, and Eastern Oromia are particularly vulnerable to drought due to unstable rainfall and soil erosion. Land division has gone to extremes in some parts of Southern Region such as Gurage and Wolayita. In Eastern and Southeastern Ethiopia, especially Somali and Afar Regions, pastoralists lead nomadic lives on sparsely populated dry land.

The problem faced by smallholder farmers is not only a supply-side problem but also a demand-side problem of finding markets as well as a quality-of-life problem that requires social-sector policies. In Ethiopia, many assistance programs are already in place. A nationwide food-aid program with large donor assistance has been established to improve food security.[5] Expenditure on agriculture and rural development is relatively high by international standards.[6] Productive support to agriculture has consistently been prioritized in the past and current national development plans. Ethiopian farmers with limited and unstable income will probably continue to support the ruling party because of benefits they receive from the government or for fear of losing them. But such vote buying which perpetuates passivity and dependency among poor farmers is hardly consistent with the grand objective of Democratic Developmentalism to create economically affluent and politically mature farmers as the engine of national development. Can Ethiopia create such dynamic farmers with the existing support measures? If agricultural productivity remains stagnant, the state will eventually face fiscal crisis and foreign aid dependency. While the Ethiopian government remains confident and optimistic, many foreign experts are pessimistic about this.

The view of Ethiopian leaders on this issue is very clear. They consider productivity breakthrough and commercialization of smallholder farmers as the central pillar of national development. They feel that a large number of policies and institutions have been introduced to support agricultural growth in the last several years and some positive results are already obtained. Among the mechanisms installed recently, the most important is the nationwide agricultural extension network that is tasked to scale up the best practices of excellent farmers to other farmers. In the previous plan period of 2005/06– 2009/2010, agricultural production grew 8.4 percent per annum on average. In the current plan period of 2010/11–2014/15, it is projected to grow 14.9 percent per annum if best practices spread to all farmers (higher-case scenario) and 8.6 percent per annum if the scaling up remains partial (base-case scenario). Diverse strategies will be applied according to crops and regions, and potentially most productive areas with stable water supply are targeted as leading regions. Surplus commodities will be exported with policy support. Agricultural commodity exchanges have been set up, and further upgrading of distribution and exchange mechanisms will be implemented and more commodities will be supplied to domestic manufacturers for processing. The government is hopeful that, backed by these measures, Ethiopian agricultural revolution is just around the corner. This will produce a large number of affluent and independent farmers in support of the current government.

The expansion of agricultural extension services in the last several years is shown in Tables 10.3 and 10.4. By 2010 Ethiopia had finished training

Table 10.3 Numbers of farmers training centers and agricultural extension workers

	Established or trained in each year						*Cumulative as of Jan. 2010*
	2004/05	*2005/06*	*2006/07*	*2007/08*	*2008/09*	*2009/10*	
Farmers training centers		1,500	2,200	2,000	1,782	. . .	9,265
Agricultural extension workers	9,368	13,899	13,383	15,095	9,404	636	61,785

Source: Agricultural Extension Department, the Ministry of Agriculture and Rural Development.

Note: As of January 2010 the number of trained agricultural extension workers exceeded the official target of 60,000. However, the number of actually allocated extension workers was less than those trained (Table 10.4). The number of operational farmers training centers as of January 2010 was 6,543.

Table 10.4 Numbers of extension workers and service delivery stations (allocated or established)

	2002/03	*2003/04*	*2004/05*	*2005/06*	*2006/07*	*2007/08*
Agricultural extension workers		9,434	23,359	34,446	49,435	. . .
Health Centers	451	519	600	635	690	826
Health Posts	1,432	2,899	4,211	5,955	9,914	11,446
Health Workers			2,737	8,901	17,653	24,571
Primary schools		10,394	11,780	19,412	20,660	23,235
Primary school teachers		105,788	121,077	203,040	225,319	253,586

Sources: Education Management Information System; Health Management Information System; Ministry of Finance and Economic Development, *Annual Performance Review*, various issues; Ministry of Health, *Health Sector Development Plan-III Annual Performance Review*, June 2008; and Agricultural Extension Department, the Ministry of Agriculture and Rural Development.

Note: The table shows cumulative assignments. Agricultural extension workers count only those actually assigned which numbered 46,451 in January 2010.

Table 10.5 Agricultural production (unit: 1000 quintals)

	2003/04	*2004/05*	*2005/06*	*2006/07*	*2007/08*	*2008/09*	*Average growth per year*
Cereals	90,062	100,308	116,242	128,798	137,170	144,964	10.0%
Edible oil	3,129	5,264	4,866	4,971	6,169	6,557	15.9%
Pulses	10,373	13,496	12,712	15,786	17,827	19,646	13.6%
Vegetables	3,879	4,320	4,502	3,451	4,720	5,989	9.1%
Root crops	16,055	16,152	13,375	14,095	15,309	12,136	–5.4%
Fruits	2,495	2,634	4,283	4,600	4,621	3,513	7.1%
Coffee	1,262	1,562	1,716	2,415	2,734	2,602	15.6%

Source: Ethiopia Central Statistical Agency, agricultural sample surveys.

and assigning three agricultural specialists responsible respectively for agricultural technology, livestock management, and resource utilization in every village (*kebele*) of the country. A farmers training center has also been established in every village. Additionally, two female health workers are being stationed in every village. Comprehensive national extension networks such as this are relatively rare in Africa. The next challenge is to fully utilize these human-resource and service-delivery networks to realize the objective of improving agricultural productivity and livelihood of rural residents.

According to the sample surveys conducted by the Central Statistical Agency, agricultural production in recent years showed an upward trend and land productivity of major crops also rose (Tables 10.5 and 10.6). This fact seems inconsistent with the pessimism expressed in the foregoing paragraphs, but there are a few catches. First, the period covered in Tables 10.5 and 10.6 were marked by relatively good weather and an increase in fertilizer use,

Table 10.6 Land productivity of major crops (unit: quintal/ha)

	2003/04	*2004/05*	*2005/06*	*2006/07*	*2007/08*	*2008/09*
Barley	11.7	12.1	12.7	13.3	13.8	15.5
Maize	18.6	17.2	21.9	22.3	21.2	22.2
Teff	8.4	9.5	9.7	10.1	11.7	12.2
Wheat	14.7	15.6	15.2	16.7	16.3	17.5
Sesame	6.7	8.5	7.3	7.1	10.1	7.8
Broad beans	11.2	11.9	11.2	12.6	13.2	12.9

Source: Ethiopia Central Statistical Agency, agricultural sample surveys.

which cannot be sustained indefinitely in the future. Second, more seriously, Ethiopian agricultural data are unreliable and may not reflect true trends.[7] This is caused partly by inadequate statistical technique and shortage of personnel and partly by the incentive to overstate output relative to targets when local officials report the results. For this reason, it must be concluded that recent agricultural performance is unknown and no basic data on which policy discussion can depend exists in Ethiopia.

The government is action-oriented and ambitious, which is commendable, but the harsh reality of Ethiopian agriculture may not allow a quick achievement of Green Revolution. Ethiopia must continue to tackle many issues before its agriculture becomes highly productive and commercialized. Nevertheless, it is an interesting feature of Democratic Developmentalism of Ethiopia that this goal is proclaimed to be the top national priority and that small farmers are regarded as the political ally of the ruling party whose voting behavior will legitimize the incumbent government.

How does this Democratic Developmentalism compare with authoritarian developmentalism observed in East Asia in the post-World War II period? The typical authoritarian developmental states were Taiwan and South Korea in the 1960s and 1970s whose outstanding features included: (i) emergence of the regime in response to a national security crisis (communist threat was the most common external crisis in East Asia); (ii) strong leadership exercised by a charismatic (male) leader; (iii) an elite technocrat group that supported and concretized the leader's policies; (iv) prioritization of developmental ideology and postponement of transition to democracy; (v) legitimacy through economic performance rather than democratic procedure; (vi) persistence of the same regime for two to three decades and social transformation that it generated (Watanabe 1995; Ohno and Sakurai 1997; Banno and Ohno 2010). Given this profile, the past experience of authoritarian developmental states in East Asia differed from the current Ethiopian model in the following ways.

First, East Asian economic development is a historically proven model with remarkable achievements in income generation and structural transformation in many countries. By contrast, the Ethiopian model remains to be tested in the future. Second, East Asian developmental states formed strong political alliance with domestic capitalists while refusing to adopt a multi-party system with free election. By contrast, Ethiopia embraces a more open political system in the early stage of industrialization. The East Asian model was justified by rising living standards for all while the legitimacy of Democratic Developmentalism will depend on both economic performance and democratic procedure. Third, social transformation triggered by high income, especially the emergence of an urban middle mass with new mindset and demands, eventually led to the end of strong states and democratic transition in East Asia in what Watanabe (1995) calls a "successful dissolution" of authoritarianism through its developmental achievements. This pattern has already run its course in Taiwan and South Korea while it is in progress in other countries. Meanwhile, how Democratic Developmentalism, with strong emphasis on producing wealthy farmers and urban small merchants and industries, will transform the society remains an open question in Ethiopia.

10.4 Agricultural Development Led Industrialization

Agricultural Development Led Industrialization (ADLI) as envisioned by the Ethiopian government can be defined as the development strategy which aims to achieve initial industrialization through robust agricultural growth and its close linkage with domestic industry. This strategy was formulated in the early 1990s and has been implemented in stages, especially from the early 2000s, in Ethiopia. ADLI is considered to be an evolving strategy subject to pragmatic experimentation and adjustments rather than an immutable principle. The revisions and expansion of policy space from the past five year plans (SDPRP 2002/03–2004/05 and PASDEP 2005/06–2009/10) to the current five-year plan (GTP 2010/11–2014/15), as discussed below, exemplifies the evolving nature of ADLI that responds to changing circumstances, evaluation of past policies, and rising policy capability of the Ethiopian government.

An early exposition of ADLI was given in An Economic Development Strategy for Ethiopia in 1994 as follows:

> The long term objective of development in Ethiopia is structural transformation of the economy in which the relative weight of agriculture, industry and service changes significantly towards the latter two. Especially, the objective is to raise appreciably the share of the industrial sector in the economy both in output and employment. This structural transformation is envisaged to occur with a high growth of agriculture which is superseded by growth of industry and services.
>
> In essence the development strategy revolves around productivity improvement of smallholder agriculture and industrialization based on utilization of domestic raw materials with labor-intensive technology. The strategy is akin to what is known in economic literature as agricultural-development-led industrialization (ADLI), framed into the Ethiopian

> context. It visualizes export-led growth which feeds into an interdependent agricultural and industrial development. Exports, be it agricultural and mineral, initiates growth thereby creating space for a process of an interdependent agricultural and industrial development (or ADLI), which increasingly becomes a self-generating process of development. Here the strategy has two layers; an outer crust of export-led growth and an inner core of ADLI . . .
>
> The strategy of ADLI in Ethiopia focuses primarily on agricultural development. This is to be attained through improvement of productivity in smallholdings and expansion of large-scale farms, particularly in the lowlands. The contribution of agriculture to economic development is conceived in two ways. On one side, agriculture will supply commodities for exports, domestic food market and industrial output, and on the other side, it will expand the market for domestic manufacture. At present, the importance of agriculture lies as a source of supply rather than demand. As industrialization picks up pace, over the long term the significance of agriculture as a source of demand will also rise.
>
> (Federal Democratic Republic of Ethiopia, 1994, pp. 8–9)

If ADLI is interpreted narrowly and strictly as the strategy to achieve early industrialization through direct material interaction between domestic agriculture and domestic industry as the main engine of growth with exports providing initial markets, the situation can be depicted as in Figure 10.1. Let us call this domestic input–output dependency Core ADLI. In this interdependence, highlighted industrial sectors are agro processing (including leather products) that uses domestic agricultural inputs as well as sectors that produce goods for rural demand such as agricultural tools and machinery, fertilizers and pesticides, construction materials, and basic consumer goods such as processed food and beverages, clothes, and simple household goods purchased by rural population.

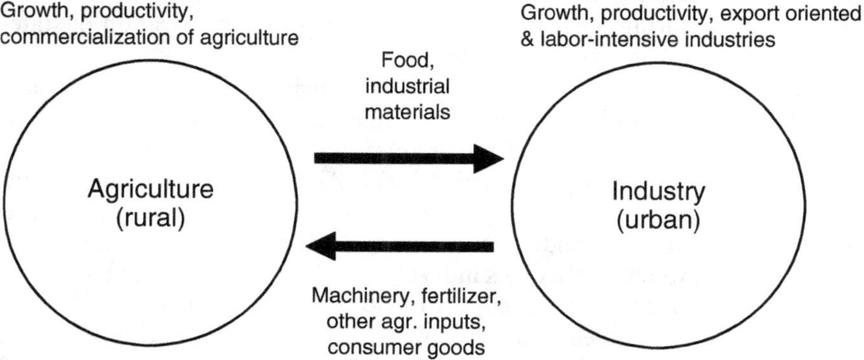

Figure 10.1 Linkages in Core ADLI

The Industrial Development Strategy of 2002 lists the following conditions under which industrialization must proceed: (i) the leading role of the private sector; (ii) parallel development of agriculture and industry through mutual dependence (i.e., Core ADLI); (iii) export orientation; (iv) focus on labor-intensive industries; (v) proper roles of local and FDI enterprises; (vi) strong state guidance; and (vii) mobilization of all social relations among government, capitalists, small farmers, labor, and management. The requirements of export orientation and labor-intensiveness should be particularly noted. Moreover, the second condition (Core ADLI) can be re-interpreted as the requirement for the maximum use of domestic resources. These three conditions are the main requirements on industry in establishing bi-sectoral interdependence. As noted above, this linkage is not a permanent one but something that can evolve into a new pattern in which industry will take the lead once the initial stage of industrialization is completed. As the Industrial Development Strategy clearly states, "When we say that we follow agriculture development led industrialization this does not mean that it will be so forever . . . if agricultural development led industrialization strategy is successfully applied it will be changed to industry led development strategy" (Federal Democratic Republic of Ethiopia, 2002, English, p. 8).

The question concerning Core ADLI is whether this strategy is powerful enough to significantly propel early industrialization in Ethiopia. True, we do have historical examples in which agriculture grew relatively strongly prior to the period of full-scale industrialization and provided resources for industrialization through taxation and foreign exchange earnings (for example, silk and tea exports in late-nineteenth-century Japan, rice and sugar production in Taiwan up to the 1960s, and the rice export tax of Thailand up to the 1980s). There are also cases in which robust agro and fishery exports ameliorated the immiserization of rural communities often associated with globalization (for example, fish and shrimp exports of Southeast Asia). Agro and fishery products may even become leading exports (for example, Chilean wine and salmon). Agriculture can also serve as an income and employment buffer at the time of economic crisis (for example, Japan immediately after World War II, and absorption of laid-off workers caused by privatization of state-owned enterprises in Vietnam in the early 1990s).

Despite all this, a historical example in which an industry which uses domestic materials as its main physical input has expanded dramatically to become the industrial pillar of that nation and contributed greatly to the structural transformation is difficult to find. Agricultural development and industrial development are usually more distinct and separable than envisaged in Core ADLI. Japanese industrialization was not based on silk and tea, and neither the Taiwanese electronics industry nor the Thai automotive industry relied heavily on the domestic supply of rice or tropical fruits.

In Ethiopia, the implementation of Core ADLI is most clearly seen in the leather and leather-product industry in which domestic animal hides and skins are procured by tanneries and manufacturers to produce finished leather or final products such as leather jackets and shoes for domestic sales and export. However, even with significant expansion in recent years, this industry still remains small. In 2008/09, the export value of leather and leather products was US$76 million amounting to 5.2 percent of total export or 0.2 percent of GDP (Table 10.2). Whether this industry will grow robustly to lead broader Ethiopian industrialization is an open question.

However, the current thinking of Ethiopian leaders is no longer confined to the framework of Core ADLI. While continuing to attach importance to Core ADLI, other strategic options and relations are also explored to promote industrialization. As noted above, PASDEP 2005/06–2009/10 highlighted growth acceleration through commercialization of agriculture and private-sector development, which is a departure from Core ADLI. Policy targets in this Enhanced ADLI were not limited to smallholder farmers in rural areas. Large-scale commercial agriculture[8] (including flower farms), urban micro and small producers, medium and large manufacturers, and foreign-invested firms all came within the purview of Ethiopian industrial policy. Many of these producers operate without much reliance on domestic agriculture–industry linkage.

The present scope of Ethiopian industrial policy is already sufficiently flexible so that all policy options for industrial development, including those not covered by Core ADLI, are freely studied and adopted. In the expanded framework of sectoral interaction, agriculture can offer surplus labor, agricultural or land taxes, cheap food ("wage goods"), and foreign exchange and export earnings for the promotion of industrialization. In turn, resources and technology can be transferred from urban sectors to agriculture through production support, supply of processed food and services, agricultural protection, or public investment (Figure 10.2). These transfers may be made

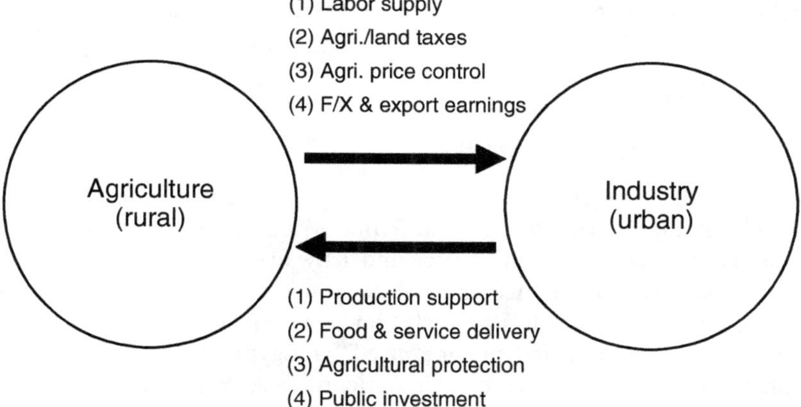

Figure 10.2 Resource transfers between agriculture and industry (other than linkages in Core ADLI)

directly as well as through fiscal and financial mechanisms of the government. Furthermore, industrial policies unrelated to agriculture, such as production of steel, cement, chemicals, and other basic materials, FDI attraction, quality and productivity improvements at factories, and establishment of industrial zones, are also being promoted.

Although policy scope was thus broadened, at least conceptually and in theory, the Ethiopian government could not immediately introduce a large number of non-Core ADLI measures. Due to the lack of policy capability and experience, additional measures had to be introduced in steps and through trial-and-error. In practice, during the period of PASDEP 2005/06–2009/10, what the Ethiopian government did mainly was to select a few export-oriented sectors and provided them with generous policy attention and financial incentives. The Industrial Development Strategy of 2002 chose meat, leather, and leather products; agro processing; and textile and garment as three export-oriented priority sectors (in addition to the promotion of construction and micro and small enterprises). Later, floriculture, an industry which emerged spontaneously from the private sector to produce cut roses in large scale for export, was added to the list.

One remaining question is regarding the meaning of ADLI when its policy scope is enlarged as much as this. The current policy scope is no different from that of any developing country in Africa or elsewhere. What is the remaining significance of ADLI, a concept which is supposed to guide the unique developmental path of Ethiopia? One possibility is that ADLI is a political statement of assurance that the interests of farmers and rural communities will not be sacrificed or forgotten no matter what industrial strategy may be adopted by the government. This may be similar to the use of the slogan of the "Socialist Market Economy" by the Chinese government in which capitalism and globalization are embraced economically while communist power monopoly is ensured politically and effort to improve the livelihood of workers and farmers are maintained nominally.

10.5 Policy learning

10.5.1 Learning from East and West

To build a developmental state with strong government guiding the private sector, Ethiopia turned to the East. Prime Minister Meles himself studied the industrial policies of South Korea and Taiwan seriously and even drafted a monograph that explained his policy stance based on the experiences of these economies. He has actively participated in research projects on Democratic Developmentalism organized by Egyptian and South African scholars as well as a series of the African Task Force meetings of the Initiative for Policy Dialogue hosted by Joseph Stiglitz of Columbia University. He has also exchanged views with other foreign scholars supportive of industrial policy such as Dani Rodrik, Justin Lin, and Mushtaq Khan. Moreover, the Ethiopian government sent several young officials to the Korea Development Institute (KDI) in Seoul to study policy formulation where they were required to copy all materials they encountered and send them back to Ethiopia. However, South Korea after the Asian currency crisis of 1997–98 "shifted to the Washington Consensus" and Ethiopia could gain little from the new teaching of KDI.[9] In addition, the Ethiopian government aggressively sought pragmatic industrial support from Western donors such as Germany, Italy, and UNIDO. In particular, at the request of Prime Minister Meles, Germany implemented the Engineering Capacity Building Program, a large-scale joint program with Ethiopia with the aims of enhancing enterprise competitiveness with benchmarking, constructing new engineering universities, building infrastructure for quality control, and strengthening business associations.

In this way, new policy tools and organizational arrangements were introduced to Ethiopia through self-learning, dispatch of students abroad, consultation with foreign experts, and technical and financial assistance of donors. These included compilation of policy documents for priority sectors; the monthly export steering committee chaired by the prime minister (copied from the South Korean model from the mid-1960s to the 1970s); productivity-enhancing tools such as benchmarking, business process re-engineering (BPR), and kaizen; establishment of sectoral institutes for priority sectors; creation of new engineering universities and TVET institutions; installation of federal and local public–private dialogue mechanisms; public administration reform; building of power and transport infrastructure; technique of scaling up of a pilot project; and strategic mobilization of ODA and FDI for these purposes. It can be said that the years after 2003 were a period of vigorous policy learning and experimentation by the Ethiopian government.

In 2008, the World Bank invited Dani Rodrik of Harvard University to Ethiopia to advise an expansion of policy scope. In the note prepared for the Ethiopian government, Rodrik argues that, while Ethiopia's "first-generation" industrial policies had achieved some success, especially in flower export, there was a need to move towards "second-generation" industrial policies aiming at both home and export markets. The existing industrial policy of Ethiopia consists of a shortlist of priority sectors which receive a variety of incentives. According to Rodrik, this narrow approach to industrialization has two limits:

> One is that many potentially successful sectors are almost certainly not on the list. There are potentially hundreds of different products in which Ethiopia can be competitive; yet it is hard to think of all of them ex ante. The most successful sector to date, floriculture, is a case in point. This is a sector that was brought to the government's attention—and made the priority list—only after private entrepreneurs had done the

> initial discovery and had come to the government for assistance. It is easy to imagine that there are many such industries that government policy fails to target simply because they are not in its list. At present, there is no mechanism in place to actively solicit "new" investment projects that may lie outside the priority list.
>
> Second, the assistance needed by investors may be highly specific to the needs of the project in a way that makes it impossible to specify ex ante. Cheap land and holidays on profits taxes may suit some investors just fine; but others may have different needs. One firm may need relief on payroll taxes, another from tariffs on inputs, and a third may want the relaxation of some regulation or legislation. In at least one instance, the prime minister has helped a large pioneer investor by agreeing to change a regulation (on qualification for DBE [Development Bank of Ethiopia] loans). But problems such as these are common at all levels, and it is unrealistic to expect that the PM himself can attend to them all. There is currently no mechanism in place to respond to such needs systematically.
>
> (Rodrik, 2008, pp. 5–6)

Rodrik proposes the following six revisions to Ethiopian industrialization strategy: (i) broadening policy scope to include more sectors; (ii) supporting "new" activities for Ethiopia rather than exports; (iii) recognition that mistakes are both unavoidable and necessary; (iv) broadening the list of policy instruments; (v) giving incentives and subsidies to "pioneers" only and not emulators; and (vi) enhancement of lines of communication and coordination with the private sector. He also adds that success depends on the change in mindset in which industrial policy is regarded as a process of collaboration and problem-solving with the private sector rather than increasing the number of incentives or the volume of exports.

Most of Rodrik's recommendations are reasonable.[10] However, it is important to recognize the fact that the proper timing of policy expansion depends on the amount of policy learning. The proposed shift from the "first-generation" to "second-generation" industrial policies was hardly possible several years ago when the Ethiopian government had just begun to promote industries with limited policy capability. At that time, selection of only a few export-oriented sectors and using simple incentive measures was natural because the government did not have sufficient knowledge to conduct sophisticated policies. By now, additional policy tools and insights have been acquired through hands-on experimentation, donor support, and interaction with foreign experts. An Ethiopian minister revealed that the expansion of policy scope was already in discussion within the government two years before the counsel of Rodrik was received. Additionally, it is also interesting to note that import substitution, which used to be summarily discredited by the Washington institutions, is now strongly recommended to Ethiopia by the World Bank through a number of US-based economists.

10.5.2 Industrial policy dialogue with Japan

Ethiopia's most systematic policy learning from the East has been through industrial policy dialogue with Japan. In July 2008, the African Task Force meeting of the Initiative for Policy Dialogue was organized in Addis Ababa by Joseph Stiglitz supported by the Japan International Cooperation Agency (JICA), where Prime Minister Meles participated in most sessions of this two-day conference. Researchers from the GRIPS Development Forum discussed East Asian industrialization (Ohno and Ohno, 2012) and offered a book to the prime minister which contained a chapter on JICA's kaizen project in Tunisia (GRIPS Development Forum, 2008b). In the following week, the prime minister requested the Japanese government to initiate bilateral cooperation with two components: a kaizen project modeled after Tunisia by JICA and policy dialogue with the GRIPS Development Forum. After a preparation period, a two-year project between Ethiopia and Japan was implemented from June 2009 to May 2011 which included eight sessions of policy dialogue together with JICA's kaizen project that aimed to improve the productivity of 30 local manufacturing companies in agro-processing, textile and garment, leather, chemical, and metal industries (Figure 10.3). These two project components were interlinked and conducted with regular and close consultation. After the completion of the first phase in 2011, both components were extended into the second phase at the request of the Ethiopian government.

Industrial policy dialogue was held at three levels: (i) prime minister, (ii) ministers and state ministers, and (iii) heads of directorates and institutes and

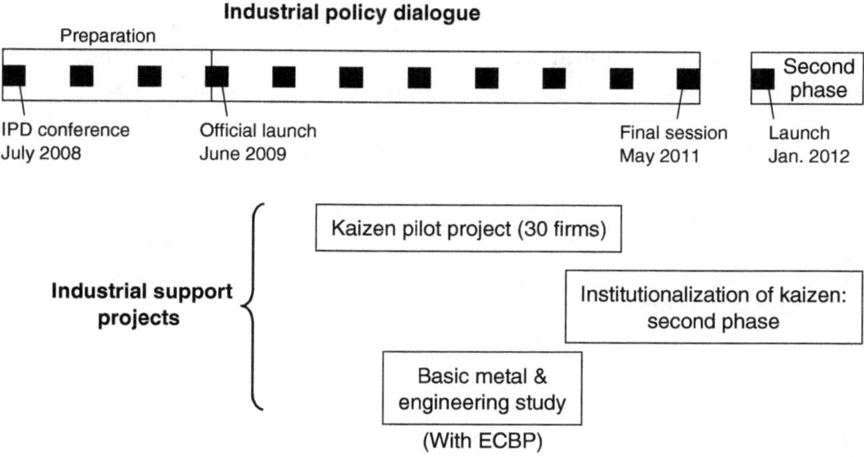

Figure 10.3 GRIPS–JICA industrial policy dialogue and industrial support projects

Note: Black squares indicate policy dialogue sessions in Addis Ababa with the prime minister, concerned ministers and state ministers, and officials and experts at operational levels. IPD stands for the Initiative for Policy Dialogue, policy oriented meetings on various topics hosted by J. Stiglitz of Columbia University. ECBP stands for the Engineering Capacity Building Program, a large-scale program run jointly by Ethiopia and Germany.

other officials and advisors in charge of project formulation and implementation on the ground. The Japanese team met with Prime Minister Meles ten times in the preparatory and first phase for substantive discussions that clarified his policy intention and defined areas of bilateral cooperation[11]. The prime minister raised various issues regarding comparison of Ethiopia's state building with East Asian developmental states, as well as East Asian experiences in technology transfer, vocational training, steel and metal engineering, agricultural breakthrough, national productivity movements, and industrial policy method and organization. Information packages on these issues were requested by the prime minister[12]. The progress of JICA's kaizen project was reported and problems encountered in its implementation were raised and solved.

At the level of ministers and state ministers, high level forums (HLFs) were organized quarterly to deliberate concrete and pragmatic issues relevant to the formulation of Ethiopian industrial policy at each point. They lasted either half day or full day and were co-chaired by the senior economic advisor to the prime minister, the minister or state minister of industry, and the Japanese ambassador. The topics of HLFs, which sometimes overlapped with the discussions with the prime minister, included the concept and practice of kaizen, basic metal and engineering industries, industrial sector orientation in the next five-year plan, methods of drafting industrial master plans and action plans, national productivity movements in East Asia and Africa, international best practices in industrial policy procedure and organization, and so on (Table 10.7). Ministers, state ministers, and heads of industrial projects from related ministries were regularly invited to HLFs or visited individually by the Japanese team in case they were unable to attend the HLF meeting. Beside these, Ethiopian officials, researchers, and business leaders were invited to Japan, Singapore, South Korea, Taiwan, and Botswana for policy study or kaizen training, and their findings were also reported at HLFs.

At the operational level, the Japanese team held numerous meetings with officials of the Ministry of Trade and Industry (the Ministry of Industry after the reorganization of government in October 2010) and other ministries, sectoral institutes and government agencies, universities and research institutions, international NPOs, and bilateral and multilateral donors. It traveled outside Addis Ababa to visit regional governments, tanneries, shoe and garment factories, metal engineering firms, food processors, agricultural cooperatives, flower farms, coffee growers, tourist establishments, and Japanese cooperation project sites.

The policy dialogue team supported the kaizen pilot project which was implemented in parallel with the policy dialogue which followed the standard format of Japanese kaizen assistance. The team monitored the progress of the kaizen pilot project and hosted open seminars on the concept and adaptability of kaizen, produced reports to introduce kaizen to Africa and review necessary ingredients for kaizen national movements (GRIPS Development Forum 2009, JICA and GRIPS 2011b), and organized internal meetings to narrow the perception gap between the two sides for smooth implementation

Table 10.7 Issues discussed at high-level forums (phase 1)

	Presentations by Japanese side	*Presentations by Ethiopian side*
1st HLF (Jun. 2009)	(1) "JICA's plan to policy dialogue and development study" (2) "ADLI and future directions for industrial development"	(1) "Evaluation of current PASDEP focusing on industrial development and related sectors"
2nd HLF (Sep. 2009)	(1) "Cross-cutting issues on industrialization and policy menu under the age of globalization: examples from East Asia" (2) "Organizational arrangements for industrial policy formulation and implementation: examples from East Asia" (3) "Planning and decision-making process for SME policies in Japan"	(1) "Comments and feedback by the Policy Dialogue Steering Committee on the presentations by GRIPS and JICA"
3rd HLF (Nov. 2009)	(1) "Designing industrial master plans: international comparison of content and structure" (2) "Industrial policy direction of Ethiopia: suggestions for PASDEP II and the next five years"	(1) "Concept for the industrial chapter of PASDEP II and the formulation plan"
4th HLF (Mar. 2010)	(1) "Basic metals and engineering industries: international comparison of policy framework and Ethiopia's approach"	(1) "Draft plan of industry sector for PASDEP II" (2) "Overview, contents of PASDEP II draft of chemical subsector"
5th HLF (Jul. 2010)	(1) "Result of basic metal and engineering industries firm-level study – parts conducted by MPDC and JICA"	(1) "Report of kaizen training for capacity building of Kaizen Unit and pilot project companies in Osaka, Japan" (2) "Report of kaizen training for capacity building of Kaizen Unit and pilot project companies in Chubu, Japan" (3) "Current status of kaizen project and institutionalization of kaizen"
6th HLF (Oct. 2009)	(1) "Singapore's experience with productivity development: internalization, scaling-up, and international cooperation"	(1) "Contents of industry sector in Growth and Transformation Plan" (2) "Singapore's productivity movement and lessons learned"
7th HLF (Jan. 2011)	(1) "The making of high priority development strategies: international comparison of policy procedure and organization"	(1) "Organizational structure of Ministry of Industry and linkage with other ministries"
8th HLF (May 2011)	(1) "Ethiopia's industrialization drive under the Growth and Transformation Plan" (2) "Achievements in the Quality and Productivity Improvement (Kaizen) Project" (3) "Overview of national movement for quality and productivity improvement: experiences of selected countries in Asia and Africa" (4) "Taiwan: policy drive for innovation"	(1) "MSE development strategy of Ethiopia" (2) "Kaizen dissemination plan and institutionalization plan" (3) "Botswana's productivity movement and its Implication to Ethiopia"

of the kaizen project. The kaizen pilot project eventually produced six "high" achievers and four "good" achievers among 28 companies that completed kaizen consultation, a result quite satisfactory by international standards. It also trained six "level 3" local kaizen consultants who could provide consultancy services on kaizen and two "level 2" assistant kaizen consultants who could guide kaizen activities. A kaizen manual, kaizen videos, and the dissemination plan for kaizen were also prepared.

Bilateral policy dialogue which is tailor-made to the urgent policy needs of Ethiopia, conducted at various levels, and linked with the implementation of concrete industrial projects, has proven to be highly effective. Since the style of Japan's policy dialogue is flexible and responsive to the needs of the student, the learning country can ask any questions related to its burning concerns instead of receiving general explanations and instructions only. Japan can also compare the best policy practices of different East Asian countries in addition to its own development experience[13].

10.6 The Growth and Transformation Plan

10.6.1 The content

In November 2010, the Ethiopian parliament approved the Growth and Transformation Plan (GTP) 2010/11–2014/15. This plan is the successor to evolving concepts, documents, and plans of the past. It incorporates the ideas of ADLI and DD and the positive and negative lessons from the past development plans while adding new issues and sectors to work with. Setting ambitious targets and calling for nationwide mobilization, the GTP aims to bring national development to a higher and more difficult stage. As the highest national policy framework, the GTP will govern Ethiopia's developmental policies, budgets, and government organizations, as well as actions of development partners and foreign investors, in the coming five years. Unlike similar plan documents in many other developing countries where much is said but little is implemented, the Ethiopian GTP is unlikely to remain merely on paper. The top leader's resolve and the government's readiness to carry out this plan and take the country to the next level of development are clearly visible. It is highly probable that the performance of every ministry, agency, or institution in Ethiopia will be judged by its contribution to the realization of the GTP.

The Ministry of Finance and Economic Development (MoFED) has the overall responsibility for preparing, implementing, and monitoring the GTP as with the previous national development plans. The drafting process took about 15 months and was managed by the Macro Economic Team of MoFED. The system of visions, objectives, and strategic pillars in the GTP is summarized in Table 2.1.

The main text of the GTP (volume I, 127 pages in the English edition) has ten chapters. Chapters 5–8 are the core chapters that contain strategic

Table 10.8 GTP's visions, objectives, and strategic pillars

Ethiopia's vision to guide GTP	"To become a country where democratic rule, good-governance and social justice reign, upon the involvement and free will of its peoples, and once extricating itself from poverty to reach the level of a middle-income economy as of 2020–2023."
Vision on economic sector	"Building an economy which has a modern and productive agricultural sector with enhanced technology and an industrial sector that plays a leading role in the economy, sustaining economic development and securing social justice and increasing per capita income of the citizens so as to reach the level of those in middle-income countries."
Objectives	1. Maintain at least 11% growth and attain MDGs 2. Education and health services for achieving social sector MDGs 3. Nation building through a stable democratic and developmental state 4. Stable macroeconomic framework
Strategic pillars	1. Rapid and equitable economic growth 2. Maintaining agriculture as major source of economic growth 3. Creating conditions for the industry to play key role in the economy 4. Infrastructure development 5. Social development 6. Capacity building and good governance 7. Gender and youth

Source: Summarized from Chapter 2 of the Growth and Transformation Plan, 2010/11–2014/15.

direction, objectives, major targets, and implementation strategies for economic sectors (agriculture, industry, trade, mining, and infrastructure), social sectors (education and training and health), capacity building and governance, and cross-cutting sectors. Under a separate cover (volume II, 38 pages in the English edition), a policy matrix gives each sector's annual targets, implementing agencies, and means of verification in a large-table format. Among the core chapters, economic sectors take up 32 percent of the main text while social sectors occupy only 8 percent. Though volume is only a partial indicator of importance, it is suggestive of the direction of policy attention. It is evident that the Ethiopian government intends to generate concrete sources of growth in the agriculture and industrial sectors under state guidance rather than confining itself to general provision of primary education, health care, and good business environment, and letting the market do the rest.

Industry is expected to grow strongly and play a key role in the economy by the end of the GTP period (2014/15). In the previous plan period of 2005/06–2009/10, industrial performance was less than expected. Real GDP grew an impressive 11.0 percent per annum but this was a result of over-achievement of agriculture (8.4 percent against the base-case target of 6.0 percent) and services (14.6 percent against the base-case target of 7.0 percent) and underachievement of industry (10.0 percent against base-case target of 11.0 percent). The share of industry in GDP remained a relatively stagnant 13–14 percent rather than rising to 16.5 percent as targeted. The exports of the three targeted sub-sectors (leather and leather products, textile and garment, and agro-processing) did grow, but were still small at US$115 million (3.8 percent of total export) as of 2009/10.

In the current five-year plan period, industry is targeted to grow 20.0 percent per annum (base case) or 21.3 percent per annum (higher case), which is much faster than the targets for agriculture, so that it will become a major engine of growth rather than a small part of the economy as it has been. Industry is expected to be the major source of employment and foreign exchange with strengthened ADLI linkage between agriculture and industry. This is to be attained by broadening policy scope from only a few export-oriented industries to both export-oriented and import substituting industries, and introducing new measures for promoting micro and small enterprises and developing eight selected medium- and large-scale industries (textile and garment, leather and leather products, sugar, cement, metal and engineering, chemical, pharmaceutical, and agro-processing). Additional policy instruments such as institutionalization of kaizen, enhancement of the TVET system, and industrial zones will be mobilized.

10.6.2 Remaining concerns

In the last session of the first phase of Ethiopia–Japan industrial policy dialogue in May 2011, the Japanese side raised four issues concerning the GTP.

The first issue was the lack of focus on quality, productivity, and competitiveness. The sectoral performance indicators of the GTP are quantities measured in tons, millions of birrs or dollars, the number of workers employed or factories established, and the like, rather than indicators of human-capital accumulation or international competitiveness. This is odd because Ethiopian policymakers always stress the critical importance of agricultural and industrial skills, engineering education, technology transfer, TVET system, and other measures to enhance industrial human capital. Similarly, previous sessions of industrial policy dialogue with Japan featured how East Asian economies raised productivity, absorbed technology, and trained workers and engineers with concrete facts and numbers. The gap between this national obsession with knowledge, skills, and technology and the absence of targets related to them in the GTP must be explained. A related puzzle is the fact that the term kaizen (factory-improvement method developed in Japan) is entirely missing from the text of the GTP, together with other productivity and efficiency tools such as benchmarking, twinning, and BPR, which will be Ethiopia's main instruments for improving industrial efficiency. This may have been because the drafting of the GTP followed the routine process where quantitative indicators were regularly adopted rather than qualitative. If that was the case, the drafting process must be revised in the preparation of the next five-year plan.

The second concern was related to how numerical targets are used. Inclusion of numerical targets is normal and even indispensable in national development plans. However, the number and scope of numerical targets must be selected judiciously and the levels at which they are set must be arrived at in a rational way that allows analysis and assessment. In the GTP, the target for real GDP growth for 2010/11–2014/15 is set at 11.2 percent per annum in the base case scenario and 14.9 percent per annum in the higher case scenario. The main difference between the two scenarios is whether agriculture would rise strongly as technology and practices of model farmers were scaled up to all other farmers (high case) or the scaling up will remain partial (base case). Either way, these are ambitious targets. Moreover, industrial targets at sector and sub-sector levels are also quite bold.[14] These growth targets may be an expression of political will and national aspiration. However, an appropriate analytical framework is needed to explain growth scenarios for logical clarity and operational flexibility so that falling short of growth targets should not lead to undesirable policy reactions that may cause allocative distortion or macroeconomic imbalance.

Growth performance is a joint product of private dynamism, policy quality, and uncontrollable shocks. While growth was higher in the first half of the previous plan period than the second half, it was not clear whether this slowdown was caused mainly by exogenous shocks (such as global recession and weather conditions) or by deterioration of policy quality or private effort. Ethiopia does not have an analytical framework to identify the main cause(s) of growth shifts and fluctuations and thus cannot address growth-related problems with appropriate policy response.

The third issue was weak policy capability. Ethiopia's industrial policy is still on a learning curve and the lack of sufficient policy capability can be a serious impediment in the implementation of the GTP. To put it more positively, clear recognition of this problem and strong resolve to overcome it in proper steps will provide Ethiopia with an excellent opportunity for further policy learning. Industrial policy dialogue with Japan identified two problems with Ethiopia's policymaking. First, Ethiopia drafts policies in great haste at the cost of quality and implementability. East Asian high-performing economies typically spend one year to revise an existing policy and two to three years to draft a new one. As a new learner of industrial policy, it would not be improper for Ethiopia to spend at least a few solid years studying international best practices, devise local adaptation, and create an appropriate policy mechanism before it adopts a new important policy such as kaizen, micro and small enterprise promotion, and industrial clusters. Second, Ethiopia needs a simple and well-designed mechanism in the central government to coordinate, monitor, and adjust priority policies. In the last several years, the country has created committees, boards, and teams more or less randomly to deal with the expanding policy scope.[15] Instead of endlessly adding new mechanisms, a central coordination mechanism comprising a national competitiveness council chaired by the prime minister, a planning commission that specializes in making development plans, and a policy think tank that supports these two bodies with action-oriented surveys, studies, seminars, and other intellectual inputs is suggested.

The fourth issue is how to kindle private dynamism. Will the Ethiopian private sector respond strongly to the industrial policy measures of the GTP? Apart from improving policy quality, latecomer countries often face the problem of a weak private sector characterized by short-terminism, job hopping, foreign-product worship, real-estate speculation, dependency on subsidies and protection, and unwillingness to explore new products, technology, and markets. In policy dialogue sessions with Japan, Prime Minister Meles asked why the Ethiopians with large sums of money invested in urban properties instead of building factories. He also inquired how East Asian governments steered the private sector away from rent seeking and into manufacturing and technology. He requested literature explaining concretely how Meiji Japan and post-World War II South Korea absorbed technology so quickly from foreign-assisted industrial projects. In partial response, the Japanese team proposed a national movement for mindset change, which is a comprehensive program of aspiration, philosophy, mass campaign, factory projects, training, certificates and awards, and institution-building that lasts for at least a decade until it becomes self-sustaining and an integral part of popular mindset (Chapter 3). A comparative study of such movements in East Asia and Africa was presented where common success factors and country-specific factors were distilled (JICA and GRIPS, 2011b). In Ethiopia, the institutionalization of kaizen will be the country's core activity for a national movement toward higher quality and productivity. Proper steps should be taken to institutionalize kaizen based on the full knowledge of international best practices.

10.7 Concluding remarks

There is much to be learned from Ethiopia's unwavering pursuit of DD and ADLI. Although the country is in a very early stage of industrialization, many weaknesses remain in its policy formulation, and the success of the GTP is not yet guaranteed, strong policy ownership and aggressive policy learning are something that all latecomer countries should study and replicate. Three final remarks are in order.

First, DD and ADLI can be understood as an Ethiopian adaptation of political and economic regimes to the reality of the early twenty-first century. The menu of development strategies is mostly common across ages and countries. It should include education and training, skills and technology, enterprise and industry promotion, agriculture and rural development, trade and investment, and power and transport infrastructure. Laws, institutions, and monetary and fiscal mechanisms that support these policies must also be established. On the other hand, international environment surrounding developing countries changes over time. During the Cold War era, any developing country belonging to one of the two ideological camps could receive a large sum of economic and military aid without intervention in the management of domestic affairs. But today, all countries are required to embrace democracy, market, and globalization. Ethiopia must also adjust to the reality of the twenty-first century so that it can secure a respectable position in the world and sufficient cooperation from investors, donors, and international organizations. The combination of DD and ADLI is innovative in that it is a proactive attempt to ignite growth with the rejection of the Washington Consensus and without counting on a large inflow of manufacturing FDI as in Southeast Asia. As a poor, landlocked, and resource-less country, Ethiopia's initial conditions are unfavorable. But policy learning started by Ethiopia and its outcome may offer important inspiration for other countries in Africa.

Second, the success of Ethiopian development critically depends on the concrete and pragmatic steps that the country will take toward the goals defined in the GTP. Among these goals, productivity breakthrough and commercialization of smallholder farmers in the agricultural sector and emergence of a strong and broad manufacturing base driven by productivity and technology in the industrial sector are crucial. Fostering of a vibrant and competitive private sector is the essence of economic development for which two inputs are required. The first is decisive and effective leadership, which Ethiopia seems to possess at the moment. However, a developmental state heavily dependent on one top leader will become vulnerable at the time of power transition. Learned policy processes and organizations must be institutionalized as much as possible to diminish this problem. The second requirement is accumulation of practical and detailed policy knowledge by ministries and agencies in charge of agricultural and industrial policies. Proactive industrial policy calls for far greater knowledge than either laissez-faire or socialist planning. To interact effectively with the private sector, officials must share up-to-date industrial information with producers and investors. They must also be well informed about the pros and cons of concrete measures adopted in other countries. Systematic policy learning must continue for years to upgrade Ethiopian policy capability toward the best international practices.

Third, policy learning and expansion of policy scope are dynamically linked in Ethiopia. This is a highly commendable feature which may be called *dynamic capacity development* (Chapter 3; also Ohno and Ohno, 2012). In most developing countries, problems are many while policy capability is limited. This makes it difficult to decide where to start development effort, and in which sequence and at what speed various policies should be introduced. International organizations used to demand a long list of difficult policy actions that must be implemented in a short time as a condition of a financial rescue package. Meanwhile, some economists argued against trying any industrial policy because the risks of policy mistake and political capture were too great. However, neither advice proved to be very constructive in breaking the poverty trap. The World Bank's 1997 World Development Report proposed a two-part strategy in which constant effort should be made to improve policy capability while adopting difficult policies gradually to match the acquired policy capability (World Bank, 1997). Ethiopia is practicing exactly what this report preached. The only difference is that the World Bank emphasized general improvements in "rules and restraints," "competitive pressure," and "voice and participation," while Ethiopia prefers to improve its policy capability through concrete problem-solving such as export promotion of leather products and establishment of a national mechanism that oversees institutionalization of kaizen. This hands-on approach is much closer to dynamic capacity development frequently observed in East Asia than the general self-improvement approach recommended by the World Bank.

Notes

1 The developmental trap

1 The closed-door policy of the Tokugawa shogunate which started in the early seventeenth century was terminated by the military threat of the American gun ships which forced Japan to sign "friendship" treaties with the US, the UK, the Netherlands, and Russia in 1854. Commercial treaties with the five Western powers, including France, were concluded in 1858, and virtually free trade began in the following year. Under these treaties, Japan did not have the right to set import tariffs unilaterally or judge foreign criminals in Japanese courts. A uniform tariff rate of 5 percent was imposed from 1866 until Japan regained tariff rights partially in 1899 and completely in 1911. Domestic sugar and cotton industries were the first victims of the inflow of Western imports.

2 Industrial policy in the age of globalization

1 Repulsion to industrial policy is often visible among conservative elites in Anglo-Saxon countries. For example, in July 2010 *The Economist* magazine hosted an e-debate on the motion that "This house believes that industrial policy always fails," with Josh Lerner defending the motion and Dani Rodrik against it. After five days of voting, 28 percent of participants supported the motion while 72 percent rejected it. However, it is not evident whether a debate of such an abstract kind adds anything useful to our knowledge on the desirability and feasibility of industrial policy.

2 Another reason to avoid it is the fact that, for ordinary students of economists, the term is strongly associated with the Ricardian theory of comparative costs, which is static. A call for sticking to one's comparative advantage can therefore easily be misunderstood as the suggestion that developing countries should forever stay with the export of energy, minerals, food, and other primary commodities.

3 As already noted in Chapter 1, a Western economist with limited knowledge of East Asia strongly protested to the statement made at a conference that Thai workers were less diligent and productive than Korean workers even under the same management. However, this proposition is supported by the majority of general directors of multinational corporations operating in East Asia and always corroborated in two separate annual surveys of Japanese manufacturing firms with overseas production conducted by the Japan External Trade Organization since 1987 and by the Japan Bank for International Cooperation since 1989.

4 It can be said that the neo-liberal paradigm failed to establish a developmental state because it denied the role of government as a leading agent for national transformation. The naïve view of "market is good, government is bad" could not create an

agent powerful enough to destroy the petrified rent seeking system in a developing country. In some cases, a policy package consisting of liberalization, privatization, decentralization, and international integration have generated a horde of new domestic and foreign rent seekers including mining companies, foreign firms, voluntary organizations, and ODA contractors and consultants who rallied for budgets, subsidies and foreign aid.

3 Ingredients of proactive industrialization

1 Apart from the technical aspect of policy methodology, the other important perspective needed to understand and promote developmental states is comparative political analysis, a topic which is beyond the present volume. For those interested in this topic, the best places to start would be Leftwich (2000, 2009); Brady and Spence (2010); and the works produced by the Developmental Leadership Program (www.dlprog.org) managed by Adrian Leftwich (York University) and Chris Wheeler (AusAid) and supported by the Australian government; and the African Power and Politics Program (www.institutions-africa.org) led by the Overseas Development Institute and funded by the UK Department for International Development and the Advisory Board of Irish Aid.

2 The exact phrase used in the World Bank report was the two-part strategy of "matching the state's role to its capability" and "raising state capability by reinvigorating public institutions." The latter included five "fundamental tasks" of (i) establishing the foundation of law; (ii) nondistortionary policy environment including macroeconomic stability; (iii) social services and infrastructure; (iv) protecting the vulnerable; and (v) protecting the environment (World Bank, 1997, pp. 3–4).

3 The Korean endeavor to teach policymaking is conducted through two channels of the Ministry of Strategy and Finance (supported by the Exim Bank and the Korean Development Institute) and the Ministry of Foreign Affairs and Trade (supported by the Korean International Cooperation Agency). These channels are not integrated, however. The term Knowledge Sharing Program is associated with the former while the latter uses various other terms. Another potential problem with the Korean approach is a trade-off between rapid quantitative expansion and assurance of quality and depth. For the policy consultation component, the number of target countries (which include both priority countries for three-year consultation and others for one-year consultation) is expanding from 11 countries in 2009 to sixteen in 2010, 26 in 2011, and 32 in 2012 (planned). For the policy module component, 100 modules are expected to be created by 2012. As the volume of knowledge-sharing activities increases, most works, which were initially managed by the Korean government, are now delegated to consultants and consultant firms.

4 The GRIPS Development Forum plans to compile documents that compare international best practices of some of the policy measures in the list and draw general lessons, such as the Handbook on East Asian Industrial Policy and a report on Industrial Policy Dialogue. The Vietnam Development Forum, a research unit located in Hanoi and associated with the GRIPS Development Forum, conducts similar research for the purpose of informing Vietnamese policymakers (Ohno, 2006b; Vietnam Development Forum and Goodwill Consultant, 2011). Separately, as part of the Knowledge Sharing Program of the Korean government, the Korea Development Institute is creating over 100 policy modules that explain the pragmatic details of individual industrial policy measures.

5 Studies in kaizen invariably note that, in both Japan and abroad, leadership of the general director is the single most important factor for successful implementation of kaizen (Imai, 1986; Kaplinsky, 1995). This is echoed by many kaizen experts

and Japanese factory managers engaged in kaizen instructions in developing countries (Vietnam Development Forum, 2007).

6 The first batch of TNI students counted 296 at entry and 225 at graduation. Among them, 166 (74 percent at graduation) had already secured jobs by the time of graduation, in September 2011, a rate quite high for Thai students. Their largest employers were IT (21 percent), auto parts (19 percent), auto assembly (17 percent), and electronics and electrical (8 percent). Japanese firms in Thailand hired 54 percent of them. Among the graduates without jobs at graduation (26 percent), 12 percent proceeded to higher education, 6 percent were in search of work, and the remaining 8 percent had other destinations (Japan–Thailand Economic Cooperation Society, 2011).

7 Interview with an executive official of the Vietnam–Singapore Technical Training Center in March 2007.

8 Interviews with the general manager and other high officials of PSDC in June 2005 and January 2006.

9 AMATA Corporation, established by Thai initiative with Japanese help but now wholly Thai owned, also operates AMATA City in Rayong Province, adjacent to Eastern Seaboard Development, and AMATA Bien Hoa in Dong Nai Province of Vietnam. One project of interest in the seventh phase of AMATA Nakorn is Ota Techno Park (OTP), a collection of small rental factory space for Japanese SME suppliers initially from Ota City of Tokyo but now accepting any Japanese SMEs with high technology. In 2006 OTP built six units of rental space ($320m^2$ each) with administrative support in Japanese language. It is now in the second-phase expansion with the total units of 17. Ota City of Tokyo provided enterprise matching but no financial support. OTP is intended to offer temporary factory space for Japanese SMEs which are expected to move out once initial success is attained. This information was obtained in an interview with executive advisor and managers of AMATA Corporation in November 2009.

10 Interview with senior officials of the Foreign Investment Promotion Division and the Cross Border Investment Promotion Division of MIDA in January 2010.

11 Interview with the deputy secretary general and other officials of the Thai BOI in March 2005.

12 I would like to thank Akio Hosono, the director of the JICA Research Institute, for providing information about El Salvador where he played an instrumental role as a Japanese ambassador to that country in strategic implementation of Japanese ODA from 2002 to 2007.

13 Due to data problems, Korea's provincial incomes prior to 1985 are difficult to estimate consistently. The gap ratios cited in the text were calculated by Huh (1995). Some of the income gap indicators using provincial data reported by Huh, which support regional income convergence, are as follows: the max/min ratio, 2.0471 (1971), 2.0143 (1981), 1.7531 (1991); the coefficient of variation weighted by economic size, 0.2873 (1971), 0.1643 (1981), 0.1572 (1991); and the Gini coefficient, 0.1597 (1971), 0.0846 (1981), 0.0644 (1991).

4 Policy procedure and organization

1 From East Asia, Banno and Ohno (2010) contributed a detailed analysis of coalition formation and re-formation among political leaders of Meiji Japan, which we called the flexible structure of politics, for the period of 1858–1881. Part of Chapter 5 of this volume is based on this study.

2 The full sentence of Vision 2011 says that "Thailand is the automotive production base in Asia which creates more value added to the country with strong automotive

parts industry." This vision remains unchanged from the previous Master Plan 2002–2006.

3 There are also examples outside East Asia. In India, the Planning Commission has been in existence since 1950 to produce consecutive five-year plans whose focus shifted over the years from massive public investments to indicative planning. In Chile, policy support was provided by Chicago Boys, or Chilean economists trained at the University of Chicago under Milton Friedman and Arnold Harberger, to the military junta which carried out free-market reforms starting in 1973.

4 Following the Korean model of the 1960s and 1970s, Ethiopia has established a monthly Export Steering Committee presided by the prime minister and attended by relevant ministers and officials. The Committee seems to work well in monitoring export performance and solving problems that may arise. However, the Ethiopian committee is narrower in operational scope than the original Korean model or other approaches explained in this section as it is not accompanied by designation of a lead ministry or agency, a secretariat, or working groups that perform various functions. Its members are confined to government ministers and officials. Moreover, it remains an implementing body rather than a policymaking body.

5 In 2001, MITI was renamed to the Ministry of Economy, Trade, and Industry (METI).

6 For more discussion on policy document structure, see Chapter 6 of GRIPS Development Forum (2010).

7 Targets are also called goals, objectives, strategies, action plans (different from "action plans" in section 4.4.1 below), and so forth. We regard all of these as "targets" as long as they set some qualitative or quantitative aims to be achieved.

8 An interview with Mr. Vallop Tiasiri at the Thailand Automotive Institute on November 5, 2009.

9 This section is based on my presentation at the Symposium on Quality of Vietnam's Economic Growth in the Period of 2001–2010 and Direction toward 2020, co-organized in Hanoi, February 2011, by the National Assembly's Economic Committee, the National Economic University, and the National Graduate Institute for Policy Studies. Fuller discussion of Vietnam's policy problems is found in Chapter 9.

10 UNIDO supports "cluster development" but targeted industries are small in size and closer to "trade villages" rather than the one proposed by the Vietnam Competitiveness Report 2010, which is essentially regional development featuring the electronics cluster in the Northern Delta, the textile and footwear cluster near Hochiminh City, and the tourism cluster in the Middle Region.

5 Meiji Japan: from feudalism to industrialization

1 The Bakufu ordered all daimyo to reside in Edo in one year and in their domain in the following year alternately. This perpetual bi-annual commuting of the han lord, accompanied by a large number of retainers, entailed a huge cost in travel and residence and strained the budget of every han. The Bakufu also imposed ad hoc public works and financial contributions to han including building and repairing roads, moats, reservoirs, and the like, and celebratory money for the birth of the shogun's son. Construction of more than one castle per han and possession of naval force were prohibited. There were other rules and regulations issued by Bakufu at will.

2 After the Edo period, Japanese calendar years coincide with the reign of each emperor. For example, the Meiji period was the years of Emperor Meiji, and similarly with Taisho (1912–1926), Showa (1926–1988) and Heisei (1988–). As a custom, emperors remain on the throne as long as they live. However, these

practices were not in place until the end of the Edo period. Until then, the Japanese calendar could be changed at any time and emperors could retire while alive.

3 Data on population and agriculture in the Edo period are fragmentary. According to the estimates of Hayami and Miyamoto (1988), the population grew from 12 million in 1600 to 32 million in 1720, then stabilized for the subsequent 150 years. In the same period, farmland expanded from 2.07 million cho to 2.93 million cho, then less slowly to 3.23 million cho by 1872 (cho is almost equivalent to hectare). Meanwhile, land productivity grew from 0.955 koku per tan in 1600 to 1.094 koku per tan in 1720, with continued improvement to 1.447 koku per tan in 1872 (koku is about 180 liters of rice and tan is about 0.1 hectare).

4 *Gosho* is a pre-modern rich merchant family in the Edo period with only one or a few lines of business. *Zaibatsu* is a conglomerate formed during and after the Meiji period, which was often family owned, with a holding company controlling a large number of subsidiaries such as banking, trade, mining, shipping, shipbuilding, and chemicals. As *zaibatsu* was disbanded after World War II by the US occupation force, new business groups without a holding company, called *keiretsu*, emerged. It was characterized by mutual holding of stocks, frequent information exchange, and business cooperation. Another type of *keiretsu* is a pyramidal production linkage between a large assembly firm such as Toyota, Honda, and Panasonic and multi-layers of companies that produce parts and components.

5 Arguments in this section are derived from Banno and Ohno (2010) and its partial English translation.

6 The plan entertained by Satsuma Han Lord Shimazu Nariakira (1809–1858) was the earliest endeavor of this kind. He had the vision of han-based *fukoku kyohei* as well as the conference of several powerful han lords as a national decision making organ although he did not reach the idea of institutionalizing a feudal assembly. His plan began to be implemented in Satsuma Han from around 1862.

7 Detailed phased accounts of coalition formations and break-ups, of which Figure 5.1 is a summary, are given in Banno and Ohno (2010).

8 Shimazu Hisamitsu (1817–1887), the de facto leader of Satsuma Han, is regarded as a han lord. Iwasaki Yataro (the founder of Mitsubishi group, 1834–1885) who was a low-level samurai close to peasantry, and Ito Hirobumi (the first prime minister, 1841–1909), a peasant's son who was given the title of lowest samurai together with his father, are counted as samurai, and similarly with Sakamoto Ryoma (1835–1867) and Nakaoka Shintaro (1838–1867) who abandoned the position of a han retainer of Tosa. Sons of han retainers who were still young at the time of the Meiji Restoration are also classified as samurai.

9 It may be argued, theoretically, that leaders selected by the author interested in the political role of samurai and han are biased. As a practical matter, however, it would hardly be possible to construct a list of prominent leaders of this period which excludes the people I have selected or which does not largely coincide with them. A minor re-shuffling of candidates would not change the conclusion that the samurai class was the main source of leaders.

10 Shibusawa Eiichi (1840–1931), one of the first officials of the Ministry of Finance of the Meiji government and later a powerful business coordinator who helped to establish hundreds of joint stock companies and economic and social institutions, came from a rich farming family in Saitama.

11 Even after the opening of ports, foreigners were confined to limited areas around the designated foreign settlements and could not travel beyond these boundaries without an official permit. For this reason, independent Japanese merchants emerged to work with foreigners to collect local products for export and distribute imported products in domestic markets. The largest among the designated foreign settlements was Yokohama, a newly reclaimed port city, and such merchants were called Yokohama merchants.

12 Another prominent feature of Japanese industrialization in the Meiji period, which has been omitted due to lack of space, was the co-existence of traditional and modern industries and their parallel growth and interaction. The existing industries from the Edo period such as mining, civil engineering, silk spinning, wood printing, and textiles, as well as small-holder agriculture, were not wiped out by the invasion of superior Western technology. Since Japan and the West belonged to entirely different cultural spheres, the daily lives of people—food, clothing, housing, etc.—did not appreciably change even with the Western impact. To satisfy household consumption which accounted for 70–80 percent of estimated national output, many traditional industries continued to expand and occupy a major position during the Meiji period. There was also a strong tendency to selectively adopt new technology to improve and scale up existing industries. By 1910, factory production systems had spread even to rural traditional industries. Studies that examine the parallel development of traditional and modern industries in this period include Nakamura (1997), Odaka (2000), and Uchida (1990).

13 Technology transfer in state-run businesses under turnkey projects in reality proceeded on a trial-and-error basis rather than as a well-planned endeavor. Masahide Yoshida, a former Bakufu samurai, recounted that he had been recruited as one of the first Japanese staff of the Telegraphic Bureau in 1869 simply because he was studying English in Yokohama. On the third day he was asked to send and receive telegrams for which he had no previous knowledge. He somehow learned the skill but eventually chose to become an interpreter of the foreign advisor who laid telegraphic cables between Tokyo and Nagasaki. As he later admitted, "any applicants were accepted and put to work immediately as there was no training institution or work procedure to instruct them. Interpretation was virtually impossible for such workers" (Uchida, 1990: 268)

14 In 1880, the Japanese returnees were working in the following government ministries (number of officials in parentheses): the Agricultural Promotion Bureau (1) and the Civil Engineering Bureau (1) of the Home Ministry; the Bureau of the Mint (2) of the Ministry of Finance; the Department of the Army (2); the Department of the Navy (14); Minister (1), the Bureau of Mining (4), the Bureau of Railways (3), Lighthouse Service (1), Telegraphic Service (2), the Bureau of Construction (3) and the Bureau of Maintenance and Repairs (1) of the Ministry of Industry; and the Hokkaido Settlement Agency (3) (Uchida, 1990). In addition to returnees, ministries also hired former Dutch scholars and domestically educated engineers. See also Table 5.3.

15 The destinations of overseas engineering students, as identified by Uchida (1990), with the number of students in parentheses, were as follows: in Britain, Royal Naval College (6), University of Glasgow (3), University of Edinburgh (2), Royal School of Mines (2), University College, London (2), and Owens College (1); in France, École d'application du génie maritime (5), École centrale des arts et manufactures (2), École polytechnique (1), and École des mines (1); in Germany, Bergakademie (3) and Technische Hochschule (1); in the United States, Massachusetts Institute of Technology (3), Rennselaer Polytechnic Institute (3), Columbia College (2), Rutgers College (1), Stevens College (1), Rose Polytechnic Institute (1), Worcester Polytechnic School (1), and Lafayette College (1).

16 In 1871, *Kogaku Ryo* (School of Engineering) was created within the Ministry of Industry, which was upgraded to a university in 1873. The university was renamed *Kobu Daigakko* in 1877.

6 Singapore: national productivity movement

1 In the first few years of the bilateral cooperation between Singapore and Japan in 1983–1990 different expectations of the two sides had to be reconciled before launching

the movement in full scale. Japanese experts wanted to begin with such basics as philosophy toward productivity and waste reduction while Singaporean counterparts demanded quick and tangible results. This discrepancy between teacher and student is a common—and not-so-serious—issue observed in many countries receiving Japanese assistance in quality and productivity improvement. See section 6.4.3 for more details.

2 In other countries, triangular cooperation often consists of slightly different groups—for example, *san-kan-gaku* (industry, government, academics) alliance is routinely stressed in Japan, and teamwork among government, businesses, and experts is emphasized in Thailand. These are perhaps the more common tripartite for industrialization than the Singaporean one which includes labor unions.

3 In Vietnam, the same phenomenon as the Queen Bee effect is called the "Canon effect" in which establishment of large printer factories by Canon attracted many supplier companies to come to Northern Vietnam.

4 This section is based on the information provided by Mr. Low Hock Meng, the Executive Director of the Singaporean Productivity Association and the former counterpart of the JICA-supported Productivity Development Project, supplemented by additional information gathered by our research team.

5 In January 2008, obligatory military service was replaced by voluntary military service in Singapore.

6 The Association of Southeast Asian Nations (ASEAN) is a regional cooperation framework established in 1967. Its current members are Thailand, Indonesia, Singapore, Malaysia, Philippines, Brunei, Vietnam, Laos, Cambodia, and Myanmar. The first five are founding members.

7 The original statement came from Kohei Goshi, the former Chairman of the Japan Productivity Center, who wrote in his letter to Prime Minister Lee Kuan Yew in September 1986, "The transformation of mankind's way of thinking can be compared to a marathon with no finish line."

8 In Singapore, an SME is defined as a company with less than S$15 million in fixed asset investment for manufacturing and a company with less than 200 workers for non-manufacturing and services. The government plans to revise these definitions to align with international norms which use revenue-based definition.

7 Taiwan: policy drive for innovation

1 Japan's per capita income in 2010 was US$42,325 but Japanese prices are much higher than Taiwan's. As a result, living standards in the two economies are similar. Using the historical real income comparison of Maddison (2003) and updating with IMF data, Japan's price-adjusted per capita income in 2010 was estimated at US$21,900 while Taiwan's was US$22,227.

2 The effective corporate tax rate in East Asian competitor countries are as follows: Japan (about 40 percent), China (25 percent), Korea (24.2 percent, to be lowered to 22 percent in 2012), and Singapore (17 percent).

3 Previously, tax incentives amounted to about NT$70 billion per year, of which tax holidays, mainly benefiting large firms, were about NT$20 billion, automation tax credits were about NT$30 billion (both of which are now abolished), and IT tax credits were about NT$20 billion (which is now halved). Under the new industrial statute, only NT$10 billion of incentives remains.

4 The DOIT is the main department of the MoEA for technology development program funding although the IDB and the SME Administration, also under the MoEA, also have budgets for industrial support. The MoEA has bureaus, departments, and administrations as shown in Figure 7.1. It seems that bureaus are larger than departments, and administrations are tasked with implementing functions.

5 These opinions were collected during the policy research mission to Taiwan in March 2011 organized by the GRIPS Development forum which contained Japanese, Vietnamese, and Ethiopian researchers.
6 The five innovation competencies are creative thinking, industrial analysis, R&D management, business development, and intellectual property management. The six technology domains are information and communication, materials and chemical engineering, electronics and optoelectronic, biomedical technology and device research, mechanical and system research, and energy and environment management.
7 The Kaohsiung EPZ was the first export processing zone in the world according to information provided by the EPZ Administration, but this claim was informally disputed by an MoEA official in Taipei. It is at least the first EPZ in the Asia-Pacific region.
8 It must also be added that land rents in Taiwan's EPZs are reasonable. Even compared with the subsidized land and factory rental fees at science parks, they are much cheaper at around NT\$9–12/m^2 per month. The exceptions are the monthly land rent of only NT\$1.33/m^2 at the remotely located Pingtung EPZ, that of the Kaohsiung Software-based Technology Park which is much higher at NT\$39.2/m^2 (reduced to NT\$19.6/m^2 after three years of plant construction), and that of the Chengkung EPZ which is set at 6.25 percent of declared land price.
9 In 1986, the share of manufacturing SMEs in total manufacturing was as follows: 96.0 percent in number, 47.9 percent in employment, 33.8 percent in production, and 31.0 percent in value-added (Industry and Commerce Census 1988 as quoted in Sumiya et al., 1992, p. 143). However, this cannot be directly compared with the current situation in the text because of different definitions (enterprises with 99 or less employees in manufacturing only). According to estimates with certain assumptions by Sumiya et al. (1992), the share of SME exports, combining exports by small and medium producers and trading houses, in total exports was 68.1 percent in 1981 which fell to 61.2 percent in 1985.
10 Japan's One Village One Product (OVOP) Movement originated in Oita Prefecture. The local development strategy, the New Plum and Chestnut Movement, started by Oyama Town in 1961 with the slogan "Let's plant plums and chestnuts and go to Hawaii" succeeded greatly in improving local income and invigorating the rural community. Based on this experience, Morihiko Hiramatsu, the Governor of Oita Prefecture during 1979–2003, launched the OVOP Movement in 1979 that featured local initiative in creating high-value specialty products while government supported it from the sideline. The OVOP model spread from Oita to the rest of Japan and by now has become a standard rural development tool for Japan's economic assistance in many developing countries including Malawi, Peru, Thailand, and Vietnam.

8 Malaysia: trapped in upper middle income

1 The nine central strategic challenges of Vision 2020 are national unity, confidence, democracy, moral and ethics, tolerance, science and technology, caring culture, economic justice, and prosperity. These are promulgated as long-term general principles details of which must be defined and continue to be modified by plan documents, budget processes, and policy actions of ministries and agencies.
2 In IMP3, the six non-resource-based manufacturing industries are electronics and electrical, medical devices, textiles and apparel, machinery and equipment, metals, and transport equipment. The six resource-based manufacturing industries are petrochemicals, pharmaceuticals, wood products, rubber products, palm oil products, and food processing. The eight service sub-sectors are ICT, construction, education and training, healthcare, tourism, distributive trade, logistics, and business and professional.

The eight functional issues are external trade, investments, small and medium enterprises, branding, enhancing domestic capabilities, human resource, ICT and other technology developments, and logistics. In addition, the halal (Islamic food) industry is also featured as a target.

3 The exact relationship between New Economic Model Part 1's SRIs and Part 2's "recommendations" remains unclear to me.

4 Quoted from the presentation of Amirsham A. Aziz, the chairman of the National Economic Advisory Council, at the inaugural seminar on the New Economic Model on March 3, 2011, Kuala Lumpur. The wording and ordering of the SRIs sometimes differ from one document or website to another.

5 The six High Impact Programs 2012–2020 are (i) one-stop registration, (ii) commercialization of technology, (iii) early stage investment financing, (iv) assistance in export (GoEx Program), (v) creation of homegrown champions, and (vi) empowering the poor and micro enterprises in rural areas. Other key initiatives include government procurement, resource pooling, reducing information asymmetry, building capacity of SMEs, specific measures for East Malaysia, etc.

6 MIDA has the following industrial divisions: ICT and electrical, electronics, transport industry, machinery and engineering supporting industries, textiles and non-metallic minerals, food, chemical, life sciences industry, wood and paper, and metal and fabrication.

7 Perodua was also established by the government in 1993 with Japan's Daihatsu as a partner. Unlike Proton, it undertakes assembly without acquiring design capability. Initially, there was a market division between Proton (over 1,000cc) and Perodua (below 1,000cc). But this division was broken and the two companies have become competitors in the domestic market. Additionally, Malaysia's local car companies include Naza which has cooperative relation with Kia, and Inokom in partnership with Hyundai.

8 The Malaysia–Japan Automotive Industry Cooperation (MAJAICO) 2006–2011 was a comprehensive official five-year support package for the automobile industry consisting of ten components, including production improvement at local vendors (part suppliers) for national car companies. In this component, called A1, 15 Japanese technical experts, mostly from Toyota, coached about 20 participating companies on lean production every six months. From 2009, 13 first-tier local suppliers were trained as model producers to teach second- and third-tier suppliers. MAJAICO was one of the cooperation projects agreed in the Japan–Malaysia Economic Partnership Agreement which took effect in 2006.

9 Vietnam: growth without quality

1 Another reason behind re-linking with the West was the withdrawal of the Vietnamese troops from Cambodia in 1989. This greatly improved diplomatic relations with China, Japan, ASEAN neighbors, and the Western countries.

2 The World Bank revises country classification annually. Based on the 2010 gross national income per capita data using the World Bank Atlas method, the classification is as follows: low-income countries (US$1,005 or less); lower-middle-income countries (US$1,006–US$3,975), upper-middle-income countries (US$3,976–US$12,275); and high-income countries (US$12,276 or more). Separately, the World Bank defines IDA-only countries to be those with per capita income of less than US$1,175 (using 2010 data) and lacking the financial ability to borrow from IBRD. IDA loans are deeply concessional but IBRD loans are non-concessional.

3 The Millennium Development Goals set by the United Nations Group for low-income countries include the following eight targets: poverty reduction, universal primary education, gender equality, reduction of child mortality, maternal health,

combating infectious diseases, environmental sustainability, and global partnership. These goals are to be achieved by 2015 and progress is monitored for each country as well as regionally and globally.

4 A Vietnamese master plan must be structured as follows: (i) significance and relevance of the sector, (ii) analysis of domestic situation, (iii) review of international market and rival countries; (iv) development strategy including perspectives, objectives, and production and investment plans, (v) solutions and steps, (vi) conclusion and policy proposals. Solutions and policy proposals are long lists of statements without backing in resources, personnel, or organization.

5 *Deus ex machina* is a Latin phrase for "god out of machine" in ancient Greek plays. This god arrives suddenly and out of context on a crane-like machine to give a forceful solution to an entangled situation.

6 Establishment of a national competitiveness council was proposed by Vietnam Competitiveness Report 2010 which was presented by Michael Porter to the prime minister (Ketels et al., 2010) as well as the present author (Ohno, 2011). In response, the prime minister instructed the Central Institute for Economic Management under the Ministry of Planning and Investment to set up this council on a trial basis with the minister of planning and investment chairing. However, this attempt is likely to fail because the key point of creating this council is to drastically reduce the number of national councils and giving highest authority to the few remaining ones. Adding one more ministerial-level council without consolidating others will aggravate the problem rather than solving it.

10 Ethiopia: the Growth and Transformation Plan

1 In 2009, Ethiopia's receipt of ODA on net disbursement basis was equivalent to 12.4 percent of GDP and 60.9 percent of gross capital formation (World Bank Development Indicators). Merchandise export, dominated by food (75 percent), especially coffee, and agricultural raw materials (14 percent), was only US$1.5 billion or 5 percent of GDP in 2008 (national data).

2 Among national leaders of the world, Mr. Meles is a unique personality. Arising from a leader of the rural guerilla fighters which toppled the previous regime, he has ruled Ethiopia for over two decades. Without notes or advisors, his lucid mind and strong memory can handle economic theory, policy debates, and technical numbers over such diverse topics as agriculture, industry, education and training, technology transfer, infrastructure, spatial development and connectivity, macroeconomy, climate change, and politics. He often represents Africa at G-20 meetings, United Nations Framework Convention on Climate Change, and other international events. He even wrote a PhD dissertation on developmental doctrine for a British university which he, however, did not finish. He spends long hours with foreign investors, academics, and organizations for substance and action, asks for technical papers and policy documents for his reading, and exchanges long letters and emails when necessary. Joseph Stiglitz of Columbia University is among his personal advisors. My Japanese team has also had the privilege of having long policy discussion with him every time we visit Ethiopia.

3 This section is based on Ethiopian policy documents noted in the text, speeches, and unpublished writings of Prime Minister Meles, and a series of discussion and an exchange of letters that the author had with Mr. Meles between October 2008 and November 2009.

4 Many studies confirm that economic liberalism does not necessarily generate growth momentum in low-income countries. Ishikawa (1990) presents evidence from China in the 1980s on the failure of liberalization policies to produce production incentives where markets are underdeveloped; Nishimura (1994) and Aoki

(1995b) show that rapid privatization in Russia created new gigantic rents and their seekers; Khan (2008) argues that capability to direct rents to productive purposes such as investment and technology absorption, rather than to eliminate rents, is needed in a country that lacks market supporting institutions; and Ohno (2009a, 2009b) contends that Washington Consensus policies can take a country to a level of income dictated by given advantages but climbing further would require a combination of more proactive policies and private dynamism.

5 After the severe drought of 2003/04, the Ethiopian government introduced the Productive Safety-net Program targeted to the most vulnerable areas and actively mobilized international aid amounting to about US$300 million annually. However, the number of farmers who have graduated from this program is limited. As of 2009, 7.57 million rural residents were in need of continued support from this program.

6 According to World Bank estimates in 2008, the ratio of agriculture-related expenditure to total government expenditure in Ethiopia is 6.7 percent, which is higher than the corresponding ratios in Vietnam (6.0 percent), Mozambique (2.2 percent), Tanzania (2.1 percent), Kenya (2.0 percent), Pakistan (1.2 percent), and Indonesia (0.2 percent).

7 Dercon et al. (2009), as well as many donor agencies in Ethiopia, stress the need to check data reliability on agricultural production and land productivity.

8 An Economic Development Strategy for Ethiopia discussed policies for large-scale commercial agriculture and policies for small farmers separately (Federal Democratic Republic of Ethiopia, 1994). However, initial focus was on the latter while concrete measures for the former were not activated until the early 2000s.

9 My discussion with Prime Minister Meles in January 2011. However, in its Knowledge Sharing Program (KSP), Korea still teaches the "old" industrial policies it practiced from the 1960s to the mid-1990s as the country's major intellectual contribution to the developing world. The two pillars of KSP are policy dialogue which includes seminars, visits, and reports, and policy modules that systematically explain Korea's developmental experiences in over 100 topics—see Chapter 3.

10 One thing that may not receive universal acceptance is Rodrik's regular insistence that only pioneer firms which take risks in "self-discovery" should be given incentives and subsidies and not copycats who come late with no risks taken (recommendation (v)). However, in reality, such selectivity is administratively cumbersome and even unfair. New activity with business risk may be undertaken not by the first nominal producer in the sector but by the tenth or the 99th. Generally, it is hard for developing-country governments to identify the producer who brought something truly new to the industry ("pioneers"). It is more reasonable and practical that any investor who satisfies certain sectoral and activity criteria, whether the first or the ninety-ninth, should be given the same incentives while they last.

11 In the preparatory and first phase of bilateral policy dialogue, the Japanese delegation met with the prime minister for substantive discussion in July, October, and December 2008; June, September, and November 2009; March and October 2010; and January and May 2011. Average length of meetings was from one-and-half to two hours. Long letters from the prime minister were received in June and July 2009.

12 At the request of the Ethiopian prime minister, the GRIPS Development Forum compiled information packages on Japanese technical education, rural life improvement movements in East Asia, information on basic metal and engineering industries, international comparison of industrial policy formulation methods, technical absorption of Japan and Korea through foreign-aided industrial projects, and basic information on the chemical industry. Separately, Introducing Kaizen to Africa, a booklet explaining the concept of kaizen as well as how it took root in Japan and how it was applied to the developing world with Japanese assistance,

was produced as an introductory reference material for those unfamiliar with the concept (GRIPS Development Forum, 2009). Handbook of National Movements for Quality and Productivity Improvement was also produced for the bilateral policy dialogue (Japan International Cooperation Agency and National Graduate Institute for Policy Studies, 2011b).

13 In the second phase of bilateral policy dialogue which started in January 2012, three-level discussions are to be held every six months in a format similar to the first phase but with more action-oriented contents. Revamping of export promotion policy and study of technology transfer are two topics that are likely to receive great attention. Meanwhile, the second phase of Japanese kaizen cooperation was initiated in late 2011 where capacity building of the newly created Ethiopia Kaizen Institute and training of Ethiopian kaizen experts through hands-on enterprise consultation would be the two main pillars.

14 For example, during the GTP period, garment export is set to expand 46 times to US$1 billion, leather and leather product export is to jump 6.6 times to nearly US$500 million, sugar production is expected to increase 7.2 fold to 2.25 million tons, cement production is to rise 10 times to 27 million tons, and sales of steel and engineering are expected to increase 17 times to over 100 million birr.

15 The prime minister personally chairs monthly committees on export, power, railroads, sugar, roads, and technical and vocational education and training. In addition, he presides over the macroeconomic committee which meets twice a month. There are other committees at the deputy prime minister level.

Bibliography

African Union (2007), "Action Plan for the Accelerated Industrial Development of Africa," African Union Conference of Ministers of Industry 1st Extraordinary Session, Midrand, Republic of South Africa, September 24–27.

African Union (2008), "Strategy for the Implementation of the Plan of Action for the Accelerated Industrial Development of Africa," Conference of African Ministers of Industry, 18th Ordinary Session, Durban, Republic of South Africa, October 24–28.

Alcock, Rutherford (1863), *The Capital of the Tycoon: a Narrative of a Three Years' Residence in Japan*, vols I and II, Bradley Co.

Aoki, Masahiko (1995a), *Keizai System no Shinka to Tagensei: Hikaku Seido Bunseki Josetsu* [The Evolution and Diversity of Economic Systems: An Introduction to Comparative Institutional Analysis], Toyo Keizai, in Japanese.

Aoki, Masahiko (1995b), "Controlling Insider Control: Issues of Corporate Governance in Transition Economies," in M. Aoki and H.K. Kim, eds., *Corporate Governance in Transitional Economies: Insider Control and the Role of Banks*, World Bank Economic Development Institute.

Aoki, Masahiko (2001a), *Toward a Comparative Institutional Analysis*, MIT Press.

Aoki, Masahiko (2001b), *Information, Corporate Governance, and Institutional Diversity: Competitiveness in Japan, the USA, and the Transitional Economies*, Oxford University Press.

Banno, Junji (2006), *Kindai Nihon Seijishi* [Modern History of Japanese Politics], Iwanami Shoten, in Japanese.

Banno, Junji (2007), *Mikan no Meiji Ishin* [Unfinished Meiji Restoration], Chikuma Shinsho, in Japanese.

Banno, Junji (2008), *Nihon Kenseishi* [History of Japanese Constitutional Politics], University of Tokyo Press, in Japanese.

Banno, Junji (2012), *Nihon Kindaishi* [History of Modern Japan], Chikuma Shinsho, in Japanese.

Banno, Junji, and Kenichi Ohno (2010), *Meiji Restoration 1858–1881*, Kodansha Gendai Shinsho, in Japanese. English translation of Chapter 1 in "The Flexible Structure of Politics in Meiji Japan," Developmental Leadership Program Research Paper no. 7, April 2010.

Brady, David, and Michael Spence, eds. (2010), *Leadership and Growth*, The Commission on Growth and Development.

Campos, Jose Edgardo and Hilton L. Root (1996), *The Key to the Asian Miracle: Making Shared Growth Credible*, Brookings Institution.

Castaldi, Carolina, Mario Cimoli, Nelson Correa, and Giovanni Dosi (2009), "Technological Learning, Policy Regimes, and Growth: The Long-term Patterns and Some Specificities of a 'Globalized' Economy," in M. Cimoli, G. Dosi, and J.E. Stiglitz, eds., *Industrial Policy and Development: The Political Economy of Capabilities Accumulation*, The Initiative for Policy Dialogue Series, Oxford University Press.

Chan, Lee Mun (2008), "Polytechnic Education," in Sing Kong Lee, Goh Chor Boon, Birger Fredriksen, and Tan Jee Peng, eds., *Toward a Better Future: Education and Training for Economic Development in Singapore since 1965*, National Institute of Education, Singapore, and the World Bank.

Chang, Ha-Joon (2002), *Kicking Away the Ladder: Development Strategy in Historical Perspective*, Anthem Press.

Chang, Ha-Joon (2010), "Towards a More Productive Debate,"*Making It: Industry for Development*, United Nations Industrial Development Organization, no. 3. pp. 23–29.

Cimoli, Mario, Giovanni Dosi, and Joseph E. Stiglitz, eds. (2009a), *Industrial Policy and Development: The Political Economy of Capabilities Accumulation*, The Initiative for Policy Dialogue Series, Oxford University Press.

Cimoli, Mario, Giovanni Dosi, and Joseph E. Stiglitz (2009b), "The Political Economy of Capabilities Accumulation: The Past and Future of Policies for Industrial Development," in Mario Cimoli, Giovanni Dosi, and Joseph E.Stiglitz, eds., *Industrial Policy and Development: The Political Economy of Capabilities Accumulation*, The Initiative for Policy Dialogue Series, Oxford University Press.

Cimoli, Mario, Giovanni Dosi, and Joseph E. Stiglitz (2009c), "The Future of Industrial Policies in the New Millennium: Toward a Knowledge-Centered Development Agenda," in Mario Cimoli, Giovanni Dosi, and Joseph E. Stiglitz, eds., *Industrial Policy and Development: The Political Economy of Capabilities Accumulation*, The Initiative for Policy Dialogue Series, Oxford University Press.

Collier, Paul (2009), *The Bottom Billion: Why the Poorest Countries Are Failing and What Can Be Done About It*, Oxford University Press.

Commission on Growth and Development (2008), *The Growth Report: Strategies For Sustained Growth And Inclusive Development*, World Bank.

Department of Statistics, Singapore (2011), *Monthly Digest of Statistics*, June 2011.

Dercon, Stephan, Ruth Vargas Hill, and Andrew Zeitin (2009), "In Search of a Strategy: Rethinking Agriculture-led Growth in Ethiopia," a synthesis paper prepared as part of a study on agriculture and growth in Ethiopia, Department for International Development, United Kingdom.

Do, Thi Dong, and Pham Thi Huyen (2010), *Shindanshi: The Japanese Business Management System*, Hanoi: The Publishing House of Transportation and Communication.

Evans, Peter (1995), *Embedded Autonomy: States and Industrial Transformations*, Princeton University Press.

Federal Democratic Republic of Ethiopia (1994), *An Economic Development Strategy for Ethiopia*, February.

Federal Democratic Republic of Ethiopia (2001), *Rural Development Policies, Strategies and Instruments of the Government of the FDRE.*

Federal Democratic Republic of Ethiopia (2002), *Ethiopian Industrial Development Strategy.*

Federal Democratic Republic of Ethiopia Population Census Commission (2008), *Summary and Statistical Report of the 2007 Population and Housing Census*, December.

Fujimoto, Koji (2011), "Brantas River Basin Development Project: A Case Study of Japanese ODA to Indonesia," a paper presented at the School of Oriental and African Studies International Workshop on Aid and Development in Asia and Africa, University of London, February.

Fujimoto, Takahiro (2004), *Nihon no Monozukuri Tetsugaku* [Monozukuri Philosophy of Japan], Nihon Keizai Shimbunsha, in Japanese.

Fujimoto, Takahiro (2006), "Architecture-based Comparative Advantage in Japan and Asia," in Kenichi Ohno and Takahiro Fujimoto, eds., *Industrialization of Developing Countries: Analyses by Japanese Economists*, 21st Century Centers of Excellence Program, National Graduate Institute for Policy Studies.

Fujimoto, Takahiro, and Junichiro Shintaku (2005), *Chugoku Seizogyo no Architecture Bunseki* [Architecture-based Analysis of Chinese Manufacturing Industries], Toyo Keizai Shimposha, in Japanese.

Grindle, Merilee (2004), "Good Enough Governance: Poverty Reduction and Reform in Developing Countries,"*International Journal of Policy, Administration and Institutions*, vol. 17, no. 4, pp. 525–548.

GRIPS Development Forum (2002), *Japan's Development Cooperation in Vietnam: Supporting Broad-based Growth with Poverty Reduction*, May, in English, Japanese, and Vietnamese.

GRIPS Development Forum (2008a), *Proposal for a New African Growth Support Initiative*, National Graduate Institute for Policy Studies, August.

GRIPS Development Forum, ed. (2008b), *Diversity and Complementarity in Development Aid: East Asian Lessons for African Growth*, National Graduate Institute for Policy Studies.

GRIPS Development Forum, ed. (2009), *Introducing KAIZEN in Africa*, National Graduate Institute for Policy Studies.

GRIPS Development Forum (2010a), "Basic Strategy of Japanese Growth Support in Developing Countries: Typology, International Comparison and Concrete Cases," a report submitted to Japan Cooperation Agency, March, in Japanese.

GRIPS Development Forum (2010b), *Policy Dialogue for Industrial Policy Formulation in Ethiopia: Interim Report Draft*, June.

Han, Sangbok (1987), "The Socio-cultural effects and Prospects of the Rural Saemaul Movement," Institute of Saemaul Undong Studies, Seoul National University, *Journal of Seoul National University Saemaul Studies*, vol. 12, no. 1, pp. 41–52, in Korean.

Hausmann, Ricardo, and Dani Rodrik (2005), "Self-Discovery in a Development Strategy for El Salvador,"*Economia*, vol. 6, no. 1, pp. 43–101, Brookings Institution Press, Fall.

Hausmann, Ricardo, Dani Rodrik, and Andres Velasco (2005), "Growth Diagnostics," mimeo, John F. Kennedy School of Government, Harvard University, March.

Hausmann, Ricardo, Dani Rodrik, and Andres Velasco (2006), "Getting the Diagnostics Right: A New Approach to Economic Reform,"*Finance and Development*, vol. 43, p. 1, International Monetary Fund, March.

Hayami, Akira, and Matao Miyamoto, eds. (1988), *Nihon Keizaishi 1: Keizai Shakai no Seiritsu 17–18 Seiki* [Economic History of Japan vol. 1: Establishment of Economic Society 17th and 18th Century], Iwanami Shoten, in Japanese.

Higashi, Shigeki (2000), "Sangyo Seisaku: Keizai Kozo no Henka to Kigyo-Seihu kan Kankei" [Industrial Policy: Business and Government in a Changing Economic Structure], in A. Suehiro and S. Higashi, eds., *Thai no Keizai Seisaku: Seido, Soshiki,*

Actor [*Economic Policy in Thailand: Policy, Institution, Actors*], Institute of Developing Economies, in Japanese.

Hirano, Katsumi (2009), *Africa Mondai: Kaihatsu to Enjo no Sekaishi* [The Africa Problem: World History of Development and Aid], Nihon Hyoronsha, in Japanese.

Hosono, Akio (2010), *Nambei Chile wo Sake Yushutsu Taikoku ni Kaeta Nihonjintachi: Zero kara Sangyo wo Soshutsu shita Kokusai Kyoryoku no Kiroku* [*Japanese who Transformed Chile into a Major Exporter of Salmon: International Cooperation for Creating an Industry from Scratch*], Diamond Sha, in Japanese.

Huh, Mun-Gu (1995), "Kankoku ni Okeru Chiikikan Shotoku Kakusa no Doko: Ikinai Soseisan no Shiten kara" [Changing Inter-regional Income Disparities in Korea: A Gross Regional Domestic Product Analysis], *Osaka Prefecture University Economic Research*, vol. 41, no. 1, pp. 133–170, in Japanese.

Ichikawa, Kyoshiro (2005), "Building and Strengthening Supporting Industries in Vietnam: A Survey Report," in Kenichi Ohno and Nguyen Van Thuong, eds., *Improving Industrial Policy Formulation*, Vietnam Development Forum and Publishing House of Political Theory, in English and Vietnamese.

Ide, Fuminori (2004), "Supporting Industry Ikusei Seisaku to Linkage no Soshutsu: Malaysia wo Jirei ni" [Policies to Develop Supporting Industries in Malaysia: Focusing on the Linkage Problem], *Ritsumeikan Kokusai Kenkyu*, vol. 17, no. 1, pp. 119–145, June.

Imai, Masaaki (1986), *Kaizen: The Key to Japan's Competitive Success*, McGraw-Hill.

Imai, Massaki (1997), *Gemba Kaizen: A Commonsense, Low-cost Approach to Management*, McGraw-Hill. Japanese edition by McGraw-Hill in 2011.

Ishihara, Minako (2001), "Ethiopia ni okeru Chihou Bunkenka to Minzoku Seiji" [Decentralization and Ethnic Politics in Ethiopia], *Africa Kenkyu*, vol. 59, pp. 85–100, in Japanese.

Ishikawa, Shigeru (1990), "Shijo Keizai no Teihattatsu to Keizai Jiyuka no Genkai" [Underdevelopment of the Market Economy and the Limits of Economic Liberalization], in *Kaihatsu Keizaigaku no Kihon Mondai* [Basic Issues in Development Economics], Iwanami Shoten, in Japanese. English translation in Kenichi Ohno and Izumi Ohno, eds. (1998), *Japanese Views on Economic Development: Diverse Paths to the Market*, London and New York: Routledge.

Japan Bank for International Cooperation Institute, "Survey Report on the Overseas Business Investment of Japanese Manufacturing Firms: Results of the 2007 (19th) Foreign Direct Investment Questionnaire,"*JBIC Institute Review*, March, in Japanese.

Japan External Trade Organization (2008), *Business Survey of Japanese Firms in Asia: ASEAN and India, Survey in 2007*, in Japanese.

Japan Historical Academy (1981), *Meiji Ishin Jinmei Jiten* (Who's Who of the Meiji Restoration), Yoshikawa Kobunkan, in Japanese.

Japan International Cooperation Agency, and National Graduate Institute for Policy Studies (2011a), *Study on Industrial Policy Dialogue in the Federal Democratic Republic of Ethiopia*, Final Report, December.

Japan International Cooperation Agency, and National Graduate Institute for Policy Studies (2011b), *Handbook of National Movements for Quality and Productivity Improvement (Kaizen)*, Project Report, December.

Japan Productivity Center (1990), *Singapore Productivity Development Project: Report on Ideal and Practice of Technology Transfer*, March.

Japan–Thailand Economic Cooperation Society (2011), *Nichi–Thai Partnership* (Japan–Thailand Partnership), No. 133, Autumn.

Johnson, Chalmers (1982), *MITI and the Japanese Miracle: The Growth of Industrial Policy, 1925–1975*, Stanford University Press.

Kaplinsky, Raphael (1995), "Technique and System: The Spread of Japanese Management Techniques to Developing Countries," *World Development*, vol. 23, no. 1, pp. 57–71.

Kawakita, Takao (1991), *Tsusansho: Keizai Sambo Hombu kara no Tenkan* (Ministry of International Trade and Industry: Conversion from the General Headquarters of Economy), Kodansha, in Japanese.

Ketels, Christian, Nguyen Dinh Cung, Nguyen Thi Tue Anh, and Do Hong Hanh (2010), *Vietnam Competitiveness Report 2010*, Central Institute for Economic Management and Lee Kuan Yew School of Public Policy, National University of Singapore.

Khan, Mushtaq H. (2008), "Governance and Development: The Perspective of Growth-enhancing Governance," in GRIPS Development Forum, ed., *Diversity and Complementarity in Development Aid: East Asian Lessons for African Growth*, National Graduate Institute for Policy Studies.

Kikuchi, Tsuyoshi (2008), "The Quality and Productivity Improvement Project in Tunisia: A Comparison of Japanese and EU Approaches," in GRIPS Development Forum, ed., *Diversity and Complementarity in Development Aid: East Asian Lessons for African Growth*, National Graduate Institute for Policy Studies.

Kikuchi, Tsuyoshi (2011), "*Nihon ni okeru Seisan Kanri Gijutsu no Donyu, Kaihatsu, Fukyu ni Hatashita Minkan Dantai no Yakuwari*" [The Role of Private Organizations in Introducing, Developing, and Disseminating Production Management Technology in Japan], *Bulletin of the Graduate School of International Cooperation Studies*, Takushoku University, no. 4, in Japanese. English translation by Japan International Cooperation Agency, and National Graduate Institute for Policy Studies, *Handbook of National Movements for Quality and Productivity Improvement (Kaizen)*, Project Report, December.

Kim, Hyung-A (2004), *Korea's Development under Park Chung Hee: Rapid Industrialization, 1961–79*, London: RoutledgeCurzon.

Kim, Kihwan and Danny M. Leipziger (1993), "The Lessons of East Asia: Korea, A Case of Government-Led Development," World Bank.

Kondo, Hisahiro (2005), *Comparative Analysis of Governance: Relationship between Bureaucracy and Policy Coordination Capacity with Particular Reference to Bangladesh*, Institute for International Cooperation, Japan International Cooperation Agency.

Krueger, Anne O. (1997), "Trade Policy and Economic Development: How We Learn,"*American Economic Review*, vol. 87, no. 1, pp. 1–22, March.

Krugman, Paul (1994), "The Myth of Asia's Miracle,"*Foreign Affairs*, vol. 73, no. 6, pp. 62–78, November/December.

Kuchiki, Akifumi (2005), "Theory of a Flowchart Approach to Industrial Cluster Policy," Discussion Paper no. 36, Institute of Developing Economies.

Kuchiki, Akifumi (2007), *Asia Sangyo Cluster Ron: Flowchart Approach no Kanosei* [Industrial Clusters in Asia: The Possibility of the Flowchart Approach], Shoseki Kobo Hayama, in Japanese.

Kuchiki, Akifumi and Masatsugu Tsuji, eds. (2008), *The Flowchart Approach to Industrial Cluster Policy*, Institute of Developing Economies–JETRO, Palgrave Macmillan.

Kurushima, Hiroshi (2003), "Kinsei no Mura no Tokucho" [Characteristics of Villages in the Edo Period], in S. Takasugi and T. Sugimori, eds., *Kinsei Nihon no Rekishi* [History of Edo Japan], Hoso Daigaku Kyoiku Shinkokai, in Japanese.

Lall, Sanjaya (1987), *Learning to Industrialize: The Acquisition of Technological Capability by India*, Macmillan Press.

Lee, Kuan Yew (2000), *From Third World to First: The Singapore Story, 1965–2000: Memoirs of Lee Kuan Yew*, Times Editions, Singapore Press Holdings.

Lee, Sing Kong, Goh Chor Boon, Birger Fredriksen, and Tan Jee Peng (2008), *Toward a Better Future: Education and Training for Economic Development in Singapore since 1965*, National Institute of Education, Singapore, and the World Bank.

Leftwich, Adrian (2000), *States of Development: On the Primacy of Politics in Development*, Polity Press.

Leftwich, Adrian (2009), "Bringing Agency Back In: Politics and Human Agency in Building Institutions and States: Synthesis and Overview Report," Developmental Leadership Program Research Paper no. 6, June.

Leftwich, Adrian (2011), "Thinking and Working Politically: What Does It Mean? Why Is It Important? And How Do You Do It?" Developmental Leadership Program presentation, March.

Lim, Wonhyuk (2011), "Joint Discovery and Upgrading of Comparative Advantage: Lessons from Korea's Development Experience," in World Bank, *Postcrisis Growth and Development: A Development Agenda for the G-20*, 2011.

Lin, Justin Yifu (2010), "New Structural Economics: A Framework for Rethinking Development," World Bank Policy Research Working Paper no. 5197, February.

Lin, Justin Yifu (2011), "From Flying Geese to Leading Dragons: New Opportunities and Strategies for Structural Transformation in Developing Countries," WIDER Lecture, Maputo, Mozambique, May 4.

Lin, Justin, and Ha-Joon Chang (2009), "Should Industrial Policy in Developing Countries Conform to Comparative Advantage or Defy It? A Debate Between Justin Lin and Ha-Joon Chang,"*Development Policy Review*, vol. 27, no. 5, pp. 483–502.

Lin, Justin, and Celestin Monga (2011), "DPR Debate: Growth Identification and Facilitation: The Role of the State in the Dynamics of Structural Change," DPR Debate introduced by Dirk Willemte Velde and with commentaries by Suresh D. Tendulkar, Alice Amsden, K.Y. Amoako, Howard Pack, and Wonhyuk Lim, *Development Policy Review*, vol. 29, no. 3, May.

List, Friedrich (1841), *Das Nationale System der Politischen Oekonomie*, Stuttgart: J.G. Cotta. English translation by G.A. Matile, J.B. Lippincott and Co. (1856).

Maddison, Angus (2003), *The World Economy: Historical Statistics*, OECD Development Centre Studies.

Maegawa, Keiji (1994), "Bunka to Bunmei no Renzokusei: Honyakuteki Tekioron Josetsu" [The Continuity of Cultures and Civilization: An Introduction to the Concept of Translative Adaptation], *Hikaku Bunmei*, vol. 10, Tosui Shobo, November, in Japanese. English translation in Kenichi Ohno and Izumi Ohno, eds., *Japanese Views on Economic Development: Diverse Paths to the Market*, London and New York: Routledge.

Maegawa, Keiji (2000), *Kaihatsu no Jinruigaku: Bunka Setsugo kara Honyakuteki Tekiou e* [Anthropology of Development: From Articulation to Translative Adaptation], Shin-yosha, in Japanese.

Mahathir, Mohamad (1970), *The Malay Dilemma*, Asia Pacific Press.

Mahathir, Mohamad (2001), *Malays Forget Easily*, Pelanduk Publications.

Ministry of Agriculture and Commerce, Japan (1903), *Shokko Jijo* [Survey of Factory Workers], five volumes, in Japanese.

Ministry of Culture and Information, Korea (1983), *A Handbook of Korea*, Korean Overseas Information Service.

Ministry of International Trade and Industry, Japan (1985), *Keizai Kyoryoku Hakusho* [White Paper on Economic Cooperation].

Mitani, Hiroshi (1997), *Meiji Ishin to Nationalism: Bakumatsu no Gaiko to Seiji Hendo* [Meiji Restoration and Nationalism: Foreign Diplomacy and Political Change in the Late Edo Period], Yamakawa Shuppansha, in Japanese.

Miyaji, Masato (1999), *Bakumatsu Ishinki no Shakaiteki Seijishi Kenkyu* [A Study of Social Politics in the late Edo to the Early Meiji Period], Iwanami Shoten, in Japanese.

Miyamoto, Matao (1999), *Nihon no Kindai 11: Kigyokatachi no Chosen* [Modern Age of Japan vol. 11: Challenge of Entrepreneurs], Chuo Koron Shinsha, in Japanese.

Miyamoto, Masaoki, and Motoji Matsuda (1997), *Shinsho Africa Shi* [Paperback History of Africa], Kodansha Shinsho, in Japanese.

Miyoshi, Yukio, ed. (1986), *Soseki Bunmei Ronshu* [Soseki's Writings on Civilization], Iwanami Bunko, in Japanese.

Mori, Junichi (2005), "Development of Supporting Industries for Vietnam's Industrialization: Increasing Positive Vertical Externalities through Collaborative Training," master's thesis, Fletcher School, Tufts University.

Mori, Junichi (2010), "Toward Technical Education that Embodies Japanese Monozukuri: The Cases of the Technology Promotion Association and the Thai-nichi Institute of Technology," in GRIPS Development Forum, "Basic Strategy of Japanese Growth Support in Developing Countries: Typology, International Comparison and Concrete Cases," a report submitted to Japan Cooperation Agency, March, in Japanese.

Mori, Junichi, and Kenichi Ohno (2005), "Optimal Procurement Strategy: Determinants of Parts Localization under Regional Linkage and Competition," in Kenichi Ohno and Nguyen Van Thuong, eds. (2005), *Improving Industrial Policy Formulation*, Vietnam Development Forum and Publishing House of Political Theory, in English and Vietnamese.

Motorbike Joint Working Group (2007), *For Sound Development of the Motorbike Industry in Vietnam*, Publishing House of Social Labor, in English and Vietnamese.

Murakami, Yasusuke (1992), *Hankoten no Seijikeizaigaku* [Anti-classical Political Economy], vol. 2, Chuo Koron Sha, in Japanese. English translation by Kozo Yamamura (1996), *Anti-Classical Political Economy*, Stanford University Press.

Murakami, Yasusuke (1994), *Hankoten no Seijikeizaigaku Yoko: Raiseiki no tameno Oboegaki* [Outline of Anti-classical Political Economy: A Memorandum for the Next Century], Chuo Koron Sha, in Japanese. English translation of Chapter 6 in Kenichi Ohno and Izumi Ohno, eds., *Japanese Views on Economic Development: Diverse Paths to the Market*, London and New York: Routledge.

Nakamura, Takafusa, ed. (1997), *Nihon no Keizai Hatten to Zairai Sangyo* (Economic Development and Traditional Industries in Japan), Yamakawa Shuppansha, in Japanese.

National Productivity Board, Singapore (1987), *Our Story: 15 Years of NPB.*

National Productivity Board, Singapore, and Japan International Cooperation Agency (1990), *Further Fields to Conquer: A PDP Commemorative Publication.*

National SME Development Council, Malaysia (2008), *SME Annual Report 2008: Rising to Meet Global Challenges.*

National SME Development Council, Malaysia (2011), *SME Annual Report 2010/11: Leveraging Opportunities Realising Growth.*

Ndulu, Benno, Stephen A. O'Connell, Robert H. Bates, Paul Collier, and Chukwuma C. Soludo, eds. (2008), *The Political Economy of Economic Growth in Africa 1960–2000*, Cambridge University Press, vol. I.

Nguyen, Thi Thanh Huyen (2004), "Is There a Developmental Threshold for Democracy?: Endogenous Factors in the Democratization of South Korea," in Asian Development Bank and Vietnam Development Forum, *Which Institutions Are Critical to Sustain Long-term Growth in Vietnam?*, Asian Development Bank.

Nguyen, Thi Xuan Thuy (2007), "Supporting Industries: A Review of Concepts and Development," in Kenichi Ohno, ed., *Building Supporting Industries in Vietnam*, vol. 1, Vietnam Development Forum, in English and Vietnamese.

Nishikawa, Shunsaku and Masatoshi Amano (1989), "Shohan no Sangyo to Keizai Seisaku" [Industries and Economic Policies of Hans], in H. Shimbo and O. Saito, eds., *Nihon Keizaishi 2: Kindai Seicho no Taido* [Japanese Economic History vol. 2: The Dawn of Modern Development], Iwanami Shoten, in Japanese.

Nishimura, Yoshiaki (1994), "Russian Privatization: Progress Report No. 1,"*Keizai Kenkyu*, Institute of Economic Research, Hitotsubashi University, vol. 45, no. 3, pp. 203–217, July, in Japanese. English translation in Kenichi Ohno and Izumi Ohno, eds. (1998), *Japanese Views on Economic Development: Diverse Paths to the Market*, London and New York: Routledge.

Noman, Akbar, Kwesi Botchwey, Howard Stein, and Joseph E. Stiglitz, eds., *Good Growth and Governance in Africa: Rethinking Development Strategies*, The Initiatives for Policy Dialogue Series, Oxford University Press.

Odaka, Konosuke (2000), *Shokunin no Sekai, Kojo no Sekai* [The World of Craftsmen and the World of Factories], new edition, NTT Publishing, in Japanese.

Ohno, Izumi, ed. (2005), *True Ownership and Policy Autonomy: Managing Donors and Owning Policies*, GRIPS Development Forum.

Ohno, Izumi, and Daniel Kitaw (2011), "Productivity Movement in Singapore," in Japan International Cooperation Agency, and National Graduate Institute for Policy Studies, *Handbook of National Movements for Quality and Productivity Improvement (Kaizen)*, Project Report, December.

Ohno, Izumi, and Kenichi Ohno (2012), "Dynamic Capacity Development: What Africa Can Learn from Industrial Policy Formulation in East Asia," in Akbar Noman, Kwesi Botchwey, Howard Stein, and Joseph E. Stiglitz, eds., *Good Growth and Governance in Africa: Rethinking Development Strategies*, The Initiatives for Policy Dialogue Series, Oxford University Press.

Ohno, Izumi, and Masumi Shimamura (2007), *Managing the Development Process and Aid: East Asian Experiences in Building Central Economic Agencies*, GRIPS Development Forum.

Ohno, Kenichi (2000), *Globalization of Developing Countries: Is Autonomous Development Possible?*, Toyo Keizai Shimposha, in Japanese.

Ohno, Kenichi (2003), *East Asian Growth and Japanese Aid Strategy*, collected essays by the author, GRIPS Development Forum.

Ohno, Kenichi (2006a), *The Economic Development of Japan: The Path Traveled by Japan as a Developing Country*, GRIPS Development Forum, in English, Japanese, Chinese, Vietnamese, and Arabic.

Ohno, Kenichi, ed. (2006b), *Industrial Policy Formulation in Thailand, Malaysia and Japan: Lessons for Vietnamese Policy Makers*, Vietnam Development Forum and Publishing House of Social Labour, in English and Vietnamese.

Ohno, Kenichi, ed. (2007), *Building Supporting Industries in Vietnam*, vol. 1, Vietnam Development Forum, in English and Vietnamese.

Ohno, Kenichi (2008a), "The East Asian Growth Regime and Political Development," in GRIPS Development Forum, ed., *Diversity and Complementarity in Development Aid: East Asian Lessons for African Growth*, National Graduate Institute for Policy Studies.

Ohno, Kenichi (2008b), "Vietnam–Japan Monozukuri Partnership for Supporting Industries: For Leveling Up Vietnam's Competitiveness in the Age of Deepening Integration," Vietnam Development Forum, August.

Ohno, Kenichi (2009a), "Avoiding the Middle-income Trap: Renovating Industrial Policy Formulation in Vietnam,"*ASEAN Economic Bulletin*, vol. 26, no. 1, pp. 25–43.

Ohno, Kenichi (2009b), *The Middle Income Trap: Implications for Industrialization Strategies in East Asia and Africa*, GRIPS Development Forum.

Ohno, Kenichi (2010), "The Shindan System: Transferability of Japan's Small and Medium Enterprise Management Consultants System to ASEAN," unpublished manuscript, GRIPS Development Forum, April.

Ohno, Kenichi (2011), "Policy Procedure and Organization for Executing High Priority Industrial Strategies," a paper prepared for the National Economics University and the National Assembly of Vietnam Symposium on the Quality of Growth, Hanoi, January.

Ohno, Kenichi, and Takahiro Fujimoto, eds. (2006), *Industrialization of Developing Countries: Analyses by Japanese Economists*, 21st Century Centers of Excellence Program, National Graduate Institute for Policy Studies.

Ohno, Kenichi, and Izumi Ohno, eds. (1998), *Japanese Views on Economic Development: Diverse Paths to the Market*, London and New York: Routledge.

Ohno, Kenichi, and Kojiro Sakurai (1997), *Higashi Asia no Kaihatsu Keizaigaku* (Development Economics of East Asia), Yuhikaku, in Japanese.

Ohno, Kenichi, and Nguyen Van Thuong, eds. (2005), *Improving Industrial Policy Formulation*, Vietnam Development Forum and Publishing House of Political Theory, in English and Vietnamese.

Oishi, Shinzaburo (1977), *Edo Jidai* [The Edo Period], Chuko Shinsho, no. 476, in Japanese.

Okimoto, Daniel I. (1989), *Between MITI and the Market*, Stanford University Press.

Okubo, Toshimichi (1876), "Kokuhon Baiyo ni Kansuru Kengisho" [Proposal Concerning Promotion of the Nation's Fundamental Capacities], in Japan Historical Document Society, ed. (1969), *Okubo Toshimichi Bunsho* (Documents of Okubo Toshimichi), vol. 7, University of Tokyo Press, in Japanese.

Ono, Goro (1992), *Jissenteki Sangyo Seisaku Ron: Nihon no Keiken kara no Kyokun* [Pragramtic Industrial Policy: Lessons from Japanese Experience], Tsusansho Sangyo Chosakai (Survey Group of the Ministry of International Trade and Industry), in Japanese.

Park, Chung Hee (1979), *Saemaul: Korea's New Community Movement*, Seoul: Korea Textbook Co. Ltd.

Rodrik, Dani (2006), "Home-grown Growth: Problems and Solutions to Economic Growth,"*Harvard International Review*, Winter version, pp. 74–77.

Rodrik, Dani (2007), *One Economics, Many Recipes: Globalization, Institutions, and Economic Growth*, Princeton University Press.

Rodrik, Dani (2008), "Notes on the Ethiopian Economic Situation," unpublished manuscript, December 22.

Sachs, Jeffrey, and Andrew M. Warner (2001), "The Curse of Natural Resources,"*European Economic Review*, vol. 45: nos. 4–6, pp. 827–838, May.

Schumpeter, Joseph A. (1934), *The Theory of Economic Development*, Harvard Economic Studies Series, vol. XLVI.

Secretariat of the Stocktaking Work (2008), *Report on the Stocktaking Work on the Economic Development in Africa and the Asian Growth Experience*, Japan International Cooperation Agency and Japan Bank for International Cooperation, May.

Serra, Narcis, and Joseph E. Stiglitz, eds. (2008), *The Washington Consensus Reconsidered: Towards a New Global Governance*, The Initiative for Policy Dialogue Series, Oxford University Press.

Shimomura, Yasutami (2005), "The Role of Governance in Development Revisited: A Proposal of an Alternative View," FASID Discussion Paper on Development Assistance, no. 5, March.

Sonobe, Tetsushi, and Keijiro Otsuka (2006), *Cluster-based Industrial Development: An East Asian Model*, Palgrave Macmillan.

Standards, Productivity and Innovation Board, Singapore (2010), *Evolution of the Productivity Movement in Singapore*.

Stiglitz, Joseph E. (2002), *Globalization and its Discontents*, New York and London: W.W. Norton & Company.

Stiglitz, Joseph E. (2006), *Making Globalization Work*, New York and London: W.W. Norton & Company.

Suehiro, Akira (2000), *Catch-up gata Kogyoka Ron: Asia Keizai no Kiseki to Tenbo* [Catch-up Type Industrialization: Evolution and Prospects of Asian Economies], Nagoya University Press, in Japanese.

Sum, Wan Wah (2000) "The Enhanced Productivity Program: the Implementation of the First Phase," dissertation for the Master of Public Administration, Department of Politics and Public Administration, University of Hong Kong.

Sumiya, Mikio, Liu jinqing, and Tu Zhaoyan (1992), *Taiwan no Keizai: Tenkei NIES no Hikari to Kage* [The Economy of Taiwan: The Bright and Dark Side of the Typical NIEs], University of Tokyo Press, in Japanese.

Takeda, Haruto (2009), "Ryo Seido no Hokai: Bakumatsu no Kin Ryushutu" [The Collapse of the Ryo System: Outflow of Gold in the Late Edo Period], *Nichigin* (Bank of Japan Journal), Summer, pp. 24–27, in Japanese.

Tanaka, Keiichi (2000), *Hyakusho no Edo Jidai* [The Edo Period of Peasants], Chikuma Shinsho, in Japanese.

Tokutomi, Soho (1889), *Kokumin no Tomo* [Companion of the People], vol. 50, Minyusha, May 11.

Tominaga, Kenichi (1990), *Nihon no Kindaika to Shakai Hendo* [The Modernization of Japan and Social Change], Kodansha Gakujutsu Bunko, in Japanese.

Tran, Tho Dat, Nguyen Quang Thang, and Chu Quang Khoi (2005), "Sources of Vietnam's Economic Growth 1986–2004," unpublished manuscript, National Economics University, Hanoi.

Tran, Van Tho (2010), *Vietnam Keizai Hattenron: Chushotoku no Wana to Aratana Doi Moi* [Development and Transition in the Vietnamese Economy: A Middle Income Trap and New Doi Moi], Keiso Shobo, in Japanese.

Tsai, Mon-Han (2006), "The Myth of Monozukuri: Manufactured Manufacturing Ideology," ITEC Working Paper Series 06–04, Doshisha University, March.

Uchida, Hoshimi (1990), "Gijutsu Iten" [Technology Transfer], in S. Nishikawa and T. Abe, eds., *Sangyoka no Jidai 1: Nihon Keizaishi 4* [The Era of Industrialisation: Economic History of Japan vol. 4], Iwanami Shoten, in Japanese. English translation forthcoming.

Ueda, Takafumi (2009), "Productivity and Quality Improvement: JICA's Assistance in *Kaizen*," in GRIPS Development Forum, ed., *Introducing KAIZEN in Africa*, National Graduate Institute for Policy Studies.

Umesao, Tadao (1986), *Nihon towa Nanika: Kindai Nihon Bunmei no Keisei to Hatten* [What is Japan? Formation and Development of Modern Japanese Civilization], NHK Books, in Japanese.

Umesao, Tadao (2003), *An Ecological View of History: Japanese Civilization in the World Context*, Trans Pacific Press.

United Nations Conference on Trade and Development (2004), *The Least Developed Countries Report 2004*, United Nations.

United Nations Population Fund (2010), *Taking Advantage of the Demographic Bonus in Viet Nam: Opportunities, Challenges, and Policy Options*, United Nations Viet Nam, December.

Vietnam Development Forum (2007), "Supporting Industries in Vietnam from the Perspective of Japanese Manufacturing Firms," in Kenichi Ohno, ed., *Building Supporting Industries in Vietnam*, vol. 1, Vietnam Development Forum, in English and Vietnamese.

Vietnam Development Forum, and Goodwill Consultant JSC (2011), *Survey on Comparison of Backgrounds, Policy Measures and Outcomes for Development of Supporting Industries in ASEAN: Malaysia and Thailand in Comparison with Vietnam*, Publishing House of Communication and Transport, Hanoi, in English and Vietnamese.

Vogel, Ezra F. (1991), *The Four Little Dragons: The Spread of Industrialization in East Asia*, Harvard University Press.

Wade, Robert (1990), *Governing the Market: Economic Theory and the Role of Government in East Asian Industrialization*, Princeton University Press.

Watanabe, Toshio (1995), *Shinseiki Asia no Koso* [Designing Asia for the New Century], Chikuma Shinsho, in Japanese. Partial English translation in Chapter 11, in Kenichi Ohno and Izumi Ohno, eds., *Japanese Views on Economic Development: Diverse Paths to the Market*, London and New York: Routledge.

Weiss, Linda (1998), *The Myth of the Powerless State*, Cornell University Press.

Weiss, Linda, and John M. Hobson (1995), *States and Economic Development: A Comparative Historical Analysis*, Polity Press.

Winters, L. Alan, Wonhyuk Lim, Lucia Hanmer, and Sydney Augustin (2010), "Economic Growth in Low Income Countries: How the G20 Can Help to Raise and Sustain It," a commissioned paper for the Presidential Committee for the G20 Summit of the Republic of Korea.

World Bank (1959), *A Public Development Program for Thailand*, report of a mission organized by the International Bank for Reconstruction and Development at the request of the Government of Thailand, Johns Hopkins Press.

World Bank (1993), *The East Asian Miracle: Economic Growth and Public Policy*, Oxford University Press.

World Bank (1996), "Governance and Public Administration (Botswana)," Findings: Best Practices Infobrief no. 9, Africa Region, World Bank, October.

World Bank (1997), *World Development Report 1997: The State in a Changing World*, Oxford University Press.

World Bank (2005), *Economic Growth in the 1990s: Learning from a Decade of Reform.*

World Bank (2007), *Ethiopia: Accelerating Equitable Growth*, Country Economic Memorandum.

World Bank (2009), *Malaysia Economic Monitor: Repositioning for Growth*, November.

World Bank (2010), "Avoiding the Middle-income Trap: Priorities for Vietnam's Long-term Growth," a paper presented at Senior Policy Seminar, Hanoi, August.

World Bank and International Finance Corporation (2010), *Doing Business 2011: Making a Difference for Entrepreneurs.*

World Economic Forum (2010), *Global Competitiveness Report 2010–2011*, edited by Professor Klaus Schwab, Geneva, Switzerland.

Yanagihara, Toru (1998), "Development and Dynamic Efficiency: 'Framework Approach' versus 'Ingredients Approach'," in Kenichi Ohno and Izumi Ohno, eds., *Japanese Views on Economic Development: Diverse Paths to the Market*, London and New York: Routledge.

Index

For Product Safety Concerns and Information please contact our EU representative GPSR@taylorandfrancis.com
Taylor & Francis Verlag GmbH, Kaufingerstraße 24, 80331 München, Germany

www.ingramcontent.com/pod-product-compliance
Lightning Source LLC
Chambersburg PA
CBHW060138280326
41932CB00012B/1555

* 9 7 8 0 4 1 5 7 0 5 8 2 0 *